THE

MARTINSYDE

FILE

Ray Sanger

An Air-Britain Publication

Published in Great Britain by

Air-Britain (Historians) Ltd
12 Lonsdale Gardens, Tunbridge Wells, Kent

Sales Dept: 19 Kent Road, Grays, Essex, RM17 6DE

Correspondence to:

J.J.Halley, 5 Walnut Tree Road,
Shepperton, Middlesex, TW17 ORW
and not to the Tunbridge Wells address

ISBN 0 85130 273 4

Printed by
Hillman Printers (Frome) Ltd
Frome
Somerset

Cover painting by Paul Monteagle

Back cover photo: Tom Edvardsson

CONTENTS

The Martin and Handasyde partnership, the First World War and expansion, post-war retrenchment and diversification, the slide into receivership, the Aircraft Disposal Company, Handasyde's subsequent career.

First machine, second machine, No.3 Monoplane, the Antoinette and Martin-Handasyde designs of 1909 and 1910 compared, 4B Dragon Fly, the fifth design, the RFC monoplane, the Military Trials Machine, the Military Monoplane, 1913 monoplane, Hydromonoplane (Waterbus) and variants, 1914 monoplane, Trans-Atlantic monoplane, other pre-war projects.

S.1, Two-seater

G.100 and G.102

RG, F.1 and F.2, F.3, F.4 Buzzard, US interest in the F.3 and F.4, other designs manufactured by Martinsyde

F.4, F.4A, F.5 and F.6, Raymor and the Transatlantic Flight attempt, Semiquaver, Type A Mks I/II/AS, England to Australia Race, Aircraft Disposal Company F.4/A.D.C.1/Nimbus-Martinsyde and A.V.1

Canada, Finland, Ireland, Japan, Latvia, Lithuania, Poland, Portugal, Russia, Spain, United States

Glider, Handasyde H.2 and A.N.E.C III, Raynham Monoplane, Desoutter I and II, British Klemm and British Aircraft Manufacturing Company Aircraft

4

Helmut Paul Martin and George Harris Handasyde taken outside the Brooklands works, April 1914.

This Martinsyde G.100, 7469, is from the second batch and was used by No.27 Squadron for the field trials of the experimental bomb sight. (Philip Jarrett)

FOREWORD

*And some there be, which have no memorial
(The wisdom of Solomon, from the Apocrypha)*

With all the great names of British aircraft manufacturers now part of history, there is a danger that some of the earliest may fade irrecoverably into obscurity, their achievements forgotten or, at best, overlooked. Once the generation that lived through the Second World War has passed on, it may be that the valiant memories of Avro, Armstrong Whitworth, Bristol, Boulton Paul, de Havilland, Handley Page, Westland -- perhaps even Hawker, Supermarine and Vickers -- will recede and dwindle into their yesteryears.

There was a time, in the early years of the century, when most British aircraft were created by men of vision and passionate determination, pursuers of ideals, above all optimists. These pioneers included in their heroic number Helmut Paul Martin and George Handasyde, the latter being one of Scotland's few early aviation practitioners. Both men had practical engineering experience in the automotive industry, then barely out of its infancy: the passion for aviation that they shared led to the creation of a series of monoplanes of outstanding elegance that enhanced Britain's aeronautical scene in the pre-war years.

These handsome Martin and Handasyde monoplanes won a deserved reputation for excellent workmanship, and flew well; yet there was no rush of would-be buyers in those lean pioneering years. Nothing daunted, the far-sighted partners designed and built in 1914 a startlingly ambitious monoplane that would have attempted an Atlantic crossing had the war not intervened.

Martin and Handasyde were not the only pioneers whose first substantial production orders came only with the outbreak of the war, though part of their output consisted of Royal Aircraft Factory designs, the B.E.2c and S.E.5a. Yet from their own Martinsyde G.100/G.102, the wryly nicknamed Elephant, the company developed a series of single-seat fighters that culminated in the superlative F.4 Buzzard of 1918, which was ordered in large numbers.

In the catalogue of British military aeroplanes, the Buzzard was one of the greatest might-have-beens of its war; but with the coming of peace it and other contemporary types came to a standstill. Blessed deliverance though the Armistice was, it spelt the end for some of those wartime builders of the aircraft that had contributed much to the attainment of peace.

The Martinsyde company did not expire immediately, but tried valiantly to carry on, building a few aircraft, attempting the transatlantic competition of 1919 and trying to stay in business by diversifying into such disparate products as motorcycles and farm lorries.

In this book Ray Sanger narrates the brief but by no means inglorious history of this pioneer company, from its tentative first products to its lingering death in the 1920s. As it is unlikely that any substantial monument to the Martinsyde company will ever be set up, this many-faceted history of dedicated endeavour, with all its successes and setbacks, will serve handsomely as an enduring memorial to two of Britain's pioneers of aviation, their skillful workers and their many fine aircraft. They richly deserve no less: let it be remembered that they made beautiful aeroplanes.

J M Bruce I.S.O., M.A., F.R.Ae.S., F.R.Hist.S.
Barton-on-Sea October 1998

6

ACKNOWLEDGEMENTS

In an article which appeared in The Aeroplane not long after Martin and Handasyde first set themselves up at Brooklands, its editor C G Grey wrote;

As public interest in aviation grew, quite a number of well-to-do men rented sheds at Brooklands and endeavoured to build experimental machines... and more and more sheds were built and by the middle of 1911 there was quite a village of sheds built in the corner between the southern boundary of the sewage farm and the curve of the track..... I know men who, possessing comfortable little incomes of say £500 to £1,000 a year, lived for years on 30 or 40 shillings a week and spent the rest on their aeroplanes.

Probably the total community of Brooklands in those days numbered a little over a hundred, but certainly not more than two hundred, and community is certainly the right word, for if anyone lacked tools or material, he merely borrowed them from another shed, and they were always lent with the greatest goodwill and without the slightest prospect of ever being returned. In fact, as a general rule the only way to secure a return of anything borrowed was to go and borrow it back.

Whether this spirit has survived in the commercial world of today I would not know but it certainly still exists between those interested in recording and interpreting the history of aviation. In writing this book I have met many, some of whom rely on aviation journalism for their income, who have ungrudgingly loaned or given precious material in the cause of furthering and disseminating our knowledge.

My involvement with Martinsyde began when for a while I was a full-time volunteer at the Brooklands Museum in its formative years. Before I left, Mike Goodall, who was destined to become one of the curators there, suggested that I carry out research into the Martinsyde Company, a project which would combine my interests in aviation and local history. Mike started me off with a selection of photographs from the Brooklands archives. As the company's records had not survived, I expected to complete the research in about six months. More than ten years later, new information is still coming to light!

Of course, the many books and articles written by Jack Bruce have been major sources of reference, his RAeS paper on Martinsyde published in 1968 being a most useful framework on which to base the book. Early contact with Jack led to fruitful correspondence with his colleague Stuart Leslie, the custodian of their combined photographic collection. Terry Fuller, then on the committee of the Woking History Society and formerly the Personnel Manager of James Walker Limited, the company that occupied the Woking factory after Martinsyde, gave me much information on the works. Through him I made contact with Chris Tait, Secretary of the Martinsyde Register and a mine of information on the company and particularly its motorcycles.

My researches led to fruitful contacts with many distinguished aviation historians including Peter Grosz, Peter Cooksley, Paul Leaman, the late Harald Penrose, Harry Woodman, the late Bert Tagg, and Philip Jarrett, the latter two in particular giving me a great deal of encouragement. Other sources of photographs were Roger Jackson, who made available his father's collection on civil aircraft, and Eric Harlin, who gave copies from Freddie Raynham's family album. I must give heartfelt thanks to one of Handasyde's granddaughters, Carolyn Pawson, who allowed myself, a complete stranger, to borrow the very precious family album. Ray Funnell, a contact from my Brooklands days, led me through the intricacies of the RAF Museum library. I also give thanks to the staff of the British Library, Royal Automobile Club Library, the Public Record Office and the Science Museum Library for their valuable assistance.

Perhaps the biggest surprise was the amount of information made available by correspondents relating to the overseas service of Martinsyde aircraft. These include Dirk Decoypere (Belgium), John Barton (Canada), Eino Ritaranta (Finland), Christophe Cony (France), Patrick Cummins and Donal MacCarron (Ireland), Robert Mikesh and Masahiro Ohno (Japan), Moshe Bukhman (Latvia), Algirdas Gamziukas and Ed Jasiunas (Lithuania), Tomasz Kopanski, Joe Tomaniewicz and K. Choloniewski (Poland), Mario Canongia Lopes and Mario Correia (Portugal), Lennart Andersson, Harry Woodman and Andrei Alexandrov (Russia), Jim Carmody, Gerald Howson, Josi Warleta and Carlos Lozaro Avila (Spain), and Bob Casari (USA).

The articles and books that I have referred to in the course of researching the book are too numerous to mention here and I thought that it would make the book too unwieldy to annotate the text. I have therefore summarised the references in an appendix at the back of the book. Many of these will be familiar to aviation enthusiasts, but some references to the Martinsyde Company and its aircraft appeared in some unexpected places and I am sure that there must be other sources that I have missed. I would of course be very interested to here from anyone that has additional material.

Finally, I must express my gratitude to Air-Britain not only for agreeing to publish my book but for the useful advice which I am sure has enhanced the value of the book. The contacts which resulted from my approach included the editor, Jim Halley, Ray Sturtivant, whose cooperation added a new dimension relating to the detailed records on individual military aircraft, and Malcolm Fillmore who put me right on the UK civil records. Major contributions have also been made by Mick Davis and David Howley who respectively prepared the scale plans and coloured side views. In the final stages I renewed contact with Jack Bruce who reviewed the text and made many valuable suggestions in the process.

Ray Sanger, Woking, February 1999

Martin checking the compression of the JAP engine of the second Martin-Handasyde outside the Humber sheds at Brooklands in the spring of 1910. (Philip Jarrett)

CHAPTER 1 - THE MARTINSYDE COMPANY

The story of the aircraft design and manufacturing activities of Martin and Handasyde began in 1908 shortly after the two men first met. Their aircraft were initially called "Martin-Handasydes" but as early as July 1911 this had been popularly shortened to "Martinsyde". It was not until the spring of 1915 that the company known as Martinsyde Limited was formed.

George Harris Handasyde was born on 30th March 1877 and was educated at Edinburgh Royal High School. His early vocational training included marine engineering experience with the firm of Ramage & Ferguson. After two-and-a-half years at sea as a marine engineer, his interest was diverted to the internal combustion engine and it is said that he owned the third motorcar ever seen in Britain - a three-wheeler Benz. He became manager of the Edinburgh Autocar Company but could not have stayed long as by the turn of the century he was in London. After seven months in charge of the garage of the London General Omnibus Company, he joined the firm of Friswells and then went on to the Mass Cars concern. Handasyde was a remarkably capable and practical mechanic and his background experience enabled him to coax the best out of the temperamental engines of the time.

Helmut Paul Martin was born in London in 1883 and was educated at Wellington College and the Central Technical College in London. He was a talented engineer with an excellent mechanical ability, coupled with a sound appreciation of scientific principles. As early as 1900, with the help of a friend, he built two motorcycle engines from designs published in the *English Mechanic*. They fitted these engines to the handlebars of their pedal cycles coupled to a V-pulley on the front wheel by a twisted rawhide belt. Martin toured Germany on his in 1901, fuelling his machine using benzine brought from chemist's shops. He travelled to Hamburg, Kassel and Frankfurt, before returning via Calais. He did not meet a single motorcar on the journey, such was the level of automotive development at the time, the only incident on the journey involving a collision with a huge dray drawn by four horses.

Late in 1901 he, with another engineer, Pierre Mauguin, made a patent application for an 'Improved Electric Igniter for Internal Combustion Engines', giving his address as 88 Boulevard de Courcelles, Paris. In 1903, after gaining practical experience at a locomotive engineering works in Glasgow and with Allens of Bedford, he took the position of assistant engineer with the Libby Company's Extract Factory at Fray Bentos in Uruguay and stayed there until 1906. Although he was an enthusiastic employee and used every spot of leave to visit the ranches and help work the cattle, the food or climate did not agree with him and he had to return to Europe. It is apparent from another patent application, for a car engine component, that he briefly returned to Paris and went into partnership with a Leon Lethimonnier, trading as Martin & Lethimonnier of 32 Rue Filicien David, Paris. However he must have quickly returned to England where he re-joined his friend from his motorcycling days and formed the engineering company, Trier & Martin, with premises at the Trinity Works, Camberwell, London, to manufacture the T & M three-jet carburettor and other automobile components. At this time Martin was living at Redcourt, Champion Hill, in south-east London.

Application was made to form the company on the 1st June 1906. The company was set up with registered offices at 101 New Church Street, Camberwell, and a nominal capital of 5000 £1 shares. The directors and principal shareholders were Frank Henry Trier, Werner Auton Trier, Helmut Paul Martin and Frank Newton Trier, the latter also being the

Martin astride a horse in Uruguay circa 1905 while working for Fray Bentos as an assistant engineer for more than two years. (Chris Tait)

company secretary. All were engineers of one persuasion or another. The other shareholders were an engineer Theodore Schneider, a chemist Edward Philip Audray (also spelt Quaduary or Audreae), and Robert Philip Martin, described as a foreign banker with a UK address at 144 Leadenhall Street, London. The total allocation of shares at that time was 4500 shares at two shillings each.

Schneider sold his shareholding to Frank Newton Trier and Robert Martin on 21 November 1907 and on 12th December Werner Trier increased his shareholding by selling two patents to the company for the consideration of 500 fully paid-up shares. In 1918, presumably on the retirement or death of Werner Trier, his shares and some of Frank Henry Trier's were transferred to relatives.

The extent to which Martin's later aviation interests affected his involvement in Trier & Martin is not clear. Certainly Martin and Handasyde aircraft were exhibited on the Trier & Martin stand at Olympia and the company has been stated to be the manufacturers of these aircraft in some literature. Also, although Martin was wholly involved with aircraft construction once the partnership with Handasyde moved to Brooklands, Martin remained a director and shareholder of Trier & Martin until its dissolution.

Very little is known of the trading activities of Trier and Martin. The accounts for the financial year ending 30th June 1908 showed a reasonable level of business but the company suffered from poor liquidity. This necessitated a call on shareholders of thirteen shillings per share on 31st December 1907 and fifteen shillings on 23rd June 1908. In the event the company ceased trading on 30th April 1919 and was formally dissolved on 3rd May 1921.

The Martin and Handasyde Partnership

With their interests, it was inevitable that Martin and Handasyde should meet in the general course of business. Handasyde had tried to interest Martin in a new type of carburettor which he had designed. The design was novel in that it atomised the fuel by passing primary air through a tube in the centre of the concentric fuel jet, the level of the fuel in the jet being controlled by a float chamber in the usual way. It seems, however, that Martin was not particularly impressed by the carburettor but was deeply interested in Handasyde's talk about the work of Lillienthal, the Wright

Advertisement from the 1911 Motor manual for the novel Trier & Martin carburettor which was an advanced design when it appeared in 1909. It embodied a throttle piston which, besides controlling the mixture flow to the inlet manifold, also progressively uncovered three jets fed with fuel from the float chamber. The first jet was for starting and slow running, the second combined with the first was for normal operation and the three together were used for acceleration and high speeds. When the throttle was closed, the jets were shut off completely and a separate air channel allowed air to the cylinders, thereby augmenting engine cooling. This could have the unfortunate effect of leaning the mixture and causing erratic running. A jacket for water or exhaust gases heated the fuel/air mixture to improve mixing at the expense of some volumetric efficiency.

Brothers and the early French aviation pioneers. From this meeting a mutual interest in aviation developed and a partnership to design and build aircraft was born, trading as "Martin and Handasyde, Aeroplane Manufacturers and Aeronautical Engineers".

The first Martin-Handasyde aircraft was a monoplane said to have been built in the ballroom of the Old Welsh Harp. Handasyde spent all of his time there building the machine and Martin joined him whenever his own business

Martin 'on safari' with friends near Buenos Aires sometime during his stay in South America. (Carolyn Pawson)

Martin with his friend Werner Trier, with whom he set up the Trier & Martin Company to market motor accessories including the T&M carburettor.

interests allowed. The hotel was only a mile or so from some land that was later to become Hendon Aerodrome. The story goes that whenever dancing was in progress, the incomplete airframe had to be hoisted up to the roof out of the way of the dancers. Unfortunately for the story, although there are photographs of the completed aircraft in the ballroom, it was in fact built in a nearby shed, possibly a boathouse. After some unsuccessful attempts at flight, during which the aircraft was wrecked, the machine was rebuilt at Barking Creek near to where Handley Page had already commenced operations. As recounted in the next chapter, the aircraft was not destined to fly.

Work was resumed at Hendon and, by the time the second machine had been completed in 1910, the partners had moved to Brooklands, where they became the first permanent tenants, initially taking up residence in the first shed that had been built there for aeronautical purposes. It had been put up in 1909 to house Louis Paulhan's Farman biplane *La Gypaète* for his demonstration flights in the autumn of that year. It subsequently became the famous Blue Bird cafe and finally, in 1914, the Officers' Mess at Brooklands. The Brooklands Automobile Racing Club (BARC) began erecting proper sheds for aviators late in 1909 and Martin and Handasyde took over No. 12 when it was ready. The rent was £100 per year or £10 per month, payable in advance. At that time Martin was still living at Champion Hill and Handasyde at 75, Oliver Road, Cricklewood, London.

Although smaller, the general layout of the partners' second aircraft was influenced by the Antoinette monoplane design. As described in much more detail in the next chapter, this layout was progressively developed through a succession of rebuilds and prototypes and, although these designs were highly thought of in the technical press of the day, the partners were not rewarded with any degree of commercial success. This was partly due to a series of unfortunate accidents involving close friends and colleagues and partly due to a reluctance on the part of the military to adopt monoplane designs.

Martin test-flew the second machine but suffered a serious accident. This discouraged him from further flying and, having decided to concentrate on running the business, employed instead an experienced pilot, Graham Gilmour, to carry out the subsequent tests on the second and third machines.

Douglas Graham Gilmour was born at Dartford in Kent on 7th March 1885. He was educated at Clifton and became connected with the automobile industry, establishing a reputation as a racing driver and motorcyclist. In January 1910, he joined the Blériot school at Pau in France, where he gained his pilot's licence on 19th April (No. 75 issued by the Aero Club of France). On his return to England, during his first flight at Brooklands he had a serious accident when the tail of his Anzani-powered Blériot grazed a telegraph wire and crashed. Luckily he was not badly hurt. He then flew another Blériot fitted with a JAP engine. After the 1910 Lanark meeting, he joined L D Gibbs & Co. and began to fly the Blériot "Big Bat" and an old Sommer at Brooklands. He then joined the Bristol Company as a pilot instructor for over a year. He flew up the Thames to London Bridge and back to Brooklands in a Bristol biplane on 5th July 1911 and two days later in the same machine skimmed the Regatta course at Henley, earning himself the suspension of his certificate for one month by the Royal Aero Club and a reputation for foolhardy flying. However, he did not merit this reputation as all his actions were carried out with due care and consideration. He started flying for Martin and Handasyde in November 1910 but was unfortunately killed little more than a year later when flying the fifth Martin-Handasyde machine.

From then on Martin and Handasyde employed two other pilots to fly their machines, Gordon Bell and Edward Petre. Charles Gordon Bell was born in London on 31st May 1889. He became a specialist in car testing at the Napier works but succumbed to the lure of flying. He came to Brooklands early in 1911 and learnt to fly on an old Hanriot monoplane, which was known affectionately to most aviators as "Henrietta". He was awarded Certificate No. 100 on 4th July 1911, after passing his flying tests the previous month. He gained experience flying Deperdussins for a time before becoming test pilot to the REP company in France, owned by M. Robert Esnault-Pelterie. He delivered several REP machines to Turkey, and in the process became the first person to fly a return journey between Asia and Europe, a deed which earned him the Turkish Order of Mejidieh. As recounted later, he earned a deserved reputation for taking risks whilst flying and was eventually killed whilst test flying for Vickers.

Edward Petre was born at Ingatestone in Essex in 1886. He was the second son of Sebastian Henry Petre and cousin to Lord Petre and Lady Furnivall, all from an old Roman Catholic family that was already well established in the reign of Henry VII. He was educated as an architect but took up aviation and began to build a monoplane in partnership with his brother Henry. They were better known in the aviation world as "Peter the Painter" and "Peter the Monk" respectively. After exhibiting their monoplane at Olympia in

Advertising the presence of the Martin-Handasyde at Olympia in 1911

Handasyde and Martin in front of their second machine, powered by a 40 hp J.A.P engine. (J M Bruce/S Leslie Collection)

Testing the propeller thrust of the JAP engine of Martin-Handasyde No 3 by registering the tension on a spring balance, summer 1911. The person ducking under the starboard wing is Handasyde. (Brooklands Museum)

1910, the brothers took it to Brooklands where they made a number of short straight flights. It somewhat resembled an Antoinette but had a pusher propeller in the tail driven by a long shaft from a centrally-mounted engine, the pilot being situated ahead of the wing. After running into financial difficulties, the brothers split up and Edward worked for a time with Howard Flanders, flying the Flanders machine regularly. He then joined Handley Page and carried out the early testing of the 50-hp machine at Fairlop in Essex, where he learned to fly properly and gained his certificate on 24th July 1912. It was after a visit to Brooklands that he was induced to carry out test flying for Martin and Handasyde. He was, however, tragically killed in one of their machines in the same year on Christmas Eve.

Martin and Handasyde built several aircraft for consideration for military use but none found favour with the authorities. This was partly due to a reluctance by the Military to consider monoplanes but the partners' cause was not helped when Gordon Bell crashed one of the machines, killing a naval passenger and seriously injuring himself. Following his recovery from his injuries, Bell returned to the aviation world as a test pilot for Short Brothers. Being an officer in the RFC Reserve, he was one of the first to go to France when war broke out and took part in the retreat from Mons and the battles of the Marne, Aisne and Ypres. He returned to Britain as an instructor and became a squadron commander at the Central Flying School before being invalided out of the RFC in 1917. After leaving the service, he again took up test flying for Handley Page and then Vickers. He had a reputation for being a headstrong character and it probably came as no surprise when he was killed at Villacoublay in France on 29th July 1918 demonstrating a Vickers F.B.16E before the French authorities.

Flight for 14th August 1914 reported that Martin and Handasyde had taken on additional sheds at Brooklands. These were larger and slightly to the west of the existing sheds. The buildings were used both for manufacturing and preparation for flight testing, the Transatlantic Monoplane

being the first new design to be built there. At this time, both Martin and Handasyde lived close to the works, Martin at Holmethorpe, Cedar Grove, Weybridge and Handasyde at The Leaders in Byfleet. Later Martin moved to Lingwood, Gower Road, Weybridge and Handasyde to The Vines in West Byfleet.

According to Tom Aspley, who was employed as an aircraft joiner on the Transatlantic, the period just prior to the War was a happy-go-lucky time, with the aviators being a closely-knit group who often took time off to watch test flights and record attempts on the track. During the hot summer of that year, time was spent cooling off by swimming in the River Wey, which wended across the land enclosed by the race circuit. For lunch, he could buy three slices of buttered bread and a cup of tea for tuppence at the famous Blue Bird Restaurant.

At this time, the partners were employing around ten workers and also Robert R Skene and Vincent Waterfall as part-time test pilots. Both pilots were unfortunate to lose their lives early in the War, Waterfall having the doubtful distinction of being the first RFC pilot to be killed on active service. Skene was born in London on 6th August 1891 and took his Aviator's Certificate (No.568) on a Bristol Biplane at the Bristol School at Brooklands on 21st July 1913. He went on a monoplane course at the Blériot School at Buc before being appointed to the RFC Reserve on 15th November 1913. Following his period with Martin and Handasyde, flying mainly the 120-hp Austro-Daimler monoplane, he was mobilised into the RFC during the second week of August 1914, following the outbreak of the War. He was killed shortly afterwards, along with his passenger, on Wednesday 12th August 1914, while taking off from Netheravon in an 80-hp Blériot two-seater. It would appear that the machine was heavily loaded with equipment and fuel for a flight to Dover, preparatory to crossing to France, and stalled whilst carrying out a climbing turn shortly after take-off. He is buried in the churchyard of St Mary, Send, near Woking. Vincent Waterfall was born at Grimsby on 25th May 1891

Martin, Handasyde and Gordon Bell in a state of undress by their tent at the Military Trials at Larkhill, August 1912 during which Bell flew the Martin-Handasyde entrant. Gordon Bell was seriously injured when he crashed on Friday 13 June 1913 in a Martin-Handasyde and never flew for the company again.

and was educated at a public school before being gazetted into the 3rd Battalion, East Yorkshire Regiment, in January 1912. He took his pilot's licence (No.461) at the Vickers School at Brooklands on the morning of 22nd April 1913, flying a Vickers Biplane. Following his period with Martin and Handasyde, he joined the RFC in July 1914 and became a Flying Officer on 5th August following a course of instruction at Farnborough. Having joined No.5 Squadron in France, he took off with an observer in an Avro 504 on 22nd August for a reconnaissance mission and was shot down behind enemy lines by ground fire near Ath, about 30 miles south of Brussels. At the time, he was buried in a grave close to where the aircraft crashed.

The partners also took on Tony Fletcher, a Cambridge graduate and formerly one of Handley Page's first two trainees, as a design draughtsman. He probably was involved in the design of both the Transatlantic Monoplane and the Pusher Biplane, neither of which were completed due to the war. The Transatlantic was being built as a contender for the £10,000 *Daily Mail* Prize. Sydney Camm, later to be known as Chief Designer for Hawkers, also joined the company in 1914. He started as a shop floor woodworker but his skill and diligence came to the attention of the management and before the war ended he had won promotion into the design office, reportedly at the instigation of the Company's Chief Draughtsman, John Stanbury. This was a considerable achievement for those times since Camm was completely self-educated in the engineering technology of the day. The partners helped to give him an excellent grounding in aircraft design and also sponsored his application to the Royal Aeronautical Society.

The First World War and Expansion

In the spring and summer of 1914, Handasyde, with the able assistance of Fletcher, had designed a sporty biplane of similar appearance to the popular Sopwith and Bristol designs. The prototype was impressed by the Government and a further sixty or more machines were built during the latter part of 1914 and early 1915. These saw service in France, Mesopotamia and with training and Home Defence units. The company also built a dozen Royal Aircraft Factory B.E.2cs, in the design of which Geoffrey de Havilland was deeply involved, for the Royal Naval Air Service under an Admiralty contract. By this time the factory area at Brooklands was around 35,000 sq ft and still growing. In the late spring of 1915, a new design appeared. This was a two-seater scout which displayed a good deal of Fletcher's influence in its design, but failed to attract orders. Before Fletcher left Martinsyde, following an argument with Handasyde, to join the London and Provincial Aviation Company at Hendon in the autumn of 1915, and later to resurface at Westland at Yeovil as part of the design team, he participated in the design of another aircraft, a rather staid reconnaissance machine. The size and lack of agility of this aircraft earned it the nickname of Elephant. This machine was much more successful and 272 were built and saw service in Palestine, Mesopotamia and the Western Front.

All major aircraft constructors were expanding their factories for the manufacture of military machines. Martin and Handasyde were no exception and converted their business partnership into a limited company under the name of Martinsyde Ltd, with registered offices at Brooklands. The Certificate of Incorporation of the Company was dated 24th March 1915 and the formal agreement was dated 19th May 1915. The company was formed with a nominal capital of 35,000 shares of £1 each. The first three shares were assigned one each to Helmut Paul Martin, George Harris Handasyde and Hamilton Fulton. The next 27,996 shares were allocated to Martin and Handasyde effective from 12th April 1915, but by 20th April a return of allotment of shares shows that some of Martin's shares had been reallocated to G H Handasyde, Hamilton Fulton, Guy Blatherwick and Martin's wife Marjorie. At the same time the Company took out a mortgage of £12,500 with the London County and Westminster Bank Limited of 41 Lothbury, London EC, using the unallocated share capital of the company as security.

The Company soon made use of its capital after its formation, for on 14th April 1915 it bought the former Oriental Institute, situated in Maybury, Woking, from the son of its founder for £4,500. Some of the land included the works of the Electric Accumulator Supply Company on a plot leased by it in 1902 for 40 years for an annual ground rent of £100.

The Oriental Institute was originally built as The Royal Dramatic College, an ambitious attempt to establish a permanent centre for the dramatic arts and incorporated facilities to accommodate a small number of retired actors and actresses. A Royal Charter incorporating the Royal Dramatic College was granted on 8th June 1859 and by early 1860 the trustees had purchased ten acres of Maybury Common for £750 from the London Necropolis Company. The building was completed by September 1862. It was designed by T R Smith in a mid-Victorian interpretation of the Tudor style and was constructed of local red brick. It had a large central hall, surmounted at the western end by a tower with a small spire.

Hubert Latham's Antoinette Monoplane after crashing on top of a Martinsyde shed in June 1911. The Martin-Handasyde No 3 was badly damaged by falling timbers and never flew again. (Les Harris)

From left to right, Alliott Verdon Roe, Spottiswoode, Bowen, unidentified person, Martin and Handasyde in front of one of Martin's cars, Brooklands 1911. (Carolyn Pawson)

The main block of sheds at Brooklands as they appeared in 1912 taken from the east by Dukinfield Jones from a Flanders monoplane piloted by E V B Fisher. (Bert Tagg)

The sheds at Brooklands, based on a plan which appeared in the March 1911 issue of Autocar. Ye Blue Bird restaurant where Martin and Handasyde briefly resided was shed 8, second from the left of the front row. Martin and Handasyde moved to the position shown (shed 12) in 1909 or 1910 and also occupied the repair shops. Martin and Handasyde had probably vacated shed 12 by mid-1912. (Bert Tagg)

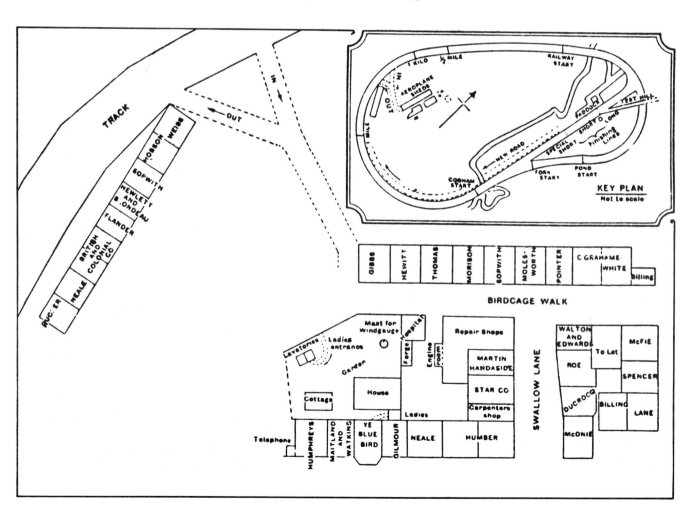

Elephants being assembled at the Brooklands works. No. 7281 went to No.23 Squadron and the remainder went to No.27 Squadron. The photograph was probably taken during February or March 1916. (Brooklands Museum)

Chabot sold it in the spring of 1884 to a Dr Gottlieb Wilhelm Leitner, a Hungarian by birth. He was fluent in Turkish, Arabic and most European languages and at the age of fifteen served as a colonel to the British Commissariat in the Crimea. After graduating from King's College, London, he was made Professor in Arabic and Mohammedan Law. After a period abroad, he returned to England with the ambition to found a centre for the study of Oriental languages, culture and history and found the vacant Royal Dramatic College very suitable for the purpose. The Oriental Institute, as it was known, prospered for a time but did not function for long after its founder's death in 1899 and the building again became vacant. Before his death, Leitner built a Mosque, which still survives, in the grounds for its Moslem students, which he passed on to the Rt Hon Syed Ameer Ali and others.

It is not clear the degree of Government financial involvement, but in order to fulfil Government contracts, Martinsyde built a large factory on the site. This spread over several acres and gave relatively unobstructed accommodation for the activities needed to supply all the components required for aircraft construction except engines but including propellers and radiators.

The College buildings were restructured, the flanks of the building were demolished at the rear but retaining the frontage in a modified form with the bay windows removed. The only part that was retained relatively unchanged was the

Vincent Waterfall who, for a short time, test flew Martinsydes during 1914 after receiving his training at the Vickers Flying School at Brooklands. He had the dubious distinction of being the first RFC pilot to be killed on active service in the Great War (Carolyn Pawson)

Along the front was a pillared cloister which provided an area protected from the weather where aged residents could sit. There were two wings either side of the main hall and entrance, each of which contained five self-contained residences housing two persons. The building was decorated with terracotta reliefs. The project soon ran into financial difficulties and on 12th November 1877 it was closed down. The property was auctioned in 1880 but did not achieve its reserve price of £5,000 at auction and was sold privately to Alfred Chabot, a land and property speculator.

Inside the Martin & Handasyde wood working shop at Brooklands with S.1s being assembled in the background. The early pattern S.1 tailplane leaning against the wall dates the photograph to late 1914 or early 1915.

The Maybury site before the Martinsyde works were built, showing the Oriental Institute in the middle background and the Maybury Laundry in the foreground separated by the main railway line from Waterloo to the south west of England. (Woking History Society)

central spire. Spoil from other construction work was spread over the site, leading to the factory being built on two slightly different levels.

With the main factory, large spans of roofing were constructed on the Warren truss principle, using internal and external bracing, to give a "saw-tooth" roof providing plenty of north light to illuminate the workspace. The factory was heated by steam and was fitted with an up-to-date ventilation system. The facilities were an engineer's dream for the period. The area was divided into a main erecting shop and machine, fitter's, welding, smith's, sheet metal and woodworking shops, the latter alone covering an area of three acres. The machine shop was fitted with electric motors which powered batches of machines. The power required for the machines and lighting totalled some 600 hp and was supplied from a power house equipped with Hornsby oil engines and a Ruston Proctor wood refuse plant, which was supplied entirely from refuse from the mill. The mill itself was fitted with machinery driven by underground shafting running on ball bearings and sawdust and shavings were extracted by fans directly to the refuse plant. Acetylene gas was piped to the welding shop from a separate generating plant outside the shop. The firm made all its own dies and press tools for drop forging, drop hammers and presses and manufactured special drills, reamers and other small tools. The sheet metal shop had forges fitted with automatic blasting and a full range of metal working machinery including aluminium welding, an advanced concept at that time. The fitter's shop was heated by steam and was well ventilated and

An aerial view of the Maybury works taken shortly after completion. The spire of the Institute remains but the eastern wing has been much modified. (Carolyn Pawson)

View of the Erecting Shop at Brooklands. The cockpit coaming in the right foreground may well belong to the prototype Martinsyde F.2, in which case the photograph would be dated the spring of 1917.

Part of the Erecting Shop at the Maybury works which covered over three acres, showing fuselages of Martinsyde F.4 Buzzards under construction. (Martinsyde Limited)

Part of the Woodworking Shop at Maybury which also covered about three acres showing wings of the F.4 Buzzard under construction. (Martinsyde Limited)

Radiator and Welding Shop. This was supplied with acetylene for welding from the work's own plant. (Martinsyde Limited)

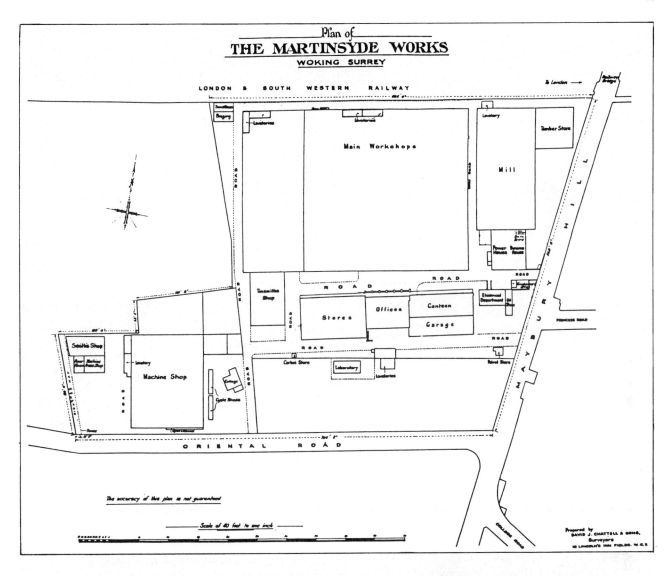

Contemporary plan of the Martinsyde works (last amendment 18.9.25), with the services and other details removed for clarity. The Institute building has been converted into stores, offices and a canteen. (James Walker Limited)

View of the Erecting shop at Maybury during the time that the Martinsyde Company was fulfilling an order for S.E.5as (Brooklands Museum)

View of the Machine Shop at the Maybury works. Groups of machines were run on separate electric motors from power generated in the works' own power house. (Martinsyde Limited)

A part of the Mill at the Maybury works. All the drive shafts for the machinery were situated underground and ran on ball bearings. Sawdust was extracted directly to the Ruston Proctor wood refuse plant. (Martinsyde Limited)

Another view of the Woodworking Shop at Maybury with F.4 Buzzard rudders in the foreground. (Martinsyde Limited)

Part of the Smiths' Shop where the firm made its own dies and press tools for drop forgings, drop hammers and presses and other special tools. (Martinsyde Limited)

Aerial view of the track, sheds and flying ground at Brooklands in the early 1930's (Flight). The former Martin and Handasyde sheds are left of centre. From left to right, the General Service sheds had been taken over by Vickers, The Brooklands Flying School and Hawkers respectively. On the right next to the track are the Hawker manufacturing sheds which replaced the old perimeter workshops (sheds 29 to 42). (Bert Tagg)

covered an area 260 by 105 feet.

The registered offices of Martinsyde Limited were moved to the Maybury works on 5th January 1917. Shortly after that, the Company raised additional finance by taking out additional mortgages with the London County and Westminster Bank of £17,500 on 19th March 1917 and £30,000 on 16th November 1917.

Early in 1916, Martinsyde took on Frederick Phillips Raynham on a freelance basis as a test pilot for its aircraft at Brooklands. As he is to figure prominently in the further narrative, it is worth dwelling here on his previous experience. He was born in 1896, the son of a Sussex farmer. He was an average student at school, with an aptitude for mechanical subjects. His interest in aeronautics was aroused by Blériot's cross-Channel flight and he was resolved to teach himself to fly. He went to Brooklands and joined A V Roe. He was not paid for his work but he was allowed to use one of Roe's planes for two hours a week, coming under the tutelage of Howard Pixton. He gained his aviator's certificate (No.85) at Brooklands in May 1911 before he was eighteen. His proficiency was well recognised as he was already instructing other pupils before he had even obtained his own Certificate and shortly afterwards was one of the first aviators to recover successfully from a spin. He took over from Ronald Kemp as Chief Instructor and Test Pilot for Alliott Roe at Brooklands in August 1911. In December he left A V Roe to become the Chief Instructor and Manager of the new Sopwith Flying School at Brooklands, but rejoined as Chief Test Pilot of A V Roe & Company during the last week of August 1912, shortly after flying the ABC-engined Flanders

aircraft at the Military Trials at Larkhill. He became very well-known for his exploits; he held the endurance record for a few hours when, on 24th October 1912, at Brooklands, he stayed aloft for 7½ hours in an Avro G before running out of oil. In February 1914, he took an Avro biplane to 15,000 feet over Brooklands, switched off the engine and glided twenty miles to Hendon, where he landed without switching on the engine. He continued to test Avro aircraft until that Company established its Design and Experimental Department at Hamble. He was loath to leave the Brooklands area and instead joined Martinsyde, being familiar with some of its prewar designs.

During April 1917, Martinsydes were the subject of an exchange in Parliament which illustrated the attitude of some in authority to women workers. A Mr T Wilson asked the Minister of Munitions if he was aware that a woman has been appointed to test the measurement of parts of aeroplanes at the Martinsyde works, and if so what qualifications did she possess that fit her for that position. Sir W Evans responded that seven women were employed by the Aeronautical Inspection Directorate at the two works of the Company and that women had been employed in these duties since July 1915 and had been found fully satisfactory. He did add the rider that the women worked under close supervision and had no discretion when carrying out their instructions.

The factory was very busy by mid-1917 as Martinsydes had become major contractors for the manufacture of the S.E.5a single-seater scout, designed by a team led by H P Folland at the Royal Aircraft Factory at Farnborough. The company constructed 600 out of the total of over 5,200 built.

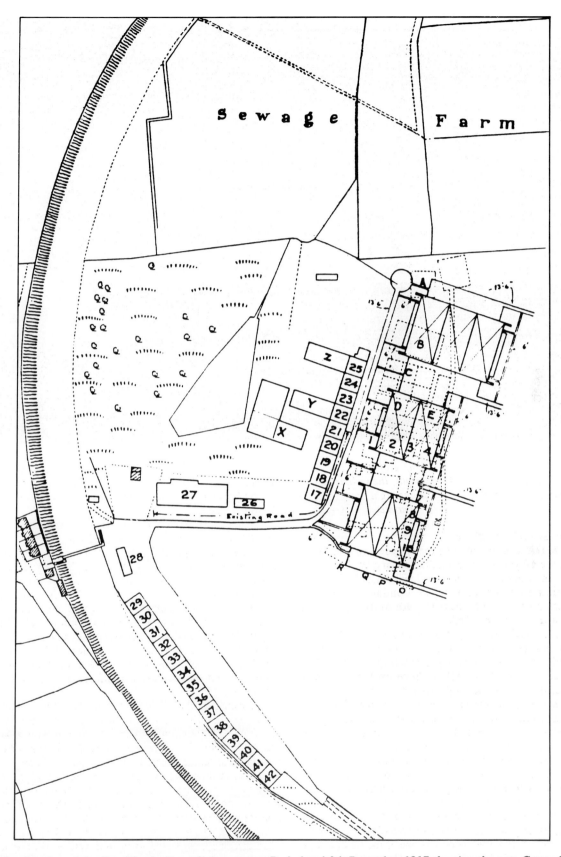

Part of a drawing of the Brooklands Aircraft Acceptance Park dated 8th December 1917 showing the new General Service Sheds built on the site of the earlier wooden flight sheds and workshops (A to E and 1 to 10), sheds 4 to 12 having burnt down earlier that year. X was a corrugated iron shed built in 1913 to make the Martinsyde Transatlantic contender of 1914 and Y was a wooden workshop also used by Martinsydes. Martinsydes and the AAP shared the old wooden sheds 17 to 25. Shed X was taken over later by the T B Andre company. Note the famous sewage farm where many intrepid early aviators force-landed and where Harold Barnwell crashed a new Martin-Handasyde. (Bert Tagg)

H R H The Duke of York (later to be King George VI) and King George V being shown the Woodworking Shop at Maybury by Hamilton Fulton and Martin during the Royal Visit on 27 April 1917. (Chris Tait)

Martinsyde lorry, based on a 1907 Berliet car owned by Martin, situated outside the facade of what was formerly the Oriental Institute. (Chris Tait)

Sybil, one of the office staff, outside the Martin & Handasyde office at Brooklands, April 1915. (Carolyn Pawson)

Despite its preoccupation with the production of the S.E.5a, the company embarked on developing their own designs, including major modifications based on the Elephant and the "F" series of aircraft designs culminating in the F.3, powered by the Rolls-Royce Falcon, and the F.4 Buzzard which, as Falcon production had been allocated to the Bristol Fighter, utilised the 300-hp Hispano-Suiza. The aircraft went into quantity production and but for the Armistice would have undoubtedly been a great success as its superior design had attracted many orders from home and the United States. Most

Frederick Phillips Raynham, who acted as test pilot for Martinsydes during the later part of the War and was pilot designated for the unsuccessful transatlantic attempt in 1919.
(Associated Newspapers)

of these were cancelled at the end of the war but some production continued for the RAF into the early part of 1919. Strenuous efforts were made to sell the aircraft and variants for military purposes overseas and for civilian use but these efforts met with only limited success. During this time the company did its best to employ ex-service pilots. These included Major C W C Wheatley, Capt R H Nisbet, E F Gill, H C Kirby, J H Clarke, J Refoy and A Wells of the RAF and Capt C W F Morgan, P Stimpson and R Reyer formerly of the RNAS. A Mr W F Savage, previously an AID Chief Inspector, also joined in a technical capacity.

Post-War Retrenchment and Diversification

The Company designed several new aircraft following the end of the war. The first was intended to once again compete for the £10,000 prize offered by Lord Northcliffe for the first non-stop crossing of the Atlantic. As described in a later chapter, this aircraft, named the Raymor after its pilot and navigator, Raynham and Morgan, crashed on 18th May 1919 in Newfoundland on its first attempt, nearly a month before the successful crossing by Alcock and Brown in a Vickers Vimy, and also failed in a subsequent attempt.

The Raymor design formed the basis for the Martinsyde Type A, the company's first truly commercial type. One of these entered the contest for the £10,000 prize for the first England to Australia flight but the aircraft came down in the sea off Corfu and the crew lost their lives. Several Type A variants were sold in Canada and the Irish Free State. The F.6, which owed something of its design to both the F.4 and the Type A, also saw service in Canada and was flown in several air races by Raynham, one being known as

"Mustardsyde" from its yellow colour. The final Martinsyde design was the Semiquaver, a single-seat racer which set up a British Speed Record for its class by achieving a speed of 161.43 mph at Martlesham Heath on 21st March 1920.

The successful sale of some aircraft to Canada was due to the efforts of R H Nisbet, who had been a test pilot and assistant designer for Martinsyde for a considerable period, *The Aeroplane* of 25th August 1920 reporting that he had been sent to Canada to try to obtain business for the Company, particularly with respect to the provision of commercial aircraft.

With the cancellation of contracts for military aircraft at the end of the war, the Company made every effort to diversify its operations. Many of its work force had woodworking skills and the Company endeavoured to make use of this experience by making farm carts. The carts were sold through sole agents, The Country Gentleman's Association of Letchworth. Unfortunately the Association's records are incomplete for this period and it has no information regarding the numbers sold. As befits a company used to precision engineering, these carts were well constructed and incorporated innovations in design. Oak and ash were used exclusively for the main framework and elm was used for the floorboards. The floor of the cart measured 11 feet by 6 feet 6 inches, and could take a load of 3 tons. One-piece steel axles supported wheels fitted with 3½- or 4-inch tyres and the fore-carriage was of the 'swinging' or double swivelling type which was designed to allow the carts to be drawn easily over rough ground. This design had to be later abandoned as it made the carts unstable and more liable to overturn. The cart could be fitted with one or two pairs of shafts and alternative types of side boards and end ladders. A similar wagon, fitted with springs, was available for road work. The wagons sold for £74 in 1919 with the optional sides extra and prices were increased by ten percent on 1st May 1920 after a pay rise had been awarded to the workers.

It is believed that the carts were tested at Dounhurst Farm, just north of Wisborough Green, where Martin had moved to sometime in 1917 or 1918.

The works also made telephone exchange cabinets for the Stirling Telephone Co but no details have been found. It has been said that the company purchased a light van/taxi chassis from Beardmore, presumably with a view to using it as a prototype for the construction of van bodies. However there is no written record of this transaction and nothing ever came of the idea. Certainly Martinsyde had some interest in car or van manufacture as the company had taken out a patent for a swivelling seat for cars. The patent shows a mechanism whereby a passenger may obtain easy access to the front or rear seats by means of a front seat which swivels about its base and is also adjustable front to rear.

As the main alternative outlet for the Company's engineering facilities, it was decided to design and manufacture motorcycle and motorcycle combinations. Howard C. Newman was retained as a consultant and the Company paid him £6,000 for the design of the engine. Newman was a leading pre-war trials rider on Ivy machines made by his family firm, S A Newman and Sons, who were also the proprietors of Brampton Forks. It has been said that he acquired the drawings for the engine from a fellow soldier, who had previously been a draughtsman for Blackburne (not to be confused with Blackburn, the aircraft manufacturer). However, according to his father in an article in *Motor Cycling* of 27th August 1915, Newman had designed and nearly completed a new V-twin four-stroke engine, which he intended to use in the 1915 TT races, before he enlisted in the

26

Advertising the Company

Kate Hockley (seated) with friend in the overalls supplied to workers at the Martinsyde works, Maybury, during the First World War. Miss Hockley worked in the fabric and doping shops. (Joan Goldsmith)

The fire at Maybury on Saturday 25th September 1920 which gutted an area of 3,000 sq ft after which the works never reopened. (Woking History Society)

Sydney Camm designed a number of detailed improvements to the machine, particularly to the AJS gearbox, which became essentially a Martinsyde design.

With its well-equipped engineering facilities, Martinsyde was able to make the whole motorcycle, including its engine, within its works. However, the engineering department adopted wasteful practices which must have contributed to the lack of profitability of the whole operation. All the engines were run-in for several hours on completion. They were mounted on wooden test stands in the open and connected to the rig's fuel and exhaust systems. Propellers were fitted to the crankshafts to act as a brake and provide additional cooling. The finished motorcycles were road-tested by driving them along muddy country lanes to Newlands Corner, a beauty spot on the hills a few miles south of Woking. After testing, each machine had to be thoroughly cleaned before despatch. Despite all this testing and the reputation for precision manufacture, individual machines were found to vary appreciably in performance, the best being reserved for favoured customers. When a motorcycle came in for overhaul, it would be stripped down, all the bright parts nickel-plated again and all the cycle parts re-enamelled, and owners had the option of having the engine rebalanced for as little as £5.

In order to break into the fiercely competitive motor-cycle market, the Company decided to enter the competition scene. As well as giving encouragement to amateur riders, both in trials and on the track, Martinsyde formed a works team. They retained a number of experienced riders, including W H Bashall, his brother J T Bashall, H H Bowen, A A Symes and E H Gifford. Both Bashall brothers and Bowen had been successful BAT riders pre-war at Brooklands and W H Bashall was also a pre-war TT winner. W H Bashall was appointed Chief Tester and Gifford was his young assistant. Symes worked under Bowen, who was in charge of the Experimental Department. However J T Bashall did not work for Martinsyde. The Bashall brothers and Symes all lived in the Ripley area near Woking and all married daughters of a Mr. Dibble, who was landlord of The Anchor public house at Ripley. The service department was run by G F Bainbridge, another rider with a reputation at Brooklands.

Over the next two years, the team members gained numerous awards in trials, hill climbs and races, the most impressive being the Brooklands 500-mile Race held on 2nd July 1921, the 1922 Six Days Trial and the Hour Record held by Bowen. Business began to pick up following these

Army in 1915. Whatever the background, he was in a position to make the design available to Martinsyde within the Company's required timescale.

The prototype Martinsyde-Newman was exhibited at the 1919 Motor Cycle Show and caused a great amount of interest. Some 6,000 orders were taken, the potential buyers being particularly impressed with the standard of the specification and the high quality of the finish. The first models left the factory in 1920 but manufacturing problems arose, despite satisfactory performance of the engine in 10,000 miles of testing in an AJS frame. These were mainly caused by a moulders' strike, requiring the cylinders to be imported from Belgium, but there was also a weakness in the design of the frame. Although these problems had been overcome by July, many orders had been lost, causing the Company heavy financial loss. In the same year, Newman left and the motorcycles subsequently produced were called just "Martinsydes". It has been said that Newman had attempted to take over the motorcycle part of the business but had been thwarted by the directors. However, there is no evidence that he was prepared or even able to take a financial stake in the company. In any event, by the middle of the following year he was actively seeking alternative outlets for his talents.

Martin with his Peugeot outside the Martinsyde sheds circa 1919. (Chris Tait)

successes and as the Company's reputation for producing good quality machines grew. The range was expanded during 1922. A 500 cc model, based on experience gained in the 500-mile race, was introduced early in the year, to be soon followed by a sports model called the "Quick-Six", featuring a slightly more powerful engine and the round tank that applied to all models of that period.

Some effort was made to export motorcycles but this seems to have been on a small scale. The principal markets were Australia (about ten) and Italy (around twenty), with one or two sold in Belgium. An Italian magazine once described Martinsyde as 'the best motorcycle factory in Europe'.

The Slide into Receivership

Returning to Company affairs, the firm became a public company and the finances were restructured during the Spring of 1920. At an Extraordinary General Meeting held on 15th March 1920, a Resolution was passed, which became effective on 19th April 1920, to increase the capital of the Company to £500,000 by creating £465,000 new shares of £1 each of equivalent ranking to existing shares. This enabled accumulated reserves to be retained by the Company by paying existing shareholders shares in lieu of dividends. This was carried out by taking out £225,897 from the Company's Reserve Account and allocating it as 225,897 £1 shares to the shareholders in proportion to their existing shareholdings (776 shares per 100 shares).

On 30th April 1920, Handasyde reallocated some of his paid up shares to others, including some newcomers. There were also some transfers of shares to Hamilton Fulton, from Martin, G. Blatherwick and Mrs. Martin, which made him third largest shareholder after the two Martins. Following a resolution passed by the directors on 14th May, the Company was made a public company on 9th July 1920. On 15th July 1920, Martin, Handasyde and Hamilton Fulton were each allocated 100 £1 shares in order to qualify them as directors.

The Company was borrowing heavily at this time to finance its day-to-day operations as on 16th September 1920 a further mortgage for £100,000 was registered in favour of the London County Investment and Parr's Bank Limited. That business was bad was confirmed by the experience of Harald

Penrose, who was later to become Chief Test Pilot at Westland. As a sixteen-year-old, his father took him for an interview with Martin for an apprenticeship. He was promised only general engineering work and no settled future.

On Saturday, 25th September 1920, a serious fire broke out in the Martinsyde works. It started at 12.30 pm, after nearly all the employees had left the works as usual. The fire was discovered at about 1.50 pm by two men who had stayed behind to finish some work on a special side-car body for a tradesman's motorcycle. It began in the fuselage shop situated towards the western end of the erecting shop, a building which extended some 125 yards along the side of the railway line and which was partitioned off into various workshops. The men immediately sounded the works fire alarm which quickly summoned the work's own fire brigade, the local Woking fire brigade, which was on the scene in a matter of minutes, and many of the workforce. The Guildford, Weybridge and Chertsey fire brigades arrived later. The delay in calling the Weybridge force was due to the station not being on the telephone while the Chertsey force had to run its hoses from the Basingstoke Canal, more than a quarter of a mile away on the far side of the railway line.

Salvage teams were quickly organised to rescue equipment, aircraft parts, motorcycles and heavy farm carts from the path of the blaze. Some of this material was transferred to remote parts of the works while partially complete airframes were pulled out to line the road at Maybury Hill. The report of "bodies" in the road led to a rumour of deaths in the fire. The fire brigades prevented the flames from spreading to the engineer's shop but were hampered by low water pressure and were unable to save the french-polishing shop, the paint shop, the dope shop and the upholstery department, all of which were gutted, an area of over 3,000 square feet. Parts of the wood store, carpenter's shop and about a third of the erecting shop were also damaged. The fire was under control by half-past three and was completely out by 4 o'clock.

The Company Secretary, F H Campkin, estimated the damage at between £20-30,000 and included the loss of 127 completed wings, some partially completed "A" type machines, fuselages, tailplanes, rudders, elevators and other aircraft parts. The cause of the fire was not determined but fortunately the loss was covered by insurance.

Martin was determined that the works should reopen as soon as possible as there was already a considerable amount of unemployment in the area, particularly of ex-servicemen. An immediate start was made to clear the wreckage, the large messroom was converted into a paint shop and every available space was utilised in an effort to restart. It was reported that *there is no likelihood of the works closing down. Despite feeling the effects of the slump in the aircraft and motor industries, Martinsyde Limited are in a good position financially, and when the industrial world is in more peaceable state they hope to have much profitable business.*

However the Company was expected to be heavily indebted to the Treasury, which through retrospective legislation had imposed a duty on excess profits made during the war. The firm's bankers, the London County, Westminster and Parr's Bank, Ltd., which held some £137,000 in debentures, appointed a receiver and manager, Mr. Daniel S Fripp of Evans, Fripp, Deed and Co. on 9th October, his appointment being confirmed by a Court Order on 2nd November 1920. The reasons behind the appointment of a receiver was explained in a letter from Martin to all creditors and other interested parties:

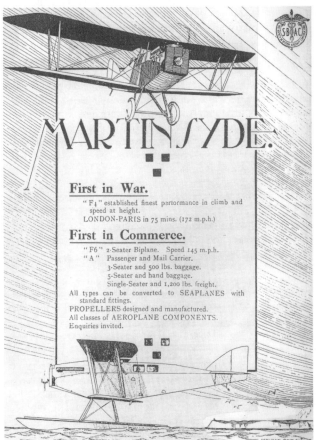

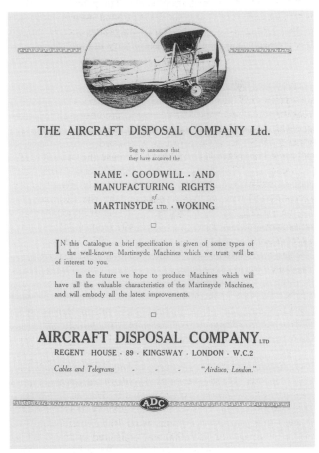

Post-war advertising for the civilian market and the take-over by the Aircraft Disposal Company Ltd.

Sydney Camm (later Sir) and his wife Hilda on a 1921 Martinsyde combination. The photograph was taken at the Hawker sports ground at Ham near Richmond in Surrey sometime in 1924. Camm may well have been given PC680 in lieu of wages.
(Chris Tait)

Dear Sirs,

In sending you the enclosed formal notice from the receiver, we take the opportunity of giving you some reasons which have led to the appointment and which we trust will ultimately result to your benefit.

Owing to circumstances over which we have no control and more particularly owing to the pressure brought upon us to pay Excess Profit Duty, our bankers felt compelled to protect their assets by taking the steps referred to which give them priority over EPD and indirectly protect the assets in your interests.

It is the bankers expressed intention that the receiver should carry on the business, in spite of the general trade depression, gives every indication that the debt due to you will be satisfied, provided that the cooperation of the creditors can be relied upon. If the situation alters to your detriment we will immediately notify you, so that you can take any steps you think necessary to protect yourselves.

We take this opportunity of thanking you for the consideration shown to us, and trust that our good relations may in no way be affected by our temporary embarrassment.

Martinsyde Limited
(Signed H.P. Martin)

However, the plant was closed down on 22nd October for an estimated period of two weeks for stocktaking. Prior to closing the works, about one hundred employees were discharged and the remainder, amounting to nearly one thousand workers, were put on part-time working, including no work on Saturday mornings. The Company Secretary told a reporter from *The Woking News and Mail* that:

Owing to the industrial depression, it is not thought likely that many men will resume work on the Monday but the whole of the workpeople at present put off will be re-employed again on full time before the end of November.

He further stated that the whole of the work output for next year had already been booked up. However, despite the management's best intentions and although a small design and drawing office was retained and some test flying continued at Brooklands, the works was never re-opened for the full-scale manufacture of aircraft.

The company was still in receivership early in 1921 and a meeting of creditors was called on 15th March at Winchester House in London to try and resolve the situation. At this meeting, Martin explained that the difficulty in which the company found itself was common to most engineering and manufacturing companies. Although it had wished to carry on in the aviation business, it had been dropped because of lack of support from the Government. Diversification into the motorcycle business in October 1919 had run into trouble because production had been delayed due to shortage of parts, partly because of the moulder's strike and railway troubles but also because the company had to rely on a number of small manufacturers of components who were also in difficulties. However great efforts had been made to make the company more efficient and the effect of this was

The first three motorcycles in March 1920 outside the Martinsyde office in Woking prior to delivery to agent's showrooms. Due to various setbacks quantity deliveries did not commence until the following July. (RAeS)

already apparent even before the Receiver had been appointed.

It was explained to the meeting that during the course of its business, the profits of the Company had been reinvested in buildings, plant and to a large extent in stock. The current assets of the Company amounted to some £354,000 against liabilities of £227,829. Present orders were being met from stocks. The value of contracts on the books amounted to some £377,000 for motorcycles alone and no difficulty was anticipated in meeting these. Due to recent losses it was likely that the claim for excess profits duty would be much reduced and perhaps even eliminated entirely. The Bank had prior claim on assets through its debenture holding but, realising that creditors would receive nothing if the company folded, were willing to take the company out of receivership provided that a suitable rescue plan could be devised which would give the Bank some cash benefit.

A resolution was carried unanimously at the meeting to appoint a committee of creditors to supervise a scheme to rescue the company. The committee so formed consisted of Mr C T Barlow of Accles and Pollock (creditors for £2,685) as Chairman, Mr Coan (£2,162), Mr Vaughan of M and L Magnetos (£4,000), Mr Turner (£1,900) and Mr Derbyshire of Bowden Wire Co (£1,516).

The scheme which emerged was accepted by the majority of the creditors at a subsequent meeting held towards the end of June. The committee had tried to obtain a cash offer for the company without success. In view of this, the bank had agreed to accept £125,000 in settlement of its claim of about £145,000, about £20,000 of which had already been found by the directors. The outstanding debentures held by the bank were taken over by a nominee of the directors, with new debentures as security. This stock carried interest at eight per cent and was redeemable after five years. Creditors whose debts did not exceed £5 were paid in cash. The remaining unsecured creditors, amounting to liabilities of £71,044 4s 8d, were given 8 per cent preference shares in lieu and this sum was transferred to the capital account. The excess profits duty, which originally had been assessed as around £35,000, was reduced significantly by the expedient of revaluing downwards the stock held by the company.

Handasyde and Fulton had already resigned from Martinsyde in the autumn of 1920. Mr J Taylor Peddie became the Chairman and Martin was appointed as technical director. Mr G Tilghman Richards, formerly chief designer at Rolls-Royce and latterly of William Beardmore, became General Manager and another man from Rolls-Royce was put in charge of the machine shop. The inspection department was also put under the control of an experienced inspector. These changes were said to have resulted in improvements in efficiency, design and relationships with customers.

Any optimism in the future of the company was not well-founded for by 19th October 1921 a new Receiver had been appointed, a Mr. Tansley Witt of Old Serjeants Inn Chambers, off Chancery Lane, London. The Company was still in Receivership late in 1923 as indicated by a letter from Messrs Donald McMillan and Mott to the Registrar of Joint Stock Companies dated 11th October 1923 as follows:

THE "MARTINSYDE" FARM LORRY

MANUFACTURED BY

MARTINSYDE, Ltd., Aeronautical & General Engineers.

THIS Lorry is built of the very best materials, oak and ash being exclusively employed for the framework.

It is fitted with Martinsyde's front under carriage which not only gives a full lock, but greater rigidity and strength than the standard type, with a considerable reduction in weight.

It is built to take double or single shaft and is well stayed with iron throughout. An exclusive feature is the swinging of the front axle, and the lorry can be drawn over obstacles without any rack to the framework, a point which not only leads to a very great increase in the life of the lorry, but also very considerably lessens the draught necessary on bad ground.

The wheels, which are of the artillery type, are fitted with 3½ or 4 in. tyres, and the steel axles are in one piece.

The floor of the lorry measures 11 ft. by 6 ft. 6 in., and is capable of taking a 3-ton load.

The lorry is supplied with detachable coal boards and one pair of shafts.

A finishing coat of paint can be applied in colour to meet buyer's wishes.

DELIVERY FROM STOCK **Price - £74** CARRIAGE PAID.

High Open Sides (as illustrated) £5 10 0 extra | Extra Pair of Shafts ... ... £5 10 0 extra
Hay Ladders - ... ... £3 10 0 .. | Draw Bar for Tractor ... ... £1 10 0 ..

Discount 5 per cent. for cash against delivery.

SOLE SELLING AGENTS (Wholesale and Retail):— APPLICATIONS FOR LOCAL AGENCIES INVITED.

THE COUNTRY GENTLEMEN'S ASSOCIATION, Ltd. (C.G.A.) LETCHWORTH, HERTS.

TELEPHONE: 41 LETCHWORTH. TELEGRAMS: "KURALNESS, LETCHWORTH."

A poor copy of an advertisement for Martinsyde farm lorries which appeared in 'The Implement and Machinery Review' of 1st March 1920. (Chris Tait)

The Receivership is still being continued under the control of the Court and a portion of the property has been realised but there still remains the freehold property and a large amount of stock and machinery which the Court has directed shall be offered for Sale by Auction in the course of the next two months.

Should the sale prove abortive, it is probable that proceedings will then be taken for foreclosure, but until the assets are disposed of it is important that the Company be kept alive, and we trust therefore that meantime you will not take any steps with a view to dissolution.

The motorcycle operation finally ceased during 1923 and the business, including the service department, was offered for sale by private treaty by the Receiver in the August. The remaining stock of parts were bought up by BAT. BAT (Best After Test) was formed in 1902 by F H Tessier and up to the outbreak of the war had produced a considerable range of models which sold well both at home and overseas. However, the company did not build on this success and failed to produce new models after the war. The company may therefore have considered that buying the Martinsyde stock was an opportunity to restore its fortunes. How BAT became involved in the take-over is not entirely clear but no doubt the long association with Bowen and the Bashall brothers must have played a part. W H Bashall had many successes at Brooklands with BAT machines and was also second in the 1908 TT on a BAT-JAP. BAT offered complete Martinsyde motorcycles and Martinsyde spares and also tried to promote a Martinsyde-BAT hybrid. By 1924 the business had passed to the two Tessier sons who did not seem to make any serious attempt to update the Martinsyde models. Despite cutting the prices of its stock, business faltered and the BAT Motor Manufacturing Company finally ceased trading in 1926.

In February 1924, it was announced that the manufacturing rights, goodwill, and all the surviving stock of airframes and components of the Martinsyde company had been acquired by the Aircraft Disposal Company (also known as Airdisco). The material went by road to Croydon to join the surplus RAF F.4 Buzzards already held there. All the assets having been disposed of, the Receiver was discharged by 12th July 1924 and the Company was formally dissolved

by a Notice in the London Gazette dated 29th January 1926.

The Martinsyde works in Woking were taken over by James Walker in 1926. In 1994 this company moved its operations to another site in Woking and the old Martinsyde factory was demolished. The site was redeveloped into a retail warehouse complex which opened in 1996.

The Aircraft Disposal Company

Although Martinsyde ceased to exist, some of its planes soldiered on for a number of years under the auspices of the Aircraft Disposal Company. This Company was formed in 1920, with Lt Col M O Darby and Lt Col J Barrett Lennard as joint Managing Directors and with Major Jack Stewart as Sales Manager. ADC was founded by a Syndicate with the express purpose of taking over all of the surplus Government stocks of aircraft, aero-engines and parts. On 18th March, Handley Page Ltd was appointed as sole agents to ADC. The proposal was to stabilise the aircraft market by establishing a fixed price list to all purchasers. In order to be fair to the remainder of the aircraft industry in Britain, all *bona fide* British aircraft manufacturers were allowed a rebate on purchases, with an additional rebate allowable on materials sold back to the original manufacturer.

The Syndicate paid the Government £1 million for the stocks and was also required to give to the Government 50% of any profits made. This represented an excellent deal for the Government, bearing in mind that the Treasury would also be taxing the Company's profits. For this money, ADC became responsible for six depots containing some 10,000 aircraft, 35,000 aero-engines and an immense quantity of engine and aeroplane spares, including between 500 and 1,000 tons of ball bearings, 350,000 sparking plugs and 100,000 magnetos. The greater part of this stock was completely new. Amongst these stocks were many Martinsyde Buzzard airframes, together with numerous engines suitable for installation in this type of aircraft. The main works were set up in the main depot at Waddon, adjacent to Croydon airport.

Over the next few years, the Company disposed of millions of pounds worth of stocks. At the same time the remaining stocks were rapidly becoming obsolete. In order to take advantage of the goodwill and reputation which the Company had earned, it was decided to change the Company from a dealer in disposals stocks to an aircraft manufacturing firm in its own right. As a result of this decision on the 30th July 1925, the name was changed to ADC Aircraft Ltd. Within the new Company, John Kenworthy became Chief Designer and Major F B Halford, later to become known for his excellent work with de Havillands, was responsible for engine development. Kenworthy had joined ADC from the aircraft department of the Austin Motor Company, where he had designed the Kestrel, Greyhound and Whippet. Prior to that, he had been at the Royal Aircraft Establishment at Farnborough, where he had assisted in the design of the C.E.1 flying boat and the S.E.5a fighter and, as chief designer, was responsible for the F.E.8 and F.E.9.

ADC marketed aircraft based on the Martinsyde F.4 in a number of variants, including re-engined versions, two-seat conversions and seaplane versions, both for civil and military use. Four were converted to racing machines and a considerable proportion of the remainder went abroad as civil machines or to various foreign air forces. The Aircraft Disposal Company ceased operations in 1930 and the three remaining Martinsyde airframes were burnt.

TELEGRAMS:
MARTINSYDE, WOKING.
CODE-5TH EDITION A.B.C.

CONTRACTORS TO H.M. WAR OFFICE, ADMIRALTY
AND AIR MINISTRY.

TELEPHONE:
WOKING 551, 552, 553.

Aeronautical & General Engineers.

MAKERS OF THE MARTINSYDE
AEROPLANES,
MOTOR CYCLE COMBINATIONS,
FARM WAGONS, ETC.

LONDON OFFICE:
CARLTON HOUSE,
REGENT STREET, S.W.1.

TELEPHONE:
GERRARD 4500.

TELEGRAMS:
MARTINSYDE, PICCY, LONDON.

AERODROME: BROOKLANDS.

YOUR REF.

OUR REF. FHC/JAG.

MAYBURY HILL,

WOKING, 18th September, 19 20.
SURREY.

AND AT BROOKLANDS, BYFLEET.

H. P. MARTIN, CHAIRMAN & MANAGING DIRECTOR.
G. H. HANDASYDE, DIRECTOR & TECHNICAL MANAGER.
HAMILTON FULTON, DIRECTOR & GENERAL MANAGER.

Messrs. The Aircraft Disposal Co.,
Claremont Road,
Cricklewood.

Dear Sirs,

<u>For Mr. Handley Page's kind attention.</u>

With further reference to our Mr. Fulton's telephonic conversations from Woking with your Office regarding the account which we have rendered for Propellors supplied to your order, we have not as yet received the cheque as promised. As we have some very heavy committments to make during the next two or three days we shall be greatly obliged if you will let us have a cheque by return.

Thanking you in anticipation to give this matter your kind and immediate attention and assuring you at all times of our best attention.

We remain,
Yours faithfully,
for MARTINSYDE LIMITED.

SECRETARY.

A letter from the Martinsyde company dated 18 September 1920 to Handley Page, requesting, indeed pleading, for payment for goods supplied. It shows already that Martinsyde was in financial difficulties. Note the change of address to Maybury Hill, Woking, the change of emphasis to general engineering and mention of the manufacture of motor cycles and farm wagons etc.

The management team at Desoutter. Left to right, M Langley (Chief Draughtsman), Marcel Desoutter, Handasyde (Chief Designer), J Fox and C G Barber. (Works Manager).

Handasyde's Subsequent Career

In 1921, after leaving Martinsyde, Handasyde and Hamilton Fulton set up a new venture, the Handasyde Aircraft Company. Raynham and Major A Graves joined the Board of Directors towards the end of the year. The company opened offices in 11a Regent Street, London, and set up a design office in a wooden hut outside The Electric Accumulator Supply Company adjacent to the Martinsyde works in Woking. Soon after the formation of the Company, Handasyde was joined by Stanbury and later by Camm, who had been one of the few employees retained by the Martinsyde receivers to help realise that Company's assets. Several machines were designed but the company was handicapped by not having a factory. This problem was overcome by the company making arrangements with the Air Navigation and Engineering Company (ANEC), at Addlestone in Surrey, to use its manufacturing facilities. This company had taken over the assets and personnel of the Blériot-Aéronautique on the same site on 1st January 1918. The Blériot company had been formed during the war to build Blériots and SPADs for the RFC and RAF under the management of Norbert Chireau.

Handasyde's first two designs, built in 1922, were a transport, intended for air mail services in Australia and a glider. These were followed the next year by an ultralight aircraft of similar layout to the glider. The company was disbanded in 1923 when it ran out of money. Raynham went to Hawker at Kingston as Test Pilot and Sydney Camm, who had become a good friend of his, followed him there as senior designer. Whereas Camm stayed with Hawkers and became Chief Designer, Raynham left in 1925 and founded the Air Survey Co. Ltd., with Ronald Kemp, another ex-Avro test

pilot. Together they built up operations in the Far East, in Burma, Sarawak and India, where they founded the Indian Air Survey and Transport Co. He returned to Britain at the outbreak of the Second World War, was given a commission in the RAFVR and joined the Accident Investigation organisation. He died on 30th April 1954.

In March 1927, Handasyde was employed as aircraft superintendent at Saunders' factory at Cowes in the Isle of Wight. Although reported to be something of a driving force, he made no progress in the company and left in 1928 to join the Desoutter Company at Croydon. The founder of the company, Marcel Desoutter, obtained his flying licence in February 1912 and thereafter flew a Blériot quite a lot at Hendon. Just before the war he had an accident in which he lost his leg. This experience led him to design and manufacture artificial legs, which were in great demand in wartime. By the end of the war, he had made sufficient money to contemplate entering the aviation industry and in December 1928 he set up the Desoutter Aircraft Company with a capital of £21,150. It was his intention to produce a small cabin machine which would be cheap to build and operate. With this in mind he obtained the world rights to the Koolhoven FK.41 and employed Handasyde to redesign this monoplane and set up jigs for mass production. The factory was situated in part of some Air Ministry sheds next to the Aircraft Disposal Company works at Waddon, adjacent to Croydon aerodrome. Handasyde first modified the aircraft to conform to British airworthiness requirements and later completely redesigned it.

Handasyde is next heard of working for the British Klemm Aeroplane Company. The parent company, Leichtflugzeugbau-Klemm GmbH was formed in 1927 as the successor to Daimler-Werke who produced the Klemm-Daimler light monoplane of 1919. Hanns Klemm became the director and chief designer. From March 1929, some twenty-seven Klemm L.25 two-seater light aircraft were imported into Britain through Major E F Stephen of S T Lea Limited, who had obtained the selling rights in the United Kingdom. In February 1933, the British Klemm Aeroplane Company was formed to build the Klemm under licence and market it throughout the British Empire except Canada. The company had works at Hanworth, Middlesex. Major E F Stephen was managing director and Lord Willoughby de Broke became Chairman. Handasyde joined as General Manager with H B Boultbee under him as chief designer, whereupon the aircraft was modified to meet British airworthiness standards and renamed the Swallow. Later Handasyde was being quoted as both works manager and chief designer. Another aircraft, the Eagle, was also put into production. The company was financially restructured in 1935 and became the British Aircraft Manufacturing Company with Handasyde as one of the directors. It put improved versions of the Swallow and Eagle into quantity production and two more designs followed, the Cupid and Double Eagle. By 1936, Handasyde was no longer listed as a director and by 1938 the company was no longer mentioned as a manufacturer of aircraft.

Table 1 - Share Allocations of Trier and Martin

	15.6.06	5.3.13	26.12.18
Werner Auton Trier	1,250	2,000	-
Helmut Paul Martin	1,750	1,000	1,000
Frank Henry Trier	748	1,498	748
Theodor Schneider	500	-	-
Frank Newton Trier	250	501	501
Edward Phillip Audreae	1	1	1
Robert Phillip Martin	1	-	-
Vernon Antony Trier	-	-	2,500
Erwin Julian Trier	-	-	250

Table 2 - Share Allocations of Martinsyde Limited

	1.3.15	20.4.15	28.5.16	17.5.20
Helmut Paul Martin	25,900	20,001	20,001	139,275
George Harris Handasyde	2,100	2,981	2,981	20,910
Hamilton Fulton		301	301	23,590
Guy Blatherwick		1,000	1,000	6,964
Marjorie Martin		4,820	4,820	33,565
Arthur Clemens Trott				550
William Sherborne				400
Frederick Horace Campton				323
Philip Morley				320

Edward Petre (Peter the Painter) with his brother. Edward was killed in a 65-hp Martin-Handasyde on 24 December 1912 trying to get to Edinburgh from Brooklands in very blustery conditions. (Carolyn Pawson)

Graham Gilmour in his own shed at Brooklands working on his sports car during 1911. He was killed flying the fifth Martin-Handasyde design on 17 February 1912.

Robin Skene, who did a considerable amount of flying for Martinsydes during 1914 after gaining his certificate with the Bristol School at Brooklands. He was the first British fatality of the Great War when he crashed at Netheravon on 12 August 1914. (RAF Museum)

Handasyde standing in front of the partially finished first machine in a shed at the Welsh Harp Hendon. Note the trailing edge extensions and the mono-wheeled undercarriage. (J M Bruce/S Leslie Collection)

CHAPTER 2 - MARTIN-HANDASYDE AIRCRAFT UP TO 1914

Despite a great deal of research by aviation historians, it is unlikely that the total number of aircraft built by Martin and Handasyde before the outbreak of the First World War will ever be accurately determined. According to the monthly journal *Aeronautics* of August 1914, the firm had by that time built "some forty machines", However diligent delving into reports from the period has failed to reveal particulars of more than seventeen aircraft of fifteen basic types. Even if all the recorded engine and wing changes are included, the total still only comes to about twenty-eight.

When they first met, Martin and Handasyde were both already experienced mechanical and automotive engineers. However in the absence of documentary evidence, it is difficult to discern how much they knew about aerodynamics and aeroplane design and construction at the time that they embarked upon their new venture. In order to put their early exploits in context, it seems appropriate therefore to review the stage at which aeronautical engineering had reached in Europe when the partners began to build their first machine in 1908.

The success of Wilbur and Orville Wright in making the first powered flight on 17th December 1903, and their subsequent mastery of controlled flight, was achieved on the back of a comprehensive literature search, a diligent four-year research and development programme and practical experience of flight, using gliders. An essential ingredient of their success was the design of a suitable engine and an aerodynamically efficient propeller.

Prior to the Wright brothers first successful flight, one of the Wrights' mentors, Octavus Chanute, had given an illustrated talk before the Aéro-Club de France in Paris in 1903, in which he described his own work and the basis for the Wright brothers successful No.3 glider. Despite this lecture, the news of the successful flights of the Wright's Flyer III in 1905 and the publishing of the Wright's patent in *L'Aérophile* in January 1906, Europeans at this time failed to appreciate either the extent of the Wright brothers' achievement or the aerodynamic principles upon which it was based. Although the pioneering work of Lillienthal and Pilcher before the turn of the century had shown the way, it was not generally understood in Europe that it was first necessary to carry out detailed research and progressive development, by means of bench studies and practical experience with gliders, before controlled powered flight could be attempted. Instead of appreciating that before one could navigate in the air it was necessary to master the principles of controlled flight, European pioneers concentrated on achieving inherent stability, a concept which led them up blind alleys, including the construction of unwieldy cellular wing and control structures based on experience with box kites.

Thus, in Europe during 1907, the longest distance and greatest time in the air were 1,030 meters and 1 minute and 14 seconds achieved by Henry Farman in the Voisin-Farman I. It was not until the summer and autumn of 1908, when the Wrights demonstrated the extent to which they had mastered controlled flight in France and the United States, that it was appreciated how far behind European efforts had lagged. Of

Martin with the first machine, the flimsy construction of which is readily apparent. (J M Bruce/S Leslie Collection)

the many lessons to be learned, two were now readily apparent. The first was the necessity for combining roll control by means of wing warping with the rudder surfaces to achieve controlled banked turns. The second was the amount of work that the Wrights had put into developing efficient propellers of sophisticated design, geared down to produce optimum thrust, which contrasted with the primitive direct drive paddles used by the Europeans.

Despite the Wright brother's ascendancy in controlled flight, it does not mean that pioneers in Europe had been totally idle and the lessons learnt from the demonstrations were soon incorporated into the mainstream of European endeavour. Although it is not meant to ignore the efforts of many others, for the sake of brevity, one might say that there were three mainstream configurations which were being developed in Europe in 1907, prior to the establishment of the Martin and Handasyde partnership, which were then progressively developed over the period 1908 to 1910, in which the partners were building their first three aircraft.

One popular configuration in 1907 was the pusher biplane similar to the Wright biplane with a forward elevator but with both horizontal and vertical tail surfaces and no control in roll. Voisin achieved his first degree of success with this type. By 1909, this type was being successfully developed with control by ailerons or wing warping not only by the Wright brothers themselves but also by Ferber, Voisin and Farman in France and by Curtiss in the United States. Another favoured layout was the tractor layout with no forward control surfaces but with stabilising tailplane surfaces. This form was used in an innovative design by

Ferber in 1904 which, by 1909, had been further developed as biplanes by amongst others Bréguet and Goupy in France and as a triplane by A V Roe in England.

However, the layout which most impressed Martin and Handasyde was the tractor monoplane, comprising main wings, fuselage and tail unit. This configuration was chosen by both Blériot for his 1907 No. VII machine and by Levavasseur for his 1908 Gastambide-Mengin I. Neither of these machines flew successfully but Blériot continued to develop this general configuration, which resulted in the Blériot XI which he used to be the first to cross the English Channel on 25th July 1909. Also Levavasseur, who was the designer of the famed series of Antoinette engines and aeroplanes, further developed his ideas into practical designs. This tractor monoplane configuration was developed into the Antoinette IV and VII, fitted with ailerons and wing warping respectively. It was engine problems and not faults in design which caused Hubert Latham's two failures to cross the Channel in July in these aircraft. As a separate development in 1906, Etrich and Els in Austria successfully flew a glider which was an inherently stable flying wing with a planform based on the zanonia seed. By early 1910, this had evolved, via a pusher powered machine with a front stabilising surface, to a tractor monoplane with horizontal and vertical tail surfaces. This was the predecessor of the elegant Taube monoplanes. As we will see below, it is possible that both Blériot and Erich made some impression on Handasyde's thinking but it is beyond doubt that the designs of Levavasseur had the greatest influence.

The completed first machine in the ballroom of the Welsh Harp Hotel at Hendon in 1909. The machine differed in significant details compared with the partially completed machine shown earlier. (Carolyn Pawson)

The First Martin-Handasyde Machine

Martin and Handasyde build their first aeroplane in 1908 at the Welsh Harp Hotel, adjacent to a lake of the same name on the northern outskirts of London, near to fields which later were to become Hendon aerodrome. Evidence of the design of the first Martin and Handasyde machine is given by four photographs, two of which were taken in the early stages of construction in a shed. The other two, which show the completed aircraft, appeared in Handasyde's own family album and were dated 1909. These were taken in the dining room or ballroom of the hotel. The aircraft shown in the pair of photographs taken in the shed seems to have been more crudely constructed than the version shown in the photographs taken in the ballroom, which suggests that the first pair of photographs were taken earlier than the second pair and not when the aircraft was later being rebuilt.

As seen from the first pair of photographs, the aircraft was a tractor monoplane with a shoulder wing mounted well forward and a tailplane and rudder assembly mounted at the rear of the fuselage and was not unlike a Blériot in general layout and the shape of the wings. According to contemporary literature, the aircraft had a wingspan of about 22 feet and weighed about 580 lbs loaded.

From the same photographs, it would appear that the aircraft was of very flimsy construction. The fuselage was V-shaped in cross-section. The two upper longerons were almost straight from behind the engine to the sternpost and curved downwards towards the front. The keel was parallel to the upper longerons for much of its length but curved upwards towards the tail. The longerons were separated by formers which were slightly staggered along the length.

The wing was heavily cambered and was of two-spar construction, the spars being joined at the centreline by a wooden sleeve. The spars seem to have been of one-piece rectangular section, tapering towards the wingtips. At the time the photographs were taken there was only a single spanwise stringer placed between the rear spar and the trailing edge. The leading and trailing edges consisted of narrow wooden slats, the former being of rectangular cross section. The ribs were heavily cambered and were of a light lattice framework construction with the upper and lower surfaces inset into the spar. The wings were wire-braced from a single king-post above and the undercarriage support below the fuselage on the centreline and from pairs of king-posts above and below the wing at about mid-span. It would appear that the wings were more or less of constant chord except for

Taube-like trailing edge extensions to the six outer wing ribs. There was no evidence of ailerons or of a control mechanism for wing warping but, in view of the wing trailing edge extensions, it was probable that wing-warping was intended.

The undercarriage consisted of a single trailing wheel on the centre line supported by two vertical supports, respectively anchored to the front and rear wing spars and to both sides of the keel. The wheel axle was supported by a strut hinged at mid-point to the bottom of the rear vertical support. It was presumably sprung at the front support by some means. One photograph shows what appears to be an outrigger skid, but this may have just been a strut propping up the wing during construction! It is not possible to determine the shape of the tailplane or fin and rudder as they do not appear in either of the photographs.

The aircraft was powered by a 12-14 hp Beeston-Humber engine taken from a Humber car. It weighed about 200 lb and drove a three-bladed propeller, with a steel boss and wooden paddle blades. Although described as a Beeston-Humber, the engine was probably made in Coventry and was probably designed around 1905 by Louis Coatalen, who was with Humber at the time. It was a T-head engine with a capacity of about two litres and was splash-lubricated. Handasyde extensively modified and tuned the engine to deliver about 29 hp. Although intended to be water-cooled, the engine was run dry because nothing more ambitious than short hops was likely to be attempted. An area of ground at Edgware, north of Hendon, was chosen for the first attempts at flight. After a few attempts at getting airborne, the propeller disintegrated and the imbalance tore the engine from its mounting.

After these abortive attempts the aircraft was rebuilt. It is probable that the pair of photographs of the aircraft taken in the ballroom were of the airframe after the repairs. If this is the case, then there were significant differences between the rebuilt aircraft and the original. As the wings were now covered, it is not possible to determine detailed differences in their construction. However the trailing edge extensions had been removed, additional spanwise stringers were apparent within the upper and lower wing surfaces and the centre kingpost now consisted of twin struts. The front fuselage was much modified with much stronger engine bearers and the undercarriage had been changed significantly. The lateral undercarriage support struts were closer together and supported a skid and twin wheels on a cross-axle. The cross-axle was stiffened by radius rods from the wheel hubs to the centre struts. It was now fitted with a two-bladed propeller.

The rebuilt aircraft was taken to Barking Creek where it

The second machine at Brooklands fitted with the eight-cylinder JAP side-valve engine and Curva propeller.
(J M Bruce/S Leslie Collection)

was taxied to and fro without getting properly airborne. Despite this lack of progress, the partners accepted a contract to give a demonstration of flying with the machine at Halifax. As Martin himself declared, the idea was not as mad as it sounds as a flying exhibition in those days was generally considered a complete success as long as the machine actually left the ground and possibly hopped over a low fence. Although packed in a crate, the aircraft suffered extensive damage due to having been dropped during the rail journey. When they arrived at their destination, they found that theirs was the only aircraft on the scene and moreover the promoters of the meeting had widely advertised a very ambitious programme in which the machine would fly over the town, descend at the zoo and fly back again. There was also a problem with the flying ground. It was situated at the highest point on the local golf course, with a built-up area more or less immediately in the line of flight. This would obviously have presented problems to Martin, the intended pilot, should the flight have run into difficulties.

Martin and Handasyde set about repairing the damage sustained to the aircraft in a large tent that had been erected on the golf course to serve as a hangar. The repairs took several days, during which the couple were generously fêted by the crowds turning up to see them working on the plane and testing the engine. The night following the completion of the repairs, the tent blew down in a gale and the aircraft was completely wrecked. Thus Martin was spared risking his life in what would have been a perilous venture. The engine and what was left of the aircraft were salvaged and the partners returned to Hendon.

The Second Martin-Handasyde Machine

The next recorded activities of the partners occurred in May 1910 after they had transferred their workshop to Brooklands, where A V Roe had earlier been active for a period in 1907-1908. They were the first to occupy a shed in a new complex built by the Brooklands authorities near the middle of the track. At Brooklands, Martin and Handasyde had moved from their relative isolation at the Welsh Harp to an area where considerable aerial activity was developing. Here they must have met many other aviators and designers and it would have been surprising if they had not been influenced by one or more of them. Also the partners must have learnt from the weaknesses in the first design because from now on they earned a reputation for the structural integrity of their designs and a high standard of workmanship.

In the event, when *The Aero* reported that the well-known carburettor firm of Tryer (sic) and Martin had a very smart little machine nearly ready for running trials, it looked very much like a baby Antoinette. The aircraft had similar general proportions, a long slender plywood-covered fuselage and the curious Antoinette control system, in which the pilot held in each hand a wheel with its axis of rotation lying spanwise. The starboard wheel controlled the elevators, the port actuated the wing warping and a rudder bar controlled the rudder. The aircraft retained the king-post method of bracing, used on both their first design and the Antoinette and which was to appear on every subsequent pre-war Martin-Handasyde monoplane. It was not until later, when detailed descriptions of the No.3 machine were published, could it be

Another view of the second machine at Brooklands showing the shallow cockpit area and control wheels.
(J M Bruce/S Leslie Collection)

discerned that the resemblance to the Antoinette was little more than skin deep.

The new monoplane began life with a Humber engine, probably salvaged from their first aircraft, with a chain drive to the airscrew. It is unlikely that the aircraft flew with the Humber engine, but by mid-June an eight-cylinder JAP side-valve engine, supplied to Martin by John A Prestwich, had been fitted with a direct drive to a Curva airscrew. Over the next several months, the engine was variously described as having outputs of 35, 40 and 45 hp, the increases in power no doubt due to fine-tuning by Handasyde.

The Aero remarked that Martin at first contented himself with "rolling practice" but was subsequently reported to have "got off the ground satisfactorily" on Wednesday 15th June. On Saturday the 25th, the aircraft met with a slight mishap on the ground, buckling a wing after a straight flight of some 400 yards. Martin was in the air again several times the following month, making many straight flights at speeds reported to be over fifty mph.

The aircraft suffered a serious accident on Saturday 30th July, damaging the fuselage quite badly. A trial modification had been made to the wing stays. This alteration caused a change in the centre of lift which could not be counteracted by use of the small elevator control surface. Martin had to cut the engine and pancake from about 60 feet. However it was flying again on 10th October with a Lang propeller, and Martin flew it on 31st October, making, according to *Flight's* reporter, "some good flights of about 300 yards".

Martin-Handasyde No.3 Monoplane

The first recorded flight of this monoplane, with Graham Gilmour at the controls, was on 2nd November 1910. Like Martin before him, Gilmour had some trouble controlling the

machine with the Antoinette style of controls and it was criticism from him that led to a change to the more conventional "Blériot" control system with a normal stick, which actuated the elevators, surmounted by a wheel for wing-warping. The tail surfaces were also enlarged. With these modifications, the aircraft was considered to be a new type and the name "No.3 Martin-Handasyde" was painted under the wings. These modifications had been made by 8th November, but the aircraft was damaged on that day because the wires actuating the wing-warping system had been inadvertently crossed. The aircraft suffered a broken propeller, wing tip and front skid. Gilmour was thrown forward onto the starboard wing, where his foot caught in a stay. He was somewhat shaken but unhurt. The aircraft was flying again by the 12th and a few days later Graham Gilmour was reported to be full of praise for the strength of the wings and undercarriage and the aircraft's natural stability. He obviously had confidence in the machine because he flew it on several occasions later that month when adverse weather conditions had grounded other aircraft. However some of the tests were hampered by engine problems. Cracks were found in two cylinders on one occasion and rough running was reported on others.

This aircraft is described in both *The Aero* for 18th January and *Flight* for 25th March 1911. The aircraft was powered by a 40-hp JAP six-cylinder engine with a direct drive to a 7-foot diameter propeller. The wing had a span of 32 feet and a chord of 6 feet 2 inches at the root and 5 feet at the tip, giving an aspect ratio of about 6:1. The thickness of the wing reduced from 8 inches at the roots to 2½ inches at the tips and the wing under camber likewise progressively reduced from 2½ inches to zero. The angle of incidence was 5 degrees at the root and effectively zero at the tip. Both journals agree that the wing, unlike the Antoinette and

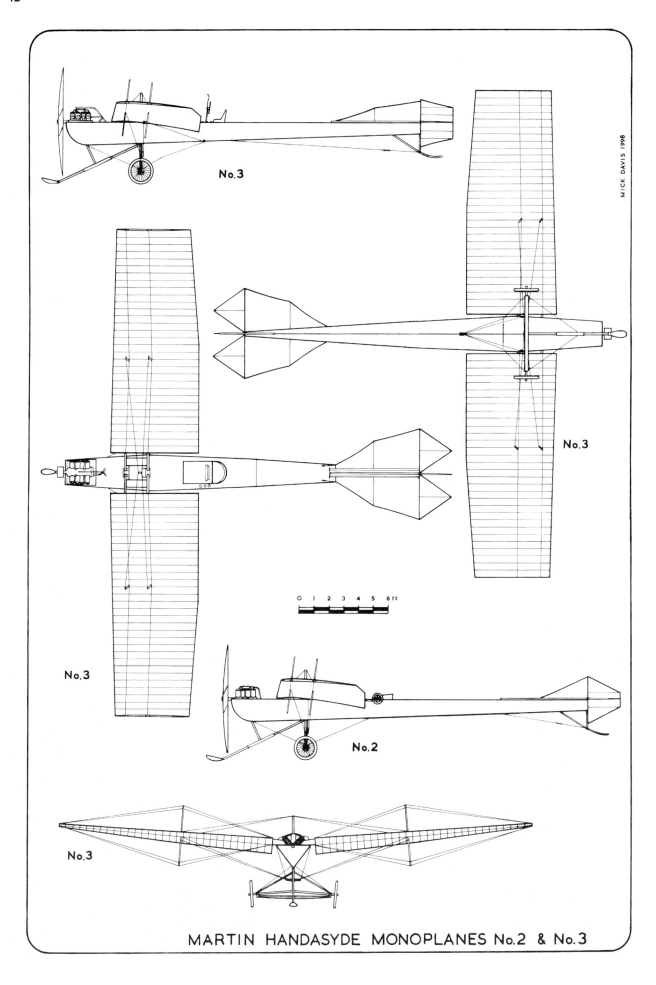

No.3

MICK DAVIS 1998

No.3

No.3

0 1 2 3 4 5 6 ft

No.2

No.3

MARTIN HANDASYDE MONOPLANES No.2 & No.3

The second machine fitted with the Lang propeller.
(J M Bruce/S Leslie Collection)

A close-up of the undercarriage and wing-warping mechanism
of the second machine. (Brooklands Museum)

subsequent Handasyde designs, was not uniformly tapered but had a chord which was parallel over the first 12 feet or so and thereafter tapered towards the tip. Each wing were built up with 31 evenly-spaced ribs onto two ⊢-section main spars, these being 2½ inches wide and 7 inches deep. The wings were braced by means of wires attached to king-posts on both spars at about mid-span from attachment points at the wingtip and fuselage. The front spar was also braced from a mast above the fuselage in front of the cockpit and from the main undercarriage support.

The length overall was 30 feet, the fuselage itself being just under 25 feet long. The fuselage was boat-shaped, with a V-shaped cross-section, the apex being slightly flattened under the pilot's cockpit to allow more room. Its girder structure was covered overall in thin ply, except for openings for the cockpit and engine. It was 1 foot 6 inches wide at the nose, widening to 2 feet at the cockpit, thereafter tapering to 4 inches at the rudder post. It was 20 inches deep at the cockpit tapering to 6 inches at the rear. The roots of the front and rear wing spars were both bolted to posts which were secured to the keel and braced to the upper longerons. The ends of the rear spars were sheathed in iron and could rotate slightly about the bolts to facilitate wing warping. Between the wing root supports was a vertical mast which passed through the fuselage and also formed the main support for the undercarriage. The top of the mast supported bracing wires to the front spars at mid-span and the upper warping wires attached to the rear spar.

The two wheels of the main undercarriage were independently sprung. The principle component of the undercarriage, which weighed some 38 lb, was a transverse leaf spring, made of laminations of lancewood imported from the Caribbean. This spring was attached to the foot of the mast by means of a casting. This casting also incorporated pivots for the two split axles, which were connected by links to the ends of the leaf spring and terminated in the wheel hubs. The links also connected two telescopic tubes, containing compressed rubber, which themselves were connected to the top of the mast. Movement longitudinally

was restricted by stays attached between the links and the fuselage and tensioned by springs. The undercarriage was completed with a skid which at the front carried a large spoon (approximately 1 foot 6 inches by 10 inches) beaten out of sheet steel.

The fin and tailplane halves were each made by stretching a single layer of fabric across a bamboo frame with edges made of wire. The bamboo frames were lashed to the fuselage through eyes in the fuselage decking. The fabric was kept taut by means of turnbuckles in the wires. The elevators were made in the same way on a T-shaped frame and were triangular in shape. The rudder was double-surfaced and built on a wooden frame. The tail skid was supported by the rudder post, which itself was strengthened by a stay tensioned by a coil spring.

The lower warping wires from the rear spar were connected together by a chain which passed between an sprocket and guard pivoted on the lower part of the mast. The sprocket was rotated by means of a long sheet steel rocking lever which was operated through a system of pulleys by turning the wheel on top of the control column. The rudder and elevators were operated conventionally by means of a rudder bar and control column. On the coaming to the left of the pilot were situated three levers operating Bowden cables controlling choke, throttle and spark advance. The control column also supported an oil shield.

At some time after 17th November, the original JAP engine was replaced by another JAP, a 35-hp ohv engine, taken from the Blériot "Big Bat" monoplane that belonged to Graham Gilmour. The machine was flown for the first time with this engine on 11th December by Gilmour. He had intended to compete for the £4,000 De Forest Prize, for the longest distance measured in a straight line flown in 1910 by a British pilot from England to the Continent, and the new engine had earlier shown its reliability by sustaining a flight of over one hour in the "Big Bat".

Sopwith tested the machine in the middle of February as a potential purchaser of the next machine already in the course of construction. The Aero reported that he made a

Close-up of the No.3 Martin-Handasyde at Brooklands. Behind is the Percival Biplane operated from Shed No.2 by the Percival Flying School. (J M Bruce/S Leslie Collection)

A close up of the undercarriage of the No.3 Martin-Handasyde. The wing-warping mechanism and particularly the rocking lever was a good deal more substantial than that on the second machine. (Philip Jarrett)

The No.3 Martin-Handasyde, fitted with a more conventional control system and a 40-hp JAP engine. (Philip Jarrett)

Another close up of the No.3 Martin-Handasyde at Brooklands. Note the oil shield, pressurised fuel tanks, the wing stays and the wing-warping wires. (Philip Jarrett)

A head-on view of the No.3 Monoplane shows the aircraft designation under the wings. (Philip Jarrett)

The Martin-Handasyde 4B Dragonfly built for T O M Sopwith on display at the Olympia Aero Show, March 1911.
(Philip Jarrett)

number of flights but he eventually broke the propeller, the front skid giving insufficient protection when he landed heavily nose-down.

The JAP engine was itself temporarily replaced by a 35-hp Green in the late spring of 1911, which involved fitting a sloping radiator behind the engine. The aircraft had the JAP engine refitted by 4th June, when it was flown by E V B. Fisher. The JAP engine emitted oil at a rapid rate, calculated to be around two gallons per hour, from auxiliary exhaust ports drilled in its cylinders, thereby covering the pilot with oil. This led the aircraft to be christened by some 'the little oil bath'. Some of this oil could be recovered by rubbing-down the pilot over a drip tray after the flight! Fisher, during his flight, was blinded by the oil despite extensive oil shields being fitted. The oil shields adversely affected performance and were removed the following day with the result reported by *Flight* that "owing to a solid stream of oil, the pilot is quite unable to see in what direction he is going".

That evening, on 5th June 1911, Latham crashed his Antoinette on the roof of the Martin &Handasyde shed and the No.3 Monoplane was damaged by falling timber. It is difficult to be certain whether this aircraft flew again for many references by the press are vague as to types and designations. In its issue of May 1913, *Aeronautics* reported "the little monoplane, once the property of the late "D.G." (i.e D. Graham Gilmour), is to be reconstructed and utilised as a school machine". This was never done; the last known report of it appears in *Aeronautics* for August 1914, that stated that the little No.3 might "to this day be seen, for the greater part intact, in the partners' sheds". However it was unlikely to have survived long after the outbreak of the war.

The Antoinette and Martin-Handasyde designs of 1909 and 1910 compared

Both types of aircraft were shoulder-winged tractor monoplanes with a trailing tailplane and a characteristic undercarriage configuration. Both also had the wings wire-braced from kingposts above and below the fuselage and at about midspan. Despite the general similarity in appearance, the two designs were considerably different in design and construction. The Antoinette was considerably larger, having a wingspan of about 50 feet compared with 32 feet for the Martin-Handasyde and it employed an eight-cylinder Antoinette engine of 55-60 hp compared with the eight-cylinder JAP engine of around 40-45 hp.

No detailed description of the actual construction of the wings and fuselage of the second and third Martin-Handasyde machines has apparently survived. However the fuselage of the Antoinette was probably similar in construction except that the Martin-Handasyde machines were ply-covered overall whereas the Antoinette was fabric covered towards the rear.

The wings however were significantly different. The port and starboard wings of the Antoinette were interchangeable, the wing section being symmetrical chordwise about the midchord and did not change in shape or incidence from root to tip. The wing structure was relatively complex with eleven main ribs between the root and the tip and with four or more lighter intermediate ribs between each main rib. The two main spars were of I-section and were evenly spaced chordwise. There were also five intermediate spanwise stringers on both the upper and lower surfaces. The wings of the Martin-Handasyde would appear to have been more

The nose of the Dragonfly with its 50 hp Gnôme engine.
(Philip Jarrett)

advanced aerodynamically. From what can be seen through the linen covering of the Martin-Handasydes, there were just two main spars and far fewer ribs. The rearmost spar was set at about mid-chord, allowing a much more flexible wing aft to the trailing edge. The wing section was more deeply concave on the undersurface, with the maximum thickness at about one-third chord. Also there was considerable washout of wing incidence from root to tip. There were also detailed differences in the configuration of the bracing wires.

The appearance of the tail units were not too dissimilar, although there were differences in shape and construction. The Antoinette had a single triangular elevator and twin rudders of the same shape; with the Martin-Handasydes, the similar layout of the first machine was abandoned for a single rudder and twin triangular elevators.

Although the undercarriage in each case consisted of a cross-axle supported from a central pillar and braced diagonally, there were significant differences in the method of shock absorption. Whereas the Antoinette relied on an oleo pneumatic system within the central support and a one-piece axle, the Martin-Handasydes had split axles supported by a laminated wooden frame with landing loads absorbed by compressed rubber in the telescopic diagonal supports of the wheel hubs. There were also readily apparent differences in the configuration of the main skid.

It is apparent that although Handasyde at first adopted the principle of the control system of the Antoinette, there were from the start differences in the detailed design of the control system, the Handasyde design for example having a more complex chain and sprocket drive for the wing-warping mechanism, and he needed little persuasion to change from the confusing twin hand wheels of the Antoinette design to the more conventional joystick.

Thus it can be concluded that although Handasyde was undoubtedly influenced by the general layout of the Antoinette machine, he clearly went his own way when designing the detailed structure and systems.

Martin-Handasyde Monoplane 4B "Dragon Fly"

In March 1911, *The Aero* reported "considerable interest is taken in the new Martin-Handasyde machines which are in the course of construction. In general outline they resemble the old JAP engined monoplane but are considerably larger, as they are two-seaters". Thus at least two new Martin-

Handasyde monoplanes were reported to be under construction but subsequent reports mention only one, the Type 4B Dragon Fly two-seater that was built for T O M Sopwith and was first exhibited at the Olympia Aero Show in March 1911 by Trier & Martin. There is no evidence that a second machine of this type was ever completed. The aeroplane was similar in concept to the No.3 Monoplane but was much larger and was fitted with a 50 hp Gnôme. It was almost certainly the most elegant aircraft at Olympia that year; its beautiful workmanship won it much praise and its detail design was excellent.

The seats were in tandem, wing span was 37 feet, average chord was 6 feet, wing area was 240 square feet, length 33 feet and the empty weight about 800 lb. The wing loading must have been about 5 lb/sq ft when loaded and the power loading of around 27-28 lb/hp (24 lb/hp if the Gnôme gave its full nominal power). The control system was similar to that of the Monoplane No.3 but the springing of the undercarriage had been improved, the wooden leaf spring being replaced by a steel cross member. *Flight* of April 29th gave a description of the undercarriage;

Another very interesting axle arrangement is that on the Martin-Handasyde machine. Here there is a central column projecting vertically beneath the body, and near the base and the head of the column are two sliding sleeves connected by steel distance pieces and pulled down together towards the lower end of the column by four elastic springs anchored to the base of the column and to the uppermost sleeve. The axle, on the extremities of which are the wheels, is divided and each half is hinged separately to the lower sliding sleeve. Diagonal telescopic struts, in which the volute springs are introduced similarly connect the axle to the upper sliding sleeve. With this arrangement, the axle can rise bodily and either wheel can ride independently.

The Gnôme engine that was fitted was the first successful rotary engine designed by Louis and Laurent Seguin and showed that the partners were keeping abreast of engine developments. Rotary engines had the advantage of light weight and as the whole engine rotated, the vibrations of the propeller were dampened without the need for a heavy flywheel. The cooling was also adequate during ground running. The engine weighed around 165 lb, had seven cylinders of 4.33 inch bore and 4.725 inch stroke and its 7.980 litre capacity gave a nominal 50 hp at 1,200 rpm (closer to 40 hp in practice). The weight, thrust and vibrational loads were taken by a tubular crankshaft, supported both front and rear in the Martin-Handasyde. Mixture passed from the carburettor through the crankshaft into the crankcase, whence it reached the cylinders through valves situated in the cylinder heads. About 25 to 35 per cent of castor oil was added to the fuel for lubrication. As exhaust gas was expelled straight to the atmosphere through a valve in the centre of each cylinder head, the result was that the head of each cylinder spewed fire and unburnt oil. The engine was also prone to dangerous backfires. As the Martin-Handasyde was not fitted with a cowling like most aircraft fitted with rotaries, the pilots were again in for an uncomfortable time! The aircraft was fitted with a small two-gallon tank reserve tank fed under pressure from the 24-gallon main tank, a sight glass between the two showing the pilot when the main tank was empty.

It has not been possible to ascertain how much flying the Dragon Fly did with the Gnôme engine but on Easter Monday, 17th April 1911, it was reported that Tom Sopwith had damaged a wing on landing. Sopwith was soon to leave for his American tour and with insufficient time to repair the

The fifth Martinsyde design with Gilmour at the controls taken at Brooklands. (Brooklands Museum)

Dragon Fly before he left, he was forced to look elsewhere for a suitable aircraft to take. By about mid-June, the Gnôme engine had been replaced by a 65 hp Antoinette, supplied by Hubert Latham, who had become interested in the aircraft during a visit to Brooklands in May. The partners came to place great reliance on this engine, as it happened at just about the time when it was going out of production.

The Antoinette engine was designed by Leon Levavasseur, the first aero-engine version being adapted from a marine engine in 1906, the basic layout being a 90-degree V-8 with the left and right cylinders being slightly offset to allow two big ends to use the same crankpin. The 60-hp version developed in 1909 had each cylinder head and barrel machined from a single steel forging and was fitted with an evaporative steam cooling system using electro-formed copper jackets. The crankshaft had gears or belts to drive the injection pumps, oil pumps and the magneto. The Antoinette engine was unusual in that it had no throttle and the petrol was injected directly into the inlet pipes by a variable-stroke pump, the only control being by means of ignition advance and retard. The engine therefore ran more or less at full power all the time, not necessarily a disadvantage as this would have been necessary to keep the aeroplane airborne.

Following Sopwith's crash, the opportunity was taken to entirely reconstruct the wings. The aircraft with the new engine was tested by Radley on 14th June and by Morison on 19th July. Gilmour, Fisher and Hamel also flew the aircraft in July and a change of propeller enhanced the performance.

On 23rd July, Morison crashed badly when a gust of wind caught the machine as he was manoeuvring to avoid the sewage farm at Brooklands. Morison was unhurt but the propeller and front fuselage were badly damaged, the engine dislodged and the fuel tanks and radiator destroyed. The machine was not rebuilt.

The Fifth Martin-Handasyde Design

The Aero of May 1911 reported that, "Martin and Handasyde have in hand a couple of monoplanes similar to the beautiful machine they showed at the Aero Show". By September, reports confirmed that one aircraft was nearly complete. As with earlier Martin-Handasyde aircraft, the fuselage was of near-triangular cross section. Its longerons were of English ash and plywood gussets were fitted about the spacers to eliminate any need for wire cross-bracing. The plywood shell of the rear fuselage was cut away, forming diamond shapes which were visible through the fabric covering, a mode of construction particular to this machine. The undercarriage was very well engineered with bungee shock absorbers mounted vertically on the central pylon to dampen the vertical movement of the undercarriage legs. The aircraft first introduced the fin and rudder profile which with slight variations appeared on nearly all subsequent Martinsyde designs. An article in *The Motor* mentioned that the aircraft "was fitted with wings of small camber with the object of increasing speed". The engine was a 65-hp Antoinette which required long radiator condensers placed along each side of the fuselage.

The new aircraft made its first flight on or about Monday, 13th November 1911, with T O M Sopwith at the controls. He continued to fly it, damaged the undercarriage on 22nd November 1911 but had it out again on the 27th, after returning from a trip to Paris, taking up a dozen or so passengers including his two sisters and Mrs. Handasyde. The next day he took up several passengers, including George Handasyde, flying altogether for nearly three hours. It was first flown by Graham Gilmour on 2nd December, the aircraft being tossed about in a wind gusting between 10 and 30 mph. Gordon Bell flew the aircraft three days later, completing twelve circuits. Subsequently on 12th December, Bell reached a height of 3,000 ft measured with an altimeter, in about 17 or 18 minutes but failed to keep an accurate note of the time taken.

The following are extracts from a contemporary account of a first flight by a passenger with more experience of sailing and motoring than flying.

The machine was wheeled out from its shed, chocks placed under the wheels, and preparations made to start the

The fifth Martinsyde design with T O M Sopwith in the pilot's seat. Sopwith damaged the undercarriage in an early flight with this machine. (Philip Jarrett)

Close up of the 65-hp Antoinette of the fifth Martin-Handasyde design. This example has a different configuration of undercarriage from those shown above.

engine. The propeller was rotated vigorously after a preparatory priming of the petrol pump and the ignition was switched on. Nothing happened. More priming and more turning of the engine by means of the propeller. Still nothing happened. More priming and more turning followed, without result. Mr. Sopwith in the pilot's seat, backed by an army of attendant experts, declared the engine to be 'flooded', so the turning was continued without the priming, but all to no purpose.

"Still flooded, turn off the petrol" said the experts, and on going to the petrol tap Mr. Handasyde found it turned off already! After that there was no more difficulty about starting, and the incident made me feel quite at home with aeroplanes; it was so exactly the sort of thing one is accustomed to on cars and boats.

The engine ran with a good healthy roar, and standing in the 80 mile-an-hour gale behind the propeller, I noticed the familiar smell that told of castor oil as a lubricant. I noticed, moreover, a very neat system of keeping the machine stationary. The elevator planes of the tail were turned down so that the tail of the machine was raised by the propeller draught, the result being that the running wheels were held down behind the chocks without any tendency to jump over them; the necessity for two or three men to hold the machine back was entirely avoided. (This method would not have been possible without a nosewheel undercarriage, otherwise the machine would have tipped onto its nose and broken its propeller).

Then came my turn, the climb into the passenger's seat and the moment or two while the engine was restarted. Away it went, the exhaust pipes in front spurting out flame, for the ignition was retarded. Then the chocks were removed, the ignition advanced, and we were off. The flame from the exhaust had disappeared and the draught from the propeller was no longer warm, only very strong and redolent of castor oil.

There was a remarkable absence of bumping as we travelled over the undulating surface of the field, the machine seeming to float from one undulation to the next. On approaching the track, Mr Sopwith put his helm hard-a-port and, after coming round, the engine was opened up. The waves seemed to get larger and easier and I thought that we were about to leave the ground, but it was not so. Directly the throttle was opened up there came a slight irregularity in the running of the engine, a cylinder was missing and Mr. Sopwith returned to the starting point to rectify the trouble though it would have been quite possible to go up with seven

out of the eight cylinders firing. The engine was slowed down as much as possible, and by retarding the ignition, it was easy to see which cylinder was at fault by the absence of flame from its exhaust. A fresh plug was put in. (It had been noticed that there had been a distinct 'beat' in the slipstream when one cylinder had been misfiring).

The plug being changed, we started once again. There followed the sensation of 'hydroplaning', then came the turn at the end of the field, and the engine was opened out. Gradually the waves became larger and easier, then the 'sea' seemed perfectly calm - and we were flying. The machine took a natural banking of her own, the right-hand wing rising and the left slanting downwards towards the ground, then, as we came up into the wind the propeller draught seemed redoubled in force and cold, though in reality it was a very warm day.

During our second round of the course we rose to about 150 feet and were flying at about 65 miles per hour, for the Martin-Handasyde is a fast machine, and, though the wind was very light, I had the experience of passing through an 'air pocket', that is an invisible down-draught. Without any pause in her flight or change in trim, the machine suddenly dropped a few feet, and the sensation was precisely that of starting downwards in a fast lift. Once more came the banking, the exhilarating rush into the wind, the gentle dipping and swaying of the great bonnet in front, and, just as I was beginning to appreciate and enjoy the sensations of flying, my first flight was over.

Darkness was approaching and Mr. Sopwith shut off his engine. The nose of the machine tipped downwards, then came again and with added force the sensation of going down in a lift, the ground rose suddenly towards us, and, once again, I seemed to be on a hydroplane at sea as the machine was skillfully piloted between the two lines of sheds to the particular one in which it was housed.

From the amount of use which the aircraft was subjected it was apparent that pilots had full confidence in it. Its excellent performance was attributed by M Chauvière, who had provided its propeller, to the engine which he estimated was producing about 90 to 100 hp at 1,400 to 1,600 rpm compared with the nominal power of 65 hp at 1,200 rpm. No doubt this was an exaggeration but it paid tribute to the abilities of Handasyde to fine-tune engines.

Sopwith flew the machine to St. Albans on 31st December, but damaged the propeller and undercarriage when landing in a small field. The machine was taken back to Hendon by road where it was repaired, the aircraft returning

The wreckage of the fifth Martin-Handasyde after Gilmour's fatal crash. (Brooklands Museum)

to Brooklands by road on 13th January 1912. The Martin-Handasyde was then used for several flights between Brooklands and Hendon. Sopwith reported that he got lost around Mill Hill, near Hendon, on the 20th. Gilmour flew from Hendon to Brooklands on 31st January, a journey which he accomplished in about 20 minutes despite a crosswind and losing his way. Graham Gilmour was flying the aircraft again at Hendon on 3rd February and on the 4th at Brooklands, Sopwith having reverted to his Gnôme-Blériot. Gilmour was the only one to be flying there that day as it was windy and snowing. He came down with frozen condensers and the aircraft covered in ice. Gilmour tested the aircraft on 13th February after it had been fitted with new wings.

On Saturday 17th February, disaster struck. Graham Gilmour was killed flying the aircraft and Martin and Handasyde thereby lost a valued friend and colleague. According to C G Grey, the editor of *The Aeroplane*, he was intending to give them some publicity by making a flight from Brooklands to the City of London by way of the Thames. Just after 11 am, he set course for London and was seen to pass over Hampton Court and Richmond Bridge. When just over the South-Western Railway, which borders the Old Deer Park, he was seen to dive slightly from about 300 feet as if about to land. A moment later the port wing was seen to give in the middle. The machine swung round, seemed to recover momentarily and then the other wing broke, the two wings folding backwards and upwards. At once the machine dropped straight onto its nose, burying the engine into the ground till only the two rear pairs of cylinders were above ground. The whole rear fuselage turned slowly onto its back, the fore part being totally smashed. Gilmour was killed instantly.

The partners reported to the press that;

The cause of the accident remains a mystery. Careful examination of the machine has shown that all the stays and wires were intact, as also control rods and wires. This makes it impossible for the wing to have folded up as stated by some. The wing spar housings were in order, though broken, or rather torn from their fastenings by the inertia of the wings at the impact. The back spar housings and compression struts across the body of the machine were torn apart in tension, all the bolts being bent outwards. This shows them to have been on the machine when it hit the ground, and the weight of the

back spars evidently pulled them apart. Thus the wings could not have folded backwards in the air.

The reasons for the accident have never been adequately explained. The excellent reputation of the manufacturer's workmanship led to the expression of considerable doubt about the reliability of the eye-witnesses statements, although these were corroborated by others who heard the sounds of the structure breaking before the actual crash. Also other engineers did not agree with the partners' interpretation of the wreckage. The weather conditions may well have been a contributory factor. It was a day of such exceptional turbulence that pilots at Hendon, Shoreham and Eastchurch had all reported alarming experiences and flying had been suspended at Brooklands.

Following this fatality, the partners subjected wings to static loading tests. These tests proved that the wing structures had a safety factor of about five, which was considered ample by the standards of the time. Nevertheless a new form of wing construction was adopted for future designs, using box spars with much greater strength than solid spars of the same cross-section.

The First Martin-Handasyde Monoplane for the RFC

Martin and Handasyde seemed to have abandoned giving their aeroplanes any logical designations by this time and it is not possible to determine with any degree of certainty from the technical press of the day how many airframes were built and how many modifications were involved.

The next machine to be reported under construction is believed to have been designed for the first official competition to select aircraft for the Royal Flying Corps, the formation of which was imminent. It was fitted with a 65-hp Antoinette and flew at Brooklands for the first time on 27th June 1912 with Gordon Bell as the pilot. It completed several straight flights despite a high wind and a misbehaving engine. Gordon Bell flew it extensively during the first half of July and also competed in the third aeroplane handicap race at Brooklands on Saturday, 15th July 1912. Starting seventh on handicap, Bell was in the process of overhauling all the other machines when he had to retire on the last lap when a water connection parted. It is not clear when it was delivered for testing by the RFC, but it was flown as a non-participant

The Chenu-powered Martin-Handasyde being prepared for the Military Trials at Brooklands. The doors of the shed have been dismantled so that the machine can be removed. (Philip Jarrett)

during the Military Trials held at Larkhill. It continued to be flown there after the Trials by Raynham, including a flight on 5th September.

The Aero for June 1912 gives a description of the construction of the aircraft. The longitudinal members of the fuselage were first clamped in templates on a special bench and when in position the three-ply wood forming the side walls was screwed into place. The vertical transverse members were then jammed up hard against the longitudinals and fixed by screws through the three-ply. The upper horizontal cross-members were assembled in a similar way, being screwed to the ply top surface, but were further strengthened by bolts parallel to the cross-members and tightened through the longitudinals. The wing chord was 8 feet 6 inches at the root and 7 feet at the tip and there was a slight wash out of about 1 to 1½ degrees both in camber and incidence between root and tip. There were two main spars 3 feet 6 inches apart. The I-section of the main spars formerly used had been replaced by box sections formed by top and bottom ash members joined by 3/16th-inch three-ply vertical pieces attached by numerous screws. Distance pieces were placed between the box members where the spar joined the ribs. There were additionally five longitudinals above and below the wing mortised into the ribs and strengthened with three-ply gussets at the joints. The aircraft was again fitted with an Antoinette engine with the radiators flanking the fuselage.

Military Trials Machine

By the middle of July, the Antoinette-powered machine was joined by larger machine fitted with a 75-hp Chenu engine driving a four-bladed propeller through a 2:1 reduction gearing. This was intended as an entry for the Military Trials due to begin on 1st August. Gordon Bell was very active flying both machines during the second half of the month. Although Gordon Bell was showing a great deal of confidence in the machine there were already disquietening reports about

the reliability of its engine. One flight terminated in an unpowered glide back to the airfield from over Weybridge. Whether the lack of power was intentional or by accident was not mentioned. A later flight ended suddenly when a leaking radiator sprayed Gordon Bell's face with boiling water. The engine was obviously a cause for concern because on 26th July, just before the aircraft was due to go to Larkhill, it was reported that Gordon Bell was testing the engine into the small hours.

The Military Trials took place during the month of August 1912 at Larkhill on Salisbury Plain. The Martin-Handasyde entrant was towed round Brooklands in its cage-like container by a steam locomotive in front of a crowd of onlookers on its way to the trials. Only nineteen of the thirty-one entries actually turned up. Of these, twelve, including the Martin-Handasyde, were monoplanes and the rest were biplanes.

The Martin-Handasyde and its engine proved to be heavier than expected and according to one report, the excess weight was so great that the position of the wings had to be changed, a major modification that affected the aeroplane's flying characteristics. The Chenu engine continued to be a great source of trouble, not only for the Martin-Handasyde but also for Coventry Ordnance, one of its two entrants having a more powerful version of the same engine. The magneto driving gear on both engines had to be completely dismantled and redesigned and the casing turned at right angles to its former position. The lugs by which the casing was bolted to the engine also failed on the Coventry Ordnance engine. The engine's reputation for staying at home earned it the appellation "Chez-Nous". The Martin-Handasyde was seldom able to fly at Larkhill and such flights that were made often terminated in engine failure.

The aircraft in the Trials had to meet a detailed specification and were expected to meet a number of performance requirements which included ease of assembly, take-off and landing runs, speed, range and endurance, and climbing and gliding ability. Due to its engine problems, the

The Military Trials machine outside Shed 17 in which it was assembled. The lorry that was used to tow it to Larkhill is visible in the background. (Brooklands Museum)

Martin-Handasyde took part only in the "Quick Assembly" and "Rough Weather" tests. In the "Quick Assembly Test", each aircraft was brought out of its packing case and assembled, after which it was required to demonstrate that it was in a flying condition. It took one hour thirty-three minutes for the Martin-Handasyde to complete this part of the test, which was about the mean compared with the shortest time of fourteen minutes thirty seconds recorded by the Avro biplane and the longest time of nine hours twenty-nine minutes by the Maurice Farman biplane. However the Martin-Handasyde did not complete the second part of the test which involved dismantling, packing away and reassembly.

The Martin-Handasyde was one of only five of the contestants adjudged to have completed the "Rough Weather" test. In this test, aircraft were required to demonstrate 'stability and suitability for use in bad weather, and in a wind averaging 25 mph 30 feet from the ground without undue risk to the pilot'. Gordon Bell completed this test on 6th August, a day which proved to provide conditions far worse than the minimum requirements. The wind gusted between 17 and 47 mph and during the day this gale ripped off the roof of the shed which housed the Coventry Ordnance Works biplane.

By 9th August, the partners had given up with the Chenu engine and apparently considered a Renault as a replacement. However a 65-hp Antoinette had been fitted by 27th September and the aircraft was flown in this configuration by Edward Petre ("Peter the Painter"). Petre continued to fly the re-engined Military Trials machine during October 1912 and made one or two cross-country flights during that month. The machine was extensively damaged on 24th October after a visit to Farnborough when Petre attempted a landing in a field after dark, hit a tree stump and overturned.

Aeronautics for November 1912 reported that the re-engined machine reposed at Brooklands and gave a full description of the Antoinette-powered machine together with a detailed drawing with the dimensions in metric units. The dimensions in the text correspond to the official ones given in accounts of the Military Trials in other contemporary

journals. However it is interesting to note that the dimensions given in the drawing were for a larger machine and corresponded exactly to those on a drawing in a French publication, *Les Aéroplanes de 1914-1915*, depicting a similar but not identical Martin-Handasyde aircraft which more closely resembled the shape of the Military Trials machine. For the record, these drawings depict aircraft with spans of 47 feet 1 inch and lengths of 37 feet 5½ inches and may well refer to models which appeared later in 1913 or even 1914.

Aeronautics reported that the fuselage of the Military Trials machine was 35 feet 4 inches long overall and again of triangular section. It was of similar construction to earlier machines except that the upper cross-members were no longer constructed of wood but of duralumin slotted into the longerons and braced diagonally with wood. The deepest section near the pilots seat was 2 feet 1 inch tapering to 7 inches at the tail. The width decreased from 2 feet 6 inches to 11 inches. The whole fuselage was covered with three-ply but the spaces behind the cockpit between the diagonal members were cut away for lightness. The engine was covered with a closely-fitting cowling of aluminium. Unlike the Chenu-powered version which had a radiator in the form of a saddle fitted behind the engine on the upper part of the fuselage above the wing, the Antoinette engine was provided with the usual condenser arrangement flanking each side of the fuselage.

The dimensions of the wings were as follows; span 42 feet 6 inches; chord 8 feet 6 inches at root, 6 feet 8 inches at tip, aspect ratio 5.5, camber 3 inches under, 7½ inches upper, angle of incidence 4 degrees, dihedral angle 6 degrees, wing area 300 sq feet. They were almost of rectangular shape, having a straight leading edge and a slightly tapered trailing edge. They were cut away at the roots to improve the pilot's downward view, the cut-out in photographs appearing to be rectangular in shape. There was a pronounced washout at the tips both in camber and incidence. The planes were built on two spars formed of a lattice girder built of two lengths of ash with the open sides covered with 3/16th-inch

The Chenu-powered Martin-Handasyde receiving a great deal of attention at the 1912 Military Trials at Larkhill.
(J M Bruce/S Leslie Collection)

three-ply. The front and rear spars were 2.75 and 2.25 inches deep respectively at the root and were both 1.875 inches wide. The wing spars were recessed or hollow at the roots to allow the insertion of stub spars which were securely bolted to the fuselage. The stub spars passed through the fuselage and were securely bolted to the upper horizontal members of the fuselage at the junction with the central king-post. The loads were further distributed to the fuselage structure by long bolts which completely encircled the fuselage. There were 10 ribs on each wing, built up with ash laths top and bottom. The rear portion of each rib had canvas glued over it to give it additional strength. Two formers of silver spruce were positioned between each pair of ribs. Each wing had six upper and six lower longitudinal formers in addition to the spars, with canvas stiffeners at the rib joints.

Due to the leverage offered by the long slender fuselage, the tail surfaces were relatively small, having a fixed tail area 30 sq feet, a fin area 7 sq feet and a rudder area 8½ sq feet. The tailplane was roughly semicircular, with the inner surface rounded to allow movement of the rudder. It was fitted flush with the upper longerons. The undersurface was flat and the upper surface was cambered. Both tailplane and fin were unbraced.

As with previous types, the king-post passed through the fuselage and also formed the main undercarriage strut. It carried two steel cables to the front and rear spars of each wing. Smaller stay masts were fitted to the spars 9 feet from the fuselage and each of these masts carried stay wires above and below the wing attached to the root and to the spars 2 feet from the tip. There were also drift wires running from the front fuselage to the rear spar and from the front skid to the main spar.

The undercarriage consisted of two 2-foot diameter wheels, fitted with 100 mm tyres, mounted on a jointed axle, connected to the main central strut by duralumin tubes and the front skid by an A-frame. The recoil of the landing was taken up by rubber springs. These were hinged to a separate attachment to the lower fuselage, relieving the lower central

strut from some of the shock resulting from a rough landing. A tail skid completed the arrangement. The undercarriage arrangement seemed to be a retrograde step from earlier designs, being unduly rigid and liable to damage from anything but a very soft landing. However this redesign with stronger springs may have been needed to satisfy the ploughed field requirement in the rules of the contest.

The controls were similar in principle to earlier designs but differed in detail. The rotary movement of the wheel on the control column was now transmitted to the warping mechanism through a bevel gear, which conferred a rotary motion to a drum below the universal joint on the control column around which the wires to the warping mechanism were wrapped. A propeller-driven pump to pressurise the main fuel tank was mounted on the undercarriage vertical post.

The weight was calculated to be around 1,000 lb empty and 1,500 lb fully loaded with pilot, passenger and 5 hours of fuel, giving a net loading of 3.3 lb/sq ft and a gross loading of 5 lb/sq ft. This resulted in a power loading with the 65-hp Antoinette of 23 lb/hp and an estimated top speed of 67 mph.

The above description, however, may have referred to an almost identical aircraft which had been completed at about this time and this may have been the monoplane that Petre was flying on Saturday 9th November 1912 when he crashed while spiralling down with the engine switched off, luckily without injuring himself. Petre was flying again, presumably with the same machine, on 17th November and he flew it to Farnborough on the 19th. It stayed there for some time and may have been the second Martin-Handasyde monoplane ordered for the RFC, which possibly had been accepted for testing despite the order that was in force at that time banning consideration of monoplanes.

On 5th July 1912, Capt E B Loraine and S/Sgt R H Wilson of the RFC were killed when their Nieuport monoplane spun in from 400 feet. On 6th September, Capt Hamilton and Lt Wyness-Stuart, whilst on reconnaissance duties connected with cavalry training, crashed in a 100-hp

The Chenu-powered Martin-Handasyde Military Trials aircraft is prepared for flight at Brooklands.
(J M Bruce/S Leslie Collection)

Deperdussin near Hitchen and four days later Lts Hotchkiss and Bettington died when their 80-hp Bristol monoplane crashed at Wolvercote near Oxford. These accidents involving monoplanes led to Colonel Seely's edict of September 1912 banning the use of monoplanes by the Military Wing of the RFC. The ban was not lifted despite a subsequent Government investigation absolving this class of machine from blame. This was a death blow to Martin and Handasyde's aspirations for supplying aircraft to the RFC. In March 1913, one machine was reported to be languishing damaged in a tent hangar at Farnborough. On 12th March in the House of Commons, Mr. Joynson-Hicks asked the Secretary of State for War, "whether any of the Flanders, Deperdussin and Martin-Handasyde monoplanes delivered during the past four months for the Military Wing, RFC, are in flying order; if so how many of each?" Colonel Seely replied that all were in flying order, but a list of RFC aeroplanes published on 1st May 1913 showed one Martin-Handasyde monoplane as "under ban". One Martin-Handasyde aircraft was given the official serial number 278, but was never officially taken over by the Military Wing and was eventually struck off charge on 29th August 1913. This may have been one of the two Martin-Handasyde monoplanes supplied to the RFC which was known to have been taken to Shoeburyness, where it was shot at and sand-tested to destruction.

Martin-Handasyde Military Monoplane

Flight reported on Saturday 7th December 1912 that "Mr. Handasyde was testing the engine of the latest Martin-Handasyde monoplane before handing the machine over to the War Office." Petre had been flying a Martin-Handasyde at Farnborough, probably the same aircraft, on 3rd to 5th December. He was then reported to be flying "the latest Martin-Handasyde" at Brooklands on Sunday 15th December, and it seems possible that this was indeed a different machine subsequently known as the Martin-Handasyde Military

The wreckage of Edward Petre's Martinsyde, following his fatal accident on 24th December 1912.
(E.A.Harlin collection)

Monoplane. Although similar in appearance to the machine delivered to the RFC, with a triangular-sectioned fuselage, this aircraft had enlarged elevators and an improved system of shock absorbers in the undercarriage, the rubber elements being housed within the central vertical pylon, which was itself supported from a large-diameter steel tube incorporated longitudinally within the fuselage structure. The Antoinette engine was given a closely-fitted aluminium cowling and was cooled by means of condensers made of aluminium tubing, 13 feet 6 inches long and nearly 70 sq feet in area but weighing a mere 9 lbs. The engine drove a Regy propeller of 2.60 metres in diameter and 1.40 metre pitch at a rotational speed of 1,150 rpm on the ground and 1,300 rpm in the air, developing around 60 hp. A padded coaming surrounded the cockpit area, which seated two in tandem. Warping lateral control was applied to the wings, the tips of which were washed-out to give better natural stability.

On Christmas Eve, Martin and Handasyde lost another

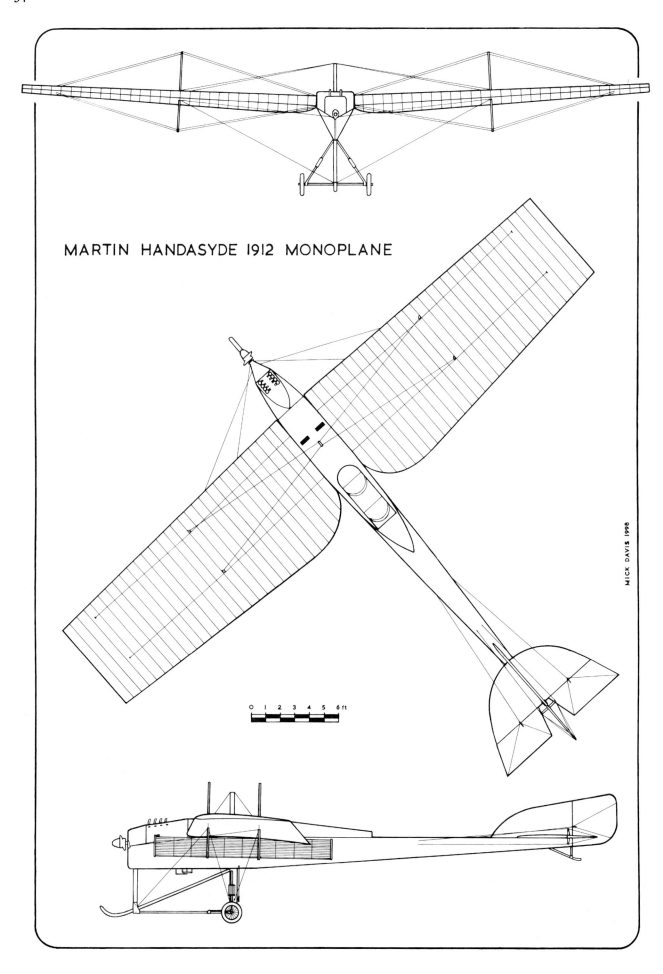

MARTIN HANDASYDE 1912 MONOPLANE

0 1 2 3 4 5 6 ft

MICK DAVIS 1998

The second machine delivered to the RFC, given the serial number 278. (Brooklands Museum)

colleague when Edward Petre was killed flying a Martin-Handasyde monoplane fitted with a 65-hp Antoinette engine and built in November 1912. This may well have been the same as the aircraft mentioned above. He had wanted to fly to Edinburgh non-stop before Christmas but had been delayed for several days by bad weather. He had eventually taken off, against his better judgment, from Brooklands at 9.10 am, hoping to get to Edinburgh in about four-and-a-half hours. The wind strengthened during the flight and blew him off course and after just over three hours flying in extreme turbulence, the aircraft had drifted as far as the coast at Marske-by-the-Sea in Yorkshire, some 250 miles from Brooklands. He evidently feared that he would not be able to get further in these adverse conditions and had tried to land. It was reported that the aircraft descended from about 500 to 400 feet, rose again and then fell to the ground. The only two eye-witnesses called at the inquest could not agree as to whether the machine had broken up in the air prior to the crash and a verdict of "accidental death" was returned. However, after the inquest other eye-witnesses reported that both wings had collapsed. It was also reported that a number of pieces of wreckage had been found several hundred yards to leeward of the crash site.

In an article in *The Aeroplane* the following week, its editor C G Grey quoted hearsay evidence, came to the conclusion that structural failure of the wings had occurred, and pontificated about the way in which this might have happened. These days such conduct would have probably have found him in court! However, an investigation conducted by the Public Safety and Accidents Committee of the Royal Aero Club also came to the conclusion that the wings had collapsed. This verdict brought the following vigorous rebuttal from Martin, which was supported by Petre's brother, who had examined the wreckage and could find no evidence of wing failure.

Sir, - Last night the Public Safety and Accidents Investigation Committee of the Royal Aero Club issued its report on the accident at Marske-by-the-Sea, in which Mr. Edward Petre lost his life while attempting a flight from Brooklands to Edinburgh.

The gist of this report is that the wings of the monoplane collapsed downwards in the air, and the Committee have come to this conclusion solely on the evidence, and second-hand at that, of four persons who maintain to have seen this actually happen.

Now, at the coroner's inquest, held on the spot and within a day of the accident, where the police were able to discriminate between what witnesses actually saw and what they thought they saw or expected to see, a verdict was returned that the accident was due solely to the terrible wind that was blowing at the time Mr. Petre endeavoured to land - a higher wind probably than has ever been flown in before.

It is curious that, though the Aero Club Committee had not only the same evidence before them as the coroner, but also the opportunity of verifying the strength and solidity of construction of the Martin-Handasyde monoplane, they should come to such a ridiculous conclusion.

As a matter of fact, the Committee did not even take the trouble to pay a visit themselves or send a capable representative to our works at Brooklands to examine similar machines which we have there; and they show their utter and complete ignorance of the subject by bracketing the design and construction of our wings with those of the Antoinette monoplane, whereas they are, in point of fact, as dissimilar as possible.

From a committee consisting of rival manufacturers, who would naturally know their business, we would have nothing to fear, but from one composed, with two exceptions perhaps, of gentlemen who are not engineers, and who certainly know nothing of practical construction, we are pained, but not very surprised, to have to put up with a report as nonsensical as it is unjust.

(signed) H.P. Martin

The 1913 Olympia Show model with the 80-hp Laviator replaced by a 120-hp Austro-Daimler at Hendon with a Boxkite taking off in the background. (J M Bruce/S Leslie Collection)

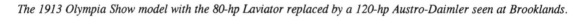

The 1913 Olympia Show model with the 80-hp Laviator replaced by a 120-hp Austro-Daimler seen at Brooklands.

Gordon Bell in the 1913 Olympia Show model at Hendon, with the 80-hp Laviator replaced by a 120-hp Austro-Daimler.

The 1913 Aerial Derby entrant at Hendon, showing the tandem cockpit arrangement and the straight-edged cutout at the wing root.

Handasyde drew a different conclusion from the evidence at the crash site. He contended that an actual landing had been made but the plane had rebounded about 40 feet into the air and out of control had come to rest about 400 feet further on, landing on its left-hand side. This was supported by the condition of the engine which had sustained only slight damage to the nose and forward left hand cylinder jacket. Also the ignition had been switched off at the time of the accident and the dashboard clock was still going. None of these things was consistent with a fall from a height. The report from one eyewitness that he "saw the wings working" was probably more consistent with the large amount of warp associated with flying on a gusty day than from any structural failure.

1913 Martin-Handasyde Monoplanes

It is not possible to determine, from contemporary reports and photographs, the number and types of aircraft constructed by Martin and Handasyde during 1913. It would appear that there were at least three but there may have been more. All that can be done is to recount the story as it unfolds in the aviation press at the time.

The loss of Gilmour and Petre and the War Office's ban on monoplanes did nothing to dampen the partners' enthusiasm for their basic design. A new monoplane exhibited on the T B Andre stand at Olympia in February 1913 was similar in concept to its immediate predecessors but with improved detail design. There was no internal wire bracing in the fuselage. The front fuselage was covered in polished plywood and in the rear half all the joints between the ash longerons and spacers were liberally gussetted with plywood, enabling the machine to be lightened by cutting away diamond shaped pieces from the ply covering aft of the cockpit. The line of the aluminium engine cowling was continued rearwards by a superstructure of ply-covered spruce which afforded some protection to the occupants, the pilot being seated behind the passenger. Duralumin was used extensively for metal parts and fittings.

According to the aviation press, the wings were constructed in a similar manner to previous models with twin box spars. These were 3 feet 6 inches apart, the front spar being 7 inches deep and 1½ inches wide and the rear 6 inches deep and 1.875 inches wide. As before, these were filled with solid blocks where the ribs joined. Further reinforcement was introduced at these points by glueing tape and strips of wood along the ribs to form a three-ply, said to double the strength. From photographs, it is apparent that this machine had straight-sided cut-outs at the roots from the trailing edge to the rear spar to improve the pilot's view.

Martin and Handasyde were seeking an engine of increased power and chose the 80-hp Laviator (the Dansette-Gillet engine renamed), having a concentric valve system with the inlet valve situated within the exhaust valve. The earlier, rather stiff, form of undercarriage design had been improved. In the new design the lower part of the fuselage-mounted king-post had been replaced by a heavy-gauge steel tube of about 3½ inches diameter. The radius rods were pivoted at the bottom and landing loads were absorbed by struts which ran from the axles to an concentric cylinder around the main strut which was sprung by internal rubber bungee. The steel undercarriage support was adequately braced by dural tubes and wire. The dural stays to the front of the skid were replaced by wires as it was supposed that people would be less inclined to rest their feet on them. There were also additional bracing wires to the king-posts on the wings. There were also duralumin tubes connecting the roots of the wing-mounted king-posts through which bracing wires could be threaded from front to rear spars without putting any strain on the wing rib. This enabled wires to be connected, for example, from the front spar to retaining points on the rear fuselage. This was reported to give a safety factor of over sixteen.

However the Laviator was not sufficiently powerful and was replaced in April by a 120-hp Austro-Daimler, of a similar type to the engine fitted to Cody's machine that won the Military Trials. The Austro-Daimler engine was an in-line six-cylinder ohv engine with twin carburettors, a bore of 4.72 inches and a stroke of 6.89 inches. The pistons were of steel and the cast iron cylinders were surrounded by water jackets of electrolytic copper. The crankshaft had a bearing between each cylinder. The inlet manifold was jacketed with hot water to improve fuel volatilisation. The manifold consisted of a circular drum inside which a concentric tube rotated, progressively uncovering the inlet ports, air/fuel supply and auxiliary inlet air, thereby keeping the mixture strength uniform independently of throttle position. All these features aided smooth running, although care had to be taken to thoroughly warm-up the engine, otherwise differential expansion of the pistons and cylinders led to a power loss. The radiator was fitted behind the engine and was cooled with air fed through three inlets, one on each side and one below the engine.

The re-engined aircraft made its first flight on 8th May 1913 in the hands of Gordon Bell. The powerful Austro-

A 1913 Martin-Handasyde with the curved wing root cutout at the trailing edge. (J M Bruce/S Leslie Collection)

The 1913 design Martin-Handasyde showing details of the 120-hp Austro Daimler engine installation, undercarriage and wing bracing. (Carolyn Pawson)

Daimler gave the aircraft a fine performance; its speed was reported to be about 82 mph. On Whit Monday, 12th May, the Martin-Handasyde was scratch machine in the Whitsun Aeroplane Handicap and came second 39 seconds behind Harry Hawker's Sopwith biplane to which it had given 69 seconds on handicap. On Sunday 25th May, Gordon Bell gave an exhibition of flying at Brooklands after returning from Hendon with a lady passenger.

The Aeroplane featured a report by a passenger of a flight in the Martin-Handasyde the previous Thursday:

In a manner similar to the Antoinette, the Martinsyde ran along before rising with the fuselage horizontal and the elevator in the normal flying position. So as soon as the speed was sufficient the machine started to rise into the air. Mr. Bell then elevated, and in a moment we had jumped to sixty feet at a steep angle. Straightening out a little, Mr. Bell then allowed the machine to rise steadily, swiftly, and at the same time almost imperceptibly to a height of three hundred feet. We then circled the track several times in a staid and sober manner with the engine well throttled down. At each turn the Martinsyde banked naturally to a proper degree.

I have made flights on a large number of aeroplanes during the last eighteen months with no other object than to watch the manner of their flying, but in none have I been quite so comfortable as on the Martinsyde. Though there is no deliberate attempt at a cowl turning upwards to throw the wind off - the deck being perfectly flat.....and about level with the passenger's shoulders - yet the draught is not strong. Even when I stood up the pressure was not high. There are many reasons - most of them highly favourable to the design - which account for this.

Tired of staid flying, Mr. Bell opened the throttle fully, and descending to within a hundred feet of the ground, began to turn in fairly small circles at full speed, banking heavily at the turns...... The Martinsyde answers its controls with great swiftness and precision. The slightest movement of the warping wheel or rudder bar was immediately responded to. The landing speed is very low, but in the absence of wind pressure I was unable to judge the speed.

In view of the ban on monoplanes for the Military Wing it was hoped to instead interest the Admiralty in the aircraft. To this end, Gordon Bell flew the Austro-Daimler monoplane to Eastchurch on 2nd June 1913 where it was flown almost daily with officers of the Naval Wing, including Commander C R Samson, as passengers. However the Admiralty never ordered any. This was probably in part due to the fatal accident which occurred with the Martin-Handasyde on its return to Brooklands from Eastchurch on Friday 13th June.

According to a contemporary account given in Brett's *History of British Aviation*, Gordon Bell flew back with Lt J R B Kennedy RN, as his passenger. They arrived above Brooklands at 5.15 pm and Gordon Bell proceeded to "shoot-up" the aerodrome. For fifteen minutes he roared in and out and around about the hangars, diving on the spectators and waving his hand to them as he almost scraped his wing tips on the grass in vertical-banked turns. Finally he flew between two of the sheds with only inches to spare, pulled up sharply to clear another hangar, went into a steep climbing turn, stalled, and dived into the ground onto his left wing tip and nose. Lt. Kennedy, who had been granted his aviator's certificate (No.423) on 18th February 1913, was crushed to death as the front seat telescoped. Mr. Gordon Bell was taken to hospital with very serious injuries, including a fractured skull, from which he subsequently recovered. All the expert witnesses who were called at the inquest were unanimous in condemning the pilot for dangerous flying and Gordon Bell was brought up before the General Committee of the Royal Aero Club four months later and cautioned as to his future flying. The aircraft was completely exonerated by the Accidents Investigation Committee. The airframe was rebuilt, fitted with a new engine and exhibited at the 1913 Olympia Show.

It seems that one or more aircraft of a similar type were built through the year. One was almost identical except that the wing root cut out was curved rather than straight. A contemporary photograph shows Handasyde standing by a wing from such an aircraft before completion. The structure of the wing differed from the description of the wing for the first 1913 machine in that the front spar was much slimmer. There was also another machine with much smaller wheels but whether this was a new or modified machine is not known.

Aeronautics reported in its September issue that a Martin-Handasyde hydromonoplane was under construction. This venture could well have been inspired by the announcement by the *Daily Mail* on 1st April 1913, of a prize of £5,000 for the first circuit of England and Scotland by a 'Waterplane'. *Aeronautics* described the float undercarriage in some detail. A single central float was to be fitted, consisting of two layers of 1/8-inch mahogany, the inner layer being set laterally and the outer skin longitudinally, with fabric between. The under surface was to be entirely flat with no step and the float was to be attached to the central pylon in a similar fashion to a conventional wheeled undercarriage. The outboard floats were to be

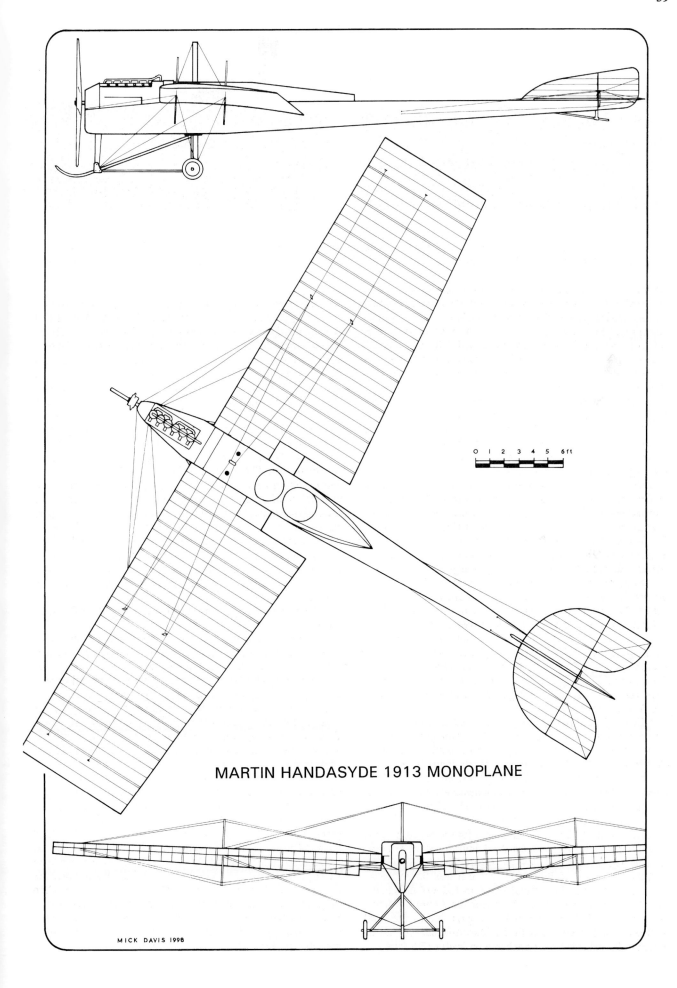

MARTIN HANDASYDE 1913 MONOPLANE

0 1 2 3 4 5 6 ft

MICK DAVIS 1998

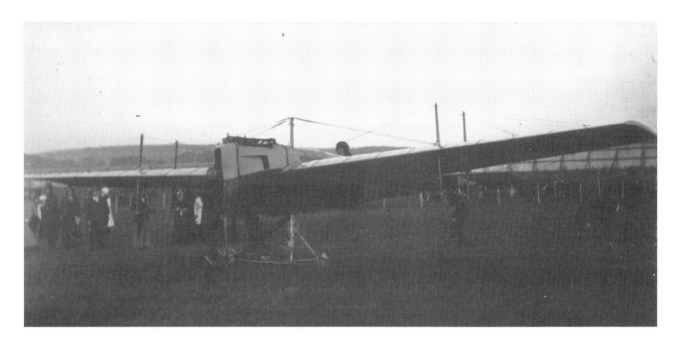

A 1913 Martin-Handasyde fitted with the small-wheeled undercarriage taken at Shoreham aerodrome with Barnwell in the cockpit

mounted on the lower ends of the wing king-posts, the front being attached through a ball joint and rubber springing.

This report also stated that ailerons were to be fitted instead of relying on wing-warping for lateral control. *Flight* reported that the aircraft had just been completed, but for the time being was to be tested with a conventional wheeled undercarriage. Following this report, *The Aeroplane* mentioned that a new Martin-Handasyde was badly damaged in a crash on 6th September. Apparently the aircraft, with Barnwell at the controls, suffered failure of both magnetos and sideslipped into the sewage farm at Brooklands. Subsequent reports from *Flight* recorded excellent flights made by Harold Barnwell in the Martin-Handasyde Waterplane, fitted with its wheeled undercarriage, on 11th and 13th September. It is not clear whether these reports refer to two separate aircraft or whether the Waterplane had been quickly repaired after a crash.

Martin and Handasyde entered an aircraft, powered by a 120-hp Austro-Daimler engine and flown by Harold Barnwell, for the 1913 Aerial Derby at Hendon on Saturday 20th September. Again, whether this was totally new or a repaired aircraft is uncertain. The aircraft was described as a very beautiful aircraft with almost all of the fuselage sides covered with plywood, thereby differing from its immediate predecessor and successor, both of which had rear fuselages covered in fabric.

On the day of the race, Barnwell flew the Martinsyde over from Brooklands in about eighteen minutes, accompanied by Hawker in a Sopwith biplane and Raynham in an Avro. It was given the racing number '12' and started two minutes in front of the scratch machine, Gustav Hamel's clipped-wing Morane-Saulnier. Barnwell had overtaken two machines by the first control point at Kempton Park and was fifth at the second control point at Epsom. Barnwell had been passed by Hamel and was lying fourth at the third control at West Thurrock but had taken the lead at Epping, Hamel having had trouble with a leaking petrol pipe. Hamel, having

Handasyde proudly posing by a 'mono wing' outside the Brooklands sheds, which seems to be for a 1913-pattern Martin-Handasyde. (Carolyn Pawson)

put his finger over the leaking pipe, drew level with Barnwell at the last control at Hertford and drew away to win by 59 seconds from Barnwell in second place. Barnwell completed the 95-mile course at an average speed of 72.39 mph.

Harold Barnwell continued to fly this aircraft for several months and participated in the London-Brighton-London race on 8th November 1913. Unfortunately he lost his way on the first leg, mistaking Newhaven for Brighton, and did not finish, landing back at Brooklands as he did not wish to risk a

The 1914 Martin-Handasyde at Brooklands. Note the retractable ladder and the streamlined undercarriage support and king-post. (Philip Jarrett)

night landing at Hendon. At the end of the year, the aircraft was modified with a pair of small wheels on the front of the undercarriage skid. On 13th November, its speed was measured to be 89 mph. At about the same time, in order to improve its performance, new wings of a different aerofoil section were fitted and several different propellers were tried. By 21st December, it was regularly flying at 90 mph over the measured 1,000-yard course at Brooklands. In 1914, it was involved in an accident when the small front wheels came off and smashed the propeller.

Aeronautics for November 1913 reported that "work on the Waterbus is at a standstill at present, but she will probably make a sudden and startling appearance in the near future." However as far as can be ascertained it never did fly in floatplane form.

1914 Martin-Handasyde Monoplane

Judging by reports and photographs, the ultimate Martin-Handasyde monoplane was an elegant machine. Although it retained the somewhat archaic king-post bracing system, it was remarkably well-engineered with fairings to the central undercarriage pylon and streamlining of the engine cowling. The tailplane structure was made with a dural frame. It possessed a number of novel features, including a folding ladder which let down on the port side and which could be stowed in a locker behind the pilot's cockpit.

Its early flights were made by Barnwell but later it was mostly flown by 2/Lt Vincent Waterfall and 2/Lt Robin Skene; the former was first reported to be flying it on 28th May and the latter on 9th June. It is sad to record that both of

these men were killed serving the RFC during the War. The Martinsyde was tested at Farnborough in April 1914 and although a speed of 97 mph was recorded its engine proved temperamental and it did not impress. The aircraft was back at Brooklands by May, where it took part in various races. In the Whit Monday race flown by Waterfall, it was hopelessly handicapped and finished well behind two very slow Boxkites. By mid-June it had been fitted with new wings which proved inferior to the originals. On 24th July, Waterfall flew the machine from Brooklands to Farnborough, picked up a Lt Lawrence and went on to Shoreham. On 2nd August, Waterfall had to return to duty with the RFC, leaving the aircraft at Shoreham as it was too windy to fly back to Brooklands. *Flight* reported that the Martin-Handasyde had been bought by visiting officials, together with a Sunbeam-powered Farman and the Avro 504 seaplane. However no official use of the machine has been reported and it is possible that the Austro-Daimler engine was cannibalised.

The Martinsyde Transatlantic Monoplane

On 1st April 1913, Lord Northcliffe, proprietor of the *Daily Mail*, offered a prize of £10,000 for the first non-stop flight across the Atlantic. The Scottish-Canadian financier and sportsman Mackay Edgar, who owned the boat in which Tom Sopwith won the 1912 International Boat Race in America, offered Gustav Hamel full financial backing for an attempt. Hamel was left to select the aircraft to be used and he chose Martin & Handasyde to design and build the aircraft. It was the intention to manufacture dual sets of all parts as a safety measure in case one set was destroyed or lost at sea on its

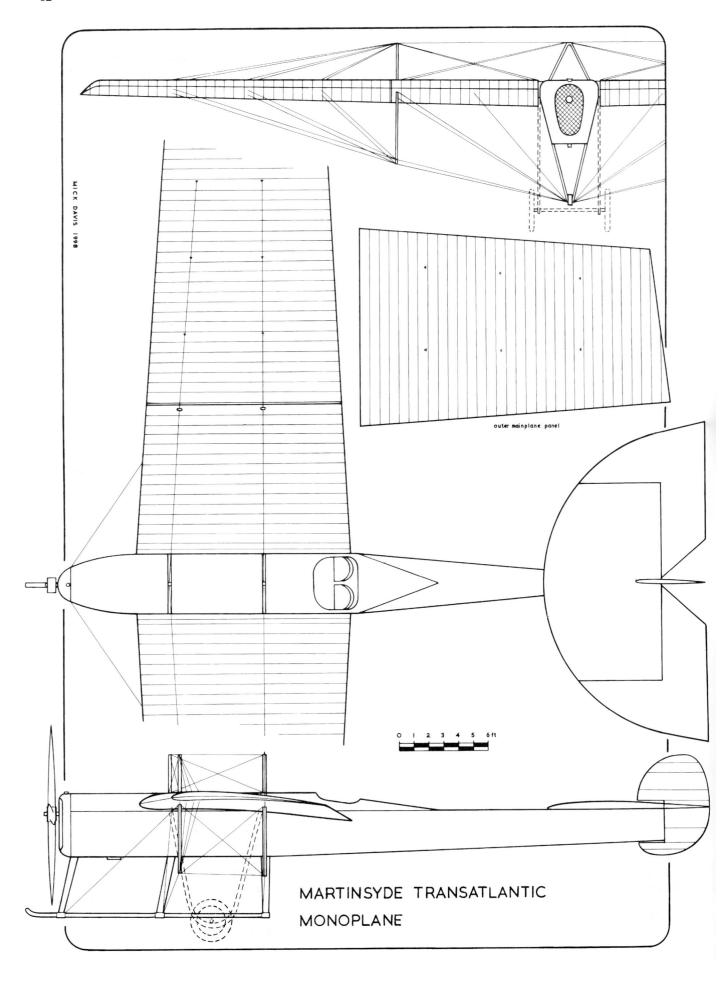

MICK DAVIS 1998

outer mainplane panel

0 1 2 3 4 5 6ft

MARTINSYDE TRANSATLANTIC
MONOPLANE

The Transatlantic under construction at Brooklands. (Philip Jarrett)

journey to its starting point in Newfoundland.

The resultant design was larger than any previous aircraft in Britain at that time. It was given high-lift, heavily cambered, wings and was estimated to weigh over two tons fully loaded. Lateral control was still by wing-warping, a rather surprising feature considering the large and stiff structure and the long and exhausting flight envisaged. Other control problems were likely to have arisen because the rudder was relatively small considering the short moment arm of the rear fuselage and the aerodynamic balances of the elevators were rather large. Emergency equipment was to include signal rockets and a telescopic radio mast.

The aircraft was to be powered by a 215-hp V-12 watercooled Sunbeam engine, which would have driven a 12-foot-diameter four-bladed Lang propeller through a reduction gear. The engine, retrospectively named the Mohawk, was developed by Louis Coatalen from the V-8 Crusader, and was the most powerful engine available at the time. It was built in considerable numbers during the early part of the war and saw service with the Admiralty in several types of aircraft, the most famous being the Short Type 184. The engine proved difficult to start and its reliability was questionable, a characteristic which may have had fatal consequences should the Transatlantic project have gone ahead.

The engine was supported by a strong girder structure forward of the centre section. From photographs it would appear that the longerons were of wood, the upper and lower longerons being separated by diagonal wooden cross-members. The side structures were joined by metal cross-bracing which also served to support the engine. All the joints were strengthened by fishplates bolted to the structure. Most of the loads would have been concentrated in a strongly-built central section, of similar construction to earlier Martinsyde designs with hickory longerons and three-ply covering. This was flanked front and rear by two bulkheads fourteen feet

apart, which formed a watertight flotation compartment capable of supporting twice the loaded weight of the aircraft in the water. The front and rear wing spars passed above the upper longerons of this compartment within an upper plywood fairing. The cockpit seated two side-by-side and was situated level with the trailing edge of the wing. The petrol tank, nine feet long and with a diameter of nearly three feet, giving a capacity of 330 gallons, was suspended from V-shaped struts attached to the front and rear wing spars which also supported the central undercarriage skid. The fuselage behind the centre compartment was a conventional wooden wire-braced structure. The total length of the fuselage was 45 feet. The aircraft was estimated to weight 2,400 lb empty and about twice this figure fully loaded.

The wings were of 66-foot span, the trailing edge being some 3 feet longer than the leading edge. The chord at the root was 14 feet 6 inches tapering to 10 feet 6 inches at the tip. The total wing area was about 770 sq feet. The two spars were of silver spruce of about one foot in depth at the roots tapering to the tip. The wing section was flat between the spars but curved downwards front and rear to form a concave under surface. The centre section spars appeared to be constructed of metal.The design employed a very strong king-post system of bracing, with cables going from the king-posts to the upper and lower longerons and to five attachment points on the outer wings. The tailplane was 21 feet in span and supported large balanced elevators. The rudder was aerodynamically balanced and without a fin.

The permanent undercarriage consisted of a central skid supported by V-struts from the wing spars and from a point near the nose of the aircraft. Skids were also mounted beneath the king-posts. A pair of wheels, supported from U-shaped struts attached to the wing spars at the roots, were designed to be jettisoned after take-off by means of a lever in the cockpit.

The fuselage, engine mounting and wings were almost

The wing structure of the Transatlantic. (J M Bruce/S Leslie Collection)

completed when the project received a fatal setback. Gustav Hamel was lost at sea on Saturday 23rd May 1914 whilst flying a new Morane-Saulnier from France to participate in the Aerial Derby on that day. On the following Monday, the partners announced to the assembled workforce, together with the company test pilot Robert Skene, that the project was to be scrapped. However, after consideration, Mackay Edgar did not immediately withdraw his support, possibly in the hope that another pilot could be found, and work continued certainly until late July. No further reports on progress have been found, although there were rumours of negotiations for a purchase and the aircraft must have been nearly complete by the outbreak of war.

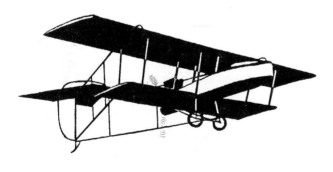

Artist's impression of what the Pusher might have looked like if it had competed in the 1914 Brooklands August Bank Holiday Meeting.

Other Pre-War Projects

Two further projects were considered before the war started. One was a pusher biplane with some resemblance to the Farman F.20. It was designed for a 65-hp Antoinette engine. The main nacelle was straight sided with steel longerons and vertical spacers and cross-wire bracing adjusted with turnbuckles. The rear fuselage was also constructed from steel tubing, converging from two points about mid-span on each wing to support the tail unit. The upper wing was of considerably greater span than the lower. It was to have been flown in the 1914 Aerial Derby by J Blatherwick but was not ready in time. It is next heard of as an entrant in the races which were due to be flown at Brooklands during the August

The only known photograph of the Martin-Handasyde Pusher. This aircraft was not completed due to the outbreak of the Great War. (Philip Jarrett)

Bank Holiday of 1914. There is in fact no evidence that it was ever completed or flown.

The other design which never went beyond the project stage was a very large monoplane. The only published reference to it in *Flight* of 7th August 1914 describes the aircraft as huge and having the pilot well aft and the passenger much further forward, about level with the leading edge of the wing.

2/Lt Vincent Waterfall in the 1914 Martin-Handasyde monoplane. (J M Bruce/S Leslie Collection)

The No.3 Martin-Handasyde fitted with the 35-hp four-cylinder in-line Green engine. Note the sloping radiator fitted behind the engine. (Philip Jarrett Collection)

Below left: Handasyde, Fisher and Pointer (left to right) testing the strength of a wing at Brooklands by the time-honoured method of loading it with sand or sandbags (Carolyn Pawson)

Right: Handasyde posing beside the rudder of the Transatlantic.

Available data on dimensions and performance of Martin & Handasyde prewar aircraft

	Martin-Handasyde (No.1)	Martin-Handasyde (No.2)	No.3 Martin-Handasyde	Martin-Handasyde 4B Dragonfly
Engine	14 hp Beeston-Humber	35-45 hp J.A.P.	35 hp J.A.P. 35 hp Green	50 hp Gnome
Span	22 ft 0 in	32 ft 0 in	32 ft 0 in	37 ft 0 in
Mean Chord root/tip		6 ft 2 in/ 5 ft 0 in	6 ft 2 in/ 5 ft 0 in	6 ft average
Length		30 ft 0 in	30 ft 0 in	33 ft
Wing Loading				5
Power Loading				27-28
Empty weight				800 lb
All-up weight	580 lb			

	Military Trials Machine	1913 Monoplane?	Transatlantic
Engine	75 hp Chenu 65 hp Antoinette	65 hp Antoinette	215 hp Sunbeam
Span	42 ft 6 in	47 ft 1 in	66 ft
Chord root/tip	8 ft 6 in / 6 ft 8 in	9 ft 8 in / 7 ft 7¾ in	14 ft 6 in / 10 ft 6 in
Aspect ratio	5.5	5.22	
Length	35 ft 4 in	37 ft 5½ in	45 ft
Wing area	300 sq ft	395 sq ft	770 sq ft
tailplane span		10 ft 3 in	21 ft
Tailplane area	30 sq ft		
Fin	7 sq ft		
Rudder	8.5 sq ft		
Wing Loading	5 lb/sq ft	6.08 lb/sq ft	6.23 lb/sq ft
Power Loading	23 lb/hp		22.3 lb/hp
Empty weight	1000 lb		2400 lb
All-up weight	1500 lb		c. 4800 lb
Maximum speed	67 mph		
Petrol			330 gal
Endurance, h	5 hr		

Martinsyde S.1 2823 with the early style tailplane and four-wheel undercarriage. (Philip Jarrett)

CHAPTER 3 - MARTINSYDES GO TO WAR

The Martinsyde S.1

Martinsyde began work on a small single-seat biplane in the summer of 1914. *Flight* of 24th July 1914 recorded that "....a tractor biplane of the small fast scouting type is now in the course of building at their Brooklands works". The aircraft was originally intended as a sporty single-seater but by the time it was ready the war had broken out and it was impressed into military service as the Martinsyde S.1.

When the aircraft appeared, it bore a strong resemblance to the Bristol Scout and Sopwith Tabloid, two machines which first appeared late in 1913 and were much admired in the aviation world. The airframe was the usual wire-braced, fabric-covered wooden structure of the period. The top decking and fuselage sides were covered with plywood as far back as the rear of the cockpit. The leading edge of the tailplane was roughly semi-circular with a straight trailing edge. The single-bay mainplanes had twin spars and sharply raked tips. Wing and undercarriage struts were connected to the fuselage longerons using bolted fish plates characteristic of Fletcher's designs.

Early production examples had a rather clumsy four-wheeled undercarriage, with skids projecting aft of the rear wheels which prevented the aircraft from sitting on its tail. Only a rudimentary tail skid was provided. With later machines, the four-wheel undercarriage was replaced by a more conventional two-wheel type, supported by V-struts.

This change was as a result of early experience in the field, where the undercarriage collapsed on a number of occasions when making forced landings following engine failure. The coaming around the cockpit was also cut down at the sides. Early in the production run, aircraft were fitted with a redesigned tailplane with a straight-tapered leading edge and tapered tips.

The unsuitability of the four-wheeled undercarriage is well illustrated by the experiences of Capt H B R Rowell while under training at Farnborough in the summer of 1915. His poor opinion of the aircraft may have been partly due to injured pride:

The only scout that existed in those days was the Martinsyde 80 Gnôme, one of the most evil little beasts that could possibly be invented. It was evidently the opinion of the experts of those times that it was impossible to land such a small machine on two wheels and so an undercarriage of four wheels was contrived for this forerunner of scouts. The machine was therefore made with this landing chassis, that would allow the machine to rest in a horizontal position with its tail up or in the normal position of rest with its tail-skid on the ground. When the machine had its tail on the ground a pair of wooden skid drags came into action alongside the rear wheels. How then was one to try to land such a beast as this? If you landed with the tail nicely down, these rear skids would catch the ground first and throw forward onto all four wheels, the front wheels would either break off or stick into soft

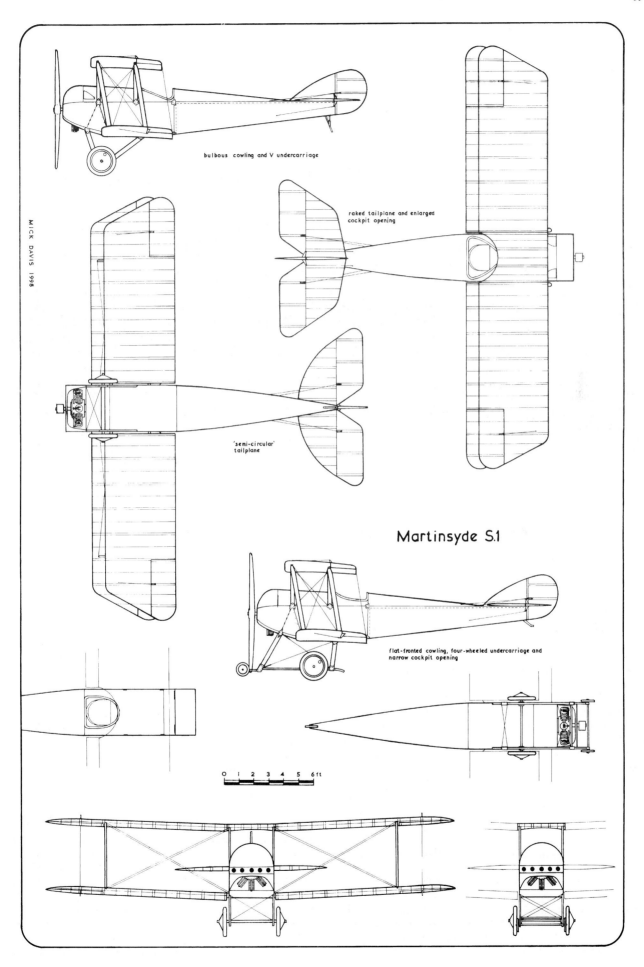

bulbous cowling and V undercarriage

raked tailplane and enlarged cockpit opening

'semi-circular' tailplane

Martinsyde S.1

flat-fronted cowling, four-wheeled undercarriage and narrow cockpit opening

O 1 2 3 4 5 6 ft

MICK DAVIS 1998

Pristine early production Martinsyde S.1s outside the sheds at Brooklands. (Philip Jarrett)

ground, with the result that everything would turn turtle. If you landed the machine on all fours, you would be going so fast by the time you came to a standstill you would have run so far that you would not have avoided hitting some small obstruction on the aerodrome, and the same inevitable result. It was one of those inventions of the devil that did my first bit of damage. I had finished my landing successfully and had turned the machine round and was heading for the hangars, the machine pitching to and fro as usual, when suddenly there was a crack. It struck a molehill. This was the only bit of damage I ever did learning to fly, and that should never have happened. However it cannot have cost 18 pence to repair.

The aircraft was powered by an 80-hp nine-cylinder Gnôme rotary engine. The engine would have appealed to Handasyde as it was beautifully built, with the crankcase and cylinders of polished steel, thin precision-made cooling fins and rows of small neat nuts and bolts. As mentioned previously when discussing the Martin-Handasyde 4B, castor oil was added as a lubricant with the fuel mixture and was thrown out, partially burnt, along with the exhaust gases. Thus a cowling was fitted not so much for aerodynamic purposes but to prevent the oil from spewing over the airframe. Unfortunately, with weight pared to the minimum, the engine was not very rugged and required constant maintenance. Only one rebore was allowed so the life of the engine was low, particularly in dusty conditions. Also fuel and oil consumption was very high and power fell off rapidly with altitude and in hot weather. As recounted later, all these features were to give real problems during the service career of the aircraft, particularly in Mesopotamia.

The flying characteristics are best described by quoting the experience of Capt L A Strange, when he was with No.6 Squadron.

....experience showed it to be a very unstable machine both fore and aft, with not much aileron control..... Although a single-seater, it was hardly superior in speed and climbing power to the Avro, which carried two men.......Whenever I encountered a Hun when flying my Martinsyde, I always had a frightful struggle to force myself up to 8,000 feet. Meanwhile the enemy would be steadily climbing, and although I found that our respective positions in the air generally suited the Martinsyde's angle of fire, I never got the chance of a surprise attack on an unsuspecting foeman.

Gp Capt Carmichael testified to the strength of the S.1 when writing about the assorted single-seat scouts received by No.5 Squadron:

A succession of these included the S.E.2, Bristol Bullet, Sopwith Tabloid and Martinsyde four-wheeler - all with 80-hp Gnôme engines. The Tabloid was a joy to fly, but the Martinsyde was the most robust - even surviving a somersault over a surprised Belgian wheelbarrow with damage only to the centre section and rudder.

Not much has been written about the armament fitted to the S.1 during its military service, but generally gun fittings were local modifications adopted by squadrons in the field. In the early days of the War, revolvers and rifles were carried. Later Lewis guns were fitted. For example S.1 2449 was equipped with a rifle when first operated by A Flight of No.4 Squadron but on the 22nd February 1915 the rifle was replaced by a stripped-down Lewis gun. The exact position of the gun is not recorded but some of the three-ply coaming was cut away to make room for it. When the same aircraft was transferred to No.6 Squadron, an additional rib was later added to the upper wing to take a bracket for a Lewis gun. A

Martinsyde S.1 2831 also had a four-wheel undercarriage. (Philip Jarrett)

similar modification was fitted to 2823 in March 1915 when in service with No.5 Squadron. Although originally fitted with an overwing gun, 1601 was later fitted, on 12th August, with a Lewis gun projecting through a hole in the left-hand side of the fuselage. Capt Strange recorded that "In my eyes all defects were outweighed by the fact that it had a Lewis gun mounted on its top plane, which could be fired forward and upward". Various modes of armament were specified for Home Defence (see later). Small bombs were known to be carried to attack ground targets and one of No.5 Squadron's aircraft, flown by Capt Carmichael, was adapted to take a 100-lb bomb, sighted through a hole cut in the floor. Previously provision had been made for 20-lb bombs under the wings.

The first machine was subjected to trial flights by service personnel at Brooklands. Lt B C Hucks, commanding D Flight of No.1 Squadron, flew it first on 25th September 1914. He was impressed with the machine despite the engine running roughly throughout. He found it slightly tail-heavy but sensitive to all controls and climbed rapidly. It flew at a speed of about 80 to 85 mph. It had a very flat gliding angle and landed comfortably, although it ran a considerable distance after touch down before coming to rest. He was very impressed with the four-wheel undercarriage as a means of preventing the machine from turning over on rough ground. He did however think that the pilot's view was restricted due to the pilot's head being just in line with the top of the fuselage coaming. Hucks flew the machine again on 2nd October after correction of the slight error in the erection of the machine which had caused the tail-heaviness. Major C

Longcroft flew the aircraft on the same day and confirmed the good flying characteristics. He was also favourably impressed with the robust undercarriage and also thought that with slight modification it should be possible to drop explosives from the aircraft.

Following these favourable reports, the first machine was impressed into military service at Brooklands on 11th October at a price of £1,050 and was given the serial number 696. Martin was convinced that the RFC would need fighting scouts and had the foresight to plan for the production of fifty machines without waiting for official orders. Therefore, when the orders came deliveries came quickly. The first to be completed, 710, was at Farnborough in the later half of 1914. 743, 734 and 1601 were recorded at Farnborough on 15th, 18th and 22nd December 1914 and 724, 741, 748 and 749 were delivered between 2nd and 26th January 1915. Those of batch 2448-2455 arrived between 17th January and 1st March, closely followed by 2820-2831 between 12th March and 5th May, 4229-4252 between 20th May and 9th August and finally 5442-5453 between 28th August and 21st October 1915. Altogether it is believed that a total of 67 were built.

As recounted below, the S.1 saw service in France and Mesopotamia and with the Home Defence Squadrons.

Service in France

The practice of the time was to allocate to each squadron in France only one or two single-seat scouts at any one time. According to official statistics, four Martinsyde Scouts, including Nos.696 and 702 at the Central Flying School, were

Martinsyde S.1 4241 with the later style undercarriage and with the curved tailplane. (J M Bruce/S Leslie Collection)

allocated to training units in 1914 and four went to France the following year. Official figures not withstanding however, it is known that at least a further seven Martinsydes went to France in 1915 (serial numbers 743, 748, 749, 1601, 2449, 2822 and 2823) and altogether served in six squadrons; Nos.1, 4, 5, 6, 12 and 16. In the Order of Battle of the RFC on 10th March 1915, two and one Martinsydes were on the strengths of Nos.5 and 4 Squadrons respectively. On 9th May 1915 Nos.1, 5 and 6 Squadrons each had just one Martinsyde on strength, No.5 Squadron having lost a second in an accident on 1st of that month. No.6 Squadron also originally had two, which had been taken on strength on 17th March. Unfortunately these squadron's records are incomplete for this period so all the movements of the Martinsyde aircraft cannot be traced. However what information that has been gleaned from squadron records and aircraft log books is given in the individual histories listing.

The first recorded action involving a Martinsyde S.1 occurred when Capt C I Carmichael of No.5 Squadron earned a DSO when sometime late in November 1914, he dropped two 112-lb bombs on Courtrai station from a height of 200 feet and returned to base with his machine riddled with rifle or machine gun bullets..

Flight reported on an action involving a Martinsyde S.1 (743) on either 21st or 23st January 1915 at a time when the only armament carried was a rifle.

Capt Holt, who was alone on the Martinsyde Scout put up a wonderful show. The German machine (Albatros) had been diving and twisting about over the airship station (at Dunkerque) for about ten minutes, trying to avoid an attack by an army B.E. Then turned out seawards at about 6,000 ft and was dived on by Holt, who had been making circles for an hour at about 8,000 ft waiting his chance. He got within three or four lengths, with the German diving away from him, dropping his controls, blazed off his rifle, and got the pilot with one shot, and two more through the cowl and thence into the water jacket round the number 2 cylinder, tearing it open. The German glided down to make a perfect landing two miles from the air station just over the Belgian frontier at Bray Dunes.

According to No.1 Squadron's War Diary, the sole Martinsyde in its charge (748) between the 17th March and 21st July 1915, was engaged in routine line patrol work and for flying practice by pilots newly assigned to the squadron. The aircraft's log book however records that on the 15th March 1915 2/Lt Bell-Irving attacked three enemy aircraft armed only with two revolvers. The War Diary also mentions that on 11th May 1915 the same pilot engaged a hostile aircraft in this machine 'with brilliant results' without specifying the actual damage inflicted on the enemy.

In his book *Recollections of an Airman* Capt L A Strange has recounted two narrow escapes while flying an S.1 in combat with No.6 Squadron. He described the first event as follows:

On the very first day it was delivered (17th March 1915) to the Squadron, I went out in it and was spotted high up over Ypres by an Albatros, which began to shoot at me while I was still a long way off and far below. I was quite pleased at the idea of the Hun wasting his ammunition at such long range, but the laugh was on the other side when a lucky bullet of his

Martinsyde S.1 2452 with the angular tailplane. (J M Bruce/S Leslie Collection)

hit the Martinsyde in a vulnerable spot, to wit, the oil tank. The bullet cut a narrow furrow down one side of the tank, which let all the oil out; I heard a big thump in the machine at the time and knew that it must have been hit, but as the controls behaved all right and the engine kept on going, I did not bother to find out what the damage was, but climbed up after the Hun.

In a very short time, however, my machine grew tail-heavy, and although I used my full elevator, I was unable to prevent it stalling. It did a tail slide and a half-turn of a spin before I could get control again, and that was the end of the fight as far as I was concerned. The Albatros came down with the intention of finishing me off, but I did not take much interest in his little attentions as I had my hands full with the job of trying to keep control of the Martinsyde.

The elevator control was none too good at the best of times, but now it seemed to be completely non-existent. If the machine's nose dropped, I was unable to pull out of the dive, and when at last, after pushing her over on her back and rolling her out of it in some way or other, I got her nose up again, it was too high, and she promptly stalled again.

Things looked bad for me, but at last I got her on to an even keel again, and kept her gingerly in position. Then I noticed castor oil all over the floor of the cockpit, and suddenly, just as I was wondering how I was going to get down without letting the nose drop too far, the engine seized and stopped dead. The next 3,000 feet were a perfect nightmare to me, as in those days we had little notion of aerobatics and considered a sideslip as something too dangerous to contemplate. But as I dared not to let the

machine's nose drop and my propeller has stopped, while I was bound to stall if the tail went down, there was nothing left for me but to manage a sideslip of sorts.

My arrival on terra firma can hardly be called a forced landing. I experienced a couple of very hectic minutes, although I cannot exactly recollect what happened in them, but the main thing I remember is the sight of the ground rushing up at me sideways in the last fifty feet or so of my descent. There seemed to be a solid mass of something or other rising out of it: in reality it was a hop field, full of high Belgian hop-poles, which I missed by a matter of inches, for somehow or other I jammed the controls over and flopped down on to a narrow trackway between the hop plantations.

The complicated old undercarriage sustained hardly any damage. When we came to investigate matters afterwards, the only feasible explanation seemed to be that the ten gallons of castor oil floating about in the fuselage must have upset the machine's centre of gravity, as all the controls were found to be in perfect order.

He was even more fortunate on the second occasion to escape with his life:

On May 10th 1915, I reached 8,500 feet when going after an Aviatik belonging to von Leutzer's Squadron from Lille Aerodrome. We were somewhere over Menin, and the Hun was still gaining height, though we were both near the tops of our respective ceilings. Not all the enemy aircraft were equipped with machine guns in those early days, but the German observer potted at me from the rear cockpit with a Parabellum pistol, and as some of his bullets came unpleasantly close, I thought it high time to retaliate, and

Capt L A Strange's mount 2449 at St Omer when he was with No.4 Squadron. Note the non-standard camouflage.
(J M Bruce/S Leslie Collection)

gave him a drum from my Lewis gun without much effect. But when I wanted to take off the empty drum and replace it with a full one, it seemed to jam, and as I was unable to remove it with one hand, I wedged the stick between my knees and tugged at the obstinate thing with both hands.

After one or two fruitless efforts, I raised myself up out of the seat in order to get a better grip, and I suppose that my safety belt must have slipped down at the critical moment. Anyhow, my knees loosened their grip on the stick just as the Martynside (sic), which was already climbing at its maximum angle, stalled and flicked over into a spin. As I was more than half out of the cockpit, the spin threw me clear of the machine, but I kept both my hands on the drum of the Lewis gun. Only a few seconds previously I had been cursing because I could not get that drum off, but now I prayed fervently that it would stay on for ever.

I knew it might come off at any moment, however, and as its edge was cutting my fingers badly, I had to get a firmer hold on something more reliable. The first thing I thought of was the top of the centre section strut, which at that time was behind and below the Lewis gun, but as the machine was now flying upside down, I had sufficient wits left to realise that it was behind and above me, though where it was exactly I could not tell. Dare I let go the drum with one hand and make a grab for it? Well, there was nothing else for it but to take the risk; I let go and found the strut alright, and then I released my other hand and gripped the strut on the other side. I was then in a more comfortable position, and at least I felt rather more part of my machine than I had done in my original attitude.

My chin was rammed against the top plane, beside the gun, while my legs were waving about in empty air. The Martynside was upside down in a flat spin, and from my precarious position the only thing I could see was the propeller (which seemed unpleasantly close to my face), the town of Menin, and the adjacent countryside. Menin and its environs were revolving at an impossible angle - apparently above me - and getting larger with every turn. I began to wonder what sort of a spot I was going to crash on. Then I got angry and cursed myself for a fool for wasting time on such idle speculations, while at the same time it dawned on me that my only chance of righting the machine lay in getting my feet in the cockpit. If I could manage it. I knew that I was bound to fall automatically into the cockpit when the machine flicked over.

I kept on kicking upwards behind me until at last I got first one foot and then the other hooked inside the cockpit. Somehow I got the stick between my legs again, and jammed on full aileron and elevator; I do not know exactly what happened then, but somehow the trick was done. The machine came over the right way up, and I fell off the top plane into my seat with a bump. I grabbed at the stick with both hands and thanked my lucky stars when I got hold of it. Then to my surprise I found myself unable to move it.

I suddenly realised that I was sitting much lower than usual inside the cockpit; in fact, I was so low down that I could not see over the edge at all. On investigation I found that the bump of my fall had sent me right through my seat, with the result that I was sitting on the floor of the machine as well as on the controls, which I was jamming. The cushion

Martinsyde S.1 (2449) of No.4 Squadron with a Bristol Scout C (1608). Note the roundel on the fuselage top decking, the relatively broad fuselage and roomy cockpit and the rounded tailplane. (J M Bruce/S Leslie Collection)

had fallen out when the machine turned upside down, along with everything else that was loose or had been kicked loose when I was trying to find the stick with my feet. Something had to be done quickly, as although the engine had stopped through lack of petrol when the machine was upside down, it was now roaring away merrily and taking me down in a dive which looked likely to end in the wood to the north of Menin. So I throttled back and braced my shoulders against the top of the fuselage, and my feet against the rudder bar; then I pulled out the broken bits of seat and freed the controls. Luckily I found them working all right, so that I was able to put the machine's nose up and open the throttle again. I rose and cleared the trees on the Menin road with very little to spare.

I did not trouble to climb any more but just flew back along the Menin road. In my efforts to find the control stick with my feet, I had smashed all the instruments on the dashboard, and as I gazed at the damage, I wondered if I could ever make anyone realise how it had been done. I had only a very hazy idea myself....

Communique No.7, one of a series issued by the RFC HQ in France based on combat reports and squadron returns, reported a combat involving the S.1 on 27th August 1915.

Lt Cooper-King, seeing a German machine in the direction of Houthulst, gave chase and opened fire at about 200 yards distance, the enemy replying with his machine gun. After discharging one drum of ammunition the Martinsyde turned away to change it and tried at the same time to get higher. In the meantime the enemy also climbed higher at a slightly greater rate, and a further encounter took place at about 9,200 ft up. When the Martinsyde ran out of ammunition it returned to the aerodrome, the enemy being last seen flying towards home.

By this time the S.1 was obsolete and the type was withdrawn from front-line service in France during the summer of 1915 with no squadron having the type by 25th September.

Service in Mesopotamia

Turkey's entry into the war on the side of the Central Powers on 31st October 1914 opened up another theatre of war in Mesopotamia. Turkey had already strengthened its forces in Lower Mesopotamia and threatened the oil installations of the Anglo-Persian Oil Company at nearby Abadan, which were considered of extreme importance by the Admiralty as a source of bunker fuel. An Indian Expeditionary Force consisting of one brigade was sent from Bahrein to establish a foothold at Fao on 6th November and, after the arrival of two more brigades, Basrah was taken on 22nd November and Qurna on 9th December. The Turks regrouped through the winter but their counterattack on Shuaiba west of Basrah on 14th April 1915 was beaten off with heavy loses and they returned to their base at Al Nasiriya. After this the British forces were reorganised as the Sixth Division.

By the end of May 1915, a decision was taken for 6 Division, now under Major-General C V F Townshend, to advance with the help of naval sloops and armed tugs from Qurna to Amara. Aerial support was given by an aeroplane flight formed in Basrah, under Capt. P W L Broke-Smith RFC. When it was formed, the Flight consisted of seven pilots, Captains Broke-Smith and H L Reilly of the Indian Flying Corps, Lt W W A Burn from New Zealand and four officers from Australia, and an assortment of mechanics, engineers and drivers from Britain, India and Australia. The aircraft consisted of two Maurice Farman Shorthorns and one Longhorn, only two of which had engines. The Maurice Farmans gave invaluable assistance with aerial reconnaissance and communication flights and by 4th June the British forces had advanced well past Amara. On 9th June, the air detachment was moved forward to Amara. In a separate thrust, Major-General G F Gorringe advanced up the Euphrates and, with the aid of aerial reconnaissance by the two Maurice Farmans and two recently arrived Caudron

Martinsyde S.1 MH6 (4244) on a lighter on the Tigris at Basrah, 1915. (E F Cheeseman)

G.IIIs, captured Nasiriya on 25th July.

The climate is quite appalling at this time of the year, shade temperatures reaching more than 50°C (122°F) with frequent dust storms whipped up by forty-mph winds. As a result, both the Maurice Farmans were rendered unserviceable with engine trouble and one of the Caudrons was lost on the 30th with its crew on its way back to Basrah. Further long flights with Caudron aircraft were forbidden as their Gnôme engines gave continual trouble in the hot and dusty conditions.

In August 1915, it was decided by the British War Office that it must take over responsibility for all aviation services in Mesopotamia from the Indian Army and all the officers of the Basrah Flight were gazetted to the RFC. It was intended to integrate the Flight with No.30 Squadron which was being formed at Ismailia in Egypt in March 1915. At this point of the campaign four Martinsyde S.1s, including 4243, 4244 and 4250, arrived in Basrah on 26th August 1915 to form the nucleus of a second Flight of No.30 Squadron. For convenience, the squadron gave these aeroplanes new numbers; MH5, MH6, MH8 and MH9. With the same Gnôme engines as the Caudrons, it was inevitable that the performance of the Martinsydes would also suffer from the climatic conditions. The first flight of one of the Martinsydes, in the hands of Capt H A Petre, was made on 29th August. It took 23 minutes to climb to 7,000 ft. At this height, its speed was only 50 mph and it consumed a large amount of petrol on the climb. Throughout the aircraft's service in Mesopotamia, the engine gave endless trouble.

When the decision to occupy Kut al Imara was taken,

No.30 Squadron sent a flight in advance to Ali Gharbi under the command of Major H L Reilly. The detachment initially consisted of a Maurice Farman and the surviving Caudron. Martinsydes MH5 and MH6 arrived on a platform lighter on 5th September 1915 and were unloaded two days later after the ramp down to the river, which was initially too steep, had been modified. MH6 was soon pressed into service, carrying out a reconnaissance to Shaikh Saad on the 13th and another upriver later that day. On the same day Farman MF1 was wrecked on landing and MH5 crashed shortly after take-off, both being returned to Basrah on a lighter the following day. The Caudron was shot down by rifle fire whilst on reconnaissance behind the Turkish lines on the 16th. This left Martinsyde MH6 as the only serviceable aircraft at that moment with Major General C V F Townshend's division. As it was vital to know the enemies dispositions, a second attempt at a reconnaissance was made on the evening of the 16th by Major H L Reilly in the Martinsyde. Major General Townshend later wrote in his book on the campaign that:

Major Reilly carried out the reconnaissance that I asked for exceedingly well... and he brought back a map and detailed information.... (As soon as) Reilly had completed his air reconnaissance and sketches...I had ample and exact information...(and) issued Battle Instructions.

The detachment moved to Sanniyat and then on to Nakhailat on the 26th, carrying out reconnaissance missions from both landing grounds. Three days before the advance began, on 26th September, aircraft reinforcements, Martinsyde MH8 and a Maurice Farman, arrived by lighter, resulting in three aircraft now being available. These had

Martinsyde S.1 being unloaded from a lighter at Basrah, 1915. (J M Bruce/S Leslie Collection)

been supplemented by two Short (150-hp Sunbeam) seaplanes from a RNAS detachment, which however proved of little use until converted to wheeled undercarriages in October. Capt H A Petre flew MH8 to the landing ground at Sanniyat but landed outside the prepared area and damaged the aircraft. This aircraft was however repaired by the 28th. Due to dust storms, mirages and the flat countryside, ground communications by semaphore were impractical and it was not until the morning of the 29th that an air observer brought back the news to Major General Townshend that the troops had entered Kut unopposed. The Turks were pursued upriver for fifty miles and Azizya was entered on 3rd October.

The detachment moved to Azizya on the 5th and Martinsyde MH6 flew there as soon as the landing ground was ready and on the following day made the first reconnaissance of Baghdad in Martinsyde MH6. Maurice Farman MF7 and Martinsyde MH8 were moved to Kut on the 8th, Capt H A Petre badly damaging the Martinsyde on landing. The accident was due to a shock absorber bobbin on the undercarriage axle moving about ½-inch, thereby exposing a nut which then sheared all the spokes off one wheel. The aircraft turned over, damaging two wings, the propeller, the engine bearers and the fin and rudder. Capt Petre badly sprained his wrist but was otherwise unhurt. It was estimated that the repair would take ten days as there were no engine bearer spares available.

On 22nd October, MH6 was used, together with two Maurice Farmans, to bomb the encampment of an Arab tribe. A total of two 20-lb, three 30-lb and sixteen 2-lb bombs were sufficient to secure the sheikh's submission. During the following week MH8 rejoined the other aircraft to carry out reconnaissances and more bombing missions on Turkish positions.

At Qurna, Amara, Nasiriya and Kut, aeroplane reconnaissances had provided the information upon which the

military plans had been based and therefore the small air detachments had exerted an influence on the campaign out of all proportion to their numbers. The air detachment at Kut was backed up by the use of a steamer and three barges. One barge was used to transport aircraft upriver and to carry damaged aircraft back to the Park at Basrah, another was used for repair work and the third as a stores and photographic dark room. Once Kut was occupied, the steamer and one barge formed there the advanced section of the Aircraft Park. At this point the available aircraft consisted of Maurice Farman MF7 and Martinsydes MH6 and the now repaired MH8. On 2nd October, MH8 was again smashed on landing by Petre. No blame was attached as it was appreciated that Martinsydes required very smooth ground for landing - 'a croquet lawn' as one harassed staff officer put it.

A lighter with maintenance equipment for three RNAS seaplanes arrived in Kut, which gave hope that the three seaplanes that were available could be made into effective machines. Also air reinforcements arrived in the shape of four B.E.2c aircraft, four pilots, mechanics and stores. The units were reorganised as No.4 Aircraft Park and No.30 Squadron, made up of A Flight at Azizya and B Flight at Kut. Preparations were made for an advance on Ctesiphon and thence to Baghdad. On 13th November, the Maurice Farman was lost in a vain attempt to cut the telegraph wires west and north of Baghdad. Thus when the advance began on the 20th, the responsibility for the reconnaissance of the enemy positions at Baghdad fell upon a Martinsyde piloted by Major Reilly.

On 21st November, when Major Reilly was flying about four miles east of Ctesiphon, his interest was caught by ominous signs of formidable Turkish reinforcements. He abandoned his Baghdad reconnaissance to make instead a detailed examination of the Ctesiphon position. He had nearly completed this survey when a splinter from an anti-aircraft

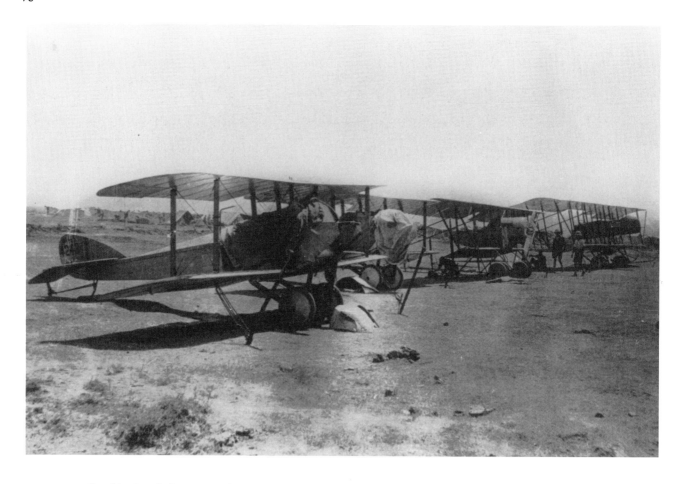

Two Martinsyde S.1s with a Caudron G.III and a Maurice Farman in Mesopotamia with 30 Squadron.
(J M Bruce/S Leslie Collection)

shell put his engine out of action. The pilot glided down and made a landing some way from the Turkish lines. He attempted to walk to the British lines but was captured by Arabs and made prisoner-of-war, his detailed maps falling into enemy hands. A second reconnaissance by an inexperienced pilot failed to reveal the true position and thus the British commanders remained ignorant of the large forces facing them.

The attack on Ctesiphon began on the 22nd, during which the last airworthy Martinsyde, MH9 piloted by Capt E J Fulton, was lost through a forced landing behind the Turkish lines, its engine having been damaged by anti-aircraft fire. The superior Turkish forces prevailed and the British retreated to Kut where they were trapped, together with three unserviceable aircraft, one of which was Martinsyde MH9. Attempts were made to supply the besieged forces by air but Kut fell to the Turkish forces on 26th April 1916. This was the end of the war service of the S.1 in Mesopotamia, but the story of the conflict continues with the relief of Kut in the section on the Martinsyde Elephant.

Service with Home Defence and Training Squadrons

Zeppelins were perceived as a threat to home defence before the War began but no effective countermeasures were formulated. On 3rd September 1914, at Lord Kitchener's request in an informal approach to Winston Churchill, the home defence of Great Britain was put in the hands of the Royal Naval Air Service. An exception was that 'vulnerable points' would remain under Army control. On 16th October

1914, it was decreed that army aerodromes would be used to assist the field army to resist a landing but surplus aircraft would be made available for RNAS use for air defence. Our defences were ill-prepared and luckily they were not called into action for nearly a year.

On 6th May 1915, just sixteen days before the first Zeppelin raid and twenty-five days before the first on London, definite instructions regarding the aircraft and the armament which should be maintained for defence purposes were laid down by the War Office. Stations made primarily responsible for Home Defence in the event of an air raid were South Farnborough, Brooklands, Hounslow, Northolt, Joyce Green, Dover and Shoreham. One machine was to be made available at each of these stations and Squadron Commanders were instructed to allocate machines for instruction and other work.

It was decided that the most suitable machine available was the Martinsyde S.1 Scout and these machines were allocated to each station concerned. The machines were to be equipped for anti-Zeppelin work with six carcass bombs with launching tubes, three powder bombs and carriers, twelve Hale's grenades and 150 incendiary darts, although the instruction added that 'it is not considered that any advantage will be gained by equipping the machines with rifles'. Sceptical over the S.1's ability to carry such a load, Major G I Carmichael of No.4 Reserve Aeroplane School test-climbed one on 24th May 1915, with the specified bomb load and an additional weight equivalent to the grenades and incendiary darts, which were not available for the trial. Even when exceeding the recommended engine revolutions he took 21½

A Martinsyde S.1 in the foreground in the rigging sheds at the School of Military Aeronautics at Oxford, showing the method of construction. (J M Bruce/S Leslie Collection)

minutes to reach 6,000 ft. Despite this evidence, it took the War Office until 29th October to be convinced that the S.1 was unsuitable for such work.

Contemporary returns to the War Office show that the Order of Battle for the defence of London included the following Martinsyde S.1s;

> Brooklands and Farnborough - two S.1s with incendiary bombs
> Dover - four aircraft including two S.1s with incendiary bombs
> Hounslow - three aircraft including one S.1 with launching tubes
> Joyce Green - four aircraft including one S.1 with incendiary bombs
> Northolt - two S.1s with incendiary bombs and Lewis guns
> Shoreham - one S.1 with incendiary bombs
> No.6 Wing - eight aircraft in reserve including one S.1

The majority of Martinsyde S.1s served with various training units but the type never achieved the popularity of the contemporary Bristol Scout or the later Sopwith Pup. Units using the aircraft for training included the Central Flying School and Reserve Training Squadrons Nos.1, 2, 3, 4, 5, 6, 7, 9, 11, 14 and 18.

Two S.1 airframes were used for ground instructional purposes at the School of Instruction at Reading, which was formed on 1st December 1915. Of the aircraft remaining airworthy, 2831 was still at Farnborough in March 1916. The first Martinsyde S.1, 710, ended its career as a target for machine gun practice at Orfordness.

Martinsyde Two-Seater

A new Martinsyde design appeared in the late spring of 1915. This was a rather ill-proportioned and ugly two-seater, two-bay biplane fitted with a 100-hp Gnôme Monosoupape engine. It was assembled in one of the London and Provincial Aviation Company's sheds at Hendon where it was presumably taken by Fletcher when he transferred to that company from Martinsyde. Its design displayed a good deal of Fletcher influence and retained the type of narrow-track four-wheel undercarriage design first seen on the early S.1 biplanes. The machine was test flown by Herbert Sykes, one of London and Provincial's flying instructors. The first flights were made on a rather bumpy evening and only two trial circuits were made.

Its intended purpose is obscure but it may have been designed as a fast unarmed reconnaissance machine as the passenger occupied the front seat and had a good downward view ahead of the wing but on the other hand it would have been very difficult for either of the crew to have used a gun effectively in combat. The aircraft was inspected at Farnborough on 9th June 1915. The results of the trials there are not known but in any case no production order was placed. It may have been that all available 100-hp Monosoupape engines were required for more favoured designs, such as the Vickers F.B.5 and D.H.2, for the two-seater later appeared with an uncowled 80-hp Anzani radial engine.

In this form it did a great deal of flying, mostly in the hands of Herbert Sykes, who had left the London and Provincial flying school in 1916 to become test pilot to the Whitehead Aircraft Company. He gave a number of aerobatic

Bill Sykes in his Martinsyde Two-seater at Hendon. (J M Bruce/S Leslie Collection)

displays on the Martinsyde. For example on Saturday 9 September he flew from Hendon to distribute thousands of leaflets over the heads of the crowds at a fête at Richmond Green. On the way, he had looped the aircraft over Kew Bridge and Richmond Bridge. The leaflets read, "Whitehead Aircraft wish every success to the Boy's Naval Brigade and the Star and Garter Fund, Richmond. Pilot H Sykes, Passenger Mr Fletcher". He then gave an aerobatic display before landing at Richmond Deer Park.

The machine had already been bought earlier by C H Stevens. Stevens was taught to fly the aircraft by Sykes that summer and took his ticket (No.3491) on it on 7th September 1916. It is unclear how long the aircraft remained in Steven's possession but Sykes was still using it in 1917, even appearing in one or two films with names like *A Munition Girl's Romance*.

The Martinsyde Two-seater spewing castor oil. The need for the rudimentary cowling is quite evident.
(J M Bruce/S Leslie Collection)

Above: The Two-seater, with a line-up of Whitehead-built Sopwith Pups, outside the Whitehead works at Feltham, Middlesex.

Below: Bill Sykes posing for the photographers with the Martinsyde Two-seater. (J M Bruce/S Leslie Collection)

Above: The Martinsyde Two-seater, in its original form powered by a 100-hp Gnôme Monosoupape engine, at Brooklands. (Mike Goodall)
Below: Not the most elegant of the Martinsyde designs! Bill Sykes taking a well earned rest on the undercarriage of the Martinsyde Two-seater. Note the fishplates strengthening the joints between the struts and fuselage longerons - a typical hallmark of Fletcher designs. (J M Bruce/S Leslie Collection)

The Martinsyde G.100 prototype (4735) with the three-bladed propeller at Brooklands. (Imperial War Museum)

CHAPTER 4 - THE ELEPHANT

The Martinsyde works built the prototype of a new single-seat biplane during the summer of 1915 at a time when Tony Fletcher was still associated there with design. Its appearance owed nothing to the ugly Two-Seater which preceded it. Instead the aircraft combined the neat appearance of the compact S.1 Scout with the elegance of the earlier Martin-Handasyde types, having a slender fuselage supporting a shapely tail unit characteristic of the earlier designs.

The aircraft acquired the unlikely nickname "Elephant" in service, but precisely how and when this occurred is uncertain. Chaz Bowyer in his book *The Flying Elephants* suggests that the name may have originated from the Brooklands factory itself. The size of the aircraft, being larger than hitherto, necessitated the use of Double Elephant-sized sheets of paper for component drawings used during production. There are more bawdy alternative stories, including a rather unfair remark made by one NCO on first seeing the aircraft that it looked like "a pregnant elephant preparing to pounce". Whatever the origins, the name stuck with various alternatives such as "Jumbo" and "Tinsides".

It has been customary to regard the Elephant as having been designed as a single-seat fighter. However at the time of its design, the concept of a small, fast and manoeuvrable aircraft specifically designed to carry the pilot and fixed armament for aerial combat had not fully taken shape. It seems probable that the aircraft was really designed as a high-speed scout or reconnaissance machine with an endurance to reach objectives well beyond the range of existing types. Hence the aircraft needed to be rather large for a single-seater

in order to carry the fuel required. Whatever the original intentions of the designers, very early in the aircraft's career it was being considered as a vehicle for carrying bombs. An official document, written shortly after the prototype had carried out trials at the Central Flying School, stated that the aircraft's bomb load was to include two 100-lb bombs carried inside the fuselage, with additional bomb carriers, designed at the CFS, under the wings.

It was destined to be produced in significant numbers in two versions. It was originally designed to be powered by a 100-hp Green engine but when the prototype appeared it was fitted with a Beardmore-built 120-hp Austro-Daimler engine with the radiator mounted behind the engine. With this engine it was designated the G.100 and later versions fitted with the more powerful 160-hp version of the same engine. were designated the G.102. The intention to fit the Green engine may account for the "G" designation, for which there is no certain explanation.

The 120-hp Beardmore was a six-cylinder in-line water-cooled engine, developed from the Austro-Daimler, which in practice could develop some 130 hp at 1,200 rpm. The bore was 130 mm and the stroke 175 mm. Each cylinder had its own copper water jacket and its own chamber in the crankcase which acted as an oil sump. The combustion chamber was domed with a slightly concave upper surface to the piston crown. Three magnetos were used, giving dual ignition and one for starting. Two carburettors each supplied fuel to three adjacent cylinders. A combination of pressure and splash lubrication was used. The increase in power to 160

An early photograph of the Martinsyde G.100 prototype at Brooklands fitted with a two-bladed propeller. The upper cowling was not fitted at this time. (Brooklands Museum)

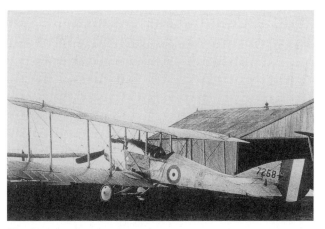

The first production Martinsyde G.100 seen at CFS Upavon, January 1916

hp was obtained principally by increasing the cylinder bore to 142 mm.

When the prototype appeared, the lower part of the engine cowling had rather an angular appearance and the fuselage upper decking behind the engine sloped slightly downwards towards the cockpit, possibly indicating the modifications necessary with the change of engine. Also there was no exhaust manifold, the exhaust ports venting directly to the atmosphere. The prototype was variously fitted with both a two-bladed and three-bladed propeller but a two-bladed propeller became standard.

The Elephant was a two-bay biplane with staggered wings of equal span and chord. Each lower wing was terminated at the root by a plywood endplate leaving a gap between the wing and the fuselage with the spars exposed. The airframe was a wire-braced wooden structure, the detailed design of which, as will be recounted later, left something to be desired. All flight surfaces and the rear fuselage were fabric covered. The decking about the cockpit and the fuselage sides between the centre section struts were plywood covered. The total fuel capacity was 50½ gallons sufficient for an endurance of about 5½ hours.

The prototype was allotted the serial number 4735 under Contract No.94/A/298. It underwent official performance trials at CFS, Upavon on 8th September 1915. The report on the trials, which were carried out both by Raynham for the Company and by a Service pilot, concluded that the machine handled admirably in the air, was easy to fly and steady in rough weather. The view from the cockpit and the cramped cockpit, which would make it difficult to fit a bomb sight with the existing structure, were criticised. The non-steerable tailskid was also criticised as it made it difficult to manoeuvre on the ground and although the landing speed was sufficiently slow it was difficult to prevent a swing on landing. The absence of a fuel gauge was commented upon as was the inconvenient position of the throttle lever. The overall conclusion was that the machine was strong and efficient and apart from these minor criticisms appeared to be a thoroughly serviceable machine.

The aircraft then went to Farnborough. It was in the AID shop there on 25th September 1915, where it was officially allotted to the Expeditionary Force. It was flown to No.1 Aircraft Depot at St.Omer on 29th October by Lt F G Dunn. After an engine change, it was flown to No.6 Squadron on 5th November by Lt Grey Edwards. From there it went to No.20 Squadron, which was otherwise flying F.E.2bs, on 1st

February 1916. As recounted later, it was to see combat with both units. The machine was returned to the Depot at St. Omer on 16th March. Reports from the field in December concluded that the machine had promise as a single-seat fighter. It had a great reserve of power and was very manoeuvrable. It was not as easy to fly as the Bristol Scout and was a little slower climbing to 8,000 feet but thereafter climbed significantly faster. The position of the bombsight again attracted adverse criticism with the rider that it would be difficult to find an alternative position without significantly altering the structure. However the view vertically downwards had been greatly improved by fitting a transparent panel in the floor.

Presumably as a result of these favourable reports from operational squadrons, the first of several orders was awarded in November for one hundred machines under Contract No. 87/A/192. For these serial numbers 7258-7307 were allocated on 12th November and 7459-7508 on 22nd November 1915. The appearance of the engine cowling of the production machines differed from the prototype. Production G.100s, the first batch of which began to appear early in February 1916, had much improved engine cowlings and a conventional two-bladed propeller replaced the three-bladed airscrew of the prototype.

The first production machine (7258) was sent to CFS Upavon, where it was test flown by Raynham. He reported (CFS Report No. 204 of 6.1.16) on several features which were to be remarked upon again and again by others.

This machine, for a design not incorporating inherent stability, is remarkably stable and easy to fly. She lands slow but runs a long way after touching down and would be improved with a claw tail skid or chassis wheels further forward to bring more weight on the tail skid.

A portion of the right hand side bodywork requires removing to facilitate sighting. The rear chassis strut on the right hand side somewhat hampers easy use of bomb sight and might be improved in this respect, The seat could, with advantage, be made adjustable to suit various pilots using the bomb sight. View ahead is bad but in other directions good.

On the afternoon of Sunday 13th February 1916, an event occurred which should have been a warning about the structural integrity of the Elephant. Raynham was test flying a newly completed production machine over Brooklands at a height of around 2,000 feet prior to flying it directly to Dover for acceptance by the RFC. He was just completing the third of a series of loops when the tail broke away but remained attached to the fuselage by a few wires and some canvas.

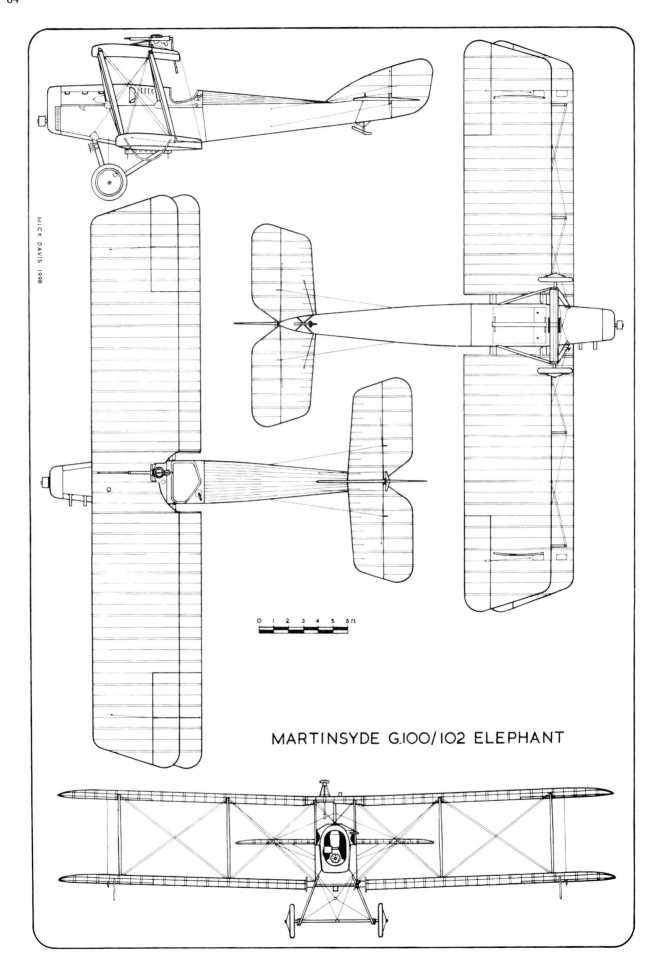

MICK DAVIS 1998

O 1 2 3 4 5 6 ft

MARTINSYDE G.100/102 ELEPHANT

G.100 (7282) from the first batch, seen here at No.1 AD St Omer on 27 May 1916, was earlier tested at Farnborough and saw service in France with No.27 Squadron. (Peter F G Wright)

The machine began to fall rapidly but Raynham managed to restart the engine and reduce the rate of descent. He was, however, unable to regain proper control of the aircraft which continued to flutter towards the ground. The machine finally crashed near Plough Bridges, close to the junction of the Byfleet and Cobham roads. Eyewitnesses, some of whom had to wade the stream, found Raynham crumpled under the overturned wreck. He was rushed to the Caen's Hill Military Hospital, Weybridge, by ambulance where he was found to be suffering from severe concussion and bodily injuries. He regained consciousness about three hours later and miraculously was soon on the road to recovery.

Although one or two machines were allocated to other squadrons, No.27 Squadron was the only one to become solely equipped with the machine in France. The design also saw service with several other squadrons in Mesopotamia and Palestine. Besides its initial use operationally as a fighting scout, its efficacy as a photographic reconnaissance aircraft quickly became apparent, this being one of the first instances of high-speed single-seaters being used in this way. For this purpose, the aircraft were fitted with a mounting upon which was fitted an 18-plate semi-automatic camera. Early experience showed that excellent photographs could be obtained from as high as 14,500 feet, almost twice the height normally used by other squadrons.

The aircraft were armed with a single Lewis gun and because a British interrupter gear was not yet available, it was mounted above the wing clear of the airscrew arc. The gun was mounted above the rear spar on a strong pyramid structure which was itself braced to the front spar. The gun was fired by means of a Bowden cable and the gun could be swung down for reloading by means of an extension fitted to the handle. Not only did this arrangement facilitate loading but it also allowed the gun to be fired at an angle upwards and slightly forwards. Although the gun could not be moved laterally, this was not considered a disadvantage as that eliminated sighting errors when firing off the line of flight. The installation became officially known as the Martinsyde No.5 Mark I mounting. A No.5 Mark II mounting is also listed which was similar to the Mark I, but had movable legs

pivoted on the underside of the rear spar.

Major A E Borton, commanding No.27 Squadron, reported to the War Office on 23rd March 1916 shortly after the squadron reached France:

This machine was originally designed for bomb dropping, the forward gun mounting being brought down to be tested at Dover about the middle of January and after minor alterations was fitted shortly before the squadron came overseas. Auxiliary sights have now been fitted, a specimen of which has been forwarded to RFC HQ. It is anticipated that extremely satisfactory results will be obtained from the mounting. There is however still some difficulty in changing the drums on this gun but this has been considerably improved by practice.

A rear gun mounting has now been fitted behind the left hand side of the pilot's seat which gives excellent field of fire from slightly behind the left hand planes round to the tailplane.

This need to augment the aircraft's armament for defensive purposes was felt less than a fortnight after the squadron's arrival in France. The second Lewis gun was clamped to a cranked pillar mounting just aft of the cockpit coaming on the port side. It was said that this fitting was first made with the help of a local French blacksmith and tested on No.27 Squadron's Martinsyde No 7271 on 13th March 1916. It was given official blessing in Supplement No.1 to the RFC Training Manual, Part 2, dated July 1916 which describes and illustrates this rear mounting as the "No.10 Mk 1 Mounting, Aircraft Lewis for use on Martinsyde 120-hp Scout and the B.E.12 Scout". As far as it can be ascertained, No.27 Squadron were the principal unit to use this particular mounting although at least one Martinsyde of No.67 Squadron in Palestine used a similar rear mounting. Although it proved difficult to manipulate and reload in combat, it did prove its worth on several occasions particularly when pilots were engaged in running battles with enemy scouts whilst attempting to return to base.

The same letter by Major A E Borton quoted above also outlined the tactics which squadron pilots were expecting to employ when using this armament:

G.102 (A1592) photographed on 22 November 1916. It saw service with training squadrons. (J M Bruce/S Leslie Collection)

I consider that the most satisfactory tactics to be employed will be to attack with the forward mounting while gliding down, in the case of a machine of the Albatros type the attack would be made from the enemy's left front - while passing directly underneath a hostile machine the forward mounting can also be used to fire upwards and forwards, in this case tracer bullets will add greatly to the range of action obtainable which will be limited if the sights were used owing to the distance from the eye.

I consider however that the most favourable position for attack will be from below the enemy's right wing, where the rear mounting will be at its most convenient angle for firing and observation and this position has also the advantage of being the least exposed to the fire of the enemy.

I consider the main disadvantages of the machine as the extremely limited view forward owing to the high cowl and low seat - with this exception I consider that the machine will prove most efficient for fighting.

Other improvements suggested by pilots of the squadrons in the field were incorporated by the manufacturer. These included strengthening the undercarriage by making the struts of ash rather than spruce, adding an extra tie-wire between the wheels parallel to the axle and replacing the wooden streamlining of the axle by aluminium as the wood continually came apart from its fixing screws. The cowling was painted light grey instead of leaving it polished aluminium, presumably to reduce glare. The portion of the fabric along the bottom of the fuselage, from the rear spar back to within 10 inches of the tail, was laced to enable ready access to the control cables for maintenance and inspection and the tap in the petrol pipe between the gravity tank and the carburettor was positioned so that it was accessible to the pilot in flight. The scoop in the cowling was slightly enlarged to allow more cooling air to reach the radiator.

Two problems of a more serious nature also required attention. Firstly the pilot's seat was made adjustable so that it could be raised to improve the view and secondly exhaust manifolds were fitted as pilots complained of nausea due to

exhaust fumes entering the cockpit. In some cases pilots required a day's rest to recover after flights as short as 1½ hours. At first the joints between manifold and the cylinder were not gas-tight and the problems continued until a field modification was adopted by the manufacturer, which consisted of an extra ring welded inside the joint and packed with asbestos.

With a top speed of over 90 mph, a service ceiling of 16,000 feet and a duration of over five hours, pilots at first felt that they would hold their own against any likely opposition. In fact, on 25th March the War Office received a request from the RFC for six Martinsydes to be allocated to F.E. squadrons to act as escorts. However early operational experience with the Elephant showed that it was not ideal for the kind of aerial combat that was being experienced by that time. Not only did its large size make it less manoeuvrable than contemporary scouts but the view from the cockpit was severely restricted, not only by the high cowling but also by the wide chord of the lower mainplane. The poor view did not help in the use of the machine in the reconnaissance role. Also the lack of a windscreen did not allow the pilot to remove his goggles so that he could use field glasses. Furthermore the cockpit was so cramped that the pilot had no convenient place to put maps or note books.

Despite these objections, Major General Trenchard, by this time the General Officer Commanding the RFC, had by the middle of April 1916 decided to use the Martinsyde as a bomber and reconnaissance aircraft and this change was formally adopted on 9th July. Provision was made for the carriage of eight 20-1b bombs under the wings and an alternative load of two 112-1b bombs mounted under the fuselage. The 20-1b racks required an additional rib on the bottom planes placed between 18 and 18½ inches from the innermost rib. Later provision was made for the carriage of a single 230-1b bomb. The first use of this weapon in France occurred on 8th April 1917 in an attack by No.27 Squadron on Hirson railway station and it was commonly used thereafter. A variety of other combinations of bombs have

G.102 (A1599) served with No.27 Squadron in France. (J M Bruce/S Leslie Collection)

also been reported such as two 100-lb bombs or one 100-lb plus four 20 lb bombs or twelve 20-lb bombs. The last combination prompted the fitment of an additional bracing strut between the front undercarriage supports.

Lt (later Sir) Hugh Chance described some unofficial modifications in his account *Subaltern's Saga*:

Our Martinsydes had no proper bombsights except for a wire contraption on the right side of the cockpit. It was impossible to fly straight whilst sighting so I asked my rigger to fix a hole in the floor of the cockpit. H.E. bombs were not the only weapons used against the Boche.... periodically a tender was sent into the nearest town and returned having denuded the shops of rolls of "Bromo" and as many china articles as possible.... over targets the rolls were hurled out followed by a china chamber pot, whilst other "lethal" weapons included broken gramophone records, soda-water bottles and other rubbish.

Meanwhile an event occurred which severely dented No.27 Squadron's confidence in the structural integrity of the machine. On 8th April, Martinsyde 7267, piloted by 2/Lt W N Thomas, was flying at 6,000 ft when one of the fuselage longerons snapped, quickly followed by the remaining three. The whole empennage together with the last two bays of the fuselage came adrift and the aircraft fell to earth taking its unfortunate pilot to his death. An inspection of the wreckage the following day showed no sign of damage due to enemy action. At first a flaw in the hickory used in the construction of the longerons was blamed with poor seasoning suspected.

The manufacturer immediately set out to strengthen the fuselage. Stiffening pieces were glued and bound to the longerons across the third to fifth fuselage bays numbered from the rudder post. The fourth bay was additionally strengthened by horizontal struts top and bottom between the longerons and additional wire ties were fitted between the top and bottom longerons in the bay behind the pilot. A load test was carried out on the new configuration on 19th April. It withstood a load of 1,000 lb on the tailplane, equivalent to 20 lb/sq inch and a horizontal load of 250 lb on the rudder post

six inches above the tailplane, although some permanent distortion resulted. By comparison, when retested with the fuselage restored to its original configuration, failure occurred just as a load of 1,000 lb was reached. It was recommended that existing fuselages should be examined, longerons replaced if necessary and the above modifications incorporated. It was also recommended that, as the vertical struts were not positively fixed to the longerons, wooden distance pieces should be bound and glued to the longerons to prevent movement of the struts along the longerons.

It was intended that new fuselages would incorporate the following modifications; the width of the rear fuselage would be increased by three inches, the section of the rear portions of the longerons would be increased from ½-inch square to 1-inch square, an additional bay would be formed by reducing the length of the existing bays by about a sixth and finally the stiffening pieces, as fitted to existing machines, would be retained but of somewhat smaller section.

The significance of the admission that the vertical struts were not positively fixed to the longerons was not lost on the pilots with No.27 Squadron and a quick response was forthcoming from the field with the suggestion that structural integrity would be undoubtedly enhanced if sockets, such as those used on F.E. and B.E. aircraft, would be used to positively anchor the struts to the longerons. This suggestion was adopted by the manufacturer on 5th May but the modification was some time reaching the squadron.

However this was not the end of the story. It was noted on delivery that two machines (serial numbers 7464 and 7465), which had been in the course of construction when the changes had been introduced, had the replacement rear fuselages of the new design butt-jointed to the forward fuselage. This had been accomplished by joining the longerons by means of steel sleeves about six inches long through which a couple of 1/8th-inch bolts had been passed. It was pointed out by No.27 Squadron that each longeron when in tension was secured merely by one bolt. It has not been recorded how the reassurance, that the fuselage would

G.102 (A3948) was used at Orfordness for miscellaneous testing. Note the experimental single exhaust stack.
(J M Bruce/S Leslie Collection)

not be in tension and the modification was AID-approved, was received at squadron level. However despite the misgivings of the squadron pilots, the two aircraft in question were reintroduced into service.

A further batch of fifty was ordered (A1561 to A1610) in June 1916. As the 160-hp version of the Beardmore gradually became available from February 1916, it was adopted as the standard power unit and the intention was to fit all Martinsydes from A1561 with this engine. With the different engine the designation was changed to G.102. The majority were so equipped but some of the later aircraft had to make do with the 120-hp engine. Deliveries from A1561 began in mid-July 1916 and in September seventy more (A3935 to A4004) were ordered, followed by a final batch of fifty (A6250 to A6299) ordered in October. All 170 Martinsyde G.102s were ordered under Contract No.87/A/487 and production lasted until the summer of 1917. From 4th August 1916, all G.100 and G.102 aircraft were fitted with a larger model of radiator.

Some of the earlier production machines were modified to take the more powerful engine and a field conversion kit was provided for this purpose. The work involved in converting a G.100 to G.102 standard needed some 90 man-hours of work and necessitated a complete change of all engine controls and a certain amount of strengthening of the fuselage to accommodate heavier bomb loads. The more powerful engine improved the top speed by about 10 mph and service ceiling by 1,500 to 2,000 ft but the heavier bomb load reduced the endurance to about 4½ hours. In these later versions, the bomb capacity was increased to one 230-lb bomb or twelve 20-lb bombs and an improved overwing gun mounting was fitted, the Martinsyde No.5 Mark II.

By September 1916, it was realised that the enlarged air scoop, which improved the air supply to cool the radiator in the summer, also exposed the rear carburettor to a chilling blast and this could lead to carburettor icing problems during the winter. Martinsyde agreed to fit an adjustable shutter which could be controlled from the pilot's seat. Additional protection was also given to the carburettor and induction pipe. About this time the manufacturer also agreed to incorporate a field modification which separated the duplicated rudder control wires. The manufacturer also reversed the position of the throttle control and the hand pump for pressurising the petrol tank as the barrel of the latter got in the way of the pilot's legs.

The aircraft's armament remained unchanged in service throughout the war. However there are official references to two alternative installations of fixed forward-firing guns. The No.8 Mark I had a fixed Lewis gun mounted on the fuselage side, offset to port within a fairing, with the propeller protected by pieces of armour plate. The No.7 Mark I installation was to have consisted of a fixed Vickers gun with the Vickers-Challenger interrupter gear, similar to the weapon installation of the B.E.12, but evidence of this latter installation has yet to be found.

On 22nd October, six Martinsydes loaned to the French for evaluation were returned to No.1 AD at St.Omer. It appears that the French were unimpressed as no order ensued.

Oliver Stewart recorded the pleasant flying but somewhat disconcerting landing characteristics in his book, *The Clouds Remember*, as the following extracts show:

As a flying machine the Martinsyde Elephant had many pleasing qualities. It ambled through the air with rather gentle burbling sound and seemed to get about the country

G.102 (A6286) a presentation aircraft 'Rhodesia III' was tested at Martlesham during July/August 1917. It was transferred from Farnborough to Orfordness where it was experimentally fitted with a 260-hp Rolls-Royce engine during July and August 1918. (Imperial War Museum)

fairly quickly. The outlook from the pilots's cockpit was somewhat restricted and the present writer, when he once got lost in one of these aeroplanes on a day when rain was falling and visibility was bad, found the restricted outlook made it difficult to recognise landmarks. But the flying quality which was chiefly attributed to this machine by the pilots of the period was that of 'floating' when landing.

Actually floating must be regarded as the responsibility partly of the pilot and partly of the aeroplane. In so far as the aeroplane is responsible, it is the testimony to sound design; for the cleaner the design, the greater the float after the approach at a given speed. The wartime machines were mostly far from clean. The biplane does not lend itself to really clean design and there were the struts and bracing wires all contributing to the drag. Pusher aeroplanes especially, had almost no float because directly the power was cut off and the aeroplane titled for the touch down, the drag pulled it up like a powerful air brake.

When a relatively clean design like the Martinsyde Elephant came out, pilots, used to things that stood still and dropped the moment the stick was brought back, were a little puzzled by it. If they approached in their habitual manner, with a big margin of speed over the stalling speed, they found the machine shooting across the aerodrome towards the opposite hedge at the moment when they expected it to be sitting down on the grass.

It was, as I say, an excellent quality in the aeroplane because it demonstrated low drag. But at the same time - and even on occasions today - pilots talk about it as if it were a fault. So the word went round that the Martinsyde 'floated badly'. I suppose the reputation of the machine was slightly damaged by the story. But in fact, directly one became familiar with the Martinsyde, or indeed with any other aeroplane with the reputation for floating, one found that the float could be prevented and the landing made in a short space provided only that the approach was adjusted so that only a small margin of speed over the landing speed was maintained.

So when we remember that the Martinsyde Elephant had this reputation for floating we remember a strong testimony in favour of the excellence of the design. As for the controls of the Martinsyde Elephant, they were reasonably good although the ailerons failed to produce as quick or as big a response as many pilots would have liked and the elevator had none of the sensitivity of the elevator, for instance, of a Camel.

The only serious fault was the poor outlook. The pilot sat just behind the trailing edge of the top plane with the trailing edge of the lower plane almost immediately below him. Forwards and upwards a big arc of view was blanked out by the top plane and downwards and forwards there was another big arc blanked out. The big chord of the wings added to the blanking effect. In addition, the forward part of the fuselage, and the cowling of the Beardmore engine, came rather high and still further restricted the forward outlook.

L W Sutherland MC, DCM, in his book *Aces and Kings* on his experiences with No.1 Squadron Australian Flying Corps in Palestine, reported mixed reactions to the attributes of the Elephant. To quote two extracts from the book;

The Martinsyde was a joy to the eye. But aloft she was sluggish, 'sloppy' on controls, and altogether a horrible machine in which to fight for your life. Her redeeming feature was that she could carry a load.

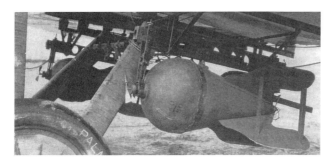

A Martinsyde with two 112-lb bombs, a very heavy load for an aircraft of its time.

Other types we had at our squadron were B.E.12a's and Martinsydes ('Tinsydes'). Old 3345, a Tinsyde, was Fred Haig's favourite bomber. Fred loved that old girl. He used to fuss over her as if she were his wealthy spinster aunt. She responded to the treatment, and, on bombing achievements, Fred was regarded as the Tinsyde expert of our show. Old 3345 was slow-footed, but she had tremendous stamina, and she was absolutely dependable. I am sure Fred will agree with me that had he been flying 3345 on 1st May 1918, he would have got away with his gallant attempt to rescue two of his brother officers who were down in the enemy lines.

Lt Stuart Campbell was less than enthusiastic about the performance characteristics of the Elephant when he was posted to No.27 Squadron in July 1917. This was some three months before they were retired from active service on the Western Front, at a time when they were being outclassed by nimble German single-seat scouts.

Soon after joining 27 Squadron, I tumbled to the fact that it was beyond doubt the most vulnerable squadron in France. Its role was long-distance daylight bombing for which it was equipped with single-seat Martinsydes. The Martinsyde was a delightful machine for leisurely pleasure flying but totally unsuitable for daylight bombing or indeed for any kind of war mission. In the ordinary way it was very slow but when loaded with bombs it became heavy, sluggish and cumbersome and took ages to answer to the controls. It was thus properly known as the Martinsyde Elephant. It was utterly useless in a scrap as fast, swiftly-manoeuvering Hun scouts could make rings round it. When a formation of Martinsydes was attacked there was only one thing it could do and that was to put noses down into a steep dive and with this added speed to zig-zag its way back home. This speedy zig-zag was absolutely essential and though far from safety proof, it did make it more difficult for the enemy scouts to register a hit.

When on long-distance raids Martinsyde flights were always escorted by scouts for a distance of roughly fifteen miles over the Line after which they had to look after themselves. Before every such raid arrangements were made in advance by telephone for the Martinsydes and the scouts to rendezvous at a given time, height and place. Thus, for example, the bombers leaving the ground at 3.30 am would have arranged to meet the escort scouts at 15,000 feet at 5.30 am over Béthune. This was invariably the rendezvous height and it will be noted that the slow, heavy Martinsydes took two hours (sometimes more) to reach this height whereas the scouts would get up there in about 15 minutes.

This criticism was rather unfair as the design had been in service already for nearly eighteen months and aircraft design and the techniques of aerial fighting had progressed a great deal in that time. Major J T B McCudden in his book *Five*

Years in the RFC recorded more favourable impressions:

I had a flight for the first time in a Martinsyde Elephant, a bombing scout that was then fitted with a 120-hp Beardmore engine. I liked this type of machine immensely, and it was very comfortable and warm, which made it very popular for cross-country flying........ At Dover I had many opportunities of flying different types of machine, and I made full use of them, but I think that the machine which took my fancy most was the Martinsyde. These Martinsydes being used for training had no war load at all and so one evening I set off from Dover to do a climb to see how high I could get. I left the ground clad only in a British warm and flying cap and goggles on Martinsyde No. 6252, and commenced climbing out towards the Goodwin Sands. Towards the end of an hour I was at 18,000 ft over Joyce Green, and by the time I had got to the machine's limit, which was 18,500 ft, I was over the south-eastern suburbs of London.

Most of the early production G.100s were delivered to No.27 Squadron, this being the only squadron to be completely equipped with this type on the Western Front. This squadron flew ten Martinsydes across the Channel to France on 1st March 1916, including 7258, 7262, 7266-7271 and 7273, and continued to be allocated Elephants until the end of 1917. The early practice of allocating one or two single-seat scouts to two-seater squadrons had not been abandoned in early 1916 and other Martinsydes went to No.6 Squadron, No.18 Squadron (7279), No.20 Squadron (7260 on 17th March), No.21 Squadron (7263 on 21st February) and No.23 Squadron (7280 and 7281 on 25th March) respectively. The Elephant also saw service in Macedonia and the Middle East in smaller numbers. In Palestine Nos.14, 67 (Aust) and 142 Squadrons each received a few Martinsydes, and in Mesopotamia some were used by Nos.30, 63 and 72 Squadrons. Martinsydes were operated by Nos.17 and 47 Squadrons in Macedonia. The Elephants performed well in these areas without making a lasting reputation and the few examples of the type remained with the Royal Air Force following the Armistice of November 1918, serving mainly in the area of Mesopotamia. After its retirement from front line duties, the Elephant was not allocated to home defence squadrons but one example was used as an engine test bed at Farnborough, Orfordness and Martlesham.

Miscellaneous War-Related Experimentation

Testing of the 260-hp Rolls-Royce engine

Martinsyde Elephant serial number A6286 was fitted with a 260-hp Rolls-Royce engine in place of its 160-hp Beardmore and was tested at Orfordness. Capt R.M. Charley first reported that he flew this aircraft, entered in his log book as "Rhodesia III", on 7th July when he commented on the uncomfortably warm airflow from the radiator. Flying it again on 1st August 1918, he choked the engine whilst taking off and as a result it ran very roughly. He was flying the aircraft again on the 3rd but, although he handled the engine more carefully, he had to cut short the test flight as the engine was overheating. Despite feeling unwell, he took the aircraft up again on the afternoon of the 8th and commented on its improved engine performance and its colossal speed in a dive. The machine was being tested on the 29th at Martlesham by its CO, Major Hubbard. However Charley flew the aircraft back to Orfordness on the 31st. On Sunday 1st September, Capt Charley was flying the Rolls-Royce-Martinsyde well above the clouds in brilliant sunlight, for the benefit of other

The rearward-firing Lewis gun installation (No.10 Mk.1 Mounting, Aircraft Lewis gun) on a G.102 of No.27 Squadron with Capt Pennell DFC in the cockpit. (A R Pennell)

pilots who were testing tinted sunglasses. He was again having trouble with the engine on the 9th, but nevertheless managed to outpace a D.H.9A in the climb, and made another short flight on the 13th.

The Martinsyde Interrupter Gear for Machine Guns

Three patents were applied for in the names of the Martinsyde Company, Helmut Paul Martin and Owen David Lucas, a consulting engineer, relating to electrically-fired ammunition. The first 124,777 dated 24th March 1916, described the means of firing the ammunition electrically, the firing being capable of being synchronised with the rotation of the propeller. The second 124,802 dated 7th April 1916, extended the scope of the ammunition for use in a modified Lewis gun and the third patent, 127,033 dated 24th March 1916, amalgamated and simplified the two patents.

The patents advocated the use of special bullets with electrically operated detonator caps instead of the normal percussion type. It was proposed that the new caps would consist of an insulated chamber containing fulminate of mercury (an unstable chemical containing mercury, carbon, nitrogen and oxygen) or a similar chemical which could be detonated by a spark between a pin, projecting internally from the base of the cartridge, and its casing. The striker of the gun would be replaced by an electrical contact which when the breech was closed would complete a circuit on contact with the round. The system would have been activated by pressing a button, the electrical circuit being broken whenever a propeller blade was in the line of fire.

The natural period of the gun would not have been affected and the gun would have taken its normal time to recoil and re-close the breech. The gun would have remained in its normal closed position until the current had been applied. A gun modified to take the electrically detonated ammunition could have been converted back to normal operation in a matter of minutes.

The device may have been tested in an Elephant and, although there were obvious advantages in replacing the complex mechanical synchronising devices with an electrical circuit, the idea was not adopted. There would have been logistic difficulties in manufacturing a specialised version of a standard item being produced in vast quantities and supplying it to the units in the field equipped with the system. Furthermore special training would have been required for fitters more attuned to mechanical systems.

Davis Gun Installation

Commander Cleland Davis of the US Navy patented (on 22nd October 1911) a design for a recoilless gun. The weapon consisted of two barrels. One faced forward and was rifled and chambered to receive the shell. The other with a smooth bore faced backwards and was joined to the first by a mechanism with a central locking handle. The second barrel could be rotated on a circumferential pivot to expose the breech. The shell consisted of a projectile with a cordite propellant separated by a wad from the recoil charge consisting of lead shot bound with black lead and grease. When the gun was fired by means of an electric primer, the shell was projected forwards and the recoil was neutralised by the lead shot being propelled to the rear.

The Admiralty became interested and, following a demonstration, ordered one 2-pounder and ten 6-pounders from the factory in America for experimental purposes, with a view to fitting them to aircraft and ships. Trials in several naval aircraft lead to a production order during October 1915. Due to inter-service rivalry, it was not until February 1916 that the RFC were able to evaluate the gun. The RFC had an urgent requirement for a gun which could shoot down German Kite balloons from a safe distance. The RFC General Officer Commanding in the Field was either unaware of, or chose to ignore, the problems which had been experienced with the Davis gun during the Naval trials, not least airframe damage caused by the effect of the propeller wash on the recoil charge of lead shot, as he suggested that the requirement might be met by mounting such a gun on the top wing of a Martinsyde.

Colonel B Hopkinson, Deputy Assistant Director of Military Aeronautics, in a memo to the GOC dated 12th April 1916, confirmed that a Davis gun firing a high explosive shell with a sensitive fuse offered a solution. It was appreciated that at that time no fuse existed which would be guaranteed to function against fabric but however one was under development which was expected would give a reasonable probability of success. The same memo related that Martinsyde were designing a barbette mounting to carry the Davis gun above the top plane of their new experimental two-seater biplane, presumably the F.1. The writer did however add the rider that the field of fire from a movable gun would always be limited and so a fixed mounting was considered to be more practical. He also stated that a contract had been placed for six guns to be delivered by mid-July and six per week thereafter up to a total of fifty.

Martinsyde were asked to design a mounting for the 2-lb version of the Davis gun on the top wing of the Elephant in place of the Lewis gun. However before the design was finalised it was realised that it would not be practical to reload the gun if it was mounted in this position and fresh instructions were sent in a memo on 18th April which is worth quoting in full:

I beg to request that you will make a service mounting to carry the mock-up model of the two-pounder Davis gun now in your possession, on the right-hand side of your 120 H.P. Scout, between the front and rear lower spars, close to the fuselage, and pointing as nearly as possible 45° downwards, but straight ahead in the longitudinal plane.

The gun should be so placed that the lever, etc, for opening the breech will be convenient for the pilot, and make for easy reloading. The actual gun is with the Officer Commanding, Chelsea Detachment, Royal Flying Corps, Ebury Bridge Road, and I shall be glad if you will send a representative to see the gun, take all necessary measurements

G.102 A6299 fitted with the Eeman triple gun installation

and get acquainted with the operations necessary to load and fire. Reloading must be done in the air, and a rack for ten rounds of ammunition provided.

I beg to enquire at what price you are prepared to supply this mounting.

A subsequent inspection found the mounting so constructed to be satisfactory provided that the positions of the sights were adjusted downwards. The price quoted by Martinsyde for the mounting was £6.15.0, hardly profiteering. Nothing further was heard of the barbette fitting to the two-seater but a memo dated 27th May 1916 from Hopkinson required a Capt Kennedy to collect Martinsyde 7301 fitted with a Davis gun from Farnborough and fly it to Orfordness where he would be given instructions as to how to proceed with testing. No record has been found as to whether the aircraft was indeed tested or even collected. What is known is that Martinsyde 7301 was lost behind enemy lines six weeks later on 9th July in the service of No.27 Squadron RFC.

The Eeman Gun Installation

There was one experimental gun installation made in an Elephant for home defence purposes. Experiments made at Orfordness showed that at night it was easier to pick out other aircraft from below compared with from the side or above. Concurrently, ballistic experts had discovered that when bullets, discharged from Lewis guns at an upward angle of about 45° from an aircraft travelling at 100 mph, follow a straight line for 600-800 yards as gravitational forces cancel out the air resistance. As a result, an experimental installation, designed by Capt L E Eeman, was made in a

G.102 (A6299). It consisted of triple Lewis guns mounted to fire upwards and forwards at an angle of 47° through slots in the centre section. The guns were laid by means of an Aldis sight. However by the time that the installation had been completed in early August 1917, it had been discovered that Gothas had been fitted with a ventral tunnel equipped with a downward-pointing machine gun. The upward-firing gun was clearly no longer practical for daylight operation, where forward pointing guns were essential, but still had merit for operations at night. Capt Eeman flew the modified G.102 on one anti-Zeppelin patrol while attached to No.39 Squadron but found nothing and the installation was never tested in combat. The aircraft crashed while being piloted by Capt Eeman at Stow Maries on 19th October 1917.

Experimental Bomb Sight

The Royal Aircraft Factory had developed a Periscopic Bomb Sight, the Mark I version of which had given excellent results in tests with No.21 Squadron flying R.E.7s when used in practice flights over a camera obscura in June 1916. It consisted of a telescopic periscope, fitted with a rubber eyecap, mounted on the right hand side of the cockpit. Before an operation, the instrument was levelled laterally and longitudinally in relation to the aircraft prior to take-off. To operate the instrument on a bombing run, the pilot first had to estimate the wind direction, usually by observing any drift of objects compared with the crosswires within the eyepiece. The pilot then had to mount his attack either upwind or downwind to avoid having to make any compensation for drift. Ground speed was estimated by measuring the time in seconds taken for an object on the ground to cross the field of

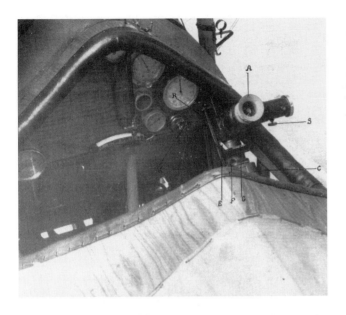

Installation of the experimental bomb sight. The eyepiece is marked A, E and F are the levelling screws for spirit level G and the height adjustment drum is C. (Public Record Office)

Another view of the rear Lewis Gun mounting. The nearest officer is Major Sidney Smith DSO, the CO of No.27 Squadron and behind him is Lt Col H C T Dowding. (Imperial War Museum)

view within the eyepiece using a stopwatch. The sight was adjusted for ground speed and height by moving a drum positioned below the instrument. The pilot looked through the sight with his right eye and kept the machine level by looking at a spirit level with his left. The pilot released his bombs when the target appeared on the crosswires set in the eyepiece.

In view of difficulties with bomb sighting experienced with Martinsydes, a Mark II version was developed for this aircraft. On 3rd July, Major Bertram Hopkinson, DADAE, reported to Major-General Trenchard that:

...it is expected that three Martinsyde machines, complete with bomb-dropping gear for 336-lb bombs and periscope bomb sights will be delivered to you in the course of the next two weeks... A further six Martinsyde periscopes are expected before July 15th. These will be fitted as soon as machines are ready for them - either with bomb-dropper or with Davis gun.

After receiving confirmation from No.21 Squadron that the periscope sight was suitable for use, on 27th July Lt-Col Caddell, ADAE, wrote to Trenchard:

Three of the Martinsyde Periscopes have been for some time fitted on machines in this country, but the machines have been held up for various causes such as engine adjustment... they will be sent out on the machines as soon as they are ready.

We expect that 25 periscopes (including the 6 just mentioned) will have been delivered by the end of August. Of these 13 are intended for R.E.7s and 12 for Martinsydes. The R.E. periscopes can, however, be altered without much difficulty into the Martinsyde pattern. Will you please let us know whether you would like this to be done?

The three Martinsydes fitted with the periscope sight were 7266, 7463 and 7469. Of these, 7266 was on the strength of No.27 Squadron when it flew to France on 1st March 1916. It was flown back to England on 15th June as a specimen aircraft for armament trials and it is assumed that the sight had been fitted by 27th June when it was re-allocated to the Expeditionary Force while still at Farnborough. It was reported at Dover in October with No.49 Squadron but it is unlikely that it returned to France. 7463 was at Farnborough

Farnborough by 26th June and although it was allocated to the Experimental Flight at Orfordness on 4th July, it was still at Farnborough on 14th August when Frank Goodden is reported to have been testing the periscope sight. It eventually was flown to Orfordness by Lt Clive Collett and subsequently saw service at Gosport, with No.49 Squadron at Dover and No.19 Training Squadron. The third Elephant fitted with a periscope sight, 7469, was allocated to the Expeditionary Force on 13th July while at Farnborough. It arrived at No.1 AD St.Omer on 12th October and joined No.27 Squadron on 20th October via No.2 AD. By then its 120-hp Beardmore had been replaced by the 160-hp version.

No.27 Squadron tested the bomb sight in the field and its CO, Major Sidney Smith, reported on 22nd October to Lt Col H C T Dowding, OC of No.9 Wing, that the bombsight was a distinct improvement over the CFS bombsight currently used, but the fact that the Elephant was unstable made it difficult to get absolute accuracy. The setting of the sight was quite simple and easy to manage. The main objection was that the sight took up a considerable amount of room within the cockpit and tended to restrict the pilot's movements when manoeuvring. Also that the eyepiece was difficult to use while wearing goggles. Practically it was found that an 'elbow piece' used to adjust the eyepiece was found to be inaccessible and a special fitment was being made in the squadron to improve matters.

Dowding annotated the report with remarks that the drum should be made smaller and the instrument should be made to be readily detachable. Also that the eyepiece should be made larger and a support made for the pilot's head while looking through the eyepiece. The response from Farnborough was that it was not intended that the instrument should be used with goggles and it would not be practical to enlarge the eyepiece. On the other hand, they were developing a suitable headrest. Farnborough also pointed out that the 'elbow piece' was in fact designed to be moved by the pilot's right elbow and not by hand and was considered suitable for its purpose.

Although ten periscope sights had been received by No.2 AD by 7th September, it is doubtful whether No.27 Squadron used the sight operationally to any great extent. Capts Vernon Brown and B M Jones of the Orfordness Experimental Station, reporting on their visit to several RFC squadrons during February 1917, mentioned in regard to No.27 Squadron that:

The Williamson camera installation on the Elephant. Also can be seen is the wooden end-plate at the wing root.
(J M Bruce/S Leslie Collection)

Three of the machines of this squadron have periscope sights but they do not consider them satisfactory owing to the aeroplane being unstable fore and aft. They are little used. I gathered that all accurate work was done from a low height, about 200 feet.

Experiments with the 336-lb Bomb

Orfordness issued a report on 4th August 1916 on the practicability of the Martinsyde Elephant as a vehicle for carrying a 336-lb bomb. It is believed that the carrier was of Martinsyde design. Certainly, at about the time that the trials were being carried out, the management at Martinsyde were resisting attempts by Handley Page to influence the Department of Military Aeronautics into getting Martinsyde to adopt the Handley Page design (which of course was the subject of prior patents!).

In the event, the original design of bomb carrier was slightly modified, a stronger release handle was fitted and the position of the handle was changed to dispense with the Bowden cable. On two occasions, a 336-lb bomb was dropped from an Elephant from 3,000 feet and both fell correctly. The Elephant when carrying the bomb was found to take 13 minutes to climb to 4,000 feet at which altitude it was able to fly at a speed of 81 mph. The problems came when trials were made on the ability of the Martinsyde to land with the bomb still attached. Two splices in the front cross bracing wires were found to have partly separated. It was concluded that landing on roughly surfaced aerodrome could cause damage to the undercarriage but that this would be acceptable in an emergency. A B.E.2c split steel axle was used in place of the standard duralumin axle for taxying tests as the latter showed signs of weakness.

It could be concluded that the Elephant had potential as a bomb carrier provided that the undercarriage could be strengthened. However the DA & QMG in the field decided, on advice from No.27 Squadron, that the aircraft should not be used for that purpose. As it happened, the trials aircraft was eventually released to No.27 Squadron without the 336-lb bomb carrier having been removed.

Despite official reluctance to use the Elephant, several 336-lb bombs were dropped operationally, both in France and Mesopotamia, using this machine.

Service on the Western Front

By the end of 1915, the British and the French had developed a battle plan by which the German reserves would be worn down by attrition as a prelude to launching an offensive. However the Germans had plans of their own and struck first on the Meuse opposite Verdun, leading to a long drawn-out battle which eventually exhausted the French. To relieve the pressure on the French, the British launched successive attacks on the Flanders front.

RFC Communique No. 27 reported an early encounter of the Martinsyde G.100 prototype on 17th January 1916. 2/Lt Bolton of No.6 Squadron sighted a Fokker biplane over Polygon Wood flying at 10,000 feet. Lt Bolton dived from 12,000 feet and overhauled the Fokker over Gheluvelt, opening fire at a range of 50 feet. After some manoeuvring at close range, a jet of flame was seen to come from the enemy's machine and the Fokker dived steeply. 2/Lt Bolton now abandoned the chase as his engine was missing badly. When last seen the hostile machine was seen still diving steeply over Gheluvelt. On 5th February, shortly after it had been transferred to No.20 Squadron, the prototype was again in action, Capt J R Howett firing a drum from his Lewis gun at a hostile machine over Clairmarais but having to break off the engagement as he was unable to change the drum.

However it was the Martinsyde Elephants of No.27 Squadron as part of No.9 Wing which took part in some of the bloodiest fighting of the war on this front from the outset of the First Battle of the Somme starting in July 1916 until its retirement from front-line active service at the end of 1917. No.27 Squadron was formed at Hounslow from a flight of No.24 Squadron on 5th November 1915, and moved to an aerodrome at Swingate Downs, just outside Dover, towards the end of that month where it received its first G.100 at the beginning of February. Within a week it had received nine more Martinsydes and the pilots began to familiarise themselves with the aircraft.

The squadron moved with its ten aircraft to St.Omer in France on 1st March 1916, one aircraft being a replacement for one damaged on take-off earlier in the day. The squadron had been allocated to 10th (Army) Wing of 1 Brigade and after a night's rest at St.Omer the pilots flew to their base at Treizennes where they familiarised themselves with the aircraft and the locality. During one routine flight, Capt Fuller wrecked his aircraft (7262) when he collided with a HT power cable. Once they were settled in the squadron started to make a photographic reconnaissance of the front covered by the First Army extending from Armentières to Souchez.

The squadron concentrated on reconnaissance and photographic missions and there were only a few inconclusive brushes with enemy aircraft during March and early April 1916. It was not until 8th April that the squadron suffered its first casualties. As recounted earlier, 2/Lt W N Thomas was carrying out a lone patrol of the La Bassée sector when the aircraft's complete tail section twisted and sheared off leaving him to spin to his death. Later the same day, Lt C A Brooks was wounded in an engagement with several Albatros fighters. On 26th April, 2/Lt S Dalrymple engaged and drove off two hostile machines and Capt Cairns engaged a hostile machine near Souchez. He fired half a drum at about 70 yards and then swerved to avoid a collision. He attacked again from behind and below, firing the remainder of the drum. The observer of the hostile machine was apparently hit, as during the second attack he appeared to be kneeling in his cockpit doing nothing, and no shots were fired. This hostile machine

This aircraft, believed to be 7459, shown during service with No.30 Squadron, carrying what appears to be a RAF 336-lb bomb. (IWM Q67952)

The upper Lewis gun mounting, shown on a Martinsyde G.102 of No.27 Squadron, was mounted off-set to the right. It proved difficult to reload in the air.

The cockpit lay-out of a G.102 Elephant. The small windscreen was a local modification in France.

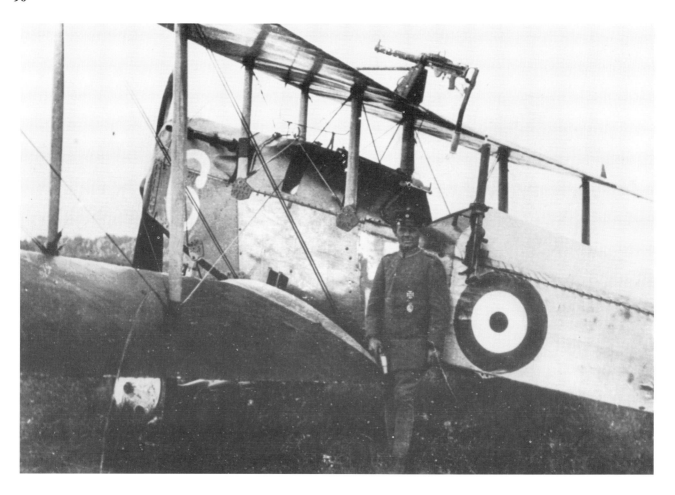

G.100 (7276) of 27 Squadron in German hands. 2/Lt S Thompson was taken prisoner after being shot down by Off Stvr Max Muller on 21 August 1917. (Philip Jarrett)

was subsequently engaged by 2/Lt Tollemache also in a Martinsyde, who fired a drum at it at about 50 yards range, driving it down towards Douvrin.

Then on 20th May, Capt Summers of No.22 Squadron in Martinsyde 7284 was one of three RFC machines which attacked an Albatros over Pozières. Capt Summers attacked the machine, firing half a drum at 30 yards range apparently without effect and it was left to Lt Tidmarsh in a D.H.2 to destroy the enemy machine. On the same day, Lt M D Basden (in Martinsyde 7278) of No.27 Squadron was killed in combat by the rear gunner of a Roland two-seater. The following day, Lt J C Turner had a hand in capturing a LVG two-seater which was forced to land at the aerodrome after losing its way on a bombing raid to Dunkerque. Later in the same day, 2/Lt A H W Tollemache had an inconclusive fight with an Albatros two-seater. In this encounter, Tollemache at 12,500 feet over Fromelles saw the Albatros below him at about 9,000 ft. He dived at it, reserving his fire till within close range. Having expended one drum, he changed it and continued the attack. The enemy twisted and turned but Tollemache managed to keep the enemy aircraft under fire at intervals. At about 4,000 ft the machines nearly collided. The enemy machine then executed a manoeuvre to escape, by side-slipping and diving vertically, flattening out near the ground close to the Citadel. Although conditions were very hazy on 31st May, two Martinsydes went out on reconnaissance accompanied by five F.E.2bs and were attacked by three Fokkers over Cambrai. The Martinsydes returned safely but one F.E.2b was lost.

At this time No.27 Squadron began to display a unit identity insignia consisting of a pair of small wooden shields, positioned each side of the fuselage mid-way between the centre-section struts, bearing a 3 inch by 3 inch profile of an elephant painted red, white and yellow for A, B and C Flights respectively.

Following Lord Trenchard's decision to change the role of the Elephant from a scout to bombing and reconnaissance, No.27 Squadron moved on 7th June from Treizennes to St. André-aux-Bois, about six kilometres west of Hesdin, to join the 9th HQ Wing under the command of Lt Col H C T Dowding. At the same time, the establishment of No.27 Squadron was increased from twelve to eighteen aircraft with twenty pilots on strength. On 19th June, No.27 Squadron moved to the aerodrome at Fienvillers with a view to supporting British ground forces in the offensive on the Somme. It quickly went into action, carrying out escort duties for other aircraft attacking captive observation balloons and also bombing raids on German communication systems, including railway stations and junctions. For example, during the evening of 30th June, when the weather had moderated after a day of low clouds and high wind, six machines of No.21 Squadron, escorted by two Martinsydes and two Moranes, bombed the munition depot and store houses at St. Sauver Station with some success.

The First Battle of the Somme began on 1st July 1916. Shortly after 6 am, a raid carried out on St. Sauver the previous day was repeated. At 8 am, six Martinsydes, escorted by two more Elephants and two Moranes, took off to bomb an enemy headquarters at Bapaume. The formation was continually attacked on the way to and over the target. With a

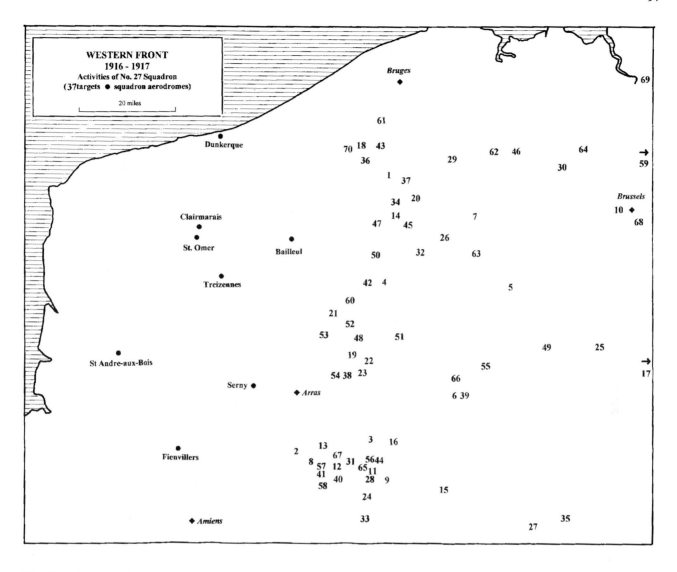

WESTERN FRONT
1916 - 1917
Activities of No. 27 Squadron
(37 targets ● squadron aerodromes)

20 miles

Martinsyde operations on the Western Front showing aerodromes and main targets;
1 Abeele, 2 Achiet-le-Grand, 4 Ascq, 5 Ath, 6 Aulnoye,
7 Audenarde, 8 Bapaume 9 Bautonzelle, 10 Berchem Ste
Agathe, 11 Beauchamp, 12 Bertincourt, 14 Bisseghem,
13 Bois de Vaux, 3 Bourlon, 15 Busigny, 16 Cambrai,
17 Cognelée (near Namur), 18 Cortemarck, 19 Courcelles,
20 Cuerne, 21 Don, 22 Dorignies, 23 Douai, 24 Epehy,
25 Epinois, 26 Escanaffles, 27 Etreux, 28 Gouzeaucourt,
29 Grammene, 30 Gijseghem, 31 Havrincourt, 32 Herinnes,
33 Hervilly, 34 Heule, 35 Hirson, 36 Hooglede,
37 Ingelmunster, 38 La Brayelles, 39 La Briquette,
40 Lechelle, 41 Le Transloy, 42 Lezennes, 43 Litchevelde,
44 Marcoing, 45 Marke, 46 Melle, 47 Menin, 48 Moncheaux,
49 Mons, 50 Mouveaux, 51 Orchies, 52 Phalempin, 53 Pont-
a-Vendin, 54 Quiey-la-Motte, 55 Quivrechain, 56 Ribecourt,
57 Rocquigny, 58 Sailly Saillisel, 59 Schoonaerde (near
Diest), 60 Seclin, 61 Sparrapelhoek, 62 St Denis Westrem,
63 St Sauver, 64 Termonde, 65 Trescault, 66 Valenciennes,
67 Velu, 69 Watermach, 69 Wijnegem, 70 Zarren.

badly-running engine and while being harried by two enemy scouts, Lt J C Turner had to make three runs over the target before he managed to release all of his 112-lb bombs. He gradually lost height but managed to reach our lines at a height of some 2,500 ft. Four more Martinsydes took off at 9.30 am to escort Major F Waldron, CO of No.60 Squadron,

on a reconnaissance over Cambrai, Busigny and Etreux. They were continually involved in battles with enemy scouts and 2/Lts Dalrymple and H A Taylor each destroyed a Roland two-seater. At about noon, Capt O T Boyd carried out a photographic reconnaissance over Bapaume and Achiet-le-Grand during an bombing raid by six R.E.7s of No.21 Squadron on Bapaume.

On 2nd July, four Martinsydes and two R.E.7s carried out a reconnaissance over the Douai-Cambrai-Marcoing-Bapaume area in the early morning, reporting some activity on the railways. After more activity by other squadrons, two more reconnaissances were carried out by Martinsydes over the same areas, supporting Moranes and Sopwiths. The two Martinsydes accompanying the Sopwiths failed to get very far, one having engine failure and one having to land on our side of the lines after a fight with a Fokker.

The first two day's operations were typical of the aerial support afforded the ground forces over the next three weeks and aerial encounters with the enemy occurred on almost every flight. On one such occasion on 6th July, Major Sidney Smith flying Martinsyde 7271 on an offensive patrol in company with Lt K N Pearson, spotted a small formation of enemy aircraft slightly below them flying westwards in pairs. Smith began climbing to get well above the enemy, but due to a misunderstanding Pearson fired a red signal and dived towards the enemy and Smith decided to follow suit. Overshooting his first target, Smith fired at the German with

G.100 (7498) forced down almost intact with 2/Lt E H Wingfield of 27 Squadron being taken prisoner.
(J M Bruce/S Leslie Collection)

his rear-mounted Lewis gun. Seeing a second enemy aircraft at about his own height, he fired three-quarters of a drum from his forward Lewis, before his adversary turned sharply to port and flicked into a vertical dive. A third German then attacked Smith from the rear, forcing him to evade violently. Having reloaded, he fired half a drum from his rear Lewis gun at this latest opponent. However his controls had become distinctly sloppy due to his port aileron wires having been shot away and he temporarily lost control. He eventually managed to regain his own lines despite the attentions of three enemy scouts which kept up harassing attacks.

No.27 Squadron continued to bomb the enemy's lines of communication to such good effect that on 9th July the squadron was advised that it would be designated solely for this task. On that date starting at 4.30 am, six Martinsydes, each armed with two 112-lb bombs and escorted by six of No.60 Squadron's Moranes, attacked trains concentrated at Bapaume, losing in the process 2/Lt R W Nicholl, who was flying Martinsyde 7301, as prisoner of war. Three-and-a-half hours later, another six Martinsydes bombed the enemy aerodrome at Velu, dropping one 112-lb bomb each, two of the bombs exploding near the hangars. They continued on offensive patrol after dropping their bombs. At 4.30 pm another raid was carried out, this time by five R.E.7s escorted by six Martinsydes and seven Moranes. On 11th July, ten Martinsydes, six R.E.7s and one B.E., escorted by Moranes and more Martinsydes, were despatched on a bombing raid but rendezvous proved difficult due to low cloud. In the event, only the Martinsydes reached their target, dropping fifty-four 20-lb bombs. Later that day, Hugh Dowding led a raid in a B.E.2c on a target near Bois

d'Havrincourt with six R.E.7s of No.21 Squadron and ten Martinsydes of No.27 Squadron, escorted by other Martinsydes and Moranes of No.60 Squadron. Although attacked by six enemy scouts, this raid was accomplished without loss to the Martinsydes although both Dowding and his observer were wounded.

Operational problems resulting from mixed formations gave rise to the following poem written by Maurice Baring during July after a Morane of No.60 Squadron had mistakenly fired at an Elephant of No.27 Squadron:

The Elephant is not a Hun

Bullets there be that can't abide
The fighting bombing Martinsyde
Without the slightest rhyme or reason
They strafe him in and out of season
The Elephant is NOT a Hun
It must not be attacked for fun
It isn't very hard to see
The crosses on a LVG
On Martinsydes the British rings
Are clearly painted on the wings
An Elephant (not very large)
Is painted on the fuselage
The GOC complains this act
Displays a grievous want of tact
And recommends that you should shoot
Your bullets on a hostile brute
Please warn your pilots every one
We're out to fight the BLOODY HUN

G.102 (A3978) No. 4 of B Flt 27 Squadron after being forced down by Flak and Lt Hess of Jasta 28 on 9 August 1917 with 2/Lt W R K Skinner being made prisoner. (via Dr Bock)

On 13 July, four Martinsydes piloted by Capt Boyd, Lt Turner and 2/Lts Pearson and Taylor, crossing the lines in cloud, bombed trains on the lines Douai-Cambrai and Denain-Cambrai. 2/Lt Taylor saw two trains, one going north and another just west of Aubigny-au-Bac. He aimed one bomb at a train from a height of 800 feet but it failed to explode. He dropped another bomb on a second train from a height of 500 feet, derailing the tender and two leading trucks. He then scattered a squadron of cavalry on the Epinoy-Marquion road and bombed a 3½-mile long convoy of transport on the Fressines-Cambrai road. Lt Turner also dropped two bombs on the same train without any apparent effect. Lt Pearson dropped two bombs on a second train on the Cambrai-Denain line near Iwuy and managed to stop it although no damage could be seen. Capt Boyd also attacked the same train with bombs and machine gun fire but only damaged the telegraph wires alongside.

On the 19th, two pairs of Martinsydes attacked rail traffic between Douai and Cambrai and between Valenciennes and Cambrai, losing 2/Lt A H W Tollemache, missing believed killed. On the following day, five Martinsydes attacked Epehy station with ten 112-lb bombs despite the attentions of three enemy aircraft which were driven off. On 21st July, six R.E.7s of No.21 Squadron, escorted by Martinsydes, dropped fourteen 112-lb bombs on Epehy station, the railway line to the north and in the town. Later in the day, an offensive patrol by six Martinsydes, piloted by Capt Boyd, Lt Usher and 2/Lts Willcox, Forbes, Joy and Letts, set out with the intention of attacking German aircraft at their base at Bertincourt. Although Boyd's guns jammed early in the patrol, he continued to lead the patrol for the whole 2½-hour flight, during which three enemy aircraft were driven down in a series of individual battles.

On 28th July, four Martinsyde Scouts set forth at about 12.30 pm to attack the railway station at Mons, carrying between them two 112-lb and eight 20-lb bombs. They were accompanied as far as St.Amand by four Sopwiths. Clouds at around 5,000 ft shielded the formation until it reached Mons at about 2.30, whereupon the machines descended to below cloud level to drop their bombs. The station was crowded with rolling stock and these and the sheds, which had been reported by agents to contain ammunition, were hit and four fires were started. All four aircraft returned safely. Later in the day four Martinsydes, each carrying two 112-lb bombs, attacked Le Transloy at 5.15 pm. A fire was started in the centre of the village and one hostile machine was driven off.

On 29th July, Major Sidney Smith took over the command of No.27 Squadron from Major Borton and on that day the squadron sent a formation to bomb the enemy airfields at Bertincourt and Velu. Eight bombs were dropped on German hangars and this was capped by the destruction of two enemy aircraft near Bapaume, Boyd shooting down a Roland and Lt B D Frost a "large Type A biplane". In the afternoon, another formation, with an escort of four Sopwiths from No.70 Squadron, bombed the enemy airfield at Hervilly. Again Capt Boyd was involved. He was attacked by a hostile machine which he first mistook for a Sopwith. His side gun jammed but he got above the enemy and fired a drum from his wing-mounted gun. The enemy side-slipped and dived. Capt Boyd lost sight of his adversary but Lt Joy saw the machine fall out of control until within 2,000 feet of the ground.

G.100 (7507) of A Flt 27 Squadron which survived the war seen at Hondschoote between 10 July and 26 October 1917 (Demerliac collection via Christophe Cony)

On the afternoon of the following day, eight Elephants, four of which were carrying two 112-1b bombs each, bombed Epehy Junction and lost two aircraft through attacks by enemy aircraft, 7471 piloted by 2/Lt L N Graham and 7404 piloted by Lt E R Farmer, both of whom were taken prisoner. One of these machines was claimed by Lt Kurt Wintgens of KekV. That evening seven Elephants, accompanied by four Sopwith 1½-Strutters from No.70 Squadron, set out to raid Marcoing. Thick mist broke up the formation and only two aircraft reached their objective. One of these was 2/Lt R H C Usher who reported back as follows:

The patrol seemed to break up just as we were crossing the Lines. As I didn't see any signals to return, and as I still had a Sopwith with me, I went on to Marcoing and dropped my bombs, both of which fell on the village. I turned quickly round and almost ran into an LVG. I gave him a drum and he went down under me. I saw the Sopwith take him on and whilst I was changing drums I was attacked again in front by a Roland. I gave him a drum and at the same time heard a machine gun behind me, looked round and saw three Rolands on my tail. I was hit in the leg almost immediately but managed to give them a drum of my side gun and they went away. My engine started spluttering and I saw a hole in my petrol tank - my engine stopped so I started gliding down thinking I should have to land. Petrol was flowing all over my left leg so I put my left knee over the hole in the petrol tank. It struck me that by pumping I might be able to get up a little pressure. By this time I was about 200 feet up - the engine started and I was about 15 miles from our Lines. I kept pumping hard all the time and managed to keep the engine going. I thought that I would have to land, but my engine just

picked up in time three or four times. I came back to the Lines for about 15 miles at an average height of 50 feet. I had lost myself and was so low that I could see very little of the country. I then picked up a Horace Farman biplane that was flying very low and followed him and eventually landed at Moreuil aerodrome - crashing the machine on landing - I was feeling very weak as I had lost a lot of blood and was exhausted by having to pump for so long. After having engaged the first machine, I did not see anything of the Sopwith. During the time that I was flying low I was subjected to a lot of rifle and machine gun fire.

In addition to its attacks on enemy communications, No.27 Squadron was often called upon to carry out raids on specific strategic targets. One such example occurred on 2nd August when three Martinsydes attacked the Zeppelin shed complex at Brussels. Smith hit one of the sheds and an electric power house with his two bombs. Captain Boyd scored one bomb on a train but missed with the other. Lt Leslie Forbes hit a train and destroyed two trucks with his bombs. The following day, two separate raids were carried out. Eight Martinsydes escorted by four Sopwiths set out to attack the Ronet Sidings at Namur and the airship sheds at Cognelée. Three Martinsydes dropped out and the escort returned after reaching Condé-sur-l'Escaut but the remainder reached their targets. At Ronet, one bomb fell in the engine shed, one in the power house, one on the main line and two on rolling stock in the sidings. In the other attack, two Elephants reached the Zeppelin sheds at Cognelée, which had been reported as being used for ammunition storage. One shed was damaged and a squad of men was machine gunned. Lt J C Turner in Martinsyde 7307 failed to return from this

G.102 (A6263) of A Flt 27 Squadron survived service in France. (J M Bruce/S Leslie Collection)

attack.

On 6th August, an offensive patrol consisting of four Martinsydes was attacked by a Fokker but in the ensuing melée the Fokker was driven down out of control and disappeared into cloud. One of the Martinsydes suffered slight damage. Around midday on 8th August, No.27 Squadron dropped forty-three 20-lb bombs on Gouzeaucourt Station, some fifteen of which were seen to hit the station and sidings, in which there was a train and some rolling stock. That evening two offensive patrols carried out by Martinsydes and B.E.12s encountered a number of enemy aircraft. In one incident, Lt Hicks of No.27 Squadron alone attacked three LVG aircraft and prevented them from crossing our lines.

Indifferent weather curtailed flying activities during the rest of August but on 12th August, seven Martinsydes dropped forty 20-lb and four 112-lb bombs on factories and the main railway at Quivrechain, just east of Valenciennes. Three buildings, two trains and an AA battery were hit. The formation was harassed by Fokker scouts on the return flight. Lt H A Taylor shot one down but Capt R H D Lee was wounded. On the afternoon of 18th August, four Martinsydes of No.27 Squadron, each fitted with eight 20-lb bombs, attacked Sailly Saillisel. Four others set out to attack the railway sidings at Annay but became separated in thick cloud. Two returned without dropping their bombs. Lt E D Hicks was forced to return with engine trouble but managed to drop his bombs close to a railway. 2/Lt B D Frost dropped his bombs on an unidentified station about 20 miles behind the lines, wrecking three coaches and damaging the station. On the 19th, during a bombing raid on Rocquigny, Lt Sherrin of No.27 Squadron attacked a hostile machine which was joined by five others. He had his radiator, petrol tank and engine damaged but managed to return safely. The squadron bombed Le Transloy on the 22nd.

On 31st August, the squadron suffered a severe setback when four Elephants set out to bomb Havrincourt Wood and not one returned. Attacked by a bevy of Halberstadts, Fokkers and Rolands over the target, Capt A Skinner in Martinsyde 7482 was shot down in flames and Capt O L Whittle in 7299, 2/Lt A J O'Byrne in 7479 and 2/Lt M H Strange were forced down or crashed and taken prisoner. One of the Martinsydes was claimed by O/Lt Hans Bethge and another by Lt Hans von Keudell, both of Jasta 1. These losses did not deter the Squadron, which continued its attacks. During the next week, raids were made on the enemy airfields at Beaucamp, Trescault and Aulnoye, destroying hangars and aircraft on the ground.

The bad flying weather continued into September. The first two weeks of the month were spent mainly in preparing for the Third Battle of the Somme. On 3rd September, eight Martinsydes encountered bad weather but six managed to drop their bombs on Sailly Saillisel. On 14th September, Lts L F Forbes and W H S Chance cornered and destroyed an LVG which had attempted to interfere with a bombing raid near Bois de Vaux. The Battle started in earnest the following day and No.27 Squadron supported the ground operations by three repeat raids on General von Bulow's HQ at Bourlon Chateau. A total of sixteen 112-lb and thirty-two 20-lb bombs were dropped and four enemy aircraft were sent down for the loss of Lt C J Kennedy in 7484, who was last seen going down close to the objective with smoke coming from under his seat. It was later confirmed that he had been taken prisoner. Other Martinsydes attacked rail communications. A report of a concentration of some forty trains in and around Cambrai resulted in the despatch of five Martinsydes at 9.45 am. Three of this formation dived on a train about to enter the station at Gouzeaucourt. Levelling out at 500 feet, the first Elephant pilot hit the engine with his bombs, the second destroyed the rear truck and dispersed his 20-lb bombs amongst the troops running from the train and the last scored a direct hit on an ammunition truck which exploded with great force. A further five Martinsydes attacked trains at Epehy and Ribecourt and a stores dump at Bantouzelle.

By 16th September, Jasta 2, commanded by Hauptmann Oswald Boelcke and boasting the presence of a Lt Manfred von Richthofen, became operational on receipt of its complement of aircraft. This unit was destined to wreak havoc with the British aircraft on this front for the forthcoming weeks.

Also on the 16th an attack was made on Cambrai station and Lt Chance, whilst piloting Martinsyde 7286, was forced to land behind enemy lines following a raid on the rail sidings at Valenciennes. In his own words:

Ordered to attack Valenciennes. Set off 7 am. When some 20 miles into Hunland, Archied heavily. Almost immediately my engine stopped. Feverish work with the auxiliary hand pump restarted the engine but it soon packed in again. I realised that a forced landing was inevitable (I had already dropped my bombs on a wood). We had just been issued with tracer bullets for our Lewis gun and were warned that the Boche were claiming that they were explosive and contrary to the Hague Convention; so before landing I fired off both machine guns and threw out the spare ammunition drums. Picking a likely-looking stubble field, I landed without difficulty and, clutching the incendiary torch with which we were equipped in case of a forced landing, jumped out - set the torch alight and poked it into the canvas of the mainplanes. This proved ineffective, so I climbed back into the cockpit, broke the glass of the petrol gauge, dipped my handkerchief into the stream of petrol which poured out, lit it from the torch and flung it back into the cockpit. There was a great gush of flame and I ran headlong to be clear of the burning plane and flung myself down as some German troops exercising some distance away started loosing off. Soon the plane was surrounded by field-grey soldiers and a German officer rode up on a horse. I saluted and we conversed in French. After a short time a staff car appeared and I was whisked off to the German HQ located in the Château du Bourlon.

Bombing raids were carried out on Quivrechain railway station on 22nd September. Later that day, fifty-six bombs were scattered on Havrincourt Wood, believed to harbour German infantry. The following day, six Elephants set out at 8.30 in the morning on an Offensive Patrol, with disastrous results as they ran into five scouts of Jasta 2. Almost immediately, Martinsyde 7481, piloted by Sgt H Bellerby, was shot down by Manfred von Richthofen for his second victory and two more Elephants, piloted by 2/Lts E J Roberts and O C Godfrey, were accounted for by Lts Erwin Boehme and Hans Reimann. The three remaining Elephants continued to fight desperately, until Lt L F Forbes, having run out of ammunition, deliberately rammed head-on the scout piloted by Reimann. Reimann spun to earth and was crushed to death, but Forbes managed to nurse his Martinsyde, with one wing near collapse and all aileron controls shattered, back to No.24 Squadron's base at Bertangles. He ran into a tree on landing and sustained a dislocated shoulder and several cracked ribs. The two remaining Martinsydes, although severely damaged, managed to return to their home base at

Fienvillers.

On 24th September, six Martinsydes took part in a sixty-aircraft offensive patrol. Lt. John Gilmour destroyed a Fokker scout but 2/Lt E.H. Wingfield in Martinsyde 7498 failed to return and ended up as a prisoner of war. On the 25th, Boyd and H.A. Taylor respectively destroyed an LVG and a "large biplane" respectively. An anonymous diary records the events of the following day:

Sept 26. Fine, mild, Easterly wind. Six machines started on Offensive Patrol. We crossed the Lines at about 10,000 ft. About quarter of an hour later running north over Velu at 11,000 ft, I was attacked by three Rolands (or LVGs). Unable to get rear gun to bear, I was pretty well peppered. When nearest had finished his drum, I turned and got half a drum into one at close range. Having lost the formation, I circled round climbing to 11,000 ft and ran south to a scrap north of Péronne. When diving I found my tail "wonky" and on looking round found several wires, struts and a longeron shot through. Came home taking much care with my landing. Tasker hit through petrol tank early in scrap, arrived before me. Sherren nearly burnt machine with Very light and Gilmour lost formation and followed two Rolands who attacked him. Pearson and Sherren completed patrol. A bombing raid in the afternoon, six of ours as escort. Fine, low clouds and windy sunset.

The Lt John Gilmour mentioned above fought the two Rolands for some 15 minutes and succeeded in destroying one. On Wednesday the 27th, Lt Roy W Chappell sent a scout down "out of control". However later in the day a patrol of six Martinsydes again ran into Jasta 2 with Boelcke leading four Albatros D.II scouts. Boelcke shot down H A Taylor in A1568. He also shared a kill with Vizefeldwebel Rudolf Reimann. This was Martinsyde 7495 piloted by 2/Lt S Dendrino who, mortally wounded in his cockpit with his control column jammed in such a way that his aircraft circled, gradually lost height to land gently near some astonished infantry. Boelcke also shot up Martinsyde 7289 piloted by 2/Lt B V S Smith. Smith managed to struggle back to base despite being wounded in the first attack and with his aircraft's petrol tank, seat, radiator, engine, mainplanes, centre section struts and controls peppered with bullets. This aircraft was made serviceable by the maintenance crews working in shifts continually for 38 hours, a feat which earned the personal congratulations of Trenchard.

No.27 Squadron continued to concentrate on bombing German communications during October. On the 20th, nine Martinsydes released a dozen 112-lb bombs on Aulnoye during a return trip which lasted four hours. No aircraft was lost although Capt O D Filley was wounded in a brief skirmish with an enemy aircraft. The following day five Elephants bombed Ath, north of Mons, where a target, believed to be an ammunition dump, was attacked with ten 112-lb bombs. On 1st November, Capt G C St P Dombasie took command of the Squadron for a month during the temporary absence of Sidney Smith. On the 10th, the squadron dropped forty-four 20-lb bombs on five enemy aircraft parked on Valenciennes airfield.

Permission was received by the squadron on 11th November to equip the Martinsydes for night flying but in the event the weather was too poor during that month for any night flying to take place. In bitter weather on the 16th, Capt Sherrin led six Martinsydes over ninety miles to drop eight 112-lb bombs on the railway station at Hirson from just 1,000 feet. Six coaches were blown off the tracks and buildings and other rolling stock were destroyed. The bad weather continued throughout the winter, causing the Third Battle of the Somme to grind to a halt after appalling casualties on the ground and in the air. By then No.27 Squadron's operations were limited to Line patrols with occasional offensive patrols. Even with the reduced level of operations, losses still occurred. Capt H Spanner was killed in action on 28th December and 2/Lt L C F Lukis died as a result of a take-off crash on 6th January 1917. 2/Lt F D Jackson was also killed on 6th January in Martinsyde 7497 when he became disorientated in cloud and flattened out too suddenly from a steep dive. The wings collapsed at the point of maximum bending loads and both the upper and lower longerons of the fuselage broke two or three bays from the tail.

A return dated 28th February 1917 shows that of the 1,116 aircraft available to the RFC in France only 26 were Elephants. On 7th March 1917, Lts J Gilmour and W T B Tasker in two Martinsydes tackled a formation of seven enemy scouts and drove them off despite severe damage to Gilmour's aircraft. On the 17th, Lts W S Caster and R W Chappell shared an Albatros C.V. Two days later a bombing raid was made on Aulnoye and during this attack a fight developed with a formation of Halberstadts. One was sent down "Out of Control" by 2/Lt E R Pennell but two Martinsydes were lost, with 2/Lt J G Fair killed and 2/Lt T W Jay wounded. Jay's aircraft (7508) was claimed by Lt Georg Schlenker of Jasta 3.

About this time, Pennell lost his Martinsyde in unusual circumstances. After bombing Hirson from 1,500 feet, he suffered problems with the engine and rapidly lost height, making a forced landing near a wood which he believed to be in Allied territory. He unexpectedly saw a party of German troops nearby and came to the conclusion that he had misjudged his position and landed on the wrong side of the lines. Surprisingly, the Germans made no effort to prevent him from destroying his aircraft which he did by setting fire to his fuel tank using his revolver and Very pistol. The reason for the enemy's lack of interest soon became apparent when some French troops emerged from the woods to make known to him that the Germans were in fact their prisoners.

No.27 Squadron carried out two particular raids on 5th April, as part of a general offensive by the RFC preparatory to the battle of Arras. In the first, a 230-lb bomb was dropped on the railway at Pont-à-Vendin and in the second, the Hirson bottle factory was attacked from 1,800 feet with 230-lb bombs, destroying factory buildings and setting fire to the engine depot. Early on the morning of 6th April, six Elephants attacked Aulnoye railway station, dropping 230-lb bombs on some sheds north of the station starting some large fires. A running fight developed between the Martinsydes and some Halberstadt and Albatros scouts, during which two Halberstadts were sent down by the combined efforts of Capt A J M Clarke, Lt W H S Wedderspoon and 2/Lt E W Kirby for the loss of two Martinsydes. Later in the morning, during a bombing attack on Ath railway station, the same adversaries fought again, but this time two Martinsydes were lost without any gain. The four pilots lost were 2/Lt J R S Proud, who died of his wounds in a German hospital, Lt Wedderspoon, who was killed in the air and Lt N A Birks and 2/Lt W T B Tasker who both became prisoners of war. The Martinsydes of Proud and Wedderspoon were claimed by Lt Joachim von Bertrab of Jasta 30.

The Battle of Arras started on 9th April in drizzling rain and poor visibility. For the first five days, the poor weather conditions prevented any long distance bombing raids, but on the evening of 13th April, twelve Martinsydes formed part of a thirty-eight-aircraft formation of bombers and escorts which attacked the de-training centre at Hénin-Lietard. 2/Lt M

Topham was killed in a Martinsyde and three F.E.2s were also lost. O/Lt Kurt Wolff claimed Topham's machine (A1564). On the 23rd, five Martinsydes were part of a force of nine aircraft which bombed a sugar factory at Lechelle, Lt. Maxwell H Coote being wounded in his right leg when his machine was riddled with bullets during a fight with Albatros D.IIIs of Jasta 26. On the following day, No.27 Squadron provided five aircraft, escorted by three SPADs, for an attack with 230-lb bombs on Ath railway station. Seven other Martinsydes flew the long journey to Hirson, where their 230-lb bombs hit the railway sheds and derailed a train. Both these missions were accomplished without loss but the Martinsydes involved in the Hirson mission had to land at widely scattered airfields due to low cloud obscuring their home base.

No.27 Squadron continued to attack rail communications until 30th April, when its attention was switched to the enemy airfields. It took part in a three-squadron attack on Epinoy airfield, the base for Jasta 12. One day later, twelve Elephants returned there, dropping a further seventy-six 20-lb bombs amongst the hangars. This time the raid was anticipated and was attacked by about twenty Albatros scouts. One Albatros was shot down in flames by 2/Lt D J Bell, without loss to the squadron. Although 2/Lt S J Stewart was badly wounded, he managed to return to the Allied lines. Throughout May, No.27 Squadron continued to attack the enemy communications network, with raids against railway stations at Orchies, Don, Queue de Boue, where a spectacular hit was obtained on an ammunition dump on the 9th, and occasional sorties against German airfields. Lt J S Stubbs was wounded in the attack on Queue de Boue. Capt D J Bell had a lucky escape on 20th May when he badly damaged his aircraft (Martinsyde 7506) on landing at Belle Vue after having his main petrol tank holed. During this period, the squadron was sometimes escorted by Sopwith Pups from No.66 Squadron. The escorts were at times of dubious benefit as the Pups had difficulty in keeping up with their charges once the Elephants had dropped their bombs. In any event there were no operational losses during May, although 2/Lt F D Holm died of his injuries after a flying accident.

On the last day of May 1917, the Squadron moved base from Fienvillers northwards to Clairmarais airfield along with other units of 9th Wing. The purpose was to support a new move by the ground forces at Ypres. Two days after the move, one of the opposing units received a new commander, O/Lt Hermann Goering.

On 4th June, No.27 Squadron received orders to attack the enemy airfield at St.Denis Westrem, which housed two Staffeln of the Gotha heavy bomber Wing, involved in mounting bomber attacks against England. The Martinsydes dropped thirty-nine 25-lb bombs without hindrance, setting fire to one hangar containing two Gothas, damaging several other sheds and generally causing havoc. Then nine Albatros scouts appeared. In the ensuing dogfights, Capt D J Bell and Lt D V D Marshal combined to shoot the upper wing off one Albatros before the former engaged a second Albatros, killing its pilot with his first burst. This aircraft looped and fell away completely out of control. Lts Marshal and M Johnson each destroyed an Albatros and Capt H O D Wilkins claimed one "out of control". Having completely routed the enemy, the squadron reformed into a tight formation and returned to base without loss. Later that day, 2/Lt A B Cort claimed a victory over an Albatros scout but the squadron lost 2/Lt D T Steeves in Martinsyde A1566, who was taken prisoner after being forced to land well beyond the lines with engine failure. For the next two days, the squadron concentrated on the bridges

An Elephant of C Flt 27 Squadron. (J M Bruce/S Leslie Collection)

over the Escaut river at Escanaffles, south-east of Courtrai, and on rail stations. On the second day, 2/Lt A B Cort force-landed at Bray Dunes with his oil tank and radiator shot through.

The squadron supported the infantry offensive against Messines Ridge by concentrating attacks on the enemy's aerodromes and, in cooperation with No.55 Squadron's D.H.4s, released a total of 335 25-lb bombs on four airfields. However the Battle of Messines was only intended to be a diversion and air activity was reduced to conserve aircraft and crews for the main offensive, scheduled to take place four miles further north beyond Ypres. Throughout June, during the lull in operations, the squadron was kept occupied with routine Line patrols and an occasional bombing sortie, mainly against German airfields in the Lys valley. During this time, opposite the Allied forces, the Germans had amalgamated four Jastas (4, 6, 10 and 11) into a single formation (Jagdgeschwader 1) under the command of Rittmeister Manfred von Richthofen.

Lt Stuart Campbell described one mission carried out during June:

The target, an ammunition dump near Ath, was some 60 miles or so over the line and as soon as the formation was clear of the AA barrage we were picked up by four Hun scouts who sat above us all the way to the objective only swooping down as our bombs were being released. I had been detailed to warn the leader of an oncoming attack and this meant diving down in front of him and firing a red Very light. I accomplished this to the tune of popping machine guns only to find as I pulled out of the dive that the formation had already turned and was streaking for home. At that moment a pop-pop-pop broke out behind me, the bullets whizzed by and I knew only too well that a Hun was diving on my tail. As I pulled up and out of his fire a second one came down from the side, his stream of lead carrying away a piece of my flying cap and making a mess of my instrument board.

By now the formation was over a mile away on its homeward journey and I was left stunting desperately, a mere 4,000 ft up, 60 miles from the line and two painted devils doing their utmost to down me. I was in no position to see things clearly as the machine was never in one place for more than one second when, suddenly, I saw one of our machines diving by me with his Lewis gun going in one long burst. I noted the pilot was bareheaded and knew at once that he was a Canadian named De Rochie. He had left the formation to turn back to what might have been certain death in order to give me a hand. His spectacular dive had scared off the enemy machine he had been firing at and though the other hung on till we reached the line he didn't attempt anything serious.

The first three weeks of July saw the Squadron dividing its attention almost equally between airfields and the railway system. These raids were frequently intercepted by German scout formations. On the 13th, Capt H O D Wilkins forcelanded in Martinsyde A1579 at Noeux-les-Mines after being hit by anti-aircraft gunfire and his machine was wrecked. On the following day, Martinsydes were sent to bomb Zarren and Quiey-la-Motte. They had just released their bombs when they were attacked by German scouts. 2/Lts T E Smith (Martinsyde 7500) and C M de Rochie (Martinsyde A6266) were killed in the first attack and 2/Lt G H Palmer (Martinsyde A1572) was shot down near Loison Harnes and taken prisoner. One of these machines was claimed by Lt Julius Schmidt of Jasta 3. The following day Capt M Johnstone was lost when returning from a raid on Moorslede. A 25-lb bomb hung up and rather than risk landing with it, he jumped from his aircraft (Martinsyde 7499) into a lake at Arques from a height of five or six feet and was killed.

Despite these losses, daily attacks continued on the German airfields at Moncheaux, Abeele, Dorignies, Sparrapelhoek and La Briquette. The longest operational flight undertaken by the squadron took place on 23rd July in difficult circumstances. Eight Martinsydes set a compass course high above the clouds to bomb Termonde. The formation broke through the clouds over Brussels and one pilot dropped his two 112-lb bombs on Watermael station. Two 230-lb and four 112-lb bombs were then dropped on the rail tracks at Termonde. All aircraft landed intact at Cormont after flying for 5 hours 5 minutes. The same afternoon, thirty-seven 25-lb bombs were scattered on the hangars at La Brayelles airfield.

The following day, six Elephants, escorted by six Sopwith Pups of No.66 Squadron, dropped three 230-lb and six 112-lb bombs on Cortemarcke station from a height of 1,000 feet. Three days later, five Martinsydes attacked the Zeppelin sheds at Berchem St.Agathe, near Brussels. Capt. Bourdillon pinpointed the target by dropping two 112-lb bombs from only 50 feet, while the remainder of the formation bombed from 2,500 to 3,000 ft. On the 28th, whilst returning from a raid on Lichtervelde and Wynghene railway stations, it was noticed that Capt H O D Wilkins (Martinsyde A3986) was gradually losing height. Although the rest of the formation tried to escort him home he had been wounded by anti-aircraft gunfire and was forced to land behind enemy lines to be taken prisoner.

At dawn on 31st July, two British armies and one French army launched an attack on the German lines and the Third Battle of Ypres began. As a prelude, on the day before two pilots of No.27 Squadron were given individual missions to attack German airfields. Capt W Smith dropped five 25-lb bombs on the hangars of Jasta 4 at low level at Cuerne and Lt Stuart Campbell released four 25-lb bombs from 3,000 feet on Heule, destroying two enemy two-seaters on the ground. Both carried out low-level strafing attacks after dropping their bombs. Capt Bourdillon made a characteristic low level attack on the Courtrai railway bridge, but although he scored a direct hit the bomb failed to explode, presumably because the vane which released the detonator did not have enough time to unwind. Lt Campbell attempted to repeat the raid on the following day but the bridge was too well guarded by enemy scouts.

On the day of the battle, the cloud base was no higher than 1,000 feet and as the day wore on light drizzle turned to heavy rain. Aircraft of No.9 Wing, including the Martinsydes of No.27 Squadron, were designated to attack the German reserve areas and enemy airfields. Each pilot was directed to attack targets of opportunity, with special emphasis on the enemy airfields. Lt R H S Hunter bombed the airfield at Marke, which was the home of Jasta 11 and the Richthofen Circus HQ, while Lt Schoones strafed Heule, the base of Jasta 10. Lt Stuart Campbell dropped a 230-lb bomb accurately on the Herinnes railway line and 2/Lt R H Ayre dropped seven 25-lb bombs on the line between Courtrai and Audenarde. Other airfields attacked were Ingelmunster by 2/Lt G Smith with eight 25-lb bombs and Grammene was strafed by Capt Bourdillon.

At 10 am that morning, aircraft of No.27 Squadron, escorted by SPADs, S.E.5s and Camels, set off to bomb the airfields yet again. Marke and Heule were each attacked by six of the Martinsydes. In each case the return journey was made at low level, with the pilots attacking any worthwhile targets with their Lewis guns. Such attacks continued during the following week. For example, on 4th August Capt Bourdillon dropped one 230-lb and four 20-lb bombs from 5,700 feet on Cortemarcke Station and on 7th August, twelve Martinsydes took off for independent sorties, each carrying a 230-lb bomb, with Capt Bourdillon overloading his aircraft

with four additional 25-lb bombs. Lt Stewart dropped his bomb from about 500 feet and blew a large hole in the railway embankment half a mile south west of Gyseghem and twisted the track, Lt Aire bombed a troop train one mile east of Schoonaerde, blowing one truck off the line, and then proceeded to machine-gun the engine and the enemy troops, who were trying to take cover. Capt Rushford and Sgt S J Clinch together bombed the railway lines leading to Menin station. Bourdillon, looking for his target, Lede station, confirmed his position by reading a platform sign and then showed his gratitude by dropping two 25-lb bombs, one close to a train and one near a shed, which he suspected was an ammunition store. He continued to Melle station, where he off-loaded his 230-lb bomb on a train carrying pit props, blowing up two of the wagons. He dropped his remaining 25-lb bombs on some new sidings north west of that station.

Two days later 2/Lt W R K Skinner was shot down in Martinsyde A3978 and taken prisoner uninjured after mixing it with four Albatros scouts from Jasta 28. Skinner was forced out of a formation of Martinsydes, flying between Lille and Roubaix, by having his ailerons damaged in a firing pass by a Lt Hess. Skinner attempted to reach the frontline in a straight glide but landed south of Quesny, hitting some trees in the process and finishing up on his nose. Despite Hess's attentions, the victory was credited to AA fire from Motor Flakzug 61.

For the following two weeks, No.27 Squadron attacked German airfields at Ascq, Mouveaux, La Brayelles and Phalempin. On 12th August, a formation of Elephants attacked Lezennes, whereupon they were intercepted by Albatros scouts from Jasta 28, losing 2/Lt S C Sillem (in Martinsyde A1573), shot down in flames near Lille by Hpt Hartmann of Jasta 28. On 16th August, sorties were carried out against rail sidings at Seclin and Courtrai and three 230-lb and twenty-one 25-lb bombs were dropped on Bisseghem airfield, the base of Jasta 6. During these raids, 2/Lt A R Baker (in Martinsyde A6261) was shot down and killed by Lt Mohnicke of Jasta 11 after a brief fight near Linselles. Five days later, on 21st August, three more pilots were lost in a dogfight with Albatros scouts which took place just east of Seclin; Capt G K Smith (in Martinsyde A6259) and 2/Lt D P Cox (in Martinsyde A3992) were both shot down and killed and 2/Lt S Thompson was forced down (in Martinsyde 7276) by Offstvtr. Max Muller. O/Lt Hans Bethge of Jasta 30 claimed one Martinsyde and Rittmeister Karl Bolle of Jasta 28 another.

For the next three weeks, enemy air activity appeared to slacken, although there was a melée when twenty Albatros scouts interrupted a bombing sortie on 27th August. Two enemy scouts were shot down without loss to the squadron. On 14th September, seven Elephants escorted by three others bombed the railway line at Courcelles and dropped four 230-lb and seven 112-lb bombs. Unfortunately, on this raid 2/Lt S H Taylor (in Martinsyde A6292) suffered engine failure and was forced to land at South Avèsnes and was taken prisoner.

Two days later the Squadron in full force successfully bombed German troop billets at Hooglede, two miles north west of Roulers. They were attacked on the return journey by Jasta 28 and lost Lt N W Goodwin (in Martinsyde A6287), who was shot down and killed near the village of Stadem. Goodwin had been attacked by Lt Hess who attacked the rearmost machine from a range of 100 yards, closing at full throttle whilst firing to around 10 yards. The Martinsyde reared-up vertically, stayed suspended for a moment before falling over to the left side, shedding its elevator in the process before spinning vertically into the ground. This loss

G.102s of C Flt No.27 Squadron. Lt Stubbs was wounded in combat in No.1 (A3991) and 2/Lt D P Cox was shot down near Seclin and killed in No.3 (A3992). (J M Bruce/S Leslie Collection)

was eventually credited as a victory to Lt Hanko, who had claimed a share in the victory. Before the sortie Skinner had lost the toss as to who would take up the dangerous last position in the formation. Lt Hess destroyed a second single-seater, almost certainly a Martinsyde flying top cover, during the same engagement. He attacked this aircraft from the rear without seriously damaging it. A fight ensued whereby each tried to out-turn the other. During a frontal attack the British aircraft was hit decisively, sideslipped and dived vertically into the ground. On the same day the Squadron also lost 2/Lt A H Skinner (Martinsyde A2651) as a prisoner of war when he was shot down by an anti-aircraft battery near Houthulst.

Another typical day dawned for No.27 Squadron on 20th September. Lt C Brown flew to Bisseghem aerodrome at a height of 500 feet and dropped two 112-lb bombs close to a hangar. Lt Aire crossed the lines above the clouds and when the ground reappeared he flew along the road and canal from Menin to the enemy aerodrome at Maerke. He dropped two 112-lb bombs from 3,000 feet on a line of two-seaters and scouts, destroying at least one. Capt E Fawcus dropped two 112-lb bombs from 3,000 feet on Abeele aerodrome and Lt Hay dropped eight 20-lb bombs from 1,500 feet on an enemy aerodrome and strafed a machine gun post. Lt E C J Elliott crossed the lines in cloud and came out over Abeele aerodrome where he dropped two 112-lb bombs from 2,000 feet and Lt H E Darrington dropped two 112-lb bombs on Heule aerodrome from 2,500 feet.

On 21st September, the Squadron Commander, Major Sidney Smith, was promoted and replaced by Major W D Beatty. Three days later, the Elephants raided Ath railway station, dropping six 230-lb and three 112-lb bombs. They were attacked by Albatros scouts on their return, shooting down one for the loss of 2/Lt W English in Martinsyde

A3976, who was taken prisoner when forced to land with a badly damaged engine. The victory was claimed by O/Lt Hans Waldhausen of Jasta 37. Bombing missions continued into October as weather permitted. On 2nd October, Lt E C J Elliott crashed Martinsyde A6268 on landing at Clairmarais after a practice flight.

On 12th October, No.27 Squadron flew eighteen Martinsydes (including 7501, 7507, A4004, A6250, A6255, A6258, A6263, A6272, A6275, A6277, A6281, A6285, A6288, A6289, A6290, A6291) and two D.H.4s to its new base at Serny. Bombing missions continued from there throughout the last three months of the year, almost to the end without loss. One particular feat worth recording was the attack by Sgt B J Clinch on the Gotha sheds at Gontrode near Ghent on 1st November. Four pilots set out in appalling weather on that day but he was the only one to find the target, the others getting lost before they had barely passed the lines. Clouds extended from 200 to 9,000 feet but Clinch, with the aid only of a lateral clinometer (little more than a spirit level), altimeter, air speed indicator and a rudimentary compass, continued on the sortie. He flew entirely by compass for 40 minutes before breaking cloud to find himself over Ghent. He followed a canal to Gontrode where he dropped two 112-lb bombs on the target from a height of 500 feet, whilst encountering heavy anti-aircraft fire, before returning successfully to base. During this period the Martinsydes were being progressively replaced by D.H.4s. The last recorded flight of this type of aircraft with the squadron was on 20th December when twelve Martinsydes were despatched on a bombing mission. Unfortunately on this mission two of the aircraft, A4004 piloted by 2/Lt N C Phear and A6277 piloted by Lt H Darrington, were lost due to a mid-air collision in cloud.

Elephant of No.14 Squadron. Note the connecting strut on the undercarriage. (J M Bruce/S Leslie Collection)

Service in Mesopotamia

Following the fall of Kut al Imara as described in the section on the Martinsyde S.1, the British forces were on the defensive and action petered out on this front until towards the end of 1916. The RNAS detachment was withdrawn by the end of June 1916, except for two naval Voisins, as the aircraft had proved unsuitable. During July, the strength of No.30 Squadron was increased from 12 to 18 aircraft with the arrival of six Martinsyde G.100s to supplement the B.E.2cs and many new pilots arrived. The opposing force also spent its time regrouping. It had strengthened its air force with German pilots flying Fokker single-seater scouts and the Turkish air force flying two-seaters. It was the enemy's intention to contain the British forces on the Tigris and make headway down the Euphrates towards Nasiriyeh.

General Maude assumed command of the British Army on 28th August 1916, and took steps to improve the lines of communication and the health of the troops and airmen, which had suffered much from dysentery, cholera and sunstroke. Besides the intense heat during the day, sandflies were a constant nuisance at night, allowing little sleep. As the year progressed and the British prepared for a new offensive, aerial activity increased with both B.E.2c and Martinsyde aircraft in action, although it is not always clear from squadron records which pilots or type of aircraft were involved. No.30 Squadron was carrying out reconnaissance duties and at the same time carried out patrols to prevent the enemy from doing the same, resulting generally in ineffectual skirmishes. Martinsydes were being used to escort the B.E.2cs on their reconnaissances and during November a Williamson camera arrived which proved very satisfactory and more than doubled the number of photographs being taken.

The Martinsydes were also used to intercept enemy reconnaissance aircraft over our own lines. Advanced warning was given by a system of emergency calls by telephone and wireless, which had priority over other transmissions, from a series of wireless stations established to signal the position of enemy aircraft as soon as they were sighted. There were many examples of this activity. Shortly after collecting a new Martinsyde on 7th November, Major Tennant chased two enemy aircraft back to their aerodrome at Kut. On 28th November, Capt J H Herring fired two drums without effect as he climbed to meet a Turkish aircraft, believed to be an Aviatik, flying towards Arab Village from the north-west. Having reached the same altitude as the enemy at 7,500 feet, he found that his Lewis gun would only fire single shots and he had to break off the engagement. Similar ineffectual combats also took place between Capt de Havilland and an Aviatik on 5th December, 2/Lt M L Maguire (in Martinsyde 7467) and an Aviatik on the 7th, Capt de Havilland (in 7466) and an Albatros on the 14th.

The British offensive preparations took on a more positive note from 12th December when ground forces began an offensive to secure and entrench a position on the Hai River close to Kut, where they were able to control the river and threaten the enemy's communications. On the 13th, Major Tennant with two other aircraft damaged the enemy's pontoon bridge over the river by dropping heavy bombs from 600 feet. Major Tennant also had an adventure the following evening. A message had come through that a B.E.2 had been forced to land in front of our cavalry with a main strut shot away. He flew with a spare and landed nearby as the cavalry were dragging the aircraft back to our lines under the constant attention of enemy Arab irregulars. Unfortunately his engine stalled and he was in danger of being overrun until a British officer rode back and swung his propeller, enabling him to take off. That night, Capt Herring dropped a total of 24 bombs in three sorties on a steamer towing elements of the pontoon bridge which was in the process of being repositioned, causing it to go aground. On the 18th, Lt

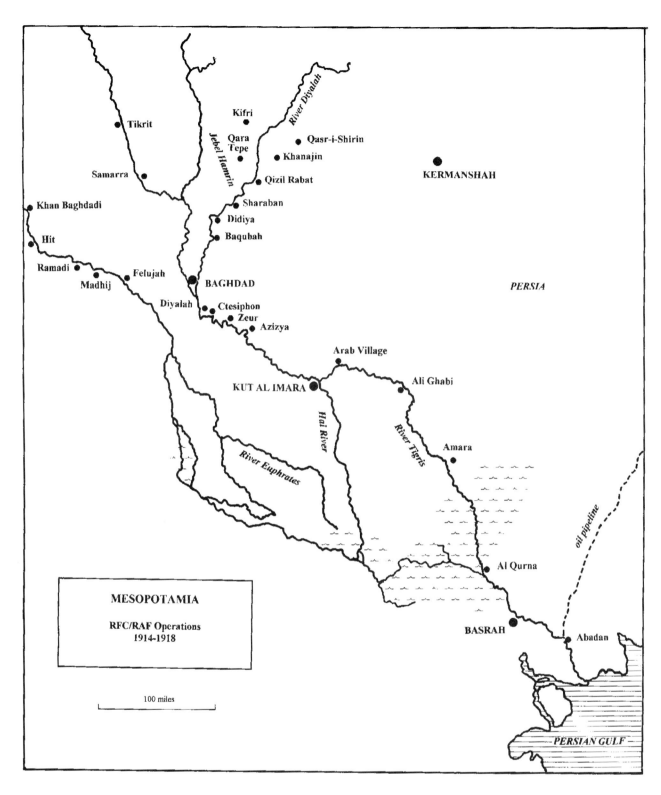

MESOPOTAMIA

RFC/RAF Operations
1914-1918

100 miles

Windsor hit a steamer, the explosion loosened her moorings and the current swung her round onto a bank. No.30 Squadron continued to support the ground forces during the succeeding weeks with bombing attacks on river targets and enemy encampments. 2/Lt Lloyd (in 7459) had a skirmish with an unidentified machine on 16th January 1917 and Lt J S Windsor with two hostile machines on the following day.

On 20th January 1917, Major J E Tennant was made temporary Lt Col and appointed Wing Commander in charge of the RFC in Mesopotamia and Capt de Havilland took command of No.30 Squadron. By this time the B.E.2cs were carrying out reconnaissances daily and were also involved in artillery spotting. The Martinsydes were still being used offensively and were carrying out bombing missions and patrols over the enemy's own airfield at Shumran, involving several instances of enemy aircraft being forced down.

2/Lt K B Lloyd (in Martinsyde 7459) was jumped by a Fokker on 24th January and was forced to land at the Atab landing ground with holes in his radiator and petrol tank. The following day Lt T E Lander (in 7468) was engaged in a bombing raid when he saw an enemy machine flying above him.

G.100 Elephant 'Bakhshi' of No.30 Squadron in Mesopotamia during 1917. This machine was made from spare parts and did not receive a serial number. (EF Cheeseman)

After dropping his bombs he climbed to attack and saw his adversary stall after firing one drum but lost sight of it whilst reloading. On the 26th, 2/Lt J S Windsor in a Martinsyde fired on an enemy aircraft as it was about to land and was fired on by another in return.

The British offensive started on 2nd February 1917 with No.30 Squadron fully involved in reconnaissance, artillery spotting and bombing. By 16th February, the Turks had been cleared from the right bank of the Tigris at Kut. On 18th February, Capt H de Havilland was awarded the DSO for shooting down a Fokker whilst escorting a B.E.2c in a Martinsyde. He saw the Fokker approaching at about 500 feet above and dropped the twelve 20-lb bombs he was carrying before getting directly underneath the Fokker. He pulled down his gun and opened fire as the enemy aircraft began to attack the B.E.2c. He followed it as it turned for its aerodrome and emptied the remainder of the drum at it. One wing came off and the other folded back against the fuselage as the enemy aircraft spun vertically into the ground. On the same day, Capt Bayly dropped a 336-lb bomb just missing barges on the river.

On the 21st, the two remaining Martinsydes were told to prevent enemy aircraft from taking off to stop them from observing the British forces throwing a bridge across the Tigris at Shumran. In this they were successful until late in the afternoon, by which time the bridge was complete and the troops were moving across. Three days later, Martinsyde pilot 2/Lt Lloyd had a brush with a Fokker.

Kut was entered on 24th February 1917. With the Turkish army in full flight, reconnaissance missions had already been flown over Baghdad by the time No.30 Squadron relocated to Azizya on 3rd March. On that day, Lt K R Lloyd encountered a Fokker whilst carrying out a reconnaissance over an enemy airfield at Dings, between Baghdad and Diala. The aircraft were flying on parallel courses with the Fokker some 1,000 ft below. They fired a couple of times at each other before the enemy aircraft dived home to his airfield. An Aviatik was also seen to take off but landed quickly.

The advance continued on 5th March and No.30 Squadron assisted with reconnaissances and by bombing the enemy's lines of communication and troop concentrations. Although hampered by high winds and a dust storm. Lt Col Tennant reconnoitred as far as Diala in a gale of wind which obscured much of the ground. He landed at Zeur which had been by-passed by cavalry and waited for the rest of the squadron to arrive from Azizya. On the following day, two Martinsydes crashed whilst landing on the very rough ground at Zeur during the storm which had continued unabated. These aircraft were manhandled across rough country to the riverbank. One aircraft was later repaired at Zeur while the other was dismantled and returned to Basrah to be rebuilt. Ctesiphon was bypassed on 6th March and Baghdad was entered on the 11th. No.30 Squadron followed soon after, occupying a former German airfield there. The British advance continued, capturing Baqubah on the Diala on the 18th and Felujah on the Euphrates on the 19th.

Thus, during the six months preceding the fall of Baghdad, Martinsydes had made a significant contribution to the effort of the RFC, which had gained superiority in the air and made incessant attacks on the enemy's ground forces. Reconnaissance machines had kept the Army fully informed of the enemy's movements, photographs had been taken of the whole of the Tigris as far as Baghdad and exhaustive reports had been made of the enemy's troops, gun emplacements and trenches.

Lt Col Tennant meeting with Russian officers and men at Mainkul on 2 April 1917. Contrary to his own account his engine was not left ticking over! (RAF Museum)

One Flight of No.30 Squadron was sent to Baqubah and another was sent to Kasirin up the Tigris. The Martinsyde Flight had been left at Baghdad for long distance communications duties. The aircraft looked weatherbeaten and dilapidated as there had been no hangars since leaving Azizya and the machines had been constantly exposed to the hot sun, wind, dust or rain. The engines had not been properly maintained and engine hours had to be conserved. This led to friction with some army officers, who had come to expect every request for support to be met, which General Maude quickly sorted out.

General Maude was concerned to link up with a Russian force, which had advanced through Persia to Kasr-i-Shirin from Kermanshah, in order to protect his right flank which was now opposed by superior Turkish forces at Jebel Hamrin. At 6 am on 2nd April, Lt Col Tennant set out from Baghdad in a Martinsyde to deliver a despatch from General Maude to General Baratoff, Commander of the Russian force. At the same time he carried out a routine reconnaissance along the route. It is worth quoting some of his impressions and his subsequent report in full.

My course took me straight out across the Jebel Hamrin to Khanikin, and over the Persian foothills to Kasr-i-Shirin. It was a lovely spring day, the country below was green, the air above cool and bracing; how good it felt to be clear of Mesopotamia. Looking back I could just discern the hill country disappearing down to the thick haze of noonday in the desert; looking ahead it seemed I was flying into a great wall of massive peaks....

At Kasr-i-Shirin the road turns almost south-east before the long thirty-five mile climb up the Pai Tak Pass, the gateway from the high plateaux of Persia down to the plains of Mesopotamia. After flying for three hours I spied a column of cavalry on the march.....not knowing if they were retreating Turks or advancing Russians, I glided slowly down. They made no movement to fire, so I glided on lower and lower till, in answer to my hand-wave, they threw their fur caps in the air; I knew at last that I was in touch with the Russians.

I landed on a patch of level ground not far off the road, and they galloped up, solemnly saluted, shook me by the hand, each in turn....Two or three junior officers were there, but not a word of any language in common. The despatch they understood, and I pointed up the pass and said `Baratoff'. I had left my engine just ticking over, and having only sufficient petrol to take me straight back to Baghdad could spare no further time; once stopped, the problem of starting again was too uncertain. They each saluted, again shook me by the hand, and as I left the ground gave a weird shout and threw their hats in the air. It had been a dramatic meeting.

With regret I dropped back into the Mesopotamian desert from that beautiful mountain region of snow and wild flowers, and after five hour's flying into what had seemed some dream country landed in the relentless heat and glare of Baghdad.

The situation on the flank was becoming more critical and on the 8th Lt Col Tennant repeated his trip to deliver despatches from General Maude to the Russians. This time he had only to go as far as Kasr-i-Shirin, about 120 miles north east of Baghdad, and felt able to leave his machine to deliver the despatches personally to the Russian officer in command within the town.

During the latter part of March and April, Martinsydes carried out reconnaissance missions along the Tigris, some sixteen hours being flown by four Martinsydes on 9th April alone. However as ambient temperatures increased with the approach of summer, Martinsydes fitted with conventional radiators could only be used around dawn as otherwise the coolant would boil away. Thus only the two Martinsydes fitted with tropical radiators could be used until spare radiators arrived at the end of the month. Even so the engine oil became very thin with the heat and offered little lubrication. Furthermore, the heat from the engine made the cockpit unbearably hot. By the end of April, frequent dust storms resulted in the machines becoming inoperable due to accumulations of dust in the carburettors and bearings.

On 10th April, Lt Col Tennant and Capt Bayly, both

Lt A E L Skinner, who had several narrow escapes with No.30 Squadron, seen here at Baghdad.
(J M Bruce/S Leslie Collection)

in Martinsydes carrying four 65-lb and four 25-lb bombs respectively, were proceeding to bomb Samarra when Capt Bayly was attacked with tracer bullets by a Halberstadt. Capt Bayly managed to fire one drum at a range of about 150 yards but was out-manoeuvered. Lt Col Tennant tried to release his bombs but two hung up. Nevertheless he was able to dive on the enemy machine and fire off a drum. The enemy machine then maintained a higher altitude and Lt Col Tennant in attempting to engage stalled, side-slipped and lost a lot of height before he regained control. The enemy machine made use of its superior height and speed to effect an escape and the two Martinsydes returned to Baghdad, the undercarriage of Capt Bayly's machine collapsing on landing due to the damage which it had received.

Capt Bayly was again in action on 12th April, accompanied by Lt Windsor. They left Baghdad in Martinsydes respectively carrying twelve 20-lb and four 65-lb bombs to bomb the enemy aerodrome at Samarra from an altitude of 3,400 feet. Although under heavy machine gun and shell fire, Lt Windsor scored a direct hit on an enemy aircraft and Capt Bayly hit rolling stock and the camp. In the same area on the 20th, Lt Lander managed to get several bursts into a Halberstadt, stalling in the process before eventually the enemy broke away and dived steeply towards its own airfield, easily outpacing the Martinsyde.

The British forces turned back a Turkish advance before occupying Samarra on 23rd April. At this stage the Flight equipped with Martinsydes was still based at Baghdad with the rest of No.30 Squadron at Baqubah. On 29th April, a Martinsyde was being flown from Baghdad to Musayab on the Euphrates, to establish whether the track across the desert was passable, when it was caught in a violent sand storm with winds reaching 70 mph. The pilot struggled for more than ten

minutes, with the aircraft out of control and at times inverted, before he managed to escape. On 4th May, the pilot of a Martinsyde crashed his machine whilst on reconnaissance in the direction of Kasr-i-Shirin. The machine was recovered by a Ford van escorted by an armoured car.

On 5th May, a Martinsyde accompanied by a Bristol Scout drove off a hostile machine which tried to attack the B.E.2c which they were escorting on a reconnaissance mission towards Tekrit. On the following day, Lt. Lander in a Martinsyde was escorting a B.E.2c in the same area, when he engaged a Halberstadt. 2/Lt Skinner in the B.E.2c had to return with a faulty engine and last saw the other two machines still fighting over Tekrit at an altitude of 3,000 feet but losing height. A subsequent Turkish radio transmission reported that the Martinsyde had been forced down barely damaged by a Sgt Major Pommerich and the pilot, wounded in the thigh, had been taken prisoner. In fact he had landed on an island in the Tigris and had crawled out of it with his leg badly smashed. Arabs had swum across and stripped him of his clothing before the Turks arrived and floated him across to the mainland on an animal skin. He was dragged out and put on a horse, arriving at Tekrit in a serious condition. It was nine months before he could walk but he survived the war, turning up in Cairo eighteen months later.

Despite this setback, reconnaissance patrols continued with the aim of producing detailed maps of the combat zone. Lt L Skinner was reported to be flying Martinsyde 7493 on such a patrol on 2nd June, this flight being his longest - some four and three-quarter hours over the mountains as far as Maidan, looking for signs of enemy activity. The Williamson film camera fitted to the Martinsyde, although unreliable, proved to be very effective for the purpose when it working. The Type 'E' plate camera was used when the Williamson

An armoured car salvaging a badly damaged Martinsyde Elephant from the captured enemy aerodrome at Tekrit Note the still visible RFC serial and the Turkish 'black square' insignia. The airframe broke its back shortly afterwards through being towed without its wheels. (Imperial War Museum)

was out of action and a total of 468 plates were taken with this camera during May. Photography grew to such a scale that demand exceeded the supply of photographic plates and the whole of India had to be scoured for stock pending the arrival of thousands of new plates from England. These deteriorated quickly in the heat and special refrigerating plant had to be imported to cool the water used for developing and printing.

During June and July, with shade temperatures reaching 50°C, the Martinsydes could not be used during the day, even if fitted with tropical radiators, as the coolant boiled away before they could climb to 1,000 feet. The old B.E.s and Martinsydes shrivelled in the sun, their fabric became bleached and loose and easily holed. One early morning attack on 3rd July, accompanied by a B.E.2c, against Beni Tamin tribesmen with bombs and gunfire was effective but a similar venture on the 11th had to be abandoned because of the heat. During this period, the pilots of A Flight began night-flying practice and became adept at taking-off by the light of flares. On 21st June, L Skinner in 7461 and Capt L J Bayly in 7493 flew a positioning flight to Samarra in readiness for an attack on the Turkish steamer *Julna* the following morning. Bayly crashed on landing at Samarra but both managed to continue and at 3.45 am found the boat moored up north of Tekrit and dropped eight 65-lb bombs from around 1,500 feet. One hit the boat on the aft deck and another exploded close by, holing the vessel on the forward side. Afterwards Skinner went to the Aircraft Park at Basrah to collect a new G.102 Elephant A3940 and flew it to Amara on 3rd July and on to Baghdad a few days later.

By this time, British troops had entrenched themselves at Samarra on the Tigris, Felujah on the Euphrates and Sharaban on the Diyalah. B and C Flights of No.30 Squadron, which

had advanced to airfields at Fort Kermea and Kuwar Reach, returned to Baghdad to refit. Meanwhile No.63 Squadron, one flight of which was partly equipped with Martinsydes, arrived at Basrah on 13th August. The intense heat soon affected most of the Squadron personnel but by 11th October they had moved on to Samarra. B Flight of No.30 Squadron, with a photographic section, moved to Felujah on 9th September 1917 and on to Madhij on the Euphrates by the 26th. The remainder of the No.30 Squadron returned to Baqubah on 13th September and, with the cooler temperatures, the Martinsydes were again becoming effective fighting machines.

Martinsydes were involved in supporting General Brooking's autumn campaign towards Ramadi, for example bombing three separate Arab encampments in the rear of our lines on 25th September. Following the capture of Ramadi on the 29th, there was a lull in the ground fighting during which No.63 Squadron took over the Tigris front and No.30 Squadron remained responsible for the Euphrates and Diyalah fronts, with B Flight at Ramadi and A and C Flights at Baqubah. Although the enemy had retired many miles, No.30 Squadron, sometimes in cooperation with No.63 Squadron, continued to operate almost on a daily basis despite having to traverse long distances in carrying out its reconnaissance and bombing missions.

On 16th October, in preparation for an advance on the Diyalah front, the enemy aerodrome at Kifri was attacked by Lts Skinner, Nuttall and Welman in three Martinsydes (nos 7494, 7493 and A3943 respectively). Six 112-lb and twelve 20-lb bombs were dropped on three enemy aircraft without scoring a direct hit. However these machines were damaged by blast and splinters and by machine gun fire directed from 2,000 feet. The pilots had to fly through considerable

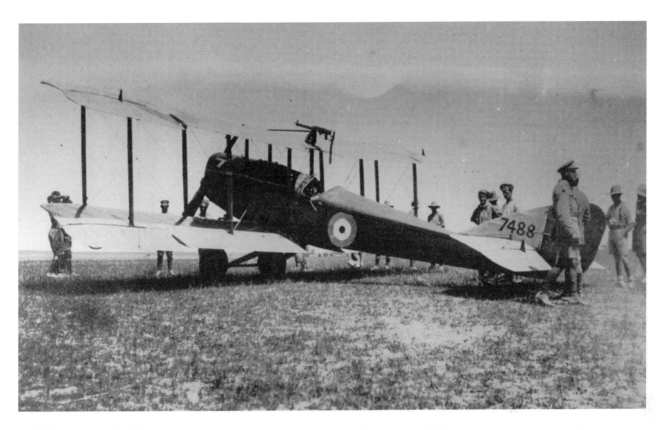

G.100 Elephant 7488. This was the machine that crash-landed on 24th February 1917 after losing a wheel on take-off while being piloted by Lt Tunbridge of No.14 Squadron. (Philip Jarrett)

machine gun fire and Lt Skinner's machine was hit in the petrol tank, spurting fuel over his legs and forcing him to land in hostile territory about 15 miles west of Kifri. He found himself under fire from an Arab and Turkish detachment at a range of about 900 yards. Despite having a water connection to his radiator damaged, Lt Nuttall attacked these forces with machine gun fire until he had to retire. Meanwhile Lt Welman landed by Lt Skinner and between them they recovered the maps and ammunition from the damaged Martinsyde but did not have time to save the Lewis guns. They set fire to the aircraft, which was soon destroyed by the explosion of one of the 20-lb bombs. After restarting the engine of Lt Welman's machine, they took off with Skinner at first perched on the wing root and later with his legs slipped into the cockpit behind Welman. Lt Nuttall just managed to reach Sharaban whereas the others were able to reach Baqubah.

On 18th October 1917, the opening day of the operations against Jebel Hamrin, Lts Skinner, Cox and Nuttall in Martinsydes A3940, A3943 and 7493, were on patrol in the vicinity of Kifri aerodrome. Cox noticed a hostile machine and fired two reds and then his forward machine gun to attract the attention of the others without effect. However Skinner then spotted the machine and in his own words:

While flying at 7,500 ft I saw a hostile machine behind and about 1,000 ft below me. I fired a red light to attract the other two Martinsydes in the formation, turned and dived to bring my gun firing down over the leading edge to bear on the EA. He then turned north towards Kifri. As EA was a two-seater with back gun mounting I tried to approach him from one side and head him off. I fired two drums from my side and top gun and then flew at 100 mph losing height but could not outdistance him, though we gradually closed in. I then turned quickly and got within 100 yds of his tail and slightly

above him, firing a whole drum into him. His observer was firing continuously at me without effect, the other two machines being slightly behind. I turned away to reload and the other two Martinsydes caught up. I fired one more drum from 150-200 yds and after the other two machines had fired at him, he dived more steeply. I followed him down to below 3,000 ft and fired one more drum. I was then unable to catch him, and we were half way between Kifri and Kara Tepe so I ceased the pursuit. EA was a two-seater Albatros with reddish fuselage and dirty coloured wings. The trailing edge of the main plane curved in towards the centre section. Pilot did not have a chance to fire but the observer seemed to be firing steadily from a back mounting with a large field of fire.

Although the enemy aircraft escaped, the incident discouraged enemy pilots from venturing forth again. On the ground, the Turkish forces avoided being trapped by retreating, offering little opportunity for aircraft to assist with artillery spotting, and by the 20th the whole of the Jebel Hamrin on the left bank of the river was in British hands. On the 20th, three Martinsydes machine gunned and dropped twenty-two 20-lb bombs on the retreating Turkish troops and bivouacs.

On 31st October, three Martinsydes, piloted by Lts Nuttall, Welman and Cox, and three B.E.2cs left Baqubah at 6.30 am to bomb a column of Turkish irregulars somewhere between Kasr-i-Shirin and Kifri. One B.E.2c was forced to land at Sharaban with a sticking contact breaker but the others, failing to find the enemy column, went on to bomb the enemy airfield at Kifri. Forming up in line astern, they dropped bombs on enemy aircraft on the ground, destroying one and damaging another. However this success was not achieved without considerable cost. One of the Martinsydes, piloted by Lt Welman fell out of formation and landed west of the aerodrome and the pilot escaped into a ravine.

Elephant of 1 Squadron AFC on a photographic sortie west of the Dead Sea, 25th February 1918. (Philip Jarrett)

Meanwhile, two enemy aircraft had taken off on the approach of our formation and circled to gain height. When one reached the same altitude as our machines, it was attacked by Lt Adams and Lt Adamson in a B.E.2c. During the ensuing melee the petrol tank of Lt Adams' machine was punctured in several places and he was forced to land on the east side of the Jebel Hamrin. He destroyed his aircraft while Lt Nuttall in a Martinsyde fired at Turkish troops surrounding him and landed nearby, picking him up without stopping, and took off again under gunfire.

In the meantime, the radiator of Lt. Cox's machine had been pierced by a piece of anti-aircraft shell. He tried to reach Diyalah but, with his engine seized and his aircraft on fire, landed 10 miles north-east of Qizil Robat, his Martinsyde being totally destroyed. He managed to walk some 18 miles to our picket lines in about 7½ hours, arriving at about 4 pm. Unaware that Lt Cox was approaching safety, Lt Nuttall, escorted by Lt Morris in a SPAD, went in search of him and found the remains of his burnt-out machine. They landed near some armoured cars, Lt Nuttall damaging his undercarriage in the process, and went to the local Sheikh in one of the cars to demand that Arabs repatriate Lt Cox without delay. The grounded machines, which in the meantime had been subjected to shellfire, were retrieved by infantry later that evening.

One Martinsyde took part in a bombing raid during the week commencing 4th November and Capt Nuttall and Capt Haight in Martinsydes powered by 160-hp and 120-hp Beardmores respectively took part in an ineffectual fight with an enemy scout later in the month. However the Squadron was being re-equipped with D.H.4s, R.E.8s and SPADs and little further mention of Martinsydes is made beyond an occasional sortie until the week commencing 13th January, when B Flight received two Martinsydes from No.63

Squadron. There were various other transfers of Martinsydes to and from No.30 Squadron during the first quarter of 1918, for example Martinsyde A3974 was returned to the Aircraft Park on 10th February and Lt Tanner brought up a new Martinsyde from the Park on 20th March.

From March until May 1918, A and B Flights of No.30 Squadron aided 15 Division at Khan Baghdadi to virtually annihilate the enemy on the Euphrates and begin an advance which ended 20 miles beyond Anah. During this campaign, on 26th March, Lts Tanner and Rose in Martinsydes bombed enemy troops and gun emplacements at Khan Baghdadi. Lt L Skinner delivered G.102 Elephant A1596 to Baqubah via Baghdad on 31st March. Its engine misbehaved, firing on three cylinders, and it was nearly dark before he arrived. It was very windy and as he landed a gust caught the machine, slewing the machine round, and it ran into a dugout and turned over.

No.72 Squadron appeared in Mesopotamia early in 1918. This squadron had been formed at Upavon from a nucleus of CFS Training Flights and was commanded by Capt von Poellnitz. The Squadron arrived in Basrah from Bombay on 14th February 1918, having first travelled overland via France and Italy and thence by ship. Two Martinsydes were transferred from No.30 Squadron to No.72 Squadron during the week starting 31st March. On 12th April 1918, one of No.72 Squadron's Martinsydes, accompanied by a number of R.E.8s, made three bombing raids on Turkish positions. By mid-April, this squadron had established itself with A Flight at Samarra, B Flight at Baghdad and C Flt at Mirjana. A Flight was equipped with D.H.4s, SPADs and S.E.5As, C Flight with Bristol Monoplanes, and B Flight with Martinsydes. It is believed that no further use was made of Martinsydes on this front.

Aircraft of No.1 Squadron AFC aircraft at Mejdel in Palestine, January 1918. The Martinsyde G.102 in the foreground clearly shows the No.5 Mk.II gun mounting for the over-wing Lewis gun. Other squadron aircraft in the background are Bristol Fighters and B.E.12as. (Australian War Memorial)

Service in Persia and Southern Russia

Although Martinsydes no longer took part in the Tigris and Euphrates operations in Mesopotamia, some of these aircraft still had a part to play in Persia and southern Russia. The military situation in this area was confused, with the Russian forces gradually disintegrating and native populations variously supporting the British or the Turks. As early as January 1918, a British force was sent to the area under Major General L C Dunsterville, this quickly becoming known as the "Dunsterforce". This consisted of an infantry brigade, a cavalry regiment, some armoured cars and an element of B Flight of No.72 Squadron with their Martinsydes.

After travelling over difficult terrain and through areas of depravation and starvation, the 'Dunsterforce' mission had established itself at Hamadan by 22nd May and at Kasvin by 1st June. From Baghdad, B Flight quickly established landing grounds at Hamadan and Kasvin and also at Zenjan in Azerbaijan and by 31st July at Enzeli on the south west shore of the Caspian Sea. The airfields at Hamadan and Zenjan were at some 6,500 feet and 3,500 feet above sea level respectively. From all these airfields throughout the hot summer, the Martinsydes flew on reconnaissance and bombing missions over many hundreds of miles, the flights extending as far as Kurdistan in one direction and to the Shiraz area in southern Persia. The Martinsydes proved reliable despite having to fly through gorges and valleys buffeted by high winds, which was just as well as landing grounds were scarce amongst the mountains.

From Hamadan on 21st June, Lt Fanshawe and Lt Pennington carried out a bombing and machine gun attack against the Jungalis tribe who were paid and officered by Germans. Lt Pennington volunteered to reconnoitre Urmia on the western side of Lake Urmia at Dunsterforce's request. There, friendly Christians of Armenian and Jhelus sects were giving assistance against the Turks. On 4th July, Capt Fuller prepared a forward landing ground with provisions of oil and fuel. On the 8th, Lt Pennington refuelled there and flew on to Urmia over the vast expanse of the lake where he landed despite being shot at from the ground. He found the people friendly and delivered despatches before returning to base. For this feat he was awarded the AFC. Further bombing on the Jungalis followed and they became sufficiently demoralised to switch sides as our ground troops entered Resht.

As part of the peace treaty of Brest-Litovsk between the Central Powers and Russia, Russia was forced to cede the three Trans-Caucasian provinces to Turkey. With the collapse of the Russian armies in North Persia and the advance of German and Turkish forces towards the oil port of Baku on the Caspian Sea, a serious threat opened up on the British flank in Mesopotamia. Baku, with its supplies of valuable oil was threatened by a large Turkish force and during August 1918 elements of Dunsterforce, including two Martinsydes, were sent to bolster the Russian forces there.

The two Martinsydes, piloted by Lt R P P Mackay and Lt M S Pope, flew to Enzali on 18th August, bombing and machine gunning Passikan on the way. At Enzali, the machines were dismantled and shipped to Baku. There they were reassembled at a Russian airfield four miles outside the town. On the 25th, a two-hour test run was carried out on Russian petrol which was found to be satisfactory. The two aircraft were employed on reconnaissance and bombing missions and for the distribution of propaganda leaflets, without aerial opposition. Any artillery cooperation had to be performed by dropping message bags as the Martinsydes were not equipped with wireless.

The British position was precarious. About an hour before daybreak on 14th September, the Turks attacked the Allied lines west of Baku. The main attack was concentrated on Wolf's Gap, a large break in the main defensive line along a ridge. At dawn Lt Mackay flew over this sector of the line and observed troops on the ridge. Because of a mist and low clouds it was not possible to identify the troops and Mackay flew on until he saw the concentration of Turkish reserves. These he attacked with six drums from his Lewis gun and returned back to base to report. Later that morning, in the same aircraft, Lt Pope carried out two reconnaissances totalling about an hour-and-a-half. During the first he emptied three drums into the troops on British Ridge, which was definitely now in Turkish hands. He then had to return to his airfield to get the gun repaired. On the second trip he fired six drums into the enemy troops which were by now half-way between the ridge and Baku.

The Martinsyde was by now full of bullet holes and unfit to fly. As the second machine was also unserviceable due to a lack of maintenance personnel, both machines were ordered to be burnt. The engines were rendered useless and the two pilots, together with the ground crew, retired to Baku, taking three Lewis guns and ammunition with them. The pilots returned to their billet at the Europe Hotel in Baku and destroyed all the photographic equipment and chemicals that they could not carry and went down to the quayside. At about 8 pm, they managed to embark on a vessel bound for Enzali just before the town fell to the enemy.

Following the Baku debacle, the Turkish forces in Persia were reinforced and the British situation became precarious. The British were forced to take up defensive positions to protect Kasvin and their lines of communications with Enzali. Lt Pennington carried out three reconnaissances in Martinsydes on 22nd and 29th August and 2nd September. An accident on take-off in a gale on 4th September prevented him from carrying out further work. On 31st August, Lt Cullen left Zenjan on a reconnaissance mission in the direction of Tabriz. He never returned and it was not until after the Armistice that it was learnt that he had been taken prisoner. Additional reinforcements were provided by A Flight of No.30 Squadron, which flew, on 17th September, three R.E.8 two-seaters some two hundred miles over mountainous country to Hamadan and thence to Zenjan. Records of operations are then sparse but mention is made of one Martinsyde accompanying two R.E.8s on an armed reconnaissance of Turkish positions into Persia on 4 October and returning with engine trouble.

Early on 6th October, Lt T L Williams in a Martinsyde lost contact with the R.E.8s that he was escorting and decided to carry out his own reconnaissance. When at an altitude of 5,000 feet near Ardibil, he noticed a train of about one hundred mules with drivers. He descended to about 500 feet and loosed off about 150 rounds. After the first pass, the engine cut and it wouldn't restart. He landed between two large villages and seeing figures approaching brandishing knives he set fire to the Martinsyde and fled. By then it was

about 7.30 in the morning and he began the long walk back to the British lines. At about 4.30 in the afternoon, he met a Persian who offered for a consideration to guide him. That night he had his uniform and flying boots stolen but managed to procure some Persian clothes. Five days later, after walking barefoot for about one hundred miles, he met up with a Gurkha officer in a car and was returned to his unit. A similar feat was accomplished by three officers, starting at about the time that Williams completed his ordeal as described below.

On 11th October, the three R.E.8s, together with an S.E.5a and an Elephant as escorts, took off at 7.35 am from Zenjan on a reconnaissance and bombing mission in the area of Tabriz. The flight was led by Capt Frank Nuttall, who had already been in Mesopotamia for about eighteen months and the Martinsyde A3973 was piloted by Lt Kenneth Misson Pennington. The flight first flew to an advanced landing ground between Sarchan and Jemalabad, well within sight of the enemy, to top up with petrol and fit the bombs. The flight took off again at 9.30 am and headed north-west and crossed the Kuflan Kuh mountains before picking up the Tabriz road near Turkmanchai. The flight ignored enemy troops and transport retreating along the road towards Tabriz but attacked a large convoy at Meamabad, losing height before dropping eighteen 20-lb bombs, four of which were from the Martinsyde. Enemy troops and transport resting on the north side of Lake Yusufabad were then attacked with machine gun fire and four bombs were dropped on another column. The flight, without the S.E.5a which returned to base as it was low on fuel, then attacked an enemy camp at Hagi Agah with machine gun fire.

Pennington in the Martinsyde by then below 1,000 feet over Mianeh, using up the remainder of his ammunition on fleeting targets, was hit by ground fire with the result that his engine cut out completely. He glided away from the road full of troops and force-landed, completely wrecking his aircraft. An R.E.8, piloted by Lt Morgan with Chacksfield as observer landed nearby to pick him up, the pilot keeping the engine running. In order to take-off again, Pennington and Chacksfield had to turn the R.E.8 around and push it several hundred yards up a slope, before they both then squeezed into the observer's cockpit. The pilot ran the R.E.8 down the slope with the engine running at full power, but just at the point of take-off the undercarriage struck a large boulder and the aircraft came to an abrupt halt, fortunately without injuring the occupants.

Capt Nuttall, who had been protecting the men from the air, had to leave due to shortage of fuel. The men were now stranded 120 miles behind enemy lines. They took the Lewis gun from the rear cockpit, frightened off a crowd of Persian civilians which had now accumulated by brandishing their revolvers, and proceeded southwards along the valley, closely pursued by enemy troops. As the enemy troops were getting closer, they hid in a hole in a nullah without being spotted until nightfall, when they started the long trek back to the British lines. Travelling mainly at night, they travelled across rough mountainous terrain for seven days, finally being picked up by a light armoured motor battery on the Mianeh road around midday on 18th October.

Fighting ended when the enemy capitulated on 30th October. Although all ground activity ceased, except for the Allies entering Mosul on 1st November, the three RAF squadrons remained in Mesopotamia for some considerable time. The aircraft participated in many long distance reconnaissance missions together with photographic work and policing operations against hostile Arab tribesmen. There is

An Elephant landing over a line up of No.1 Squadron AFC aircraft during 1917.

little mention of Martinsydes in action, although 7461 is reported at Bushire with C Flight of No.30 Squadron on 31st January 1919 and on 6th March Capt Adams in a Martinsyde was shot in the head and crashed during a revenge attack on a village after he had been fired on by tribesmen when reconnoitring Khun. In April 1919, No.30 Squadron was disbanded, to be followed by No.72 Squadron in September. No.63 Squadron maintained a detachment in Kasvin for several months until it too was disbanded in February 1920.

Service in Egypt, Arabia and Palestine

At the beginning of the war, in order to secure the passage of shipping through the Suez Canal, Britain took steps to secure Egypt against the Turkish forces occupying Palestine and their Moslem brethren in the Western Desert and the Sudan. Several campaigns took place which temporarily removed these threats. However, following the evacuation of Gallipoli in January 1916, attention of the British and Turkish forces, the latter reinforced with up-to-date German aircraft, re-focussed on the Canal Zone and the Sinai Peninsula.

Air support for the British forces at about this time comprised No.14 Squadron RFC, No.17 Squadron RFC and No.1 Squadron Australian Flying Corps. No.14 Squadron was formed at Shoreham, Sussex, from a nucleus of personnel from No.5 Wing on 3rd February 1915 and was initially equipped with Maurice Farman biplanes and a few Martinsyde scouts. The squadron, now equipped with B.E.2cs, sailed for Egypt on 7th November 1915, arriving in Alexandria on the 17th. Shortly after Christmas, after a brief stay at X Aircraft Park, Heliopolis, the squadron was moved to Ismailia. The Australian squadron, which was renumbered No.67 (Australian) Squadron RFC on 12th September 1916,

comprised 28 officers and 195 other ranks but was without aircraft or equipment. The unit had embarked from Melbourne on 16th March and had reached Suez on 14th April 1916. The men were distributed for training amongst the various RFC detachments and most of the officers were sent to England for final training. By June 1916, it had been decided to reorganise the RFC squadrons in the Middle East and East Africa under a central command in Egypt, known as No.5 Wing within the Middle East Brigade.

Having by this time secured its rear in the Western Desert, the British repelled the Turkish advance along the coast from Palestine at Romani in early August 1916 and, with the threat on the Canal removed, began to regroup. Several engagements by single-seat scouts (in all probability Martinsydes) in support of the ground forces have been reported over this period. By November the British forces had advanced more than half the distance from Qantara to the Palestine border. The Australian squadron, with one Flight each at Suez and Heliopolis, relocated A Flight from Kharga oasis in the Western Desert to Qantara on 8th November 1916. On the same day, No.14 Squadron moved its A Flight from Ismailia to Salmana, replacing it at Ismailia with B Flight moved from Suez. The RFC units now had to protect a line from a point seventy miles east of the Canal in the northern sector, in a wide semicircle back to the canal at Qantara and from there along the canal to the Red Sea.

The two squadron's B.E.2c aircraft had been reinforced with a number of Martinsyde G.100 Elephants, with one Martinsyde attached to each flight. Constant aerial reconnaissance and occasional bombing raids were carried out. For example, on 30th October two B.E.2cs, escorted by Guilfoyle in a Martinsyde, took twenty photographs of Masaid and on 6th November a B.E.2c, again escorted by

G.102 Elephant A3953 of No.22 Training Squadron at Aboukir, autumn 1917. (J M Bruce/S Leslie Collection)

Guilfoyle, photographed the line between El Arish and Magdhaba. On 11th November, a Martinsyde escorted five B.E.2cs in an attack on the enemy airfield at Beersheba. The Martinsyde dropped a 100-lb bomb in the centre of the airfield and subsequently helped to repel an attack by a Fokker and an Aviatik which had risen to meet the force. A similar formation later attacked Turkish camps at Bir Lahfan and at Magdhaba in the Wadi El Arish. On 2nd December, Freeman in a Martinsyde had to rescue Minchin, who had been shot down while reconnoitring Gaza and Beersheba. Minchin had landed in enemy territory near Rafah with holes in his petrol tanks and burnt his machine. Freeman drove off the Fokker and landed alongside. Minchin sat himself astride the cowling and Freeman flew them both back to Mustabig. On 14th December, Muir in a Martinsyde helped to repel enemy reconnaissance machines, injuring the observer of an Aviatik and pursuing the machine some twenty miles beyond El Arish.

No.67 Squadron moved from Qantara to Mustabig on 17th December. The aircraft on strength included three Martinsyde G.100s, thirteen B.E.2cs and four Bristol Scouts but during December the B.E.2cs were progressively replaced by B.E.2es and shortly afterwards these B.E.2es were replaced by B.E.12as. British forces entered El Arish unopposed on 21st December and on the following day four Martinsydes from No.67 and two from No.14 Squadrons, each carrying two 112-lb bombs, were sent to bomb an important railway bridge over Wadi Ghuzze at Irgeig, north west of Beersheba. No tangible results were achieved and the force had to repel the attentions of two Fokkers and an Aviatik in the process. One of No.67 Squadron's machines, piloted by Jones, was badly riddled with bullets and its elevator was damaged by shell-fire.

By the end of the year, the demoralised Turkish forces in the area of El Arish had either withdrawn or surrendered and all of the Sinai peninsula was in British hands. Aerial reconnaissance and bombing operations, in which Martinsydes participated, continued in support of the advance out of El Arish into Palestine. The enemy airfield at Beersheba was bombed five times during January 1917 in support of the attack by ground forces on the Rafah area. On the 8th, Beersheba was bombed by three Martinsydes, escorted by three Bristol Scouts. On the 9th, while two Martinsydes, escorted by three Bristol Scouts, were bombing Bir Saba, another Martinsyde was on its way to Beersheba and involved in a running fight with three enemy scouts, two of which were Fokker biplanes. Its pilot was wounded three times in as many minutes and his plane shot up to the extent that he was forced to land in the sea north-east of Rafah. He was captured by Bedouin but rescued later by a New Zealand patrol. On the 15th, eleven aircraft attacked the airfield despite heavy anti-aircraft fire, one a Martinsyde, piloted by 2/Lt F H McNamara of No.67 Squadron, dropping two 100-lb bombs. On 19th January, a B.E.12, escorted by two Martinsydes piloted by Murray Jones and Ellis, carried out a reconnaissance deep into the rear of the Turkish army, covering Bethlehem, Jerusalem and Jericho.

These attacks continued through February and March. In retaliation, an enemy plane bombed the El Arish area on 28th February. Several machines took off in pursuit and one of No.14 Squadron's machines, piloted by Lt Tunbridge, lost a wheel on take-off. Ground signals were put out to acquaint the pilot of the problem and he managed to land without injuring himself, although the aircraft turned over onto its back, breaking its propeller.

During March, each flight was strengthened by having

Data on dimensions and performance of the S.1 and Elephants

	S.1	G.100 Elephant	G.100 Elephant	G.102 Elephant
Engine	80 hp Gnome	120 hp Beardmore	120 hp Beardmore	160 hp Beardmore
Airscrew, (diam)		Avro Y120, (2895mm)	LP.920, (9 ft6 in)	LP. 2400, (9ft 6½in)
Dimensions				
Span	27 ft 8 in	37 ft 7 in	38 ft 0 in	38 ft 0½ in
Chord	4 ft 9 in		5 ft 11½ in	5 ft 11½ in
Gap	4 ft 6 in		5 ft 8 in	5 ft 8 in
Stagger	10 in		1 ft 6 in	1 ft 6 in
Dihedral	2° 30'		2°	2°
Incidence	2° 30'		3°	3°
Length	21 ft 0 in	27 ft 3 in	26 ft 6 in	27 ft 0 in
Height		9 ft 6 in		9 ft 8 in
Tailspan		14 ft 1 in	13 ft 6 in	13 ft 6 in
Wheeltrack			6 ft 5/8in	6 ft 5/8 in
Tyres (mm)			700 x 100 mm	(700 x 100)
Surface Areas				
Wings	280 sq ft		410 sq ft	410 sq ft
Ailerons	4 x 7 sq ft		4 x 10.5 sq ft	4 x 10.5 sq ft
Tailplane	20 sq ft		26 sq ft	26 sq ft
Elevators	13.33 sq ft		21 sq ft	21 sq ft
Fin	2.5 sq ft		4.75 sq ft	4.75 sq ft
Rudder	5.33 sq ft		10 sq ft	10 sq ft
Tankage				
Petrol		50 gal		
Oil		6 hrs		
Performance				
Weights				
empty			1759 lb	1793 lb
loaded			2424 lb	2458 lb
fuel and oil			421 lb	389 lb
load and crew			244 lb	276 lb
Maximum Speed				
sea level	87 mph	100.2 mph		103.1 mph
2000 ft				104 mph
3000 ft				103.7 mph
6000 ft	102 mph			
6500 ft			95 mph	102 mph
10000 ft			87 mph	99.5 mph
14000 ft				93.5 mph
Minimum Speed		50 mph		
Climb to,				
1000 ft		1 min 30 sec		1 min
3000 ft		4 min 20 sec		3 min 30 sec
6000 ft		9 min 30 sec		8 min 5 sec
6500 ft			10 min	
10000 ft			19 min	15 min 55 sec
12000 ft				21 min 10 sec
14000 ft				29 min
16000 ft				40 min 45 sec
17000 ft				49 min 30 sec
Service Ceiling			14,000 ft	16,000 ft
Take off run				100 yds
Landing run				160 yds
Endurance			5½ h	4½ h
Reference		CFS 204, 6.1.16	Tech Notes etc	M.80, Jan 1917

M.130, Aug 1917 (M/S with Eeman guns)

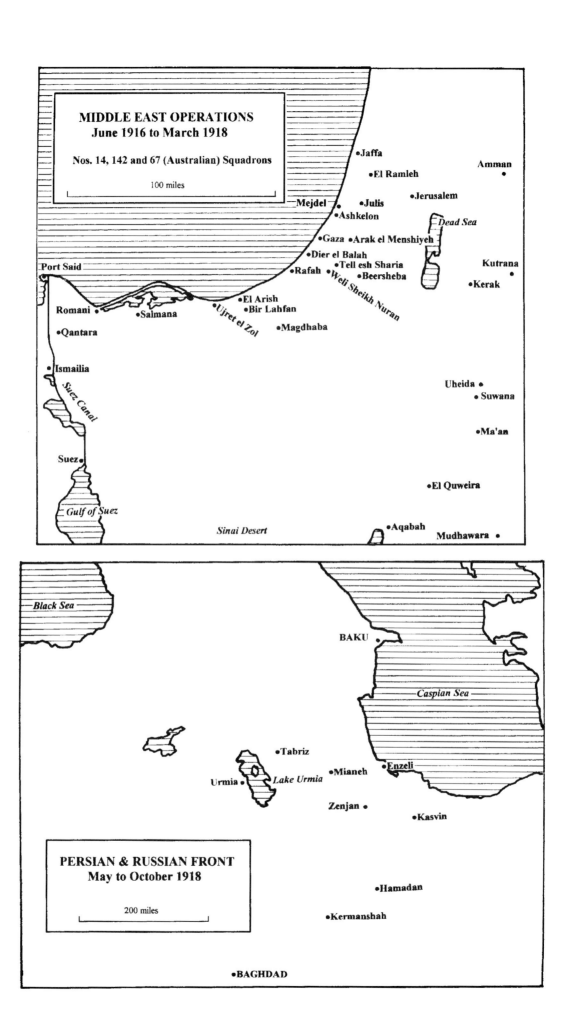

MIDDLE EAST OPERATIONS
June 1916 to March 1918

Nos. 14, 142 and 67 (Australian) Squadrons

100 miles

•Jaffa
Amman •
•El Ramleh
•Jerusalem
Mejdel •
•Julis
•Ashkelon
Dead Sea
•Gaza •Arak el Menshiyeh
•Dier el Balah
Kutrana •
•Tell esh Sharia
Port Said
Rafah •
•Beersheba
•Kerak
Weli Sheikh Nuran
•El Arish
Romani •
•Bir Lahfan
•Salmana
Ujret el Zol
•Qantara
•Magdhaba
•Ismailia
Uheida •
Suez Canal
• Suwana
•Ma'an
Suez •
•El Quweira
Gulf of Suez
Sinai Desert
•Aqabah
Mudhawara •

PERSIAN & RUSSIAN FRONT
May to October 1918

200 miles

Black Sea
BAKU •
Caspian Sea
•Tabriz
Enzeli •
Urmia •
•Mianeh
Lake Urmia
Zenjan •
•Kasvin
•Hamadan
•Kermanshah
•BAGHDAD

Martin & Handasyde No.3
Believed first flown with a 40 hp
JAP engine by Graham Gilmore
in November 1910 and scrapped
on the outbreak of war.

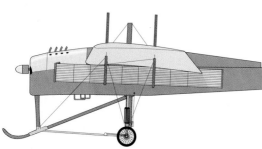

Martin & Handasyde Military Trials machine.
Shown after its Chenu engine had been replaced
by a 65 hp Antoinette in October 1912, after
unsuccessfully competing in the Military Trials in August.

Martinsyde S.1
2451, with early British markings,
Farnborough 1916.

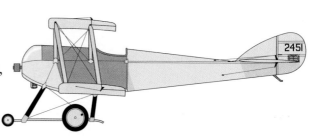

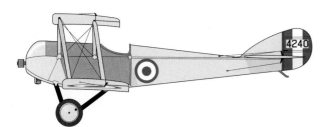

Martinsyde S.1
4240, as seen at Farnborough June 1916.
The roundels and fin stripes reflect the need
for better national identification adapting the
French pattern, with reversed colours.

Martinsyde Elephant
A6264, 1 of "A" Flight,
No.27 Sqn., France,
July 1917.

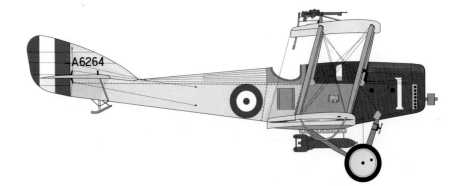

Martinsyde Elephant
A3999, formerly of "X" Flight,
later with No.23 TS Aboukir,
12 June 1918.

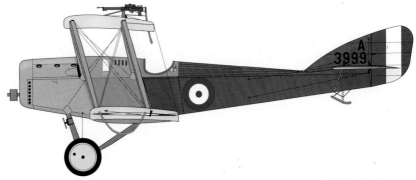

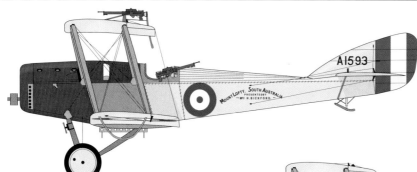

Martinsyde Elephant
A1593, "A" Flight, No.67
(Australian) Squadron, Middle
East, circa Summer 1917.

Martinsyde Elephant
A6299, fitted with the Eeman
triple-gun, attached from
Farnborough to No.39
(Home Defence) Sqn.,
19 October 1917.

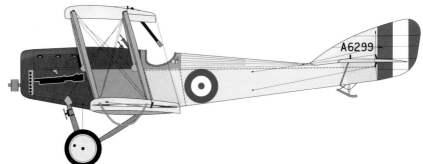

Martinsyde Buzzard
H7781, used for trials at
Martlesham Heath from
October 1920 to April 1921.

Martinsyde Semiquaver
G-EAPX, Raynham's entry for
the 1920 Aerial Derby, flown
into first place by Frank Courtney.

Martinsyde Raymor
Martinsyde's entry for the £10,000
Daily Mail Prize for the first to
cross the Atlantic son-stop, crewed
by F.P. Raynham and C.W.F. Morgan.
Crashed Newfoundland 18 May 1919.

Martinsyde F.6
G-EBDK, when owned by
Leslie Hamilton in 1925,
still in F.P. Raynham's
"Mustardsyde" colours.

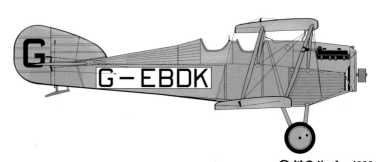

© M.D.Howley 1999

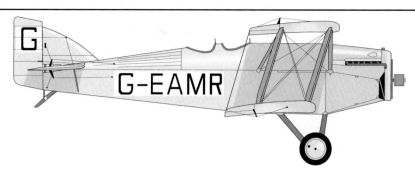

Martinsyde Type A.1 Mark 1.
G-EAMR, Martinsyde's entry for the
£10,000 England to Australia race,
sponsored by the Australian
government. Capt. C.E. Howell and
Sgt. G.H. Fraser died when it crashed
at Corfu on 9 December 1919.

Nimbus Martinsyde
G-EBOJ, one of two built by ADC
and entered in the King's Cup Races
from 1926 to 1928.

Martinsyde A.D.C.1.
G-EBKL, fitted with a 385 hp Jaguar
engine, later entered in the 1925
King's Cup Race with the racing
number 8.

Martinsyde Type A MarkII(AS).
G-CAEA, operated for two years by
Price Bros. And Dominion Aerial
Exploration Company in Canada.
Written off in a fatal accident on
12 July 1923.

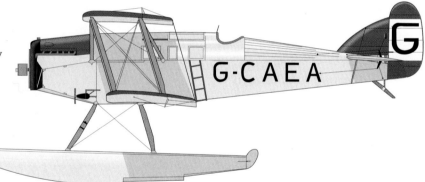

Martinsyde F.4 Buzzard
MA-24, the only surviving Martinsyde
aircraft, supplied to the Finnish Air Force,
on 26 March 1927.

Martinsyde Type A MarkII.
"The Big Fella", named after
Gen.Michael Collins. Purchased to
enable his escape should the
Anglo-Irish Peace talks fail,
December 1921.

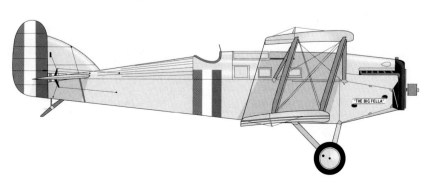

Martinsyde A.D.C.1
Supplied to the Latvian Air Force
in 1926, destroyed in a fatal crash
summer 1928.

Martinsyde F.4 Buzzard
The only F.4 operated by the Polish Air Force,
delivered on 29 January 1921 and written
off in a training accident 9 July 1926. Shown
as the personal aircraft of General
Wjodzimierz Zagorski.

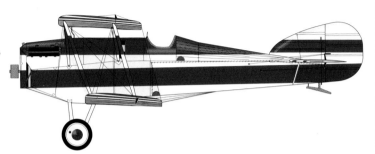

Martinsyde F.4 Buzzard
One of three used by the Portuguese
Air Force from 1923 to 1934. The
greyhound is the symbol of Air Base No.3.

Martinsyde F.4 Buzzard
One of a number used by the
Soviet Air Force from 1923 to 1931.

Martinsyde F.4 Buzzard
One of a number of F.4s, F.4As
and F.6s used by the Spanish Navy,
from 1921 to 1936, in the colours
applied in July 1936.

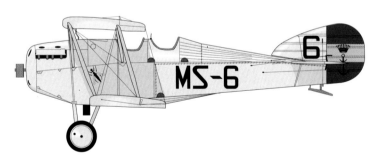

Martinsyde Type A, Mark II.
One of two operated by Pitcairn
Aviation in the USA during 1924.
The fin colour may be orange/red.

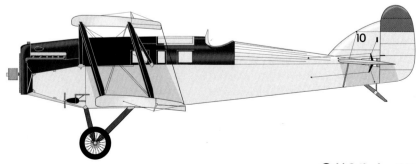

The ultimate Martinsyde fighter, the F.4 Buzzard.

CHAPTER 5 - THE BUZZARD

Martinsyde RG

Once it was realised that the Elephant was not sufficiently compact and agile to hold its own in the type of aerial combat which had evolved by 1916, the Martinsyde company made an attempt at revising the design to overcome its deficiencies as a fighting machine. A standard Elephant fuselage was fitted with single-bay wings of substantially reduced span. Unfortunately no details have come to light regarding its dimensions, weights or performance but presumably it retained the 160-hp Beardmore engine. That this variant was not tested in any depth was probably due to the expectation that a new more powerful engine would become available, the 190-hp Rolls-Royce water-cooled V-12 engine, later to become known as the Falcon.

The Martinsyde design office evolved a single-bay development of the Elephant designated the RG to take this engine, fitting it with a rectangular nose-mounted radiator and a two-bladed propeller. However, whereas the cockpit of the Elephant was situated behind the trailing edge of the upper wing, on the Falcon-powered aircraft the pilot was seated under the centre section, thereby restricting his upward view. Much of the Elephant's fuselage was retained but the sternpost was made deeper, resulting in a fin of reduced area whilst keeping the Elephant's rudder. Armament consisted of a Vickers gun mounted externally on the upper port longeron of the fuselage outside the centre section struts and a Lewis gun on the starboard side, although overwing mounting of the latter was thought possible.

The Martlesham Heath test report (M.81 of 28.2.1917) recommended several design changes to improve the aircraft and pilot safety. It was proposed that the air intake to the carburettor should be fitted outside the cowling as the pilot would otherwise almost certainly be injured if a backfire occurred. Also the exhaust pipe should be extended to prevent the pilot and his seat from being sprayed with oil from the exhaust and valve guides. It was thought that the pilot would be given greater freedom if the plywood fairing behind his shoulders were cut back.

The aircraft was fitted with an airspeed indicator, aneroid, rev counter, oil pressure and radiator temperature gauges. However there was insufficient room in front of the pilot to fit a compass. Nevertheless the flying controls were found to be conveniently placed. The machine was found to be very light and easy to manoeuvre with good lateral, longitudinal and directional control. The view was considered not to be sufficiently good and could have been improved by raising the pilot's seat and fitting a small windscreen. It would have been further improved by covering the centre section of top plane and the innermost twelve inches of the lower planes with transparent Cellon. The throttle control would have been more convenient if placed on the control

The Martinsyde RG in its original form with the cockpit positioned under the centre section. (J M Bruce/S Leslie Collection)

column and the petrol cocks needed to be brought forward as they could easily be knocked by the pilot's left elbow. Differences in trim between engine on and engine off could be readily accomplished by adjusting tailplane incidence. Take-off run to unstick was 80 yards and it was easy to land with a run of about 150 yards. The overall conclusion was that the high speed and rapid climb of this machine at heights should make it a valuable fighter.

However, shortly afterwards on 9th March 1917, Brig. General Brooke-Popham wrote to the Director of Aircraft Equipment at the War Office; "GOC instructs me to inform you that he considers this machine is useless in view of its moderate performance on trials and its small petrol capacity."

The Company quickly took note of the criticisms of the earlier design and produced an extensively modified and improved aircraft. This was designated the "RG" by the company. How this designation came about has not been established and it was not recognised by the authorities. The aerofoil section of the Elephant was retained but otherwise the construction and dimensions of the wings were modified, with the lower wing being smaller in chord and span than the upper. As a consequence, the spars of the lower wing were built slightly closer together than those of the upper and the interplane struts were raked slightly outwards. Ailerons were fitted to both upper and lower wings and were given curved taper towards the tips.

The fuselage was much modified, with the cockpit now positioned behind the centre section struts. The trailing edge of the centre section was cut away to improve the view and a pair of synchronised Vickers guns were mounted ahead of the cockpit within easy reach of the pilot. Behind the cockpit, the top decking was tapered upwards to form a head rest for the pilot. The configuration of the fin and rudder of the earlier Falcon-powered prototype was retained. The engine was a 275-hp Rolls-Royce Falcon III fitted with a frontal radiator and driving a four-bladed propeller.

Late in June 1917, the RG was sent to Martlesham Heath for just a day and during this brief period was flown by several pilots whose collective opinion was that "...if the view is improved by placing the pilot higher, the exceptional performance, combined with ease of control at all speeds, and ease of landing will make the machine superior to any other existing type of fighting scout." The official report (M.112 of 27th June 1917) was equally enthusiastic:

The performance of this machine is far and away better than any other machine yet manufactured. The machine manoeuvres extremely well and could almost hold her own in this respect against even a rotary-engined scout. She has a very good point in being able to be turned even at very high speeds. She is remarkably light on the controls and with the help of the adjustable tail will fly hands off at any speed. There is no doubt that as a fighter she would be invaluable..

The machine is very easily landed and few crashes would result from this even on bad aerodromes. There might be difficulty in getting into a small field or aerodrome surrounded by trees as the machine has a long glide....

Vision a little worse than the S.E.5 but far better than the previous 190 Martinsyde. It is understood that in a future model the pilot's seat will be raised so that he can see easily over the top plane.

Just to make sure that the point about the excellent performance was appreciated, the Martlesham report was given an appendix in which the performance of the RG was compared with the S.E.5a and Dolphin. This showed that the time to an altitude of 15,000 feet was 12.8 minutes compared with 18.8 and 17.3 minutes respectively and once at that height the top speed of the RG was 127½ mph compared with 121 and 116 mph and the rate of climb was 725 ft/min compared with 465 and 495 ft/min.

Despite its excellent performance and favourable reports the RG was not chosen for production. Unfortunately the Falcon engine had been earmarked for the Bristol Fighter, which was already in quantity production, and an official decision had also been taken to produce the S.E.5 and Sopwith Camel as the standard single-seat fighter aircraft.

Not to be beaten, the Martinsyde company had another

The modified Martinsyde RG showing its raised Vickers guns. (E A Harlin Collection)

design under consideration to be powered by a B.H.P. engine, which it is assumed was the standard 230-hp version. However this type was never built, presumably because this engine, with its six in-line configuration, did not have the development potential of the Falcon. In the event the next Martinsyde fighter type to appear was the F.3.

Martinsyde F.1 and F.2 two-seaters

The F.1, known as the "Father" in the Martinsyde works as it was the first of the "F" series, was classed as a two-seater fighter, although bearing in mind its seating arrangements it probably started out as a reconnaissance machine. The aircraft was powered by a 250-hp Rolls-Royce Mk III engine driving a four-bladed Lang propeller. The two-bay wings were of unequal chord and, like the Bristol Fighter, the fuselage was placed about midway between them. The lower wing was uncovered immediately below the fuselage and was supported by an open structure of struts. But there any resemblance with the Bristol Fighter ended. The fuselage and tail assembly were basically similar to the Elephant but the former was strengthened and enlarged to take the more powerful engine. Unlike the seating arrangement of the Bristol Fighter, which had the observer immediately behind the pilot, allowing excellent communication between the crew and an unrestricted field of fire upwards and rearwards, the observer of the F.1 occupied the front cockpit between the mainplanes some distance from the pilot and had a very restricted view.

These crew arrangements were severely criticised in the official report when the prototype F.1 (A3933) was sent to the Testing Squadron for evaluation in July 1917:

The observer is in the front seat, and there is no fixed gun firing forward. The testing squadron suggested it would be a decided improvement, in extent of view and fire, if the positions of pilot and observer were reversed, while machine would be better able to resist a strong attack from below. Flying qualities, stability and controllability good; magneto, carburettors, tanks, etc., very inaccessible.

Not unexpectedly the F.1 did not receive a production order. However whilst at Orfordness, the prototype F.1 was fitted with an experimental gun arrangement for the purpose of combating the Gotha raids. This system was similar to the Eeman system fitted earlier to the Elephant. The F.1 was fitted with an upward sight for the pilot, developed by Melvill Jones, and two Lewis guns angled at about 45° to fire above the propeller arc. The proposal was for the pilot to fly the aircraft into the correct position for an attack and then signal to the observer, who was lying on his back in the front cockpit, to open fire.

The planned operational trial with the upward-firing guns unfortunately came to nothing as the crew failed to locate a target. Piloted by Capt L J Wackett, a highly-skilled and experienced night pilot, with Lt H H Hussey as observer, the F.1 patrolled from Rochford on two successive nights 29/30th September and 30th September/1st October 1917. It was planned that nominated searchlight crews would indicate the general position of a raider without necessarily illuminating the target. On the first occasion observers on the ground distinctly heard a Gotha bomber with the Martinsyde in the vicinity but no contact was made. This was probably due to the Martinsyde being at a much greater height than the raider, as Wackett firmly believed that Gothas flew in at around 14,000 ft. However, according to post-war German

132

The unsuccessful Martinsyde F.1, A3933. (Philip Jarrett Collection)

accounts, these aircraft approached their targets at altitudes of between 4,000 and 8,200 ft and only gained height on their outward journeys after dropping their bombs.

The F.2 two-seater owed more in its development to the RG than the F.1. It was a single-bay biplane with the same overall dimensions as the RG single-seater. Unlike the F.1, the fuselage was situated with the lower longerons in line with the lower wing and with the pilot's and observer's cockpits situated close together and with the pilot in front just to the rear of the wing leading edge and the observer behind just forward of the wing trailing edge. The pilot, situated between the wings, had a very restricted view especially for landing. He was provided with a fixed synchronised Vickers gun mounted slightly port of centre. Martlesham suggested that the view could be improved by moving the dashboard forward into an empty space behind the engine and cutting back the three-ply covering at the sides. This modification would also improve access to the gun. The observer, however, who was provided with a Lewis gun mounted on a Scarff ring, had a

much improved view compared with the F.1. Fuel was contained in two tanks of 23 and 10 gallon capacity, one in front of the pilot between his legs and one behind the pilot's seat. The position of the forward tank was criticised because it restricted the pilot's movements.

A Martlesham report (M.98 of 1st May 1917) found that the aircraft had good longitudinal and lateral but only fair directional stability. It had good controllability on all axes and in taxying. The take-off and landing runs were found to be 80 yards and 100 yards respectively. Besides criticising the pilot's view, the report was also critical of some of the control arrangements. In particular, the pilot's rudder controls were channelled via the observer's rudder bar, which was very poorly supported and could easily be trodden on and broken. The F.2 was smaller and lighter than the F.1 and, apart from duration and range, had a much improved performance despite being fitted with a Hispano-Suiza engine of only 200 hp.

The F.1 at Rochford showing the supports for two upward-firing Lewis guns firing through the centre section. (J M Bruce/S Leslie Collection)

The nose of F.1. A3933. (Eric Harlin collection)

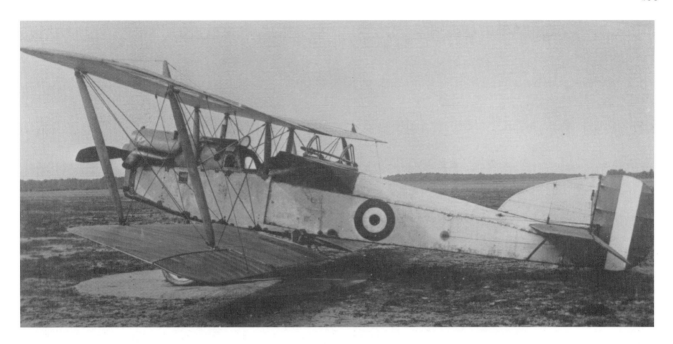

The Martinsyde F.2 at Martlesham Heath. (J M Bruce/S Leslie Collection)

Unfortunately, even with these improvements, the F.2 still had no material benefits to offer compared with the Bristol Fighter, which was already in full production and earning itself a good reputation on the Western Front, and therefore did not go beyond the prototype stage.

The Martlesham weekly report for 14th July 1917 mentions a two-seater Martinsyde being fitted with a 200 hp Sunbeam Arab engine at the engine manufacturer's works at Wolverhampton. This was the F.2 with its 200 hp Hispano-Suiza replaced by an Arab (engine number 9008). The aircraft was reported at the Sunbeam works on 7th July having its exhaust pipes and oil tank altered. It made its second flight on 18th July (date of first flight not known) and was repaired at the Sunbeam works after being badly damaged on landing. The aircraft with the Arab engine arrived at Martlesham on 11th August, where engine tests were interrupted by water leaks. A Sunbeam representative had overhauled the engine and carried out alterations to the cooling system by 15th September. Engine tests took place the following week, whereupon the aircraft was flown back to Wolverhampton on 1st December. The engine was subsequently transferred to an S.E.5a.

The Martinsyde F.2 fitted with the 200 hp Sunbeam Arab engine. (Eric Harlin Collection)

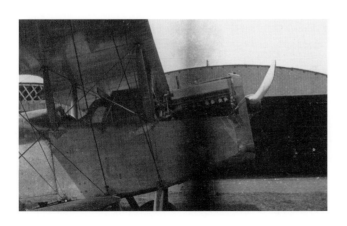

Martinsyde F.3

A new fighter emerged from the Martinsyde works at Brooklands during the autumn of 1917, designated the F.3 and christened "Mother" by the workforce. Whereas the F.1 two-seater was something of an anachronism, both the F.2 and the F.3 owed much to the RG in their lineage while at the same time incorporating a much more compact and pugnacious aspect to their designs. That this is so was probably attributable to the influence of Emile Bouillon, who joined the Martinsyde Company as an assistant to Handasyde, who was still regarded as Chief Designer. Bouillon was a French engineer who had worked for Louis Bréguet in France and for Messrs Hewlett & Blondeau in England, where he had worked on the detail design of the Dyott Battleplane and played a leading part in the design of that company's single-engined bomber of 1916.

The Falcon engine of the F.3 retained the frontal radiator, four-bladed propeller and the distinctive exhaust manifold arrangement of the RG, which might suggest that the installation had been transferred directly from the RG to the F.3, a not unreasonable assumption considering the shortage of Falcon engines at that time. However the engine fitted was apparently non-standard as in official reports it was referred to as a "Falcon Experimental" with an output of 190 hp at 2,100 rpm. A two-bladed propeller soon replaced the original four-bladed one. From an early stage, the water-cooled V-8 240-hp Lorraine de Dietrich 8Bb engine was considered as an alternative.

The fuselage was made in two parts, each with solid hickory longerons with spruce spacers. The two parts were butt-jointed at about half-way along the fuselage. The forward half had solid spruce diagonals and the sides had no cross-bracing wires, these rendered unnecessary by birch three-ply covering. Transversely, cross-bracing was by wire and tubular stays and horizontally the bottom was cross-braced with wire. The rear half consisted of nine bays, wire-braced throughout. The longerons were made of hickory and were tapered and the spruce spacers were spindled out. The cowling was made of aluminium sheeting supported by angle-section formers. Sections of the cowling were hinged or

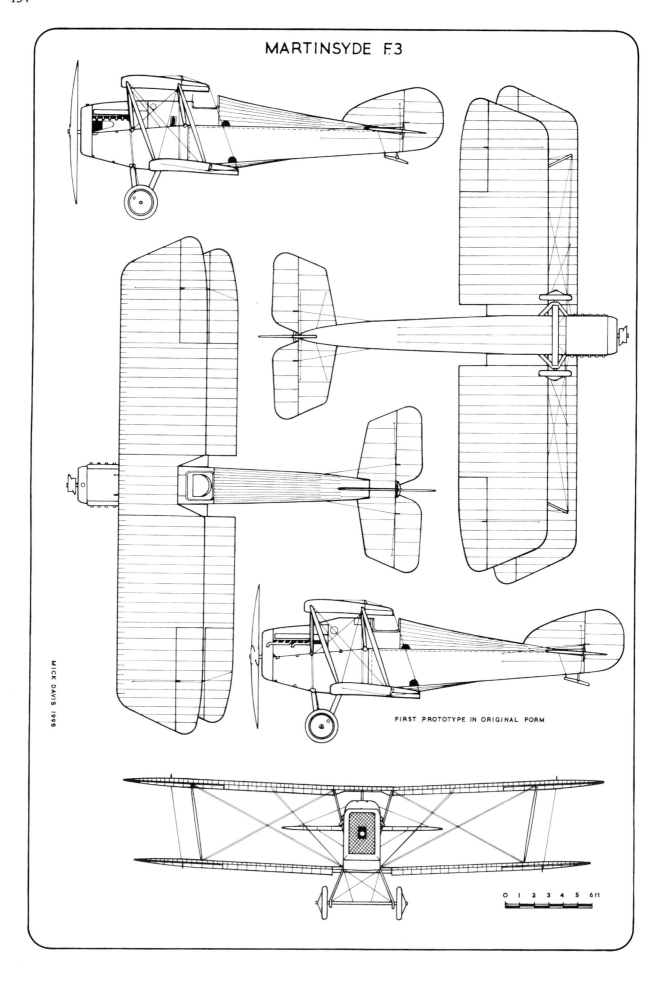

MARTINSYDE F.3

MICK DAVIS 1998

FIRST PROTOTYPE IN ORIGINAL FORM

0 1 2 3 4 5 6ft

The Martinsyde F.3 with the original hump over the guns forward of the pilot. (E A Harlin Collection)

detachable for access.

Criticisms of earlier designs, particularly of the pilot's view, had been taken to heart and as a result the pilot's seat had been raised so that the trailing edge of the centre section was only a few inches above eye level, allowing an excellent view overhead. This resulted in a much deeper fuselage than had been previously seen in Martinsyde designs. This good work was partly undone by enclosing the breeches of the two Vickers guns in a humped fairing which, while protecting the pilot from the slipstream, significantly restricted his view directly forward and therefore his ability to sight the guns. The problem was soon appreciated and the fairing over the guns was soon removed, thereby improving the pilot's view along the nose. A little later, the top decking ahead of the cockpit was reskinned and large outlets for spent cartridges and belt links were provided in the shoulders of the decking, just in front of the centre-section struts. The fuselage fairing behind the cockpit headrest was also modified from a rounded shape to a more pointed one.

The single-bay wings of the F.3 were of equal chord but of slightly unequal span. As on the RG, the interplane struts were raked slightly outwards as were the centre-section struts, due to the centre section being appreciably wider than the fuselage. The flying wires were duplicated. The lower mainplanes were attached to a form of centre section, the spar members of which were attached to the undersides of the lower longerons, necessitating a belly fairing which added to the depth of the fuselage. This space was utilised by housing the oxygen equipment. The wing spars were built up of three laminations of spruce, which were spindled out at intervals. Each wing panel had four compression ribs of box section, with four spacing ribs between each. Wooden strips were run along the top and bottom edges of these ribs, enclosing the spars. For added strength, diagonal wire bracing between the spars was also provided, the wires passing conveniently through the cutouts in the ribs. The upper surface of the leading edge of each wing was covered in 1/16th-inch ply to 12 mm behind the front spar. Ailerons were fitted to both upper and lower wings and had the characteristic taper of those fitted to the RG. Their spars, ribs and trailing edge were all made of spruce. The fairings between fuselage and wings were made of three-ply formers and stringers and covered in fabric.

The tail unit was made predominantly of wood, with the horizontal surface built on a fabric covered box spar. The fin was built integrally with the stern post of the fuselage, which was constructed of duralumin tube, and supported an unbalanced rudder. The incidence of the tailplane could be adjusted in flight from -3½° to +6° through a screw jack actuated by means of a cable running to a control wheel in the cockpit.

The undercarriage was supported by V-struts set at an angle of 22½°. They were made of spruce and attached to the longerons by means of brackets bolted between reinforcing plates of duralumin. Each wheel was on a half-axle, pivoted from near the centre of the spreader bar which was made of duralumin. Each pivot point was wire-braced to the longerons. Rubber shock absorbers, each made of 25 feet of 3/8th-inch cord were housed between two 10-swg duralumin side plates attached to the angle of the support struts.

Manufacturer's trials were reported as complete by mid-September but in fact they were extended until the end of that month. It may be that the Martinsyde company had thought it

The F.3 with the Rolls-Royce Falcon engine and four-bladed propeller with the original hump over the guns.
(Eric Harlin Collection)

The cockpit area of the F.3 with the hump over the guns removed. (Eric Harlin Collection)

prudent to obtain the advice of a pilot with combat experience before the aircraft was sent for official trials, as an RFC Captain flew the aircraft early in October while it was still at Brooklands. His report of 3rd October does not seem to have survived but it was officially noted that the aircraft had been criticised for a somewhat restricted downward view. These remarks were to adversely affect consideration of the aircraft later but at the time Martinsyde sensibly refused to make cut outs in the lower wings to improve the view as they knew the extent to which such modifications could adversely affect performance. By 20th October, it was reported that the Vickers guns and interrupter gear were to be fitted at Brooklands, but in spite of two weeks elapsing, the interrupter gear was not fitted at that time.

The F.3, still without armament and without radiator shutters fitted, finally reached Martlesham Heath on 9th November 1917 and testing began shortly afterwards, following the repair of some leaks in the fuel tanks. The prototype went to France for evaluation by an RFC unit on 28th November but its stay was brief as it had returned to Martlesham Heath by 8th December and during the following week it was returned to Brooklands for modifications.

Martlesham was unstinting in its praise of the new fighter. To quote from Report No. M.158 dated 26th November 1917:

Suitability of machine: Very good indeed; the machine is considered a great advance on all existing fighting scouts. Not only has it an exceptionally good performance, but the visibility is very good indeed, the guns are well placed and easy to get at, and the manoeuvrability is excellent for a

machine of this size and power. The landing speed is slow.

The aircraft's stability and controllability in all axes was recorded as unequivocally good, as was its behaviour while taxying, there being "very little tendency to swing when getting off the ground". The performance was excellent as evinced by the figures given at the end of this chapter. Otherwise any criticisms about the layout of the controls and structure were minor and capable of ready modification. Some of the recommended changes to the structure were to improve access to the guns for maintenance and to allow cross-feeding of the ammunition belts, should one gun jam.

An experienced service pilot, Major W J C K Cochran Patrick, then commanding No.60 Squadron, was given the opportunity to evaluate the F.3 and commented as follows in his report of 4th December:

This machine has undoubtedly a very fine performance in speed and climb. Below 12,000 feet, however, I consider that these advantages are outweighed by slowness in handling and bad view forward and down. The view above and level is very good and the view down and to the sides is not nearly as bad as might be expected, considering the large chord of the planes, but the view forward and down is very badly obstructed by the breadth of the fuselage. On the other hand, I consider that above 12,000 feet this machine would be very much better than any existing type, as it would not only have the advantage of speed and climb, but would also be able to out-manoeuvre the ordinary machine, owing to its ability to turn without losing height. The gliding angle is very good indeed and the landing speed low. On the other hand, it would be difficult, owing to the flatness of the glide, to get the machine into a small field over trees. The arrangement of the

The Martinsyde F.3 with the original hump over the guns forward of the pilot. (E A Harlin Collection)

guns is exceedingly good and very handy for correcting jams.

Although not as uncritical as the Martlesham report, the general tenor of the findings was reasonably favourable.

It was quickly decided to build the F.3 in a quantity sufficient to equip and maintain two squadrons. A batch of 150 aircraft was ordered under Contract No.A.S.36686 in addition to six development aircraft under Contract No. A.S.29238. Serial numbers D4211-D4360 and B1490-B1495 were respectively allocated in response to an official request on 5th December.

Major General Hugh Trenchard, Commanding the Royal Flying Corps, was aware of the order because on 6th December he wrote to the Director General of Military Aeronautics:

1. *I have seen the Martinsyde Scout with the Rolls-Royce engine tried.*
2. *I understand two squadrons of this machine have been ordered and I would be glad if you would inform me when they will come out.*
3. *I think that a third gun ought to be put on the top plane to fire upwards; it need not fire straight forwards*
4. *The machine only carries 300 rounds of ammunition per gun at present. This is not really enough, and even this amount of ammunition is only carried with great difficulty. This should be improved if possible.*
5. *I should like to have one of these machines out to use and get to know long before the Squadrons arrive. Would you kindly let me know when I may expect one machine.*

That the Martinsyde was still strongly in official favour is shown by the minutes of a meeting called by Sir William

Weir, Controller of Aeronautical Supplies in the Ministry of Munitions, to decide on the forward manufacturing and supply programme up to the middle of 1919. In respect of single-seat fighters, it was decided that 56 squadrons would be needed and the new equipment should consist of:

"a. Martinsyde, with 190 Rolls-Royce or 300 Hispano-Suiza engines and
b. New type of machine to take B.R.2 engine".

The mention of the Hispano-Suiza engine in the context of the Martinsyde may have been due to the fact that the meeting knew that "...we will have available 2,000 300-hp Hispano-Suiza engines, for which at present there is no machine designed, nor any stated requirements, and a decision should be made as to the utilisation of these".

During December 1917, Trenchard underwent a change of heart regarding the Martinsyde F.3. At a meeting held on 31st December under the chairmanship of Sir William Weir to further consider the design and supply of aircraft he was minuted as saying:

Regarding the Martinsyde single-seat fighter with Rolls-Royce engine, General Trenchard stated that in the experiments they have carried out, it appears that this machine is short of petrol, has a bad view, and is not handy, and it does not appear that it will ever become a satisfactory machine. Sir William Weir pointed out that this opinion was diametrically opposed to the advice given to the Air Board by the Technical Department and on which the two squadrons were ordered. It was therefore suggested that this type should not be further developed.

It was stated, however, that it is very desirable that a single-seat fighter should be developed to take the Rolls-Royce

The F.3 prototype at Martlesham Heath. (J M Bruce /S Leslie Collection)

Falcon and/or the 300-hp Hispano-Suiza with better view than
the Martinsyde and, if possible, this should be considered
along with the four experimental types of rotary-engine single-
seater fighters, which are at present being constructed.

Sir William Weir stated that the quantity of Falcon
engines is limited and a discussion ensued as to what other
type of engine could be discontinued to enable additional
quantities of Falcon engines to be produced.

One can only conclude from Trenchard's remarks that he
must either have been badly briefed or that he had confused
the F.3 with some other type of aircraft, perhaps even the
original 190-hp Falcon Martinsyde which had been justifiably
rejected by Brooke-Popham in March 1917. Fortunately these

*Martinsyde F.3 B1490 with the revised forward fuselage
coaming. (J M Bruce/S Leslie Collection)*

remarks were largely disregarded and the production of the
F.3 went ahead, apparently with the intention of commencing
deliveries during February 1918 as the following extract from
the official Statement of Aeroplanes (No.4) dated 23rd
February 1918 indicates:

Martinsyde F.3

150 of these machines have been ordered. Deliveries should
commence in February and extend to July. Two squadrons are
to be equipped and maintained with these machines and
adequate provision for spares should be made.

The question of the engine to be fitted in these machines
is undecided. It is improbable that the 190-hp Falcon Rolls-
Royce will be fitted, and the machines may be stored
temporarily and fitted later with the 300-hp Hispano, in which
case spares provision will require careful consideration.

The decision to adopt the Hispano-Suiza as an alternative
had been taken sometime around 9th January 1918. It was
already apparent that the production of Bristol Fighter
airframes was already outstripping the supply of Falcon
engines and that it would be prudent to find another engine
for the Martinsyde. By that date, an official request had been
made to the company to install a Hispano-Suiza engine and at
the same time, in deference to Trenchard's wish to improve
the pilot's view, a request was also made to reduce the chord
of the lower wing. The company responded on 14th January
proposing to fit either the Lorraine or Hispano-Suiza and to
reduce the chord of the lower wing, designating the modified
aircraft as the F.3A.

At about this time, during the week ending 5th January
1918, the Martinsyde F.3 was given the designation X2. This
followed a directive requiring prototypes to be given serial
numbers in a special category, after the procurement of

The prototype F.3, now with its serial X2, at Brooklands. (J M Bruce/S Leslie Collection)

aircraft becoming the responsibility of the Ministry of Munitions earlier in the year. Then it was decreed that manufacturers would not be allowed to construct or carry out experimental work on airframes or engines without licence from the Controller of Aeronautical Supplies at the Air Board.

On 25th January, Department T.6 reported to the Controller of the Technical Department that:

the position of the Martinsydes with the Falcon engine is well known. With the 300-hp Hispano-Suiza the machine should perform equally well, if not better; though probably it would not be so reliable. Modifications to the lower planes so as to improve the downwards view are to be incorporated. The firm is at present engaged in fitting the Lorraine-Dietrich engine, the purpose of which is not quite clear to me.

However as future events proved, Martinsyde were quite right not to rely on the delivery of Hispano-Suiza engines in good time. The engine of the prototype was changed in early January and by the middle of the month Constantinesco synchronising gear for the guns was being fitted. The aircraft then underwent maker's trials at Brooklands from the end of January until mid-February.

Despite the supply difficulties with the engines, some fanciful ideas on the ability of Martinsyde to supply aircraft remained. The Director of Aircraft Equipment wrote to Trenchard to say;

... it is expected that one Squadron of this machine will go out in April, and the other in May. It is hoped, however, to let you have one of this type of machine early in March in order that you may be able to use and get to know it before arrival of the Squadrons.

This proposed production schedule was totally unrealistic. If powered by the Falcon, the F.3 could only be produced by severely restricting the output of the Bristol

Fighter powered by the same engine, an option which had not been seriously contemplated by the authorities. And there was no immediate prospect of obtaining supplies of the 300-hp Hispano-Suiza. On 24th February 1918, Major J P C Sewell, reporting from France about the French aircraft industry recorded that, "the 300-hp Hispano-Suiza engines have only just finished their bench tests." By 24th April, he could only report that, "ten of these engines have been built up to the present and are destined for various machines, such as the new Nieuport monocoque, the Bechereau, etc. One only is running (at 2,200 rev/min giving about 275 hp) for endurance tests on a reinforced SPAD."

It appears that the prototype was not returned to Martlesham. Instead the first production machine (B1490), fitted with a Falcon, arrived there on 26th April 1918. Due to engine problems and lack of spares, trials did not commence until the middle of May. These were concluded by 1st June and the aircraft then went to Orfordness for armament trials about a week later. There the ammunition load was increased by 400 rpg and the airframe was fitted with oxygen equipment, these modifications increasing the all-up weight by 120 lb.

The report could find little wrong with the aircraft. Although the mountings for both the guns and the Aldis and ring and bead sights were adjustable at the rear, it was suggested that the front mounting for the sights should also be made adjustable. On the other hand the ability to slide the windscreen forward and the provision of clips on the top wing, to hold the rear gun covers when opened, was welcomed as these features facilitated the clearance of stoppages.

The increased weight reduced the performance slightly but the excellent handling qualities were unaffected as shown by the following extracts from an undated official report.

F.3 B1492 at Biggin Hill. (J M Bruce/S Leslie Collection)

This machine for its size and weight has extraordinary good manoeuvre, and can turn almost as quickly as a Camel. She answers very quickly to rudder, elevation and aileron controls. Petrol tanks are between pilot and engine....

I am confident that the enemy has not at present got a machine which could out-manoeuvre the Martinsyde. In test flights here, with both a Camel and a Wagtail against the Martinsyde and after changing pilots, it was found practically impossible to get on the Martinsyde's tail in a good firing position. A great point is that it turns so quickly and can be made to climb at the same time. With its speed, climb and good manoeuvre, this machine I am sure would do splendid work (on the Western Front) both at heights and low down. No bomb racks are fitted.

The view from the pilot's seat is very good. It has the usual blind spots below the fuselage and tail plane. The pilot is in a comfortable position, and the machine is not at all difficult to fly or land.

The above report was probably based on mock combats, reported by Capt W H K Copeland on 22nd May 1918, at the time when he was seconded from his duties as Flight Commander with No.60 Squadron. In these trials, the F.3 showed a marked superiority over the Camel and Wagtail as the following extracts indicate.

Camel (110 Le Rhône) v. Martinsyde:
This fight was started at 3,000 ft and ended up just above the tree tops, the Martinsyde forcing the Camel down. Manoeuvring to get on each other's tails, the machines seemed to turn about the same pace. The Martinsyde could easily outclimb the Camel in a climbing spiral and thus always had the advantage of height. The Martinsyde appeared to come off one bank into another as quickly as the Camel. On points the Martinsyde has undoubtedly the advantage over a Camel as a Fighting Scout.

Martinsyde v. Wagtail:
This fight was started about 4,000 ft and ended up at about 1,000 ft, the Martinsyde forcing the Wagtail down. On trying to get on each other's tails, the Wagtail appeared to turn slightly quicker, but the Martinsyde could easily outclimb it on turns, thus having the advantage of height. The Wagtail came off banks slightly if anything quicker. The Martinsyde could have broke off the fight any time and got away but not so with the Wagtail.

Capt Copeland also reported upon the Martinsyde that day.

The Martinsyde as a fighting scout is very good; not only has it a good performance, but the visibility is good, and it manoeuvres quickly, answering controls at once. On controls this machine is light as compared with an S.E. The guns are in a very good position in front of the pilot, and are easily got at for clearing stoppages. All instruments are easily seen and all controls conveniently placed. When fully clothed the pilot is quite comfortable and nothing fouls his legs or arms.

It is difficult to make a comparison with the S.E. as the Martinsyde is so far superior. Compared with the Camel she can turn just as fast. The landing speed is slow and the angle is very flat.

Further mock combat trials were carried by B1490 during the week ending 19th October, as a replacement for a F.4 which was delayed by engine problems. The Wagtail did not in fact participate on this occasion but the Martinsyde again outclassed the other opposition consisting of a B.A.T. Bantam, Sopwith Snipe and Fokker D.VII. The Fokker was beaten with respect to manoeuvrability, speed and climb. It also outperformed the agile Bantam at altitude and all contestants were superior to the Snipe. B1490 remained at Martlesham until the end of November after which it disappears from the record.

F.3 B1491. (J M Bruce/S Leslie Collection)

The first 300-hp Hispano-Suiza to arrive at the Martinsyde works was Engine No. 200010, which was test run on 15th March 1918, producing 305 hp at 1,800 rpm but deliveries did not begin in quantity until the first week of July, when 18 built by the parent company were despatched to the Regent's Park depot. Apparently this completed the pilot order for 20 from Hispano-Suiza, the follow-on contract for 1,935 engines for British use being undertaken by the Mayen company of Paris. The first Mayen-built engine arrived at Farnborough during the week ending 27th July and only 14 had arrived in England by the end of August. Deliveries of a further 2,250 Hispano-Suiza engines from other suppliers did not begin until October 1918. There was no hope of completing even the first contract for 150 machines before the end of the war.

In the event, only seven F.3s were built with Falcon engines, the prototype X2 and six from the first batch with series B1490 to B1495. Four went to RAF Home Defence squadrons in 1918, including Nos.39 and 141 Squadrons. All other production was completed as F.4s.

The Martinsyde company suggested to the authorities that the Rolls-Royce version should retain the F.3 nomenclature and that Hispano-Suiza powered versions should be designated F.A.3. In the event it was mutually agreed that the latter should be designated F.4 and all further production was of this type. It was not until 9th September 1918 that Martinsyde were notified that the aircraft would be officially known as the Buzzard.

F.3 B1490 at Martlesham Heath. (IWM)

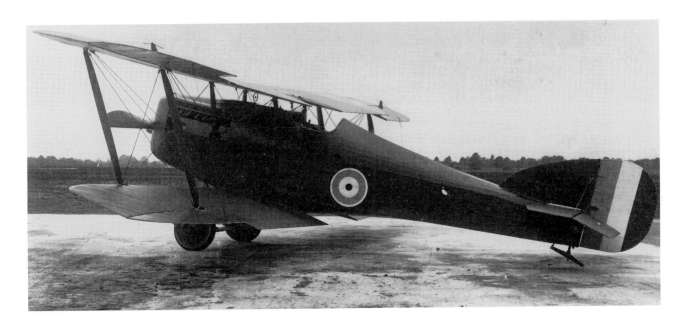

Martinsyde F.4 Buzzard with a Rolls-Royce Falcon engine, possibly the prototype. (J M Bruce/S Leslie Collection)

Martinsyde F.4 Buzzard

By 21st March 1918, it was expected that deliveries of the 150 production models would begin in May. This was still the case on 9th May when according to the fifth official Statement of Aeroplanes, the use of the 300 hp Hispano-Suiza engine was confirmed. By mid-August, plans included the provision of nine squadrons of F.4s. The Programme of Development for the period ending 1st June 1919 allowed for 13 squadrons of the type with the RAF in France. The first unit was not now expected to join the Expeditionary Force in France until November 1918. Nos.89 and 95 Squadrons, also equipped with Martinsydes, were expected to follow in December. The plans expected two S.E.5 squadrons to convert to the type by January 1919, with two more following in February. A new squadron was expected to go to the Front in March followed by another in April. Two Dolphin squadrons were also expected to re-equip with the type in April, followed by another two in May. This programme required a substantial increase in orders. In September 1918, 600 more F.4s (H7613 to H8112) were ordered from the parent company and 350 (H9763 to H9112) were ordered from Boulton & Paul. A few weeks later, further contracts were allotted; 150 (J1992 to J2141) from Boulton & Paul, 200 (J3342 to J3541) from Hooper & Co Ltd and 300 (J5592 to J5891) from the Standard Motor Co Ltd.

The definitive F.4 differed somewhat from the F.3. Besides the inevitable modifications due to the change of engine, the pilot's view was improved by reducing the chord of the lower wing by six inches and by moving the cockpit rearwards by one bay (10 inches). The structural strength was increased by extending the plywood covering by one bay and the cross-bracing was modified. The resultant space in front of the cockpit was used for additional fuel and ammunition. An additional diagonal member was added to the rear bay of the forward fuselage which was attached to the lower longeron above the rear spar of the lower centre section. This spar had been moved forward as a result of the reduction in chord of the lower wings. At the Ministry's insistence and despite resistance from the manufacturers, the laminated spars between the ribs were taped with linen to protect against moisture and guard against the failure of imperfectly glued joints. The twin Vickers guns were located side-by-side immediately ahead of the cockpit and completely housed within the top decking. The front fairing was lowered by two inches. Also the longerons of the rear section were changed from hickory to spruce and were wrapped in fabric. The engine bearers were now formed of two duralumin plates joined by duralumin webs. A minor difference was that whereas the wing fabric on the F.3 was stitched and taped at every rib, on the F.4 this was done on alternate ribs only. Following criticism in later Martlesham trials, from 6th January 1919 the tailplane hinges were fabricated from steel instead of aluminium, in order to strengthen them against side loads.

The first Hispano-Suiza engine received by Martinsyde was fitted to F.4 D4256 and this aircraft was despatched to Martlesham in June 1918, where it was immediately subjected to performance trials. As originally built, it was fitted with a cooling system based on twin Gallay honeycomb blocks with two shutters moving on vertical hinges behind the blocks. These were soon condemned as inadequate and were replaced by conventional vertical shutters mounted in front of the engine. The overflow pipes, one to each radiator block, were led up the centre section alongside the bracing wires to the centre section. These were however too small in bore and froze up at altitude, causing two forced landings. Suitably-lagged larger bore tubing solved this problem. Heaters were also installed in the pipes leading from the water pump to the cylinder jacket. However the problem of leaks from the dual radiator blocks were never satisfactorily solved. Also the oil tank was found to be too small, resulting in high oil temperatures during the climb.

In his book *Martlesham Heath*, Gordon Kinsey quotes some experiences of Wg Cdr A R Boerce in testing the F.4 there which illustrates the difficulties that were encountered

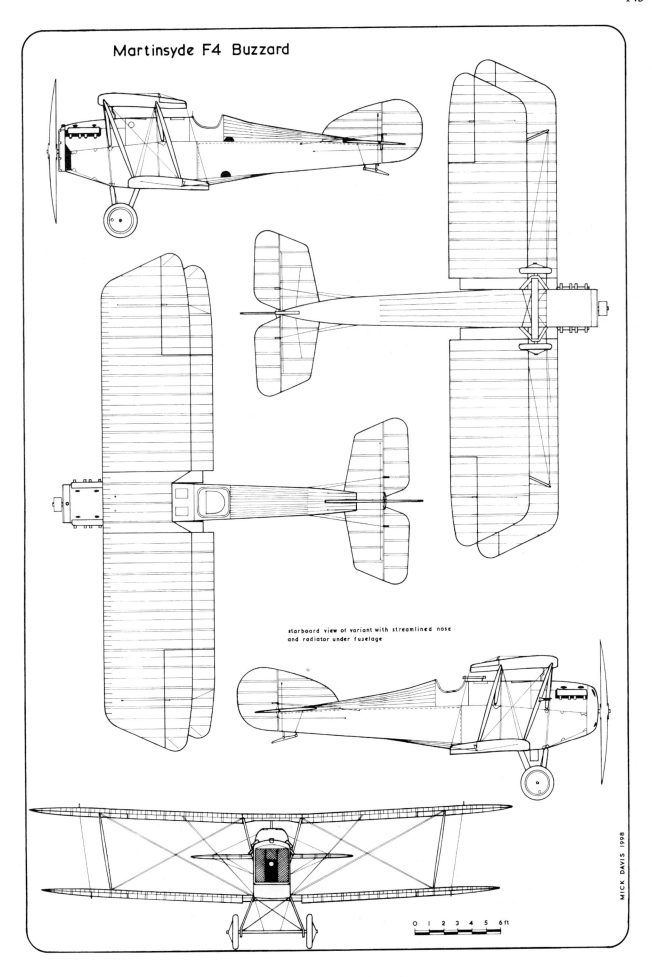

Martinsyde F4 Buzzard

starboard view of variant with streamlined nose
and radiator under fuselage

MICK DAVIS 1998

0 1 2 3 4 5 6ft

Martinsyde F.4 D4353 fitted with a Rolls-Royce Falcon engine and a four-bladed propeller. (J M Bruce/S Leslie Collection)

with the cooling system.

About May 1918, I had a straight-forward job to do in taking Martinsyde F.4 Scout with a 300-hp Hispano Suiza engine on an altitude test with full load of guns and ammunition. Ceiling, climb and speed test with pilot's weight made up to 180 lbs. At 31,000 feet, on aneroid (27,000 feet corrected to standard atmosphere) the water-cooled engine froze solid so I had to glide down. The curve of the climb would have continued to a genuine 31,000 feet if the coolant had functioned. I could see the Wash over one shoulder and dirty London with the misty Thames over the other, and if I had dropped like a stone, I could not say if it would have fallen on Ipswich, Stowmarket or Felixstowe. Open cockpit, three pairs of gloves, the silk ones electrically heated as was the waistcoat and boot feet. The speed was calibrated, 120 mph at 20,000 feet and 153½ mph at ground level.

During 1918, I crashed a Martinsyde F.4, later called the Buzzard, with a 300 hp Hispano-Suiza water-cooled motor. As with many crashes, I must confess it was due to carelessness. I was haring across the aerodrome 'full-out' - 'grass-cutting' - preparing to do some stunts. My speed was between 125-130 mph. The one almost fatal mistake was that I forgot that there was a gentle cross-slope in the airfield surface. One of my wheels touched the ground and I catapulted over and over several times, wrapping the wings round the fuselage. I quickly grasped the guns to steady myself. My nose went through the small windscreen and I got two beautiful black eyes and was slightly concussed, but was able to crawl out and walk away. Quite a few accidents happened in those days by what today would be called foolishness - in the interests of progress.

D4256 was flown to France on 17 July 1918, primarily it would seem for evaluation by the French authorities and Capt G McKerrow, an Experimental Officer from Orfordness, reported seeing it there on the 25th. On arrival at Villacoublay, its radiators were found to be leaking yet again. Also the good performance figures achieved in England could not be reproduced, probably due to the quality of fuel available in France. When it was subsequently flown with fuel supplied from Britain, small fragments of aluminium from a cracked piston and a piece of steel cage from a crankshaft roller bearing were found in the sump. Not surprisingly, all the pistons were found to be badly scored and the engine was sent back to Hispano-Suiza. The overhaul proved beneficial but the radiators continued to leak. Deemed irreparable, these were replaced by new radiators from England with a better finish.

Despite these difficulties, the French authorities expressed satisfaction with the aircraft's performance in the trials, which compared favourably with the similarly-powered Sopwith Dolphin, Nieuport 29 and Spad 21, all of which were being considered for the future equipment programme of the Aviation Militaire. Apparently the four French pilots involved in the trials reported favourably on the manoeuvrability and excellent view from the cockpit. Following a request from the French, the aircraft was returned to Martlesham on 6th August for confirmatory performance tests. No order from the French ensued but the particulars of the F.4 described as a Martinsyde C.1 powered by a Hispano 8Fb appeared in a list of French aircraft dated October 1918 supplied by the Section Technique de l'Aéronautique.

D4256 was returned to the works on 15th August. Martlesham were expecting D4262 in October for evaluation in mock combat tests but this aircraft was delayed by engine

Martinsyde F.4 Buzzard D4260 with a Fokker D.VII in the background. (Aeroplane Monthly)

problems and the tests were carried out instead by F.3 B1490 as described earlier. F.4 D4260 was eventually flown to Martlesham as a replacement on 12th October 1918.

Martinsyde had been reluctant to accept that the twin Gallay radiators were unsatisfactory, but eventually the company bowed to criticism and installed a single flat radiator with 7 mm water tubes, fitted with Chelsea-type radiator shutters. The original shutter installation consisted of three vertical banks covering the entire face of the engine except for the part under the airscrew hub. However, in practice the entire centre bank was sometimes omitted. This radiator was first used in August 1918 but the timing of its introduction on the production line remains obscure. Certainly D4301 had the new radiator but D4263 was still fitted with the Gallay type as late as January 1919.

The fuel system was also the subject of late changes. The original design used an air pressure feed system, which would have serious disadvantages in the event of battle damage. However, in late August, the authorities prevailed upon Martinsyde to install a positive feed system, first suggesting that Martinsyde incorporated the new M.I.D. self-sealing tanks and Vickers fuel pumps but three days later proposing that the Badin petrol system be adopted, incorporating a Weyman hand pump for start-up and emergency use. However the design of the aircraft did not permit the installation of the large gravity tank required by the latter system and another system was finally adopted. This utilised a Vickers wind pump with a Weyman hand pump as back-up. A small gravity tank was kept filled automatically and came into use when the forward speed was too slow for the wind-driven pump to be effective.

The operations of the Independent Force indicated a clear requirement for a long-range escort fighter but the forward programme for aircraft procurement announced in the spring of 1918 did not specifically include such a type. Perhaps seeing the Buzzard as a successor to the Elephant, the RAF requested on the 17th August that the oil tank capacity of the F.4 be increased from 4 to 7½ gallons, whilst allowing ½-gallon ullage space. The oil tank was also raised to allow gravity feed to the pump, to ensure that the pump was always primed. In a letter dated 27th August, Martinsyde was requested to fit tanks of this capacity to the 25th and subsequent aircraft off the production line. As an initial step, the Design Branch of the Technical Department requested that three F.4s (H6540 to H6542) be fitted with the tanks of increased capacity and they were notified by the manufacturer on 2nd October that the construction of the three tanks was proceeding and the first aircraft would be ready in about ten days.

The fuel capacity was also to be increased to a total of two 28-gallon tanks located in the fuselage, giving an endurance of 3½ hours. The construction of the tanks was changed form aluminium to steel because of the difficulty of repairing aluminium welds in the field. In the event, the Armistice reduced the urgency of the work and the modifications to H6540 were not completed until the early spring of 1919. The standard and long range versions were designated the Buzzard Mark I and Ia respectively. At least two long-range Buzzards were completed. The fuel system of the second (H6541) was being tested at Farnborough on 20th October 1919 and it was still there being tested in mid-December. Because the Hispano-Suiza engine tended to vibrate, the company refused a Ministry request to fit olives in all the joints of the oil and water pipes as it would make the joints too stiff and fractures might result.

Steps were taken before the war ended to increase the firepower of the aircraft. It was officially agreed on 25th September to increase the ammunition capacity to 770 rpg. It is not known whether this modification had been carried out before the end of the war, but it was likely to have been incorporated in D4260 which went to Martlesham on 12th February 1919. This aircraft was 100 lb heavier than D4256 and its performance was inferior as a result. It was also requested that the manufacturer should modify the chute for expended cartridge cases and links.

Unfortunately, the delivery of the Hispano-Suiza engines did not match the production schedule and the formation of No.95 Squadron and the re-equipment of three squadrons with F.4s was cancelled. It had been expected that deliveries of F.4s would have totalled 25 by 2nd November 1918 but only seven had been delivered and of these three had no engines. Although 39 Mayen-built engines had reached England by that time, there were another 44 airframes in store awaiting engines. It is believed that eventually all 156

Buzzard D4256 at Martlesham Heath. (IWM Q63808)

aircraft from the first batch and at least 174 from the second batch were completed by the parent company. All other production contracts were cancelled following the Armistice. Of the 330 or so produced, 276 were still on charge with the RAF on 31st December 1919, although few of these were operational.

Why the Sopwith Snipe, with a much inferior performance (see table below), was adopted by the RAF as its post-war fighter instead of the Buzzard is not clear. Several reasons have been put forward, none of which is entirely convincing. It is true that the Snipe was powered by a British rather than a foreign engine, the Bentley B.R.2, but the D.H.9A, which was also adopted by the RAF, also used an engine manufactured overseas, the American-built Liberty. In any case the Buzzard could easily have been re-engined with the Falcon Mark III as indeed several were. A more likely explanation was one of cost. The Snipe airframe cost £945.17s.0d and its engine £880, giving a total of £1,825.17s.0d. The Martinsyde F.4 airframe cost £1,142.2s.0d, to give a total with the Falcon engine of £2,352.2s.0d and at least £2,146 with the Hispano-Suiza.

Although the Armistice prevented the F.4 from being used during the war, four F.3s were allocated to Home Defence squadrons in 1918. Two were known to have been with No.39 Squadron at North Weald Bassett on 8th June 1918 and B1492 was at one time with No.141 Squadron at Biggin Hill. B1494 was also used on Home Defence duties.

Several Buzzards were also used for experimental work after the Armistice. Between July and October 1920, the first Buzzard Ia (H6540) was tested at the Isle of Grain with two Lewis guns to supplement the twin Vickers. The additional guns were partially let into the upper surface of the lower wing outside the airscrew arc and therefore could not be reloaded in flight.

Comparative performance figures of the F.4 Buzzard and Sopwith Snipe

Height (ft)	Speed (mph)		Time to height (min)		Rate of climb (ft/min)	
	F.4	Snipe	F.4	Snipe	F.4	Snipe
6500	-	-	4.7	5.2	1165	970
10000	-	121	8.1	9.4	920	710
13000	137	117	11.8	14.4	710	515
15000	132	113	15.0	18.8	570	390
16500	130	108	17.1	23.2	460	290
19500	124	-	26.0	-	250	-

The cockpit of a Buzzard during construction. (J M Bruce/S Leslie Collection)

The fin and runner, showing the tailplane control runs and the space under the fin to allow for tailplane adjustments.
(J M Bruce/S Leslie Collection)

Martinsyde F.4a H6541 at the 1921 RAF Pageant, one of three Buzzards fitted with long range fuel tanks.
(J M Bruce/S Leslie Collection)

In November 1920, H7781 was subjected to official trials. It is likely that this aircraft was the in the standard configuration of the long range type at higher greater gross weight than tested previously and the performance suffered as a result. The official report noted that

The performance obtained is much below the standard results obtained with this type of Scout in 1918 and 1919 although the engine from actual test is well up to its power. This difference can only be explained by the greater total weight of the aircraft in test and by variation in diameter and pitch of the propeller.

The Royal Aircraft Establishment also tested several Buzzards. D4263 arrived there from Brooklands on 6th January 1919 and this had been joined by D4264 by 25th April and D4287 by late October. One of its last recorded jobs was to test the AM Design Flowmeter Mark I in February 1922, involving flights of up to five hours duration.

A list of aircraft available for disposal on 21st May 1919, drawn up on behalf of General J B Seely of the Air Ministry, included 50 Martinsyde F.4s (called F.3s) without engines.

United States Government Interest in the F.3 and F.4

During the first three years of the First World War, the United States Government pursued a policy of not getting involved. The direction of military policy therefore was towards defending the country and its possessions against attack, a commitment which required few of the types of aircraft engaged in the war in Europe. Furthermore such a neutralist stance did not encourage its future allies to divulge details of their experience in designing aircraft to meet the demands of the conflict. This, coupled with a lack of urgency on the part of the Government and the resultant lack of funding for development and procurement, meant that the United States Army was ill-prepared to fight an aerial war in Europe when it finally entered the fray on 6th April 1917.

Prior to entering the war, the Army's experience with scouting or fighter aircraft was to have ordered 13 unarmed aircraft from four manufacturers and another 12 armed with twin Lewis guns. Of these, only one, an unarmed Sturtevant 8, had been completed up to the time of entering the war and this crashed before delivery. Otherwise, out of the total, only five machines of Curtiss manufacture were delivered by the war's end and all were obsolete compared with the types in use in France and of no interest to the Service. Thus on entering the war, there were no suitable airframes or engines of American manufacture nor equipment such as interrupter gear for synchronising machine guns.

Although the country was to be at war for 19 months, there was much less time to equip the American Expeditionary Force (AEF). It was two months before the US even agreed to to furnish a combat air force in Europe. A further two months elapsed before the Bolling Aeronautical Mission, sent to Europe to choose suitable French or British designs for manufacture in the US, made their selection.

Although two SPAD types were finally chosen for production in the US, an interest was also shown in several British types. At a meeting on 5th September 1917, the Aircraft Board resolved to order D.H.9s, Martinsydes, Bristol Fighters and Bristol Scouts. The same meeting approved that orders be placed at once with the Curtiss company and with Dayton-Wright for 1,500 Martinsydes each. In the event, only the order for 1,500 from Dayton-

Martinsyde F.4 fitted with the experimental four-gun installation. (J M Bruce/S Leslie Collection)

Wright was placed. The Martinsyde in question was the F.3 which was only available in prototype form.

On 16th September, Col Bolling in Cable No.163-S sent preliminary performance figures to the US on the Martinsyde with the "290-hp Rolls-Royce engine" and added that drawings were not yet available. Obviously drawings were needed to get the aircraft in production and on 24th September, Cable No. 209-R was sent to the AEF requesting that a man be sent urgently to Martinsyde to get them.

The order with Dayton-Wright for 1,500 Martinsydes was dated 8th October 1917 and the fighter was to be redesigned for the 8-cylinder Liberty engine of about 290-hp. The Liberty engine was specified because it had become evident that it would be impossible to build sufficient quantities of the Rolls-Royce engines in the US to support such a huge programme. Cable No.20 was sent early October to the AEF notifying them of this decision. On 15th October, Col Gorrell wrote a memo to Col Bolling while both men were in France stating that it would be impossible to get the Martinsyde with the Liberty engine in production in the US because the British had said that it is "purely an experimental machine, and that its successful tests are due entirely to the Rolls-Royce engine". He also stated that he had been informed by the British that the machine was not yet ready for production in England in its present form. This statement was probably made because of the shortage of Rolls-Royce engines which led to the F.3 being redesigned as the F.4 to take the 300-hp Hispano-Suiza engine. As a result the order with Dayton-Wright was cancelled and all plans to produce the Martinsyde F.3 in the US were dropped.

Interest was later transferred to the Martinsyde F.4. On 14th April 1918, Cable No. 916-S from the AEF to the US said that several sample fighters were to be sent to America, including the Martinsyde and mentioned the engine to be the Rolls-Royce 275-hp Falcon. On 13th June, the British Embassy in Washington requested information on five aircraft types, including the Martinsyde F.4 with the Hispano-Suiza engine, and the details for the Martinsyde were sent two weeks later. On 5th August 1918, the head of the Bureau of Aircraft Production wrote a memo to the Department of Military Aeronautics (the operational side of the US Air Service) to the effect that a sample Martinsyde F.4 would be shipped to the US from Britain that month with three more to follow. Also the Lockhart mission, which had been sent to Europe in the summer of 1918 to select planes for US production in 1919, sent a number of aircraft specifications to the US, including those for the Martinsyde F.4. However no airframes were ever sent and nothing further materialised.

Detail of the Lewis gun fixture on the experimental four-gun installation. (J M Bruce/S Leslie Collection)

In the event the intended production of foreign types in the US was unsuccessful. The SPAD production programme failed to materialise and the only British types produced in the US were a single S.E.5 with a 180-hp Hispano-Suiza engine intended as a trainer and 27 O-1 aircraft built by Curtiss, based on the Bristol Fighter and fitted with the Liberty 12 engine. The British were still trying to sell up to 500 machines to the US late in 1919, but were promoting the Snipe in preference to other machines.

Other Designs Manufactured by Martinsyde

The Royal Aircraft Factory, based at Farnborough, lacked the manufacturing capacity to produce sufficient of its designs to meet the demands of the RFC. Furthermore there was always pressure on the Government to give consideration to private companies at the expense of this Government enterprise. The Martinsyde Company had gained a reputation for its workmanship and it came as no surprise that it should be one of several manufacturers awarded contracts to manufacture aircraft designed by the Factory. This production was carried out by Martinsyde while it was also manufacturing its own designs.

Royal Aircraft Factory B.E.2c

In 1911, although the Army Aircraft Factory at Farnborough, the forerunner of the Royal Aircraft Factory, was not officially allowed to design or build aircraft, a Voisin was 'reconstructed' there into a wholly new aircraft by Geoffrey de Havilland and designated the Blériot Experimental No.1 or B.E.1. The B.E.2, a very similar aircraft but powered by a Renault engine instead of a Wolseley, appeared in February 1912. Although it did not actually win, it clearly performed better than the other aircraft at the Military Aeroplane Competition at Larkhill in the following August. Thereby finding favour with the authorities, it became the progenitor of a series of aircraft, principally the B.E.2c, 2d and 2e, which gave sterling service during the war. Martin and Handasyde built only twelve, out of over eleven hundred B.E.2cs delivered. These were built for the RNAS under Contract No.C.P.58232/14 and were given serials in the range 988-999. They mainly served with home defence squadrons and training establishments.

A Royal Aircraft Factory B.E.2c manufactured by Martinsyde. 992 was delivered to RNAS Great Yarmouth on 20th July 1915 and saw service from Great Yarmouth and its auxiliary airfields at Bacton and Holt. It went to Eastbourne Naval Flying School on 8th April 1916 and moved on to Eastchurch on 14th October. On 30th March 1917 it went to Cranwell where it was deleted on 17 January 1918. (J M Bruce/S Leslie Collection)

Royal Aircraft Factory S.E.5a

The S.E.5, along with the Sopwith Camel, was designed to meet a requirement drawn up during the latter half of 1916 for a faster and more manoeuvrable single-seater fighter. It was a completely new design and the first two batches, fitted with the 150-hp Hispano-Suiza engine, were manufactured at Farnborough. Some of the second batch were fitted with the 200 hp version of this engine and this variant, when incorporating other detailed modifications, was designated the S.E.5a. The manufacture of the first batch of 200 of the new version was awarded to Martinsyde under Contract Number 87/A/1616 dated 1st February 1917. These were given serial numbers in the range B1 to B200 and most were manufactured at Brooklands and delivered to No.10 Aircraft Acceptance Park there between July 1917 and February 1918. Many further contracts were awarded to other manufacturers, including Vickers at Weybridge and A.N.E.C. at Addlestone.

Three further follow on batches of 100 each, with serial numbers in the range D3911 to D4010, E3154 to E3253 and F5249 to F5348, were awarded to Martinsyde under Contract

Nos. 35A/222/C.137, 35A/222/C.137 and 35a/1265/C.1164 respectively. The manufacture of the batch with D serials was completed by May 1918 and delivered to No.10 AAP by the beginning of October 1918. According to Ministry of Munitions records, the last two batches were completed by August 1918 and March 1919 respectively. However information as to the fate of the last batches is scant and most must have gone directly into store. One or two saw combat, several were the subject of Imperial Gifts to Australia and Canada and some were given civil registrations in Britain. A final contract for 100 machines, Contract No. 35a/1651/C.1325, was cancelled. All surplus stock eventually went to the Aircraft Disposal Company.

The detailed history of both these types of machine is outside the scope of this book. Anyone wanting more information should consult *British Aeroplanes, 1914-1918* by J M Bruce, published by Putnam in 1957 and *The S.E.5 File* by Ray Sturtivant and Gordon Page, published by Air-Britain in 1996.

Royal Aircraft Factory S.E.5a from the Martinsyde Contract 87/A/1616. It was one of several that replaced Bristol Fighters with No.111 Squadron in Palestine during December 1917. The Bristol Fighters were in turn were passed on to No.1 Squadron AFC to work alongside Martinsyde G.102s. (M O'Connor)

Rear fuselage of F.4 showing tailskid, bungee rubber shock absorber and the chain drive to the rudder post.
(J M Bruce/S Leslie Collection)

Left: Details of the front fuselage showing the engine installation, main fuel tank, gun mountings, undercarriage and centre section with wing fittings of the F.4.
(J M Bruce/S Leslie Collection)

Fuselage showing wire-braced longerons and spacers, plywood covering and strengthening fishplates.
(J M Bruce/S Leslie Collection)

K152 sporting its racing number 10 in the 1919 Aerial Derby at Hendon in which it came second piloted by R H Nisbet. (P Jarrett Collection)

CHAPTER 6 - POSTWAR MARTINSYDE AIRCRAFT

Martinsyde F.4, F.4A, F.5 and F.6

Following the Armistice, Martinsyde for a time continued to manufacture F.4s for the RAF, producing more than 300. Most of these went directly into store. Like other British manufacturers, the Company made every effort to adapt its wartime expertise to the civilian market. In the times of financial stringency which followed the end of the War, the F.4 was too highly-powered and expensive to gain wide acceptance as a civil sporting or touring aircraft. However, the Buzzard's high performance held promise of success in competitive flying, with the prospect of bringing the product to the attention of potential customers and the public at large.

With this in view, an F.4 was stripped of all its military equipment, fitted with a 275-hp Rolls-Royce Falcon III engine without radiator shutters and given the civil registration K-152. As recounted below, it was entered into the 1919 Aerial Derby with Lt R H Nisbet as pilot and other F.4s were entered into subsequent races during the 1920s. Four standard F.4 fighters, G-EANM, G-EAUX, G-EAYK and G-EAYP received temporary civil registrations for overseas demonstrations. One of these, G-EANM, was flown to Spain and Portugal by Raynham with a view to interesting the military there.

The Martinsyde F.4A was an adaptation of the F.4 single-seat fighter intended as a civil two-seat touring machine, express mail carrier or high-speed trainer, with the passenger seated in front of the pilot. It could be fitted with either a wheeled or float undercarriage. It was of standard Martinsyde construction for the period, the fuselage being made of spruce with the front portion ply-covered and joints reinforced with external duralumin fishplates. The wings had fabric-wrapped laminated spruce spars with strap-type interplane fittings. The space between the front spar and the leading edge was covered with thin three-ply strip. The twin floats, when fitted, consisted of single-step pontoons, with sewn 'Consuta' plywood skins built on full-length longerons.

Three of these machines were built. One registered G-EAPP was flown by Sqn Ldr T O'Brien in the 1920 Aerial Derby. Its performance was essentially the same as the F.4 but its range was marginally reduced if dual controls were fitted. An example was exhibited at the 1920 Olympia Show but no orders materialised. Later two military versions of the F.4A were built. With these, the pilot sat in front of the observer. One version had single-bay wings and the other two-bay wings of increased span with increased bracing and provision for a Lewis gun on a Scarff ring mounting for the observer. A small number of these machines were supplied to Spain.

It is doubtful whether the F.5 ever existed, unless the designation should have applied to all demilitarised F.4s (such as K-152). The designation appeared in the 1920-21 Aircraft Standard Catalogue in the British Exporter Series, which contained many factual errors, and was described as an unarmed sporting single-seater.

The F.6, also dubbed the 'Tinsyde', was contemporary with the F.4A and was produced as as a two-seat passenger or reconnaissance version. It was designed to be fitted with either a 275-hp Rolls-Royce Falcon or a 300-hp Hispano-Suiza. It was an extensively redesigned F.4 with a short-span centre section and shorter wings with smaller ailerons. The upper wings were built without dihedral. The cabane struts

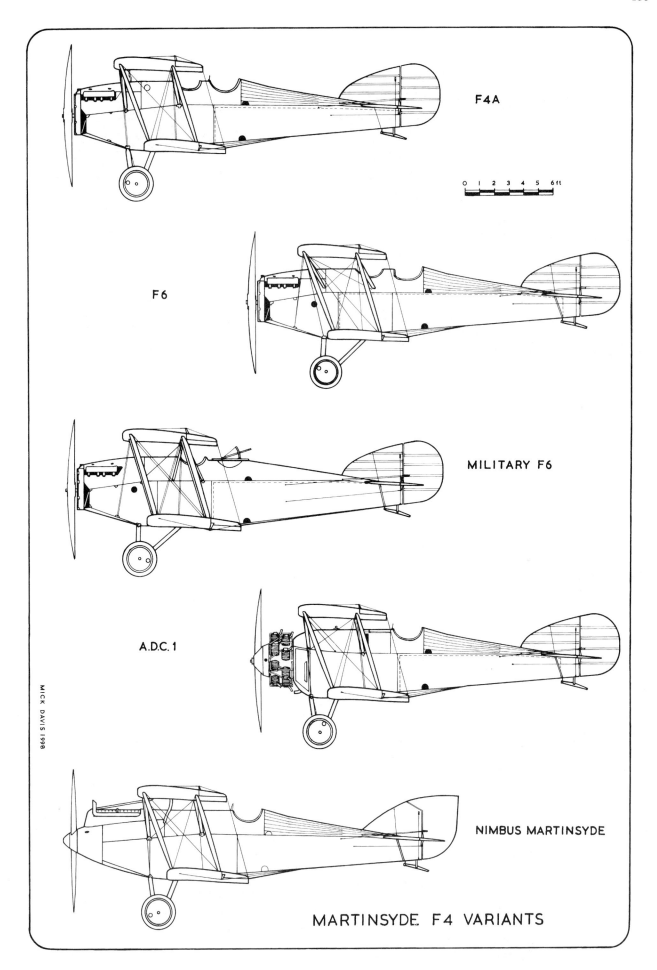

F4A

0 1 2 3 4 5 6 ft

F6

MILITARY F6

A.D.C. 1

NIMBUS MARTINSYDE

MICK DAVIS 1998

MARTINSYDE F4 VARIANTS

K152, the first civil F.4, was fitted with a Rolls-Royce Falcon III engine. (J M Bruce/S Leslie Collection)

were revised to have similar stagger to the interplane struts and to be vertical as viewed from the front. The undercarriage struts were also revised with vertical forward struts and the rear struts inclined rearwards at 15°. A twin-float seaplane version was advertised but it is doubtful whether it was ever built or flown. Only three F.6s found their way onto the British civil register, G-EAPI, G-EATQ and G-EBDK. G-EAPI, fitted with a Hispano-Suiza, took part in the 1920 Aerial Derby before going to Canada where it was joined by a second of the type, probably G-EATQ.

G-EBDK, bought by Fred Raynham for £15, was a low-powered version, fitted with a 200-hp Wolseley Viper. He flew it in the 1922 and 1923 Kings Cup Air Races as a two-seater. By 1922, Raynham himself had painted it bright yellow with black trimming on the edges of the wings and fuselage, which attracted a great deal of adverse criticism and the appropriate nickname - "Mustardsyde". Mr. L C G M (Gerald) Le Champion of Brooklands bought it from Raynham in 1924 and sold it on to Leslie Hamilton at Croydon in 1925, who operated it as an air taxi. It was then sold it to Major J C Savage at Hendon in 1927. This aircraft was dismantled in Dudley Watt's shed at Brooklands in April 1930 and lay there for several years.

Air Race Entrants

Martinsyde F.4 K-152 was entered into the 1919 Aerial Derby. This was the fourth such event and, being the first following the War, was billed as the Victory Derby. It was held on 21st June over a course of 189 miles, made up of two laps of a circuit from Hendon to Kempton Park, Epsom, West Thurrock, Epping, Hertford and Epping again before

returning to Hendon. There were thirteen starters from sixteen entries, four of which did not complete the course. The Martinsyde Company test pilot, R H Nisbet, came second, to Capt G W Gathergood in a Airco D.H.4R, in 1 hour 27 minutes 42 seconds at an average speed of 129.34 mph, winning the Shell Trophy and £100 in the process.

Martinsyde F.4 G-EAXB, piloted by Major E L Foot, was entered into the Sixth Aerial Derby, held at Hendon on 16th July 1921 but was unplaced, the race being won by J H James in the Gloucestershire Mars I powered by a 450-hp Lion II at an average speed of 163.34 mph.

The Club Handicap at the Easter Monday meeting at Croydon on 17th April 1922 attracted thirteen diverse entries, including two Martinsyde F.4s, piloted by Ft Lt W H Longton and Ft Lt H O Long. Neither of the Martinsydes were placed, the race being won by Capt R H Stocken in a D.H.9A. A Martinsyde F.4, piloted by Major E L Foot, was again unsuccessful in the First Sprint Handicap over eight miles held at the Whitsuntide Races at Waddon, Croydon, on 3rd June 1922, this being won by Cobham in a Puma-powered D.H.9B. A Martinsyde Buzzard was entered into the Handicap Race at the Royal Air Force Pageant held at Martlesham Heath on 24th June 1922, but was unplaced, the race being won by an Avro Aldershot (J6852) piloted by F/O C E Horrox. Raynham flew his own Martinsyde F.6 G-EBDK in the seventh Aerial Derby held at Waddon and came third at an average speed of 107.85 mph, the winner again being J H James in the Mars I in the fastest time at 177.85 mph. Capt R H Stocken flew F.4 G-EATD entered by ADC but was forced to retire.

The year 1922 was also the first occasion in which the King's Cup Race was held. This was a handicap race starting

F.4 G-EAXB, formerly D4279, crashed at Croydon on 5th May 1922. (J M Bruce/S Leslie Collection)

at 9 am on 8th September from Croydon. On the first day, the entrants flew to Renfrew, Glasgow, via Birmingham and Newcastle and after resting overnight flew back to Croydon via Manchester and Bristol, a distance of some 810 miles. The only Martinsyde entrant of 21 starters was Raynham in his F.6, G-EBDK. Raynham was eleventh on handicap, being allowed 117 minutes 7 seconds compared with the scratch machine, an A.W. Siskin flown by F T Courtney. Starting eleventh, he had already improved six places by Birmingham and was in first place by Newcastle but had been overhauled by F L Barnard in a D.H.4A by Glasgow. Although nearly caught on the return journey by A J Cobham in a D.H.9B, he held on to retain second place at the finish with a total flying time of 7 hours 43 minutes 43 seconds.

Raynham also entered his machine in the second King's Cup race held on 13-14th June 1923, which this time started at Hendon. He had Thomas, a correspondent of *The Motor* with him as a passenger. He made an emergency landing at Leeds on the second leg between Birmingham and Newcastle as one of his main lift wires broke. He landed very carefully 'as he thought that lift wires are rather necessary'. The race was won by Capt F T Courtney in a A.W. Siskin II, with A J Cobham second in a D.H.9 and Capt H S Broad third in a D.H.9C. Raynham also entered G-EBDK in the Aerial Derby starting at Croydon over the August Bank Holiday. Starting sixth on handicap, he finished fourth on handicap and fourth overall.

Raynham's F.6, now owned by Le Champion, was repainted in a yellow colour and, flown by J R King, was also unplaced in the third King's Cup starting at Martlesham Heath on 12th August 1924, which was won by Alan Cobham in a D.H.50. On the August Bank Holiday Monday of 1925,

the same machine was entered by Leslie Hamilton into the International Handicap at the Lympne Air Meeting but performed so badly that it flew the last lap all alone as the rest of the machines had already landed. Luckily Raynham did not witness this unfortunate episode as he was preparing to leave to join the Aerial Survey Company to survey Sarawak and North Borneo. Raynham's old F.6, now owned by Hamilton, was entered in the various handicap races making up the Royal Aero Club's August Meeting, held from 1st to 3rd August 1925, but no success resulted, the handicappers apparently favouring the low-powered entrants.

The Raymor and the Transatlantic Flight Attempt

It was as long ago as 1st April 1913 that Lord Northcliffe, editor of the *Daily Mail*, first announced his offer of £10,000 to the first person or persons to fly across the Atlantic Ocean non-stop. However the War intervened and it was not until four months before the war ended, on 17th July 1918 that the *Daily Mail* renewed the offer for a flight from any point in the USA, Canada or Newfoundland to any point in the United Kingdom within a 72-hour period. If a seaplane was entered, it would be allowed to alight on the sea and still be eligible for the prize if it took off and completed the flight without outside aid. The offer was considered premature and both the Air Council and the Royal Aero Club of Great Britain, which would regulate the conditions for the flights, disallowed any flights until there was peace. The prize was subsequently boosted by offers of £1,000 from a businessman, Lawrence Phillips, and £2,000 from the Ardath Tobacco Company.

As has been recounted in an earlier chapter, Martinsyde were building an aircraft to make an attempt when the War

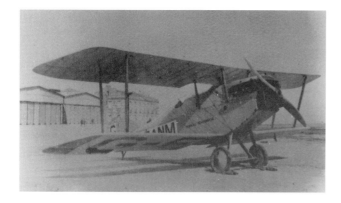

Civil F.4, G-EANM (ex-H7692), which was delivered to the Portuguese Air Force in January 1923.
(The A J Jackson Collection)

F.4 G-EATD, formerly D4267, was registered to Handley Page at Cricklewood and was grounded after the 1922 Aerial Derby. (J M Bruce/S Leslie Collection)

began. When peace returned, Martin and Handasyde revived their interest but now there was considerable competition in the offing. Because of the prevailing winds, it was easier to fly eastwards from America to Britain and St John's in Newfoundland, being the most easterly point of the North American continent, was the logical place from which to make the attempt. Now that there were serious preparations being made, the Air Ministry arranged with the US and Canadian authorities to make meteorological information available and the Marconi Company was asked to co-operate by collecting and transmitting all relevant information from land stations and ships. The Admiralty asked all shipping to look out for aircraft attempting the crossing and render all help possible.

Several manufacturers were secretly in the process of building special machines or modifying production models for the attempt. The Martinsyde machine bore a strong resemblance to the F.4 Buzzard but was larger, with a two-bay wing with a span of 43 feet 4 inches compared with 32 feet 9 inches and a length of 27 feet 5½ inches compared with 25 feet 6 inches. It was powered by a very reliable Rolls-Royce Falcon III engine of 275 hp. The choice of a single engine rather than two caused considerable controversy, two engines being considered to be safer by some. However Handasyde argued that in any case a twin-engined aircraft, being larger, could not maintain height should one engine fail.

The pilot was seated behind the navigator, with the large fuel tanks situated between the engine and the front seat. The fuel capacity gave the aircraft an endurance of about 27 hours at a cruising speed of 110-117 mph. The fuselage was painted bright red, so that it was more readily visible should it be forced down in the sea; the rest of the machine, being clear-doped, had a yellowish tinge. However, no special equipment was fitted for overwater operation, Raynham the chosen pilot being quoted as saying that he intended "to cross the Atlantic not fall into it". The navigator, Capt C W F Morgan, (known as Fairfax or just 'Fax'), was equally straightforward -

I'm afraid life-saving gadgets are of little use. For myself, I have decided that I may as well take one deep breath if we strike the sea. We will be a very small speck in a big ocean out there.

The aircraft was christened *Raymor* after Raynham and Morgan. Raynham was, of course, the principal test pilot for Martinsydes during the war and Morgan, formerly of the RAF and the RNAS, was himself an accomplished pilot and experienced in navigation and wireless. Despite having lost a

leg, Morgan was of a cheery disposition and was not beyond playing practical jokes and making fun.

The Sopwith company were also building an aircraft, called the *Atlantic*, for the event and both Sopwith and Martinsyde were well aware of the other company's intentions as Hawker and Raynham, the pilots chosen by their respective companies, were close friends. Two other contestants remained from the ten original entries, Capt John Alcock and Lt Arthur Whitten-Brown in a Vickers Vimy and Admiral Sir Mark Kerr, Major Herbert Brackley and Major Gran in the Handley Page *Atlantic*.

Martinsyde was the only entrant that considered it worthwhile to reconnoitre Newfoundland beforehand for a suitable landing ground. The Company sent Morgan across the Atlantic in January 1919. He arrived in St John's in freezing conditions, with the harbour blocked with ice and the ground covered under several feet of snow. He had contracted influenza on the voyage and had to be carried ashore on a stretcher. When he had recovered, Morgan quickly discovered that there was no ground entirely suitable as an airfield within sixty miles of the capital. After probing the snow with a long pole he finally chose a field at Quidi Vidi. The field was a narrow strip of ground near a lake. Between the strip and the sea in the direction of take-off was a line of cliffs about 300 feet high with intervening streams, scrub-trees and rocks. He was warned that the field could become swampy with the spring thaw but nevertheless it was the best that he could find.

Towards the end of March 1919, tests on the Raymor were finally concluded at Brooklands with a ten-hour flight. This was followed by a simulated flight during which the aircraft was secured to the ground in a large hangar with Raynham and Morgan occupying their seats in full flying gear and provided with just the food and drink that they would carry with them. The petrol and oil tanks were filled to capacity and the engine was run at continuous full power until the fuel ran out after about twenty-four hours. The engine was stripped and found to be in perfect working order.

The Sopwith aircraft was the first to be shipped and the Martinsyde followed on board the SS *Sachem*, arriving at St. John's on 11th April. Morgan paid particular attention to part of the cargo consisting of a large crate marked 'Martinsyde Transatlantic Flight. Aircraft Spares. Handle With Care'. However the crate contained not spares but two dozen bottles each of brandy, gin, rum, whisky, sherry and port. During his earlier trip, Morgan had found that alcohol was totally prohibited in the Dominion, and he made sure that he would

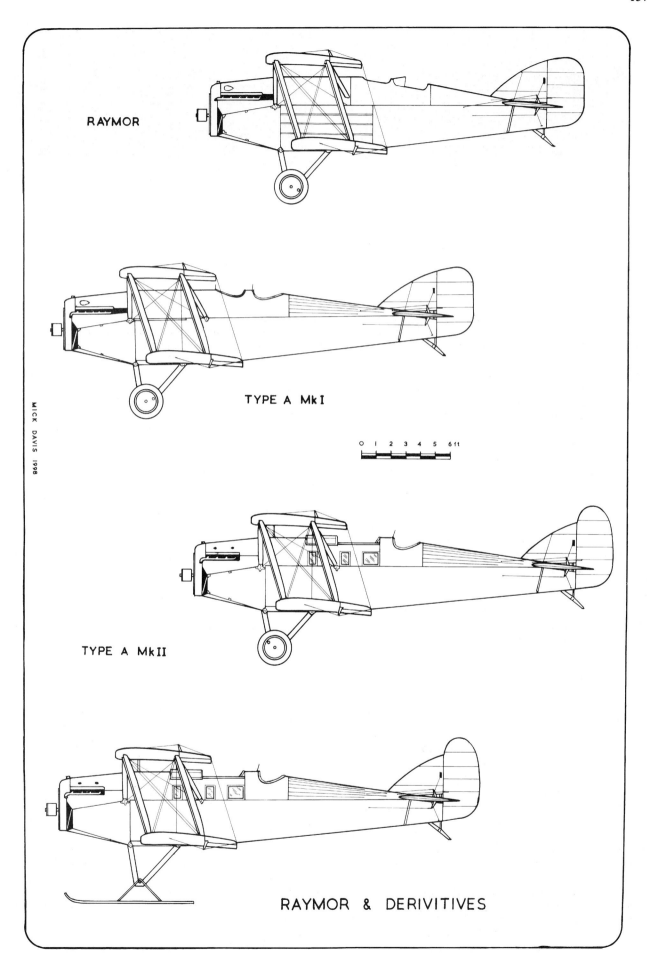

RAYMOR

TYPE A MkI

0 1 2 3 4 5 6ft

TYPE A MkII

MICK DAVIS 1998

RAYMOR & DERIVITIVES

The Raymor transatlantic contender under construction at Brooklands. (The A J Jackson Collection)

not suffer as a consequence! The Martinsyde crew first established a base at Pleasantville, a suburb of St. John's, and quickly re-erected the aircraft in a hangar in the field selected by Morgan at Quidi Vidi. The fliers from all the teams, when they arrived, booked in at the Cochrane Hotel, a large four-storey building on the side of the hill leading down to the harbour. Although dubbed "The Cockroach" by Hawker, it in fact offered an excellent standard of comfort with clean bedrooms, a well-appointed dining room and a billiard room where the fliers could relax after their day's work.

On the 15th, the weather deteriorated and a gale blew up. Raynham and Morgan had to leave their warm beds and rush to secure their hangar from destruction. On the following day, a short lull in the storm enabled them to make their first test flight. The Raymor was wheeled across the road from its tented hangar to the grass strip. Raynham and Morgan, wearing leopard-skin hats in addition to the more conventional flying suits and fleece-lined boots, climbed aboard and took off. They flew over the town, out through the Narrows, up the coast to the village of Torbay and returned to make a perfect landing, flying altogether for about three hours. It was deceptively easy when not carrying the full load of fuel!

However the weather remained totally unsuitable for making the Transatlantic attempt for a month. Even when the weather over the Atlantic moderated, sodden ground, local fog and adverse winds made an attempt inadvisable if not impossible. Hawker and Raynham spent much time keeping an eye on each other's preparations. As days stretched into weeks, they came to an understanding that each would advise

the other of any impending departure. On Sunday 18th May, Lt Clements, the weather expert sent by the Air Ministry, gave the news that the storms were abating. It was just past the full moon so at last there was a chance. The next few hours confirmed that the conditions were improving. It was Harry Hawker, and his navigator, Lt Cdr Kenneth Mackenzie-Grieve RN, in the Sopwith *Atlantic* who made the first attempt. They took off at 3.40 pm on that day from their base, the Mount Pearl Flying Field at St John's.

On that day, the direction of the wind was such that Raynham would have to take-off cross-wind, making the take-off marginal with such a heavy weight of fuel on board. He waited another hour hoping for a shift in the wind, which sometimes happens late in the afternoon, but felt unable to wait any longer. The engine was running smoothly as Raynham taxied out in front of an expectant crowd. As the aircraft accelerated it hopped a couple of feet in the air two or three times as it passed over bumps but it never gained flying speed before the undercarriage buckled under the strain. The aircraft ran forward a few yards, ran into a soft spot and tipped forward. The fuel tanks burst and the machine, crew and the surrounding ground were soaked in petrol, but luckily no fire resulted.

Raynham was struck by the control column in the abdomen and cut his eye. Morgan's cork leg got jammed and the other one was severely bruised, his left eye was cut and he had a long gash down one cheek. Neither of them moved for several minutes, then Raynham managed to extract himself and Morgan was helped out. Raynham recovered his composure sufficiently to inspect the aircraft and arrange for

The Raymor at Brooklands. (J M Bruce/S Leslie Collection)

it to be returned to its hangar, then he washed his face and went back to the Cochrane for supper. Capt John Alcock and Lt Arthur Whitten-Brown, the crew of the Vickers Vimy, on returning to the hotel after searching all day for a take-off field for their aircraft, found Raynham remarkably cheerful despite bandages and plaster, busy planning the repair of the Raymor for another attempt.

Morgan was however in shock. He was put in a car and taken to the home of a friend, where he was given a careful examination. Four stitches were put in his left cheek and two over the eye. His left shoulder and leg were badly bruised. He was in intense pain and given morphine. He had become blind in one eye, which the doctors believed was due to the bruising. What the doctors did not know was that he had a small piece of shrapnel enter the eye during the war and specialists in England had been afraid to remove it in case he lost its sight in the process. He was still blind in that eye a few days later and what is more another examination found a sliver of glass from the compass embedded in his skull. It was decided that Morgan should not be allowed to fly ever again and arrangements were made to sent him home on the next available vessel, the *Corsican*, which left St. John's on 24th May.

Before he left, Morgan wrote a letter which was published in the *Evening Telegraph*:

I take this opportunity of saying farewell to my friends in Newfoundland. Unfortunately, it has not turned out the way of leaving I prayed for, namely, waving to you 'au revoir' as we sailed over the hills on the long trip east.

It is said that a sailor can never leave the sea, and the

man who said it was fairly right, and the good old sea will take me away.

It is now almost four months since I came to St. John's. Many wonderful things have happened during that time. Newfoundland and St. John's have become centres of attraction.

Although your country is far, far from being an ideal place for flying, no better place in the world could have been chosen for the kindness given to an airman. It was even said in Halifax papers some time ago that an Atlantic flight wouldn't take place for a few days since the airman had several social engagements. If that was true, who knows. But it is true that none of us airmen was ever in want of hospitality.

Yet it was a very big strain, always thinking of what the weather would be, and with all the disappointments. Perhaps at some times we may have answered abruptly, but I think most people of average intelligence would understand.

The doctors have rung the death knell on my ever flying again, but the Raymor will fly again, and a better man than I am. You will be blessed by seeing her rise again. My heart and thoughts will always be with her, and perhaps I shall have but the greater pleasure of seeing her land safely in England - the air conqueror of the Atlantic.

Meanwhile there had been no news of Hawker and Grieve in the Sopwith and they were presumed lost at sea. However on 25th May a small Danish steamer, the *Mary*, hove-to off the Butt of Lewis and signalled with flags to the Lloyds station that she had these two airmen on board, having rescued them from the sea some 700 miles off the coast of

View of the Martinsyde hangar at Quidi Vidi. (National Aviation Museum of Canada)

The Raymor attracting a great deal of attention before its Transatlantic attempt. (National Aviation Museum of Canada)

The Raymor at Quidi Vidi prior to the Transatlantic attempt. (D Thompson)

The Raymor outside its tent hangar at Quidi Vidi prior to the Transatlantic attempt. (D Thompson)

The Raymor about to take off on its ill-fated attempt to cross the Atlantic. (National Aviation Museum of Canada)

Raynham descending from the Raymor a few minutes after the crash. (Philip Jarrett)

The Raymor after its crash on its first attempt. (National Aviation Museum of Canada)

The rebuilt Raymor renamed 'Chimera' in its hangar at Quidi Vidi. (D Thompson)

The Martinsyde Semiquaver G-EAPX.
(The E A Harlin Collection)

Ireland a week earlier. The Vickers Vimy arrived on a day of driving rain on the 26th May and on 9th June the Vimy undertook a satisfactory test flight of about 40 minutes.

In the crash, the Martinsyde's fuselage behind the pilot's seat had been undamaged but the engine had to be replaced along with the undercarriage. It was estimated that repairs would take a further ten days. Morgan's replacement as navigator was Lt C H Biddlescombe, who arrived in Newfoundland on 14th June. He was a qualified master mariner and also a pilot so was an excellent choice. On the day that he arrived, Alcock and Brown took off in the Vimy at 4.28 pm GMT (12.58 local time) and sixteen hours twelve minutes later landed at Clifden in Ireland, a distance of 1,800 miles, thereby becoming the first to fly the Atlantic non-stop.

Following the successful flight of the Vimy, press interest in the aftermath declined and it is difficult to fill in any details of subsequent events. Although the prize had already been won, it was decide to continue with the preparations with the Martinsyde in an attempt to better the time. As the name *Raymor* was no longer appropriate, the aircraft was renamed the *Chimera*. Repairs were completed in a garage on the outskirts of St.John's. Trial flights were made on 4th and 14th July and Raynham and Biddlescombe began the second attempt on the 17th at 3.15 pm. The plane managed to struggle into the air after about 300 yards. Before it had reached a safe altitude, it was caught by a side gust of wind and a wing dipped and touched the ground. Although Raynham straightened the aircraft, it hit the ground on an even keel and the undercarriage, propeller, lower wing and part of the fuselage were badly damaged. The crew escaped without serious injury but this time the aircraft was damaged beyond repair. The remains of the aircraft were packed up and sent back to Woking aboard the SS *Grampian*.

Some twenty or thirty items of mail with special postmarks were aboard the *Raymor* on its first flight and about twenty-five additional envelopes were added for the second flight. Raynham took this mail back with him to London by sea, flung it into a corner when he reached home and forgot to hand it in until reminded early in the following year.

Martinsyde Semiquaver

A few months after the Transatlantic attempt, Handasyde designed a new racer, very much like a scaled-down F.4 in appearance. After the 1919 Aerial Derby, Handasyde was heard to remark that the F.4 "was no machine for racing - it was too big to be fast". With this reservation in mind, he fabricated a racing machine by modifying an existing fuselage

and fitting new wings. It resulted in an extremely strong aircraft, powered by the 300-hp Hispano-Suiza engine fitted with a frontal radiator and driving a two-bladed propeller. The fuel tank was placed aft of the engine at the point of the centre of gravity.

The single-bay wings were built up on spars formed of a laminate of a thin centre layer and thicker front and back layers spindled out to form an I-section. The interplane struts rested on duralumin supports to prevent deformation of the spars. The streamlined bracing wires and interplane struts were attached by means of metal straps wrapped round the spars. The fuselage completely filled the gap between the mainplanes with upper wing was directly attached to a hump in the fuselage, eliminating the need for cabane struts. The lower wings were of marginally less span and chord than the upper. The undercarriage was of the normal V-type, with an undivided axle and struts made of oval tube. The aircraft was painted red, with a black registration G-EAPX on a white rectangular background painted on the fuselage sides aft of the cockpit.

The British Record

Fred Raynham flew the brand new racer at Martlesham Heath on 21st March 1920 to an official British Speed Record of 161.434 mph (259.75 km/h) over four measured one-kilometer passes. This attempt was still 13 mph short of the world record and this British record was broken within three months by Folland's L.S.3 Goshawk racer.

The 1920 Aerial Derby

Raynham entered the Semiquaver into the 1920 Aerial Derby, which took place on 24th July. It was one of sixteen entrants, of which fourteen actually took part in the race. Late on the eve of the race, Raynham telephoned his close friend, Frank Courtney, explaining that he had wrenched his knee while flying another aircraft and to ask if Courtney would take his place, a suggestion which was accepted without hesitation. Courtney did not take Raynham's advice to make a one-hour familiarisation flight before the race, which would have been prudent considering that flight tests had not been completed and furthermore the aircraft was only at that moment being re-erected at Hendon following its appearance at Olympia. As events proved, to ignore this advice was unwise.

The scratch aircraft was Mr Tait-Cox's Goshawk, which gave the Semiquaver one minute on handicap and the other Martinsyde entrants, R H Nisbet in an F.6 and Sqn Ldr T O'B Hubbard in an F.4, 11 and 10 minutes respectively.

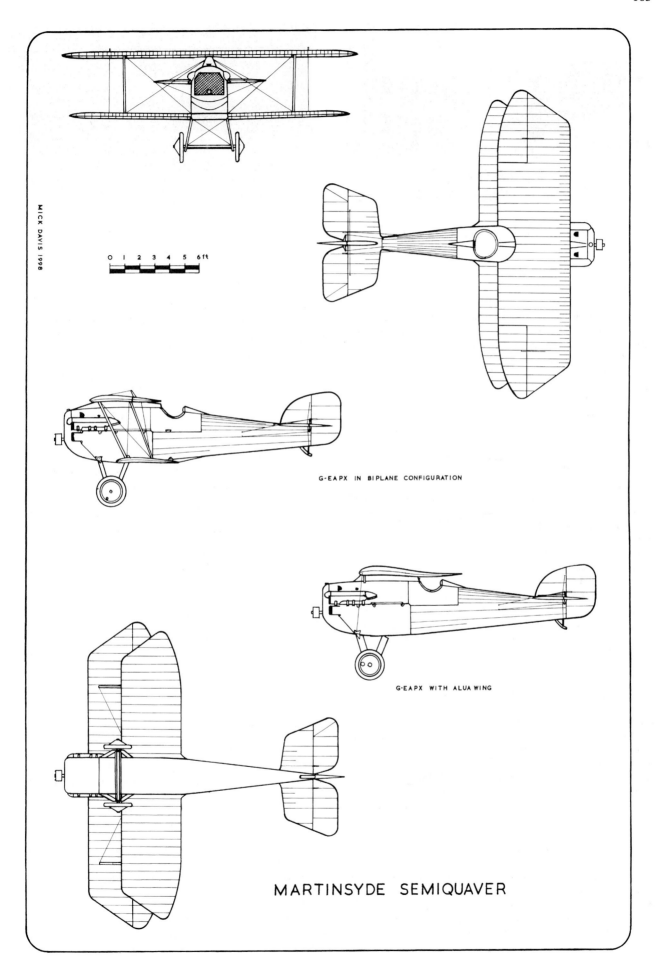

MICK DAVIS 1998

0 1 2 3 4 5 6 ft

G-EAPX IN BIPLANE CONFIGURATION

G-EAPX WITH ALUA WING

MARTINSYDE SEMIQUAVER

The Martinsyde Semiquaver G-EAPX. (The A J Jackson Collection)

When his turn came in the race, Courtney took off, swung low around the central pylon and sped off towards the first turning point at Brooklands, some twenty miles to the south. It immediately became apparent that the pitch of the propeller was too high, resulting in the engine becoming overloaded. Despite cutting the revs, the coolant temperature soared and scalding water was sprayed into the cockpit from an overflow pipe on the undersized radiator. Courtney recalled that he had a "three-handed job" of manipulating the joystick, throttle and maps. The main occupation was to control the throttle in order to maximise the power while keeping the coolant below boiling point. While rounding the Hendon pylon to finish the first lap, Courtney blacked out from the centrifugal forces. This was Courtney's first experience of this phenomenon and frightened him to such an extent that he kept quiet about it for months, fearing that the licensing authorities would withdraw his licence as being medically unfit.

As he approached the finishing line after the second and final circuit, Courtney decided to pull out all the stops and pushed the throttle fully open. Clouds of steam emerged as the Semiquaver passed the home pylon to win the race. Fearing that throwing caution to the winds in this way had drained the radiator of water, Courtney headed at once to land. Unbeknown to him, the shock absorbers of the landing gear had been tightened so that the aircraft could stand rigid on its undercarriage at the Olympia show and no one had remembered to slacken them off prior to the race. As a result, when the Semiquaver hit a small ridge hidden in the grass, it bounced into the air, staggered and hit the ground with its left wingtip. It came to rest upside down. Courtney had been saved from serious injury by the fuselage hump and the stout rudder post both of which remained relatively intact and he was able to squirm free, much to the relief of the St.John's Ambulance men who had rushed to the scene with stretchers.

Despite this debacle, Courtney had won the race at an average speed of 153 mph, with J H James second in a Nieuport Nieuhawk (320 hp ABC Dragonfly) and C F Unwins third in the Bristol Bullet (450-hp Bristol Jupiter). Nisbet and Hubbard in the other Martinsydes came fourth and fifth respectively.

Following the Aerial Derby, the Semiquaver was tuned up and made even more racy by having its wing area further reduced. It was entered into the Gordon Bennett Race at Etampes. The British were confident, too confident as it happened, that they would win. Raynham secured the aircraft by its tailskid to his car and accompanied by his friend McGeagh, towed the aircraft all the way via the Southampton - Le Havre ferry. The only damage incurred to the aircraft during the trip was a chafed shock absorber and a punctured tyre. However, he flew the race with the same tyres.

As soon as he arrived at Etampes, Raynham gave the aircraft a short trial flight. On the day of the Cup, he left the aircraft in its shed until late afternoon, so that it would be cooler and the air less bumpy, a wise precaution as the radiator capacity had not been increased. His main rival, the Frenchman Sadi Lecointe, befriended him and went out of his way to make him feel at home, lending him tools and mechanics.

Raynham's special fuel, which he had ordered in advance, had not arrived, so Col Bristow of Ogilvie and Partners, then in Paris, sent a lorry to Rouen to obtain the proper brew. When the fuel finally arrived, it had a specific gravity of 0.68 whereas the carburettor had been tuned for a figure of 0.70. Although the discrepancy might have caused the engine to overheat, Raynham did not risk making the tricky adjustment necessary.

At 4.30 pm, Raynham had the Semiquaver wheeled to the starting line and with no further fuss he took off, using a take-off run far less than anyone else and sped past the pylon into the setting sun. His British supporters started to get anxious when he did not reappear after 25 minutes as expected. When he finally did return his engine was misfiring

The Martinsyde Semiquaver G-EAPX at Etampes. (The E A Harlin Collection)

badly and the fuselage was covered in black oil. The packing had blown in a joint in an oil pipe. Instead of claiming the trophy as expected, he calmly hitched up the Semiquaver to his car and made his way back to England.

The "Alula" Wing

The Semiquaver finished its life as a test bed for a new type of wing, dubbed the "Alula" wing by its inventor, A A Holle. Holle was a Dutchman, who had previously designed an unsuccessful parasol monoplane during the First World War called the Varioplane. He had now formed a company, the Commercial Aeroplane Wing Syndicate Ltd., of 34 Gresham Street, E.C.2, to develop this wing form. It was not intended that the company would build aircraft except for experimental purposes but rather to act as a consultancy to other companies. He believed that it would produce lift in proportion to the cube of the velocity - rather than in proportion to the square of velocity as nature's laws would dictate. The venture was partly financed to the tune of £30,000 by Robert Blackburn. Another Dutchman, a Capt Vertholen, also invested a considerable sum into the venture. Blackburn was anticipating utilising the load-carrying capabilities of the wing for a four-ton aerial lorry called the Pelican. This was to have been a large cantilever monoplane with two 460 hp Napier Lion engines and an all-up weight of nearly eleven tons. It was projected to carry its load over a distance equivalent to London-Paris at a cost of 2.6 pence/lb.

Holle's wing had a straight trailing edge and a swept leading edge, tapering to a point at the wing tips. A large incidence at the centre line gradually modulated to a negative incidence at the tip, giving zero lift at this point, a feature which was supposed to eliminate span-wise airflow with its resultant losses of lift at the tip.

Tests with a 4 x 36 inch model wing in a wind tunnel at the East London College was said to give encouraging results and full-scale tests began in Yorkshire at Sherburn-in-Elmet, near Leeds. With the first attempt, a flimsy example of Holle's wing was mounted unbraced as a parasol onto a

Getting ready to tow the Martinsyde Semiquaver back to England after the Gordon Bennett Race at Etampes.
(The E A Harlin Collection)

The Semiquaver with the 'Alula' wing. (Imperial War Museum)

D.H.6. Unfortunately, the weakness of the wing structure allowed aeroelastic twist of the wingtips, rendering useless the conventional ailerons that had been fitted. After his first test pilot had almost killed himself, Holle provided two hinged slats in the leading edge for lateral control, which in the event proved to be rather too sensitive. It was this device which probably provided the origin of the "alula" name - an alula being an auxiliary digit on the leading edge of a gull's wing which can be extended to form a slot and delay premature leading edge stall during slow flight. Holle, refusing to face the truth, blamed the cumbersome D.H.6 for inhibiting the wing's performance and looked around for a more aerodynamically efficient mount.

Holle managed to persuade Handasyde to part with the Semiquaver for an undisclosed sum, most probably provided by Capt Vertholen. Although the basis of the earlier claims for the wing were for its load-carrying capability, Holle set about adapting the "Alula" wing for racing. The shape of the wing precluded the use of span-wise spars. The resultant wing structure consisted of only thin span-wise stringers and chord-wise formers covered by eighth-inch mahogany veneer. It was claimed that the wing had a load factor of 7, but as might be predicted, when sent to Farnborough on 11th June 1921, the wing was found to be too flexible and failed the load test, having a load factor of only 1.75. After a delay during which some redesign took place, a second wing was sent in July to the French Institut Aérotechnique at St-Cyr. Either the third or the fourth set replaced the biplane wings of the Semiquaver.

The "Handalula" or "Semi-Alula-Quaver" was assembled at Addlestone and towed to Northolt where Frank Courtney was to test it prior to flying it in the 1921 Aerial Derby the next day. After a few taxi runs, during which its top-heaviness and instability on its narrow undercarriage was duly noted, Courtney declined to fly it. His decision was no doubt aided by an aside from Handasyde, who was taking more than a passing interest, to the effect that 'the pilot who takes up this machine comes down dead'. Holle was forced to look for

someone else, and just a couple of hours before the race managed to tempt Count Bernard de Romanet, who was looking for a mount in the race, from London to Northolt. However the Frenchman confirmed Courtney's assessment of the aircraft as did another freelance pilot, Christopher Draper, and the aircraft did not race.

The aircraft was flown shortly after, probably about five days after the Derby by Reginald W Kenworthy, a man of independent means, who Courtney described as "a fine fellow but not known for his technical judgment or reasonable caution". Courtney witnessed the flight and described it as harrowing.

According to Kenworthy, he was holidaying in Scarborough when he received a telegram asking if he would test the machine. He agreed that he would carry out the test for a fee of 100 guineas, apparently the going rate for such a task, subject to his inspection of the aircraft. On arrival at Northolt, despite being appraised of the doubts of others over the airworthiness of the machine, he duly looked it over and took it out for a taxying test. During this run he found the controls to be very sensitive and the aircraft showed no signs of leaving the ground at 90 mph, a speed achieved at quarter throttle. He asked for the throttle quadrant to be changed from its position on the starboard side of the cockpit to a more normal position on the port side while he considered the proposition over lunch. Deciding to carry out the flight, he asked the manager of the flying school at Northolt to suspend flying while he took the machine up. The director was apparently all too willing to remove his school machines away from danger. Kenworthy described the test some years later in the October 1937 issue of *Popular Flying*:

Now for the test! I tested all the controls from beginning to end and taxied to the far end of the aerodrome to face the wind, nearly to the hedge, to have as long a run as possible. Now we are off. I opened the throttle wide; 50-60-70-80-mph. She bumps terribly on the uneven aerodrome surface - hope the chassis will stand it! No lift yet! 90-100 and still not off! 105-110- bumping ceases, she is airborne! She shoots up into

The Semiquaver with the 'Alula' wing. (J M Bruce/S Leslie Collection)

the sky, right wing is down, correct it with the joystick immediately she nearly turns over on the left wing. Jove! she is sensitive! Must stay up and get used to her before landing; all the time we are climbing at 150 mph, she is fast all right. I stay up for about 20 minutes till I feel that I have got her properly tamed. I find her stalling speed is about 110 mph, which tells me I must touch down well over 100 mph to maintain control to the end. I do 175 mph. I dare not find her top speed on this flight, wires may have become loose and so I land carefully at 110 mph. She bumps terribly but stands it. So the machine is taken back to the sheds for a two-day examination and thorough overhaul.

Three months later, on 12th October, Holle set up a demonstration flight for almost a dozen of Britain's top aviation men, including the Secretary of State for Air and Lord Trenchard. The demonstration was supposedly of "an aircraft destroyer" designed to show how the high speed and lift characteristics of the "Alula" wing could be adapted for aerial fighting. The promised "aircraft destroyer" turned out to be the Semiquaver with its undercarriage strengthened and track widened from 3½ to 6 feet. It is not clear whether the wing structure had been strengthened but the ailerons were again positioned on the trailing edge but located on this occasion at mid-span. Kenworthy was again the pilot.

The demonstration was totally unconvincing. The performance of the machine was compared directly with an old Bristol Fighter which took off at the same time. The Semiquaver was undoubtedly faster and climbed quicker than the Bristol, but the performance margin was no more than might be expected considering that the Bristol was carrying two people on the same engine power. Kenworthy took no chances with the structure of the wing and did not demonstrate the machine's manoeuvrability, but gingerly carried out a few steeply banked turns at about 3,000 feet. Kenworthy then made a long and gentle descent to a careful landing, at a speed adjudged by C G Grey of *The Aeroplane* to exceed that of the standard British fighters of the time.

Although B D Thomas, designer of the Thomas-Morse

racers in the States, was influenced by the concept, the project was effectively dead and the Semiquaver towards the end of 1921 was abandoned at Northolt aerodrome and left to rot - an unseemly end for such a promising machine.

Martinsyde Types A Marks I, A Mark II and AS

The Martinsyde Type A was designed to meet a demand for an efficient commercial aeroplane and owed its ancestry directly to the F.4 and the Raymor transatlantic aircraft. Although fitted with an engine of similar power, it was a larger machine than the F.4 with more than double the carrying capacity but with an inevitable reduction in performance. Because Martin and Handasyde believed that at that time it was not possible for a two-engined machine to sustain flight if one engine failed, they considered that a machine with a single engine of a tried and trusted type would be more reliable. They also calculated that a single-engined machine would have a lower capital cost and would be easier to maintain. Furthermore these machines were smaller, more manoeuvrable in the air and more easily handled on the ground than a twin-engined machine.

The Type A was produced in two forms - the Mark I and Mark II. Both Marks were fitted with either the 275-hp Rolls-Royce Falcon engine or the 300-hp Hispano-Suiza and could also be fitted with floats or skis as an alternative to wheels. The machine was known as the Type AS when fitted with floats, which were of wooden construction, with flat bottoms and two steps. The aircraft were of conventional layout with two-bay staggered wings of equal span. Besides the pilot, the Mark I was arranged to carry two passengers, normally in an open cockpit, and 600 lb of freight or mails. The Mark II was similar in all essentials except with the arrangement of the fuselage which was designed to carry four passengers in an enclosed cabin situated in front of the pilot. Without passengers, it could carry up to 1,200 lb of freight.

Considerable attention had been paid to ease of construction and maintenance. All parts were cut on jigs and

Type A Mark I G-EAMR, with Capt C E Howell and G H Fraser aboard, about to take off from Hounslow aerodrome on its ill-fated attempt in the England-Australia Race. (A J Jackson Collection)

standardised. The engine was easily accessible and airframe parts were readily replaced, frames and all fittings being standardised and drilled on jigs. The fuselage, of the usual braced girder type, was built of spruce throughout. It was made of four sections; the nose with the engine bearers which extended to the forward undercarriage strut, the cabin section extending aft of the main planes, the cockpit section and the tail portion which contained the pilot's cockpit and extended to the stern post. Any of these sections could be repaired or replaced independently of the others. The engine bearers were of tubular duralumin and a fireproof bulkhead separated the engine compartment from the cabin. The main petrol tank was placed in the lower portion of the fuselage behind the engine bulkhead with a small gravity tank mounted in the centre section of the mainplane. The four-piece nose radiator was fitted with shutters. The front and cabin sections were not wire-braced but covered with three-ply, except for the upper decking of the cabin which was made of mahogany. The ply was glued and screwed to the frame and reinforced at each joint with fishplates. The rear portion of the fuselage was covered with fabric and doped with 'Cellon'. The space inside the cabin was divided into two pairs of side-by-side seats. The front pair of seats were reached by stepping over the backrest. To assist entry, the front part of the roof of the cabin slid forward on guide rails and the rear part was hinged. Glazed windows were provided at the sides and the top was covered in fine gauze which let in light and gave ventilation without being draughty.

The wings were built on laminated spruce spars, the layers being glued together and bound with doped fabric. Metal fittings enclosing the spar were fitted with tongues to which the forked ends of the interplane struts were secured by means of a single bolt. Bracing wires were secured to lugs on the same fittings. The ribs were laminated at points were the load was taken by strips of veneer glued on either side of the web. The fabric was stitched rather than pinned to the structure at the leading and trailing edges and at each rib, the lacing being covered by linen tape. The lower main planes were attached to the fuselage by means of two forged box fittings on the fuselage and were held fast by a steel rod passing through the boxes. The upper planes were attached to the centre section in the same way. The main plane struts were attached by means of a shoe which engaged a duralumin block fitted to the spar. The centre section struts were similarly fitted.

The tailplane was attached to the fuselage by means of two hinge bolts at the front spar and the incidence could be varied by adjusting the position of the rear spar by a wheel in the cockpit.

The undercarriage comprised a pair of solid V-struts bolted at the wheel base with duralumin butt plates. The struts were attached to the fuselage by means of a fork end fitting and eye bolt, the latter also acting as an anchor for the undercarriage bracing wires. The bungee shock absorbers were streamlined by the front struts and a fairing. The split axle was pivoted at the centre and could easily be replaced by withdrawing a split pin and bolt.

Only six were built and all were exported, five to Canada and one to Ireland. One was briefly on the British civil register as G-EATY before going to Canada. After operations with Martinsydes ceased in Canada, two of the Martinsyde Type As reappeared in the United States.

Capt Howell aboard G-EAMR just prior to take-off in the England-Australia Race

The England to Australia Air Race

In March 1919, the Australian Government announced a prize of £10,000 to be awarded to the first Australian nationals to fly from Britain to their homeland within an elapsed time of 720 hours. It was further stipulated that the aircraft must be British and that the contestants must depart from the seaplane station at Calshot or from Hounslow aerodrome. Following the announcement, there was official disquiet over allowing competitors to risk their lives over a route which had few facilities and had not been properly surveyed, particularly beyond Calcutta. It was decided between the Air Ministry and the race organisers that no competitor should be allowed to start until it had obtained reliable information about the latter part of the route. Brig Gen A E Barton DSO and Capt Ross Smith of the Australian Flying Corps were sent to carry out a survey. Their findings were reported on 15th September to the effect that the only suitable landing grounds between Calcutta and Port Darwin were the racecourses at Rangoon and Singapore and an area at Bandoeng in the Dutch East Indies. There was no suitable landing ground between Bandoeng (in present-day western Java) and Port Darwin, a distance of 1,750 miles. In the event, another landing place was established in Timor, reducing the distance of the final leg to about 600 miles. The Australian Government arranged for weather forecasts for the last leg to be sent from Port Darwin to Timor and cabled from there to Batavia, where the British Consul would transmit the messages to the aviators.

Martinsyde entered a Type A Mark 1 on 15th August, nominating a Capt Howell as the pilot. The arrangement with Howell was that should he win the prize, he would repay £8,000 to the Martinsyde company and remain in its employ for at least six months afterwards. Exactly a month later, it was announced that he would be accompanied by a Sgt Fraser, acting as navigator and mechanic.

Capt Cedric Ernest Howell DSO MC DFC was born in Adelaide, South Australia, and was educated at the Church of England Grammar School in Melbourne. He was refused entry into the AIF at the outbreak of the war as he was under-age. Instead he enlisted as a private in the regular army, joined 14 Battalion and served in Gallipoli where he contracted malaria. He later took part in the early battles on the Somme as a sniper. He managed to get into the RFC in 1917 and carried out his initial training at Denham before going to No.17 Training Squadron at Port Meadow in Oxford. His first solo flight took place in a R.E.8 on 24th July 1917. From Oxford he went to Yatesbury to complete his training before being posted to Italy, where he flew Sopwith Camels. During his service, he was credited with destroying thirty-two aircraft, of which seventeen were confirmed, and numerous balloons and kites.

George Henry Fraser was born at Coberg, Victoria, in 1879. He enlisted early in 1917 into the AFC as a mechanic and sailed to England during August 1917. After the Armistice, he took a course in aerial navigation at Andover, thereby gaining the necessary qualifications to enter the Race.

Type A Mark I G-EAMR being tested on floats prior to the England to Australia Race. (The E A Harlin Collection)

The Martinsyde aircraft, registered G-EAMR, was a standard Type A Mark 1 fitted with a 275 hp Rolls-Royce Falcon engine. The only major modification was an enlarged fuel tank to give an endurance of about ten hours. About 1,000 lb of spares were stowed aboard the aircraft, including a spare propeller. Despite the extra load of fuel and spares, the performance of the aircraft still had an economic cruising speed of around 100 mph and a safe landing speed of about 40 mph. A special pattern of main compass was fitted, otherwise the instrumentation carried was completely standard.

The Martinsyde Company carefully laid plans for the trip. Fuel supplies were arranged at all the likely stopping places beyond India. Arrangements had been made to convert the aircraft to a floatplane for the stages between Calcutta and Port Darwin by despatching in advance by sea metal-clad floats to Calcutta and a spare undercarriage to Darwin. Preliminary test flights showed that the floats did not materially affect performance, the aircraft taking off from water quickly without tending to "porpoise". The floats were fully interchangeable with the wheeled undercarriage and added about 400 lb to the all-up weight.

Martinsyde were the sixth of the seven entrants to actually attempt the flight. The start was delayed for a week by bad weather. Howell left Brooklands for Hounslow on the 2nd December, circling low over the Martinsyde works at Woking on the way to say farewell. They eventually took off from Hounslow at 9.34 am on Thursday 4th December 1919. Only a small group of people saw them off, mainly Royal Aero Club officials, some representatives from Martinsyde and some members of the press. It was reported that after a few hasty farewells, the crew shouted "Ta ta boys, we are off" as they taxied away from the hangars and into wind for take-off. They carried a number of letters for their compatriots in Australia, including one for Prime Minister Hughes. Messages for a safe trip were received from HRH Prince Albert, Mr Winston Churchill and Major General Sir F H Sykes.

They headed across the Channel in bad weather. Some trouble with a fuel pump in Paris delayed them for two hours so they had to abandon their target of reaching Lyons that night and stopped instead at Dijon, after again encountering bad weather. They had great difficulty in getting down safely. Just north of the town, whilst in thick cloud, they just managed to clear a mountain ridge at the end of a valley, narrowly missing some trees. Howell broke six inches off the tailskid in a heavy landing.

After sampling French hospitality in Dijon, the crew took off the next morning heading for Pisa. The aircraft was blown off course by gale force winds and they had to settle for landing at Toulon as conditions worsened. After two hours, the weather improved and they flew over the Gulf of Genoa to land at Pisa at about 3.30 pm. The airfield at Pisa was drenched with rain and waterlogged. Fraser set to work to make a new tailskid out of a block of timber purchased locally, using a hacksaw and a pocket knife. Night fell before he could complete the task and, as the workshop on the airfield was without lights, he had to wait until the following morning to complete the job. Both airmen were unhappy about the delay as their request to include a tailskid amongst the spares carried aboard had been ignored by Martinsyde.

The next day, 6th December, they were able to take off from Pisa and landed at Naples at 3.30 pm after a flight lasting two hours, being unable to reach the original target of Taranto in the time available. Despite pouring rain and strong winds, the crew were able to take off on the following day with a view to reaching Taranto. However flying conditions were treacherous and both men were airsick. They got as far

Martinsyde F.4 G-EAWE, owned by Handley Page Ltd just prior to its delivery flight to Poland. (Philip Jarrett)

as Salerno but conditions made a landing attempt too risky and the men had to turn back to Naples where they spent the night. They reached Taranto the following day without mishap.

On 9th December, the Martinsyde left Taranto at 11.15 am with the intention of reaching Athens, a distance of some 400 miles, which they were expecting to reach in little more than four hours. However the aircraft never arrived. The Lloyds agent at Corfu telegraphed on 13th December: "Information just received, British aircraft wrecked off St. George's Bay, Corfu, December 10th; no hope of survivors; log book washed ashore; certificate number 332; identification mark GUMR, Capt C R Howell, Melbourne; number of licence 412; Hounslow for Melbourne. Leaving to investigate"

The previous day, the British Consul at Corfu had received information that a British aeroplane had landed in the sea three miles off St. George's Bay. Capt Bullaid was with the British Consul at the time and suggested that his tug, *Norma*, should go out and search for the men. The following day, the tug searched the coast three miles off-shore for a distance of 45 miles and then returned hugging the shore but found nothing.

In the meantime, the Lloyds agent, Mr. Woodley, went overland in a motor car to St. George's Bay. He took a small boat and examined the aircraft which was lying in about 12 feet of water some 300 yards off shore. The machine appeared intact, with one wing and the rudder projecting out of the water. He could see no sign of bodies in the machine. A day or so later, locals attempted to salvage the machine but, when discovering that it was not Italian, abandoned it

near the rocks on the northern side of the bay, where she eventually broke up.

According to the innkeeper at nearby Prunella, at about 7.30 on the night of 9th December an aeroplane was heard flying overhead. It circled St. George's Bay about four times endeavouring to find a landing place. He saw the aircraft land in the water about 250 yards off shore and heard two people crying for help. He was unable to launch his boat due to rough seas but set out a lantern to show the direction of the shore. After an hour or so, the cries ceased. The following morning, as soon as it was daylight, he saw the aircraft still afloat but no one on aboard. Later Capt Howell's body was washed ashore. He was dressed in two sweaters and pants, but he had taken his flying suit and boots off. His watch was also found on him, which had stopped at 2.50. Lt Fraser was never found.

Howell's wife was travelling to Australia in the liner *Orsova* at the time of the flight. News of his death was telegraphed to the ship but was withheld from her until after the boat had docked in Adelaide, when the bad news was broken to her by Howell's father. Howell was first buried in Corfu but his body was later disinterred and transported by an Italian tramp steamer to Melbourne. He was buried with full military honours at the Heidelberg Cemetery in Victoria on 22nd April 1920. Capt H A Rigby, who originally intended himself to take part in the race but withdrew, was one of the pallbearers.

St. George's Bay is only about 150 miles from the aircraft's starting point at Taranto and should have been overflown within two hours, i.e. before 2 pm. Why it did not appear before 7.30 in the evening and what happened in the

Martinsyde Type A Mark II G-EATY prior to being shipped to Newfoundland for the Aerial Survey Company.
(The A J Jackson Collection)

interim remains a mystery. Although it is possible that the crew made an intermediate landing to effect repairs or confirm their position, no report of such has ever come to light. It is also possible that the crew lost their way and expended all their fuel looking for a landfall. Another theory advanced was that due to strong headwinds, Capt Howell tried to reach the African coast directly but had to turn back.

Six months after the crash, Capt Howell's father was still not satisfied that the true circumstances of the tragedy had been established. In the first place, the accident had not been reported for three days, yet communications on the island were not that bad. His theory was that Capt Howell had landed safely but was murdered for his money by the locals and his body and machine had then been pushed into the sea. This theory was supported by the fact that Howell was not wearing his Sidcot jacket or his flying boots when he was found. Also, although 10/6d in small change and several small articles were supposed to have been found on the body, his pockets were full of sand when examined in Australia and it was unlikely that the sand would have been replaced after the original examination. Furthermore the £100 in cash and a considerable sum in credit notes, which Howell was carrying when he left England, were never recovered, although several small items of little value and Fraser's diary were later found inland.

The winners of the Race were Capt Ross Smith as pilot, his brother Keith Smith as navigator and two mechanics Sgts J W Bennett and W H Shiers in a Vickers Vimy (G-EAOU), who took off from Hounslow on 12th November and arrived in Darwin on 10th December after covering 11,080 miles in an elapsed time of 668 hours 20 minutes. Thus they were making their triumphant arrival about the time that the Martinsyde men met their deaths.

The Aircraft Disposal Company F.4, A.D.C.1, Nimbus-Martinsyde and AV1

Martinsyde F.4

When Martinsyde was finally wound-up, the Aircraft Disposal Company Limited bought the aircraft manufacturing rights, goodwill and remaining stock of airframes and components. This material joined a large stock of RAF surplus F.4s already held by the company. ADC's Martinsyde catalogue issued shortly afterwards contained a number of retouched photographs of several F.4 variants. ADC continued to sell standard F.4 Buzzards and small numbers were sold to the Irish Free State, Russia, Lithuania, Poland and Japan. One variant had the frontal radiator replaced by two Lamblin underslung radiators and the nose was faired over. Several of this type were sold to Spain.

Five became civil aircraft in the United Kingdom. As mentioned above, two were used for racing and demonstrations, G-EAXB being flown by Major E L Foote in the 1921 Aerial Derby and G-EATD by R H Stocken in the 1922 Aerial Derby. Three more received civil registrations, G-EBDM, G-EBFA and G-EBMI.

G-EBMI, one of the last to be made airworthy, became the only privately owned F.4. It eventually became the property of E D A Biggs at Woodley in March 1930 and was lost a few months later due to the failure of the tailplane spar whilst under test in a high speed dive. The pilot, S W 'Pat' Giddy, the Phillips & Powis instructor, was killed in the crash. In about 1929, while at Shoreham, this aircraft was the subject of a rather bizarre incident involving F G Miles as recounted by his friend and colleague D L Brown in his book *Miles Aircraft since 1925*:

Martinsyde F.4 G-EBMI. (The A J Jackson Collection)

(The Martinsyde) had been lying dismantled in the back of a hangar at Croydon for many years, but we decided that provided it was restricted to straight flying it should be safe enough. For the next few weeks we busied ourselves with assembling it. When it was about three-quarters complete, we wheeled the aircraft out of the workshop onto the aerodrome with a view to starting the engine. However, this proved to be a good deal more difficult than we anticipated. There was, of course, no electric starter. It needed three people to join hands and pull the propeller round while the pilot wound a starter magneto inside the cockpit. This sort of exercise went on for several weeks without getting so much as a kick out of the engine. We did everything we knew to get the engine going, but without success. We tried priming it with petrol, sucking in and sucking out, still without any sign of life. We worked in relays, taking turns to swing the propeller, while one of us sat in the cockpit operating the switches and starter magneto. As the days went by still without result, we became more and more despondent, finally even postponing the assembly of the aircraft because it did not seem much use as the prospect of flying a really high-powered aeroplane melted away and it looked as if there was not much we could do about it. At last, in desperation, we tried priming the engine with oxy-acetylene. Even then nothing happened.

One afternoon we were making a last effort to get it started. Miles was sitting nonchalantly on the side of the cockpit with one leg inside and one out while three of us were pulling at the propeller, when suddenly, without any warning at all, the engine started with a terrifying roar and the Martinsyde leapt forward over the baulk of timber which, because we could not afford chocks, we had placed under the wheels. The Martinsyde was pointing straight at the petrol pumps and, as it leapt forward, Miles snatched back the throttle but without effect. Hurriedly sliding down into the cockpit, he pushed the rudder round and slewed the machine

so that it just missed the petrol pumps and a moment later, to everyone's horror, he was in the air.

Two of the four ailerons were disconnected and were flapping loose; the aircraft had no tyres, no windscreen, no safety belt and Miles was wearing no helmet, no goggles, not even a jacket. It was a terrifying moment. Finding himself in the air, Miles did a hurried circuit of the aerodrome, tried to throttle back but found the throttle was adjusted wrongly so that he could not close it, so he did the obvious thing and flicked off the ignition switches but, to his amazement, the engine still continued to run. The ignition switches were disconnected so that when we had all thought the switches were off, they had been on contact all the time. Miles found himself flying round unable to either throttle back or switch off. It seemed to Miles that the only course open to him was to turn off the petrol and hope that the engine would stop when in a suitable position for landing.

Here again, there were difficulties. First of all, the Martinsyde had a very complicated petrol system involving quite a number of fuel cocks and Miles did not know which one to turn off. Furthermore he had no means of knowing how long the engine would keep running after turning the petrol off and thus it was almost impossible for him to judge his distance relative to the aerodrome so as to be in a position in which to land. However there was nothing for it but to try, and so, summoning up his courage, he turned off all the fuel cocks he could find. As he approached the aerodrome he waited for the engine to stop, but it kept running till eventually he was too close to the aerodrome to land and, of course at that moment the engine stopped. Feverishly he turned on all the fuel cocks and prayed that the engine would pick up, which mercifully it did. In the course of this flying around he had found that, due to the disconnected ailerons, he had hardly any lateral control, particularly at low speeds; yet, with the small size of our aerodrome and the fact that the

174

The Martinsyde A.D.C.1 powered by a Armstrong-Siddeley Jaguar engine. (J M Bruce/S Leslie Collection)

aircraft had no brakes, he obviously had to approach fairly slowly.

By now he had a rough idea of how long the engine would run after the petrol was switched off, so this time he approached the aerodrome he wondered whether the engine would stop just too soon or whether again it would stop too late so that he would overshoot. But this time he had judged it correctly, although even now it was not easy because he had to glide fast enough to retain lateral control and yet slowly enough to enable him to pull up in the 400 yards length of the aerodrome. Those who were watching from the ground held their breath as they saw the Martinsyde coming in to land, but Miles judged it perfectly, touching down gently on the bare wheels.

Martinsyde A.D.C.1

Designed by John Kenworthy, who had been taken on as Chief Designer by ADC, the second variant appeared in November 1924. Designated the A.D.C.1, it was a mating of the standard F.4 airframe with an 425 hp Armstrong Siddeley Jaguar engine. This was a radial engine with two staggered banks of seven cylinders each. One novel feature of the engine was a fan located in a casing to the rear of the engine which forced carburetted fuel mixture into the cylinders and at the same time acted to cool the engine oil. The propeller was fitted with a wide diameter boss.

With the exception of the fuselage forward of the pilot's cockpit, the engine and some of the equipment carried, the machine was almost identical to the F.4. The principal alteration was the rearrangement of the longerons between the centre section struts, where the upper longerons sloped upwards instead of downwards and the lower longerons were straight. These supported a firewall made of asbestos sheet sandwiched between two sheets of aluminium. Forward of the

firewall, the engine bearer plate was supported by a tubular structure and was the standard Armstrong-Siddeley design except for a slight alteration in the angle of the four bolt slots. The engine could be removed as a unit by undoing these four bolts and disconnecting the various engine and fuel connections. The petrol tank, of 55 gallons capacity, was fitted immediately behind the firewall. The fuel supply to the engine was gravity fed and the engine was primed by means of a separate line fitted with a primer pump. The engine controls were operated by push rods passing through the firewall. Oil was supplied from a tank mounted below the fuselage floor, hot oil being circulated around the bottom of the tank which was exposed to the air for cooling purposes. A thermocouple was fitted to the oil tank and a petrol level gauge was fitted to the tank in clear view of the pilot.

The aircraft was fitted with twin Vickers guns with Constantinesco interrupter gear. Access to the gun mechanism was by two sliding doors. Steel guards were fitted between the guns and the main fuel tank.

The aircraft proved to have an exceptional performance, significantly better than the Gloster Grebe then entering RAF service. Considerable foreign interest was shown in the type and visitors to the ADC works included delegations from Argentina, Japan, Portugal and Spain. However just one order resulted, that from Latvia for eight aircraft.

Martinsyde A.D.C.1 G-EBKL, fitted with a 385 hp Jaguar engine, was entered into the 1925 King's Cup race based at Croydon on 3rd and 4th July 1925 by Lt Col M O Darby. It was given the racing number 8 and was flown by Sqn Ldr Walter Longton DFC AFC. This entry afforded the opportunity to compare the Martinsyde with machines with the same engine, such as the Armstrong Whitworth Siskin, which had been designed since the war. Longton got away well and disappeared into thick mist but nothing more was heard of him until much later that night. Apparently some

The Nimbus Martinsyde powered by an ADC Nimbus engine developed from the Siddeley Puma. (A J Jackson Collection)

special carburettor jets, which had been fitted to the engine for high rate-of-climb trials, had not been replaced for the event. These gave a very high petrol consumption of about 35 gallons per hour. Consequently, after flying through thick fog around Luton and Bedford trying to find an opening, he ran out of petrol and managed to make a landing on Nottingham Race Course. It was three hours before he could find enough petrol to refill his tanks. He got as far as Harrogate before deciding that it was useless to continue as the tanks would not hold enough petrol to enable him to cover the longer stretches of the course.

Nimbus Martinsyde

Another re-engined variant, also created by John Kenworthy, appeared with a closely cowled 330 hp in-line six-cylinder water-cooled ADC Nimbus engine that had been developed from the Siddeley Puma. The development work was carried out by Frank Halford, who also designed the original B.H.P. engine from which the Puma was developed while he was at Beardmores, utilising a number of Puma engine components. Like previous F.4 variants, the fuselage was of tie-rod-braced timber construction of rectangular cross section with curved upper decking. The single-bay wings had two routed-out spruce spars with wooden ribs. Ailerons were mounted on all four wings. Apart from plywood forward of the cockpit, the structure was fabric covered. A modified fin with a horn-balanced rudder was fitted. Despite its racy appearance and clean lines, the overall performance was slightly inferior to that of the standard F.4. The impetus behind fitting the Nimbus engine was the large stock of Puma engines and components held by ADC. The Puma engine was obsolescent by the end of the war and was never particularly reliable. It is not surprising therefore that the design never attracted military orders and the company were never called upon to fit

the twin Vickers guns which the company claimed that it could carry.

Only two Nimbus Martinsydes were built and these were given civil registrations G-EBOJ and G-EBOL. Both were entered in the 1926 King's Cup Race which was held over the two days, 9th and 10th July. Raynham's old Mustardsyde was entered by Leslie Hamilton but it was withdrawn before the race. This time the course totalled 1,464 miles, comprising four circuits each day. Of the fourteen starters, only five crossed the finishing line. Capt F T Courtney in G-EBOL retired after the first circuit. G-EBOJ, piloted by H H Perry, survived until after the sixth circuit and then retired while in third place. G-EBOJ was also unplaced in the Bournemouth Summer Handicap at the Bournemouth Summer Aviation Race Meeting held on 21-22nd August 1926 but had better fortune in the Boscombe High Power Handicap over two five-mile laps at the same meeting, Wg Cdr W S Douglas coming second to a D.H.37A piloted by A S Butler. This aircraft was withdrawn from the 1927 King's Cup Race held on 30th July but won the Hucknall Stakes High Power Handicap on 1st August at 141.2 mph. G-EBOJ was entered in the Morris Open Handicap of the Whitsun 1928 Hampshire Air Pageant and was flown by Capt N Stack. It won the second heat with an average speed of 134½ mph from a handicap of 11 minutes 56 seconds and went on to win the final at an average speed of 129½ mph from a handicap of 20 minutes 14 seconds. It then took part in the 1928 King's Cup Race, starting at Hendon on 20th July, piloted by Squadron Ldr H W G Jones, but was unplaced. The same aircraft was entered in the 1929 King's Cup Race but did not participate. As far as can be ascertained, this was the last entry of a Martinsyde aircraft in any major national event.

In 1927, G-EBOJ was streamlined by having its undercarriage struts faired over and cylinder-head fairings fitted. When the Aircraft Disposal Company ceased trading in

Amherst Villiers in his Martinsyde A.V.1. (Janie Villiers)

1930, G-EBKL and G-EBOJ were scrapped. G-EBOL was sold to Air Taxis Ltd in March 1927 and crashed at Epsom Downs on 7th October 1927.

Martinsyde A.V.1

However, that was not the end of the Martinsyde story as, in the following year, ADC Aircraft Ltd., the successors to the Aircraft Disposal Company, produced the Martinsyde A.V.1. Registered G-ABKH, it was externally similar to the two-seat F.4A but incorporated many detailed modifications to the airframe and engine devised by its owner, C Amherst Villiers. One of these modifications, apparent from photographs, was the provision of two streamlined fuel tanks above the upper wing, supported by the cabane struts. He christened the aircraft *Blue Print* and had it painted in two or three vivid shades of blue.

Villiers was of an inventive mind without being entirely practical or worried about technicalities. Apparently on one occasion he was having problems with high oil consumption and as a result was having difficulty in getting a certificate of airworthiness or permit to fly. In order to check this, the inspector asked Villiers to fly the aircraft for an hour or so. According to his story, the engine cut shortly after taking off from Heston and Villiers was lucky to find a field in which to land. After a few minor adjustments to the engine, he persuaded several youths to hold the aircraft down while he swung the propeller. The engine started first time and he flew back to Heston. By this time the required hour had elapsed and on his return it was found that the oil problem had been miraculously cured.

G-ABKH was hangared at Brooklands until sold to C B Field in October 1932. Following an accident, in which it hit a telegraph pole and crashed at Bekesbourne in February 1933, it lay derelict at its owner's aerodrome, Kingswood Knoll, Surrey, until scrapped in 1935.

Martinsyde F.6 G-EAPI. This was cancelled on the British register when it was sold to the Canadian Government and became G-CYEQ. (The A J Jackson Collection)

Martinsyde Semiquaver G-EAPX (Philip Jarrett)

Fitting the Alula wing to G-EAPX. (P Jarrett Collection)

Freddie Raynham's F.6 G-EBDK, which passed through several owners before being dismantled at Brooklands in April 1930.
(Philip Jarrett)

The late-registered F.4A G-ABKH, designated the AV.1 by the Aircraft Disposal Company

Data on dimensions and performance of the late- and post-war aircraft

	R.G.	R.G.	F.1	F.2
Engine	190 hp Falcon I	275 hp Falcon III	250 hp RR Mk III	200 hp Hispano-Suiza
Airscrew, diameter	Lang 3090	Lang	Lang 9334	Lang 3290, 9 ft 2½ in
Dimensions				
Span, upper / lower	32 ft 0 in / 30ft 0 in	32 ft 0 in/30 ft 0 in	44 ft 6 in / 44 ft 2 in	32 ft 0 in / 30 ft 0 in
Chord, upper / lower	5 ft 0 in	5 ft 0 in	6 ft 8 in / 5 ft 10 in	6 ft 0 in
Gap	5 ft 6 in	5 ft 6 in	6 ft 0 in	5 ft 3 in
Stagger	1 ft 10 in	1 ft 10 in	1 ft 7 in	2 ft
Dihedral	2° 30'	2° 30'	3°	2°
Incidence	3°	3°	3°	2° 30'
Length	25 ft 8 in	25 ft 10 in	29 ft 1 in	25 ft 0 in
Tailspan	12 ft 0 in			
Height	9 ft 11 in		8 ft 6 in	8 ft 2 in
Tyres (mm)			750 x 125 mm	700 x 100 mm
Surface Areas				
Wings	310 sq ft	310 sq ft	467 sq ft	334 sq ft
Ailerons	32 sq ft	32 sq ft	54 sq ft	48 sq ft
Tailplane	23 sq ft	23 sq ft	26 sq ft	24 sq ft
Elevators	18 sq ft	18 sq ft	21 sq ft	19 sq ft
Fin	4 sq ft	4 sq ft	5 sq ft	4.25 sq ft
Rudder	11 sq ft	11 sq ft	11 sq ft	9.75 sq ft
Tankage				
petrol	26 gal	26 gal	66 gal	33 gal
oil	3 gal	3 gal	5½ gal	3¼ gal
water	5 gal	5 gal	6 gal	gal
Performance				
Weights				
empty	1730 lb	1740 lb	2198 lb	1547 lb
loaded	2234 lb	2261 lb	3260 lb	2355 lb
fuel and oil	214 lb	240 lb	517 lb	263 lb
load and crew	290 lb	281 lb	545 lb	545 lb
Maximum Speed				
sea level	130 mph			120 mph
6500 ft	126.5 mph	132 mph	109.5 mph	
8000 ft	125 mph			
10000 ft	122 mph	130 mph	104.5 mph	114 mph
12000 ft	119.5 mph			
13000 ft			98.5 mph	
15000 ft	115 mph	127.5 mph	94 mph	107 mph
16500 ft			89 mph	
18000 ft	108 mph			
Climb to				
1000 ft	45 sec		1 min	1 min
3000 ft	2 min 20 sec			
6000 ft	5 min 15 sec		6 min 55 sec	
6500 ft	5 min 55 sec	4 min 10 sec		7 min 42 sec
10000 ft	10 min 20 sec	7 min 20 sec	13 min 40 sec	13 min 30 sec
12000 ft	13 min 30 sec		18 min 35 sec	17 min 42 sec
14000 ft	17 min 15 sec		25 min 20 sec	23:min
15000 ft	19 min 20 sec	12 min 50 sec		26 min 18 sec
16000 ft	21 min 45 sec		36 min 20 sec	30 min30 sec
18000 ft	27 min 30 sec			
19000 ft	30 min 55 sec			
Service Ceiling	22,000 ft	23,500 ft	16,500 ft	17,000 ft
Endurance	1¾ h	2 h	3¾ h	2½ h
Reference	M.81, Feb 1917	M.112, Jun 1917	M.115, Jul 1917	M.98, May 1917

	F.3	F.3	F.4 prototype	F.4 production
Engine	190 hp Falcon exp	275 hp Falcon III	305 hp Hispano-Suiza	300 hp Hispano-Suiza
Airscrew, diameter	Lang 3770	Lang 3770	Lang 5270, 8ft 8 7/8 in	Lang 5270B, 8ft8 7/8in
Dimensions				
Span, upper/lower	32: ft 0 in / 31 ft 6in	32 ft10 in / 31 ft 6 in	32 ft :9 3/8in / 31 ft2 3/8 in	32 ft 9 3/8 in / 31 ft 2 3/8 in
Chord, upper/lower	6 ft	6 ft	6 ft 0½ in / 5 ft 6¼ in	6 ft 0½ in / 5 ft 6¼ in
Gap	5 ft 3 in	5 ft 3 in	5 ft 2 5/8 in	5 ft 2 5/8 in
Stagger	2 ft 0 in	2 ft 0 in	2 ft 0 in	2 ft 0 in
Dihedral	2°	2°	2°	2°
Incidence	2°	2°	2°	2°
Length	25 ft 8 in	25 ft 6 in	25 ft 5 5/8 in	25 ft 5 5/8 in
Height	8 ft 8 in	8 ft 8 in	10 ft 4 in	10 ft 4 in
Tailspan			11 ft 2½ in	11 ft 2½ in
Surface Areas				
Wings	320 sq ft	320 sq ft	320 sq ft	320 sq ft
Ailerons, upper/lower	2x11.75 / 2x9.25 sq ft	2x11.75 / 2x9.25 sq ft	2x11.75 / 2x9.25 sq ft	2x11.75 / 2x9.25 sq ft
Tailplane	20.25 sq ft	20.25 sq ft	20.25 sq ft	20.25 sq ft
Elevators	16.5 sq ft	16.5 sq ft	16.5 sq ft	16.5 sq ft
Fin	6.5 sq ft	6.5 sq ft	6.5 sq ft	6.5 sq ft
Rudder	9.75 sq ft	9.75 sq ft	9.75 sq ft	9.75 sq ft
Tankage				
petrol	2x15+1x3=33 gal		38 gal	38 gal
oil	3 gal		3½ gal	3½ gal
water	6 gal		4 gal	4 gal
Performance				
Weights				
empty	1790 lb	1859 lb	1710 lb	1811 lb
loaded	2325 lb	2446 lb	2289 lb	2398 lb
fuel and oil	254 lb	283 lb	298 lb	306 lb
load and crew	281 lb	304 lb	281 lb	281 lb
Maximum Speed				
sea level	142 mph		145 mph	
6500 ft			144 mph	
10000 ft	138 mph	129.5 mph	142.5 mph	142.5 mph
13000 ft			139.5 mph	
15000 ft	132.5 mph	123.5 mph	136.5 mph	132.5 mph
16500 ft	130.5 mph		134 mph	
19500 ft			127.5 mph	
20000 ft			126 mph	
Landing speed				45 mph
Climb to,				
5000 ft			3 min 00	
6000 ft	3 min 35 sec			
6500 ft	4 min	4 min 40 sec	4 min	4 min 40 sec
10000 ft	6 min 45 sec	8 min 5 sec	6 min 40 sec	7 min 55 sec
13000 ft	9 min 35 sec		9 min 30 sec	
15000 ft	11 min 55 sec	15 min	11 min 45 sec	14 min
16000 ft	13 min 15 sec			
16500 ft			13 min 40 sec	
19500 ft			18 min 30 sec	
20000 ft	24 min 30 sec		19 min 20 sec	
Service Ceiling	24,000 ft	21,500 ft	25,000 ft	24,000 ft
Endurance	2½ h	2¼ h	2½ h	
Reference	M.158, Nov 1917	M.200, May 1918	M.210A, Jun 1918	various

	F.4A	F.6	Type A Mark.I	Type A Mark.II
Engine	300 hp Hispano-Suiza	300 hp Hispano-Suiza (200 hp Wolseley Viper)	275 hp Rolls-Royce Falcon III	300 hp Hispano-Suiza
Dimensions				
Span, upper/lower	32 ft 9 3/8 in	31 ft 11¼ in / 29 ft 4 in	43 ft 4 in	43 ft 4 in
Gap			5 ft 6 in	5 ft 6 in
Chord upper/lower		6 ft 0½ in / 5 ft 6¼ in	6ft 6 in	6ft 6 in
Length	25 ft 5 5/8 in	24 ft 6 in	29 ft 1¼ in	29 ft 1¼ in
Tailspan			12 ft 4 in	12 ft 4 in
Height (without airscrew)	8 ft 10 in	9 ft 1¼ in	10 ft 6 in	10 ft 6 in
Surface Areas				
Wings	328.5 sq ft	310 sq ft	512 sq ft	512 sq ft
Tailplane			23.4 sq ft	
Elevators			18.6 sq ft	
Fin			6.68 sq ft	
Rudder			10.0 sq ft	
Wing Loading	7 lb/ft^2	7.25 lb/ft^2	7.75 lb/ft^2	7.75 lb/ft^2
Power Loading	7.5 lb/hp	7.5 lb/hp	14.5 lb/hp	14.5 lb/hp
Tankage				
petrol	36 gal	52 gal	105 gal *	105 gal*
oil	4 gal	6¾ gal	8 gal	8 gal
water	10 gal	3½ gal	6 gal	6 gal
Performance				
Weights				
empty	1,811 lb		1,800 lb	1,800 lb
all-up	2,300 lb	2,300 lb	4,600 lb	4,600 lb
useful load	100 lb		600 + 2 passengers	1200 or 4 passengers (capacity 40 cu ft)
Maximum Speed,	142 mph		125 mph	123 mph
Cruising Speed	115 mph		100 mph	100 mph
Landing Speed	44 mph	40 mph	40 mph	40 mph
Initial Climb			650 ft/min	650 ft/min
Climb to,				
5000 ft			8 min	
10000 ft			18 min	
Service Ceiling	24,000 ft		16,000 ft	16,000 ft
Range	295 miles	450 miles	700 miles *	700 miles *
Endurance	2.5-3 h	4.5 h	7.5 h*	7.5 h*
Reference	A.Eng 14.7.20		A.Eng 14.7.20 & *manufacturer	A.Eng 14.7.20 & *manufacturer

	Raymor	Semiquaver	A.D.C.1	Nimbus Martinsyde
Engine	285 hp Rolls-Royce Falcon	300 hp Hispano-Suiza	395 hp Armstrong Siddeley Jaguar III	330 hp A.D.C. Nimbus
Dimensions				
Span	41 ft 0 in	20 ft 2 in	32 ft 9 3/8 in	32 ft 9 3/8 in
Chord upper/lower		4 ft 10½ in / 4 ft	5 ft 11in	
Length	26 ft 0 in	19 ft 3 in	25 ft 0 in	26 ft 10 in
Tailplane			11:2	
Height		8 ft 2 in	9 ft 6 in	9 ft 6 in
Surface Areas				
Wings			320 sq ft	320 sq ft
Ailerons			41 sq ft	
Tailplane			21 sq ft	
Elevators			16.5 sq ft	
Fin			6 sq ft	
Rudder			9.5 sq ft	
Wing Loading			8.28 lb/ft^2	
Power Loading			7 lb/hp	
Tankage				
petrol	370 gal		55 gal	
oil			4.5 gal	
Performance				
Weights				
empty			1,865 lb	2,014 lb
all-up		2,025 lb	2,650 lb	2,665 lb
military load				160 lb
Maximum Speed				
sea level		165 mph	163 mph	150 mph
10,000 ft			154 mph	
Cruising Speed	100 mph			131 mph
Landing Speed			52 mph	50 mph
Climb to				
5,000 ft			2 min 25	
10,000 ft			5 min 30	7 min 30
15,000 ft				14 min
20,000 ft			17 min 30	25 min
Service Ceiling			27,000 ft	23,500 ft
Endurance		2.5 h	3 h	2.5 h
Range				327 miles
Reference	variuos	variuos	variuos	variuos

Martinsyde Type A Mk II on floats or Type AS G-CAEA, operated by Price Brothers & Co. (K M Molson)

CHAPTER 7

MARTINSYDE AIRCRAFT IN POST-WAR OVERSEAS SERVICE

Canada and Newfoundland

The Aerial Survey Company Limited

Major F Sidney Cotton, an Australian pilot who had served in both the RNAS and RFC, went out to Newfoundland in November 1920 to fulfil a contract with a company formed to spot seals for the sealing fleet. After the first season, Cotton, together with Alan S Butler as partner, bought out the company and its assets but met with only very limited success due to difficulties in obtaining the confidence of the sealing companies. In addition to its sealing operations, the company provided intermittent mail services to many Newfoundland outposts, some as far north as Cartwright, Labrador. It also set up its own lumber business with a view to supplying pit-props to mining companies, made aerial surveys and carried out some prospecting operations.

Botwood on the Exploits River was selected during the first winter as the headquarters because of its geographical location and its railway connection to St Johns. A second base on the Quidi Vidi Lake at St.John's was added the following

winter and a further base was set up at Hawkes Bay in connection with the timber project. The first year Cotton used a D.H.9 inherited from the original company and a Westland Limousine, powered by a Napier Lion engine salvaged from his own D.H.14A which had been written off earlier when competing in the 1920 Aerial Derby. The D.H.9, G-EAMX, was written off at the beginning of the second year and the secondhand engine of the Westland gave endless trouble. However Cotton had already bought a Martinsyde Type A Mark II (G-EATY) and had ordered a second which was due to be delivered early the following year. The Martinsyde, however, was not used during the first season as it was damaged when one ski went through some thin ice. To these he added two smaller Westland cabin biplanes. All the aircraft could be equipped with skis or floats for operating from lakes and rivers, which of course were frozen over in the winter. As the two Martinsydes were not photographed together, it is uncertain whether they were similar in configuration or even whether the second was ever put into operation.

At least one of the Martinsydes was fitted with additional

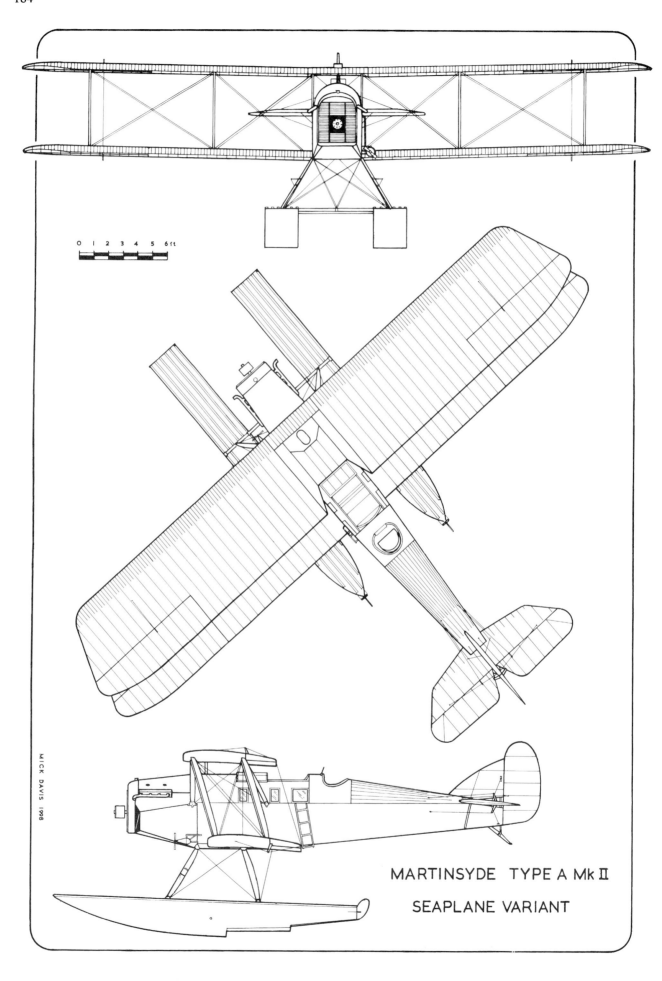

0 1 2 3 4 5 6 ft

MICK DAVIS 1998

MARTINSYDE TYPE A Mk II

SEAPLANE VARIANT

A Martinsyde Type A Mk I G-CAAX belonging to Price Brothers & Co on floats. (K M Molson)

equipment. A special windscreen was fitted to reduce the amount of cold air entering the open cockpit. Additional instrumentation was fitted, including a Vickers-Reid gyro turn indicator. A wireless was fitted above the main petrol tank and could be maintained on the ground by removing an outside panel. It could be operated by a crew member through a hinged door in the wooden panel ahead of the front seats. An aerial camera was mounted in the floor near the front wall. The cabin was heated by means of air piped from a funnel behind the radiator which then passed close to the port engine exhaust pipe. The amount of heat was controlled by means of a small lever mounted on the table in front of the wireless panel. The aircraft was never registered and flew without markings.

The airmail services are reasonably well documented through official sources. Most of the flights were between small isolated outposts, which but for aerial services were virtually cut off in the winter. The mail was collected at certain points and held until a means of transport became available. Scheduled flights were often delayed by the weather or by mechanical problems and sometimes mail intended for aerial transportation ended up by going by train or ship. Even so, during the winter months air transportation was the only means of delivery, particularly to the frozen wastes of Labrador.

Only three mail flights were made or attempted in Newfoundland during 1921 and only one to Halifax, Nova Scotia. None of these flights was made by the Martinsyde, which had been damaged when one of its skis broke through thin ice on the lake in December. The Martinsyde was repaired early in the New Year, and Cotton used it once to deliver mail to the sealing fleet whilst attempting a seal-spotting demonstration. Although some success in spotting seals was achieved, the sealing companies were not impressed and this type of operation was abandoned.

Some twelve mail deliveries were made in 1922, most of which were carried out by Major Cotton in the Martinsyde. On 23rd February, Major Cotton flew the Martinsyde from St.John's with three passengers and mail for Clarke's Beach, Bay Roberts and Harbour Grace. Mail was picked up from all points and a direct flight was made back to St.John's from Harbour Grace. Mail which had accumulated between 24th January and 27th February was flown by Major Cotton in the Martinsyde from Botwood on 3rd March for St.Anthony, arriving at 12.45 pm. Three hours later, the Martinsyde flew on to Battle Harbour, Labrador, arriving at 5.30 pm. On landing, one ski was damaged. Although the ski was quickly repaired, the onward flight to Cartwright was delayed by bad weather until the 6th. Major Cotton and his mechanic, J R Stannard, left Cartwright at 10.00 am on 12th March for the return flight to St.John's, stopping en route at St.Anthony at noon, at Seldom-Come-By at 1.30 pm, at Botwood at 2.45 pm and ended at Quidi Vidi, St.John's at 5.05 pm. The local press hailed this flight all in one day as a great achievement.

On 14th March, Cotton flew from St.John's to the Trinity Bay district and later flew back to Botwood, the mail going on to St.John's by rail. On 16th March, Cotton and Stannard flew mail to Twillingate, Fogo Island and district in the Martinsyde and five days later, Cotton carried out a flight in search of the Westland, which had failed to arrive the previous day at these destinations on a flight from Botwood. The Westland was located at Charles Brook, where it had force-landed, a mere 12 miles from Botwood. The mail was delivered promptly but it is not known who completed the flight. Cotton set off for Cartwright from St.John's on 28th March in the Martinsyde but was forced to return. He did not

Type A Mk II operated by Sidney Cotton for seal spotting and mail carrying in Canada (J M Bruce/S Leslie Collection)

start off again until 9th April when he flew to Botwood. A return mail flight was made from Botwood to the Hawkes Bay-Ingornachoix Bay area on 10th April. He then left Botwood on 20th April at 10.15 am, arrived at St.Anthony at 12.30 and continued on at 1.10 pm. He arrived over Battle Harbour at 2.30 pm but due to bad ice conditions there, he landed a few miles away at Hoop Hole Cave. Due to bad ice conditions reported at Cartwright, he returned to Botwood the same day, the Cartwright mail having to proceed by surface means and not arriving until 23rd June. Some mail was picked up on the return journey from St.Anthony to St.John's but mail at Battle Harbour was rejected due to its excess weight and did not arrive at its destination until 24th July. No more winter flights were made that year due to the unsuitability of the ice for aircraft landings.

Butler and Cotton split up during the Spring of 1923, Butler taking over the lumber business and Cotton continuing with the mail and aerial survey operations with his five machines.

The 1923 airmail season started by Major Cotton making a return trip from Botwood to the St.Barbe district which included Port Saunders, Hawkes Bay. On 8th February, Major Cotton in the Martinsyde and a pilot named Basedon in a newly-imported Westland, left Botwood for St.John's. The Westland crashed near Quidi Vidi, but Major Cotton completed his flight carrying mail, including some carried on from the Hawkes Bay trip. About this time, plans were being made to use the company's aircraft in the Labrador Gold Fields rush. Major Cotton in the Martinsyde flew mail to Hawkes Bay on 23rd March and continued on to Flower's Cove and Forteau, Labrador, before returning to Hawkes Bay. Bad weather prevented Cotton from flying back to Botwood on 2nd April, but he was back there by the 12th, when a successful flight was made to St.John's. On 7th May, Major Cotton returned to Labrador. On 3rd May, three

aircraft from the company made a trip from Botwood to Hawkes Bay with the intention of making an aerial map of the gold fields in Labrador. The return flight was made to Botwood on 16th or 17th May.

Towards the end of the sealing season, Cotton decide to make one more attempt to interest the sealing companies. When he was far out over the ice floes and some two hundred miles from land in the Martinsyde, the engine began to run roughly and it was only with difficulty and a good deal of luck that Cotton managed to get back to Botwood. This incident made him realise that it was not worth taking further risks in view of the limited potential of the operations and he decided to wind up the company. He sold the three Westland aircraft in Canada and later sold the two Martinsydes, presumably to Pitcairn Aviation in Pennsylvania.

Price Brothers Limited

Price Brothers Limited, with its head office in Quebec City, set up an aircraft division of the company in order to survey its timber limits, situated in the Lake St.John's district of Quebec, and to afford protection against forest fires. H S Quigley was appointed in charge of this division. The first aircraft, a Curtiss JN-4 (Canadian) Jenny fitted with a single Hoffar float proved unsuitable. Despite the ready availability of cheap war-surplus aircraft, the company purchased three Martinsyde Type A aircraft between 1920 and 1921. These aircraft were purchased through the agency operated by R H Nisbet in Quebec City.

Operation of these aircraft in 1923 was passed to a new company formed by Capt Quigley, the Dominion Aerial Exploration Limited, which flew under contract for both Price Brothers and for the Quebec Provincial Government. The operations were confined to the summer months and covered the whole of the Lake St.John's district, including

An unmarked Canadian Type A with a land undercarriage snowed-in. (A J Jackson Collection)

trips up many of the rivers such as the Mistassini, Peribonka, Shipshaw and Saguenay. The operational report for 1922 gives an example of the extent of the operations. This states that the operations started on 14th May and continued until 15th September. Sixty-seven flights were made totalling 124½ hours flying time and the services performed included aerial photography, survey and forest reconnaissance and fire protection.

The first of the Price Brothers' Martinsydes was G-CAAX, a Type A Mark I (c/n 15/1) powered by a Rolls-Royce Falcon III engine (serial 2947). It was officially registered on 21st July 1920. This machine had a very brief career, being written off on 18th August 1920. It was being piloted by P B Morency and had P Nesbitt and P Gauthier as passengers. Apparently the pilot took off from the dam at Lake Onatchiway without noticing that the tailplane was at the extreme of its adjustment. At a height of 1,000 feet, he tried to alter the angle of incidence but could not do so on account of the chain having come off the sprocket. While the pilot was trying to replace the chain the aircraft stalled and went into a spin. The pilot did not recover in time to clear some trees. The pilot and Nesbitt were seriously injured and Gauthier was killed instantly.

The second Martinsyde (G-CADG), another Type A Mark I (serial 15/2) was also registered on 21st July 1920. This aircraft was written off the following year on 30th May. Just prior to taking off, at a speed of about fifty mph, the machine struck one of the buoys marking the channel of the river Chicoutimi. The impact tore off the float undercarriage and the aircraft finished on its side. The aircraft became a total wreck during a careless salvage operation. Both the pilot, who was again Morency, and his passenger, A Sewell, were uninjured.

The third Martinsyde operated by Price Brothers was a Type A Mark.II (G-CAEA, serial 216-1). This aircraft was registered on 12th June 1921 and was operated for over two years by both Price Brothers and the Dominion Aerial Exploration Company. It was written off in an accident on 12th July 1923. Apparently during the absence of the manager of the company, the engineer in charge, a John Oldham, took the machine up without permission, with a fellow mechanic, Lee Evans, as passenger. Oldham was not the holder of the necessary pilot's certificate and was not in any case qualified to fly this type of aircraft. On reaching a height of approximately 300 feet, the machine was observed to be apparently out of control and immediately spun down into shallow water. The body of the passenger was found some hours afterwards but the body of the pilot was never recovered. The Court of Enquiry established that both men had been drinking heavily and surmised that if the manager had been present, the accident would not have happened.

One of the Martinsydes owned by Price Brothers shed a propeller during a winter flight sometime in the 1920s. The incident is reported to have occurred not far from Grandes Bergeronnes, some distance from Chicoutimi. The aircraft landed safely on a nearby lake without further mishap and the propeller apparently fell into some snow, from which it was recovered by local Indians the following spring. The propeller now resides in the Aviation Museum at Sainte-Marie-de-Beauce, Quebec.

Other Martinsydes in Canada

A Martinsyde F.6, formerly with the British registration G-EAPI (C/n given as E4500), was sold to the Canadian Government and taken on charge as G-CYEQ on 9th October

Finnish Martinsyde F.4 MA-33 at Utti in the winter of 1928/29. (J M Bruce/S Leslie Collection & Eino Ritaranta)

1922. It was struck off charge on 4th November 1925. A second F.6, with the British registration G-EATQ, was almost certainly the aircraft sold to Bishop-Barker Aeroplanes, Toronto, and flown by Lt Col W A Bishop VC, who was uninjured when it crashed at Armour Heights Aerodrome, Toronto, on 25th October 1920, before it had been allotted a Canadian registration. This registration may have been G-CYER, which was allocated to a Martinsyde F.6 but was never issued.

Finland

In April 1923, a Martinsyde F.4 Buzzard was acquired by the Finnish Air Force for evaluation tests. It was purchased from the Aircraft Disposal Company and was given the serial number 8E1 on its arrival in Finland in April. The Fokker D.X and Gourdou-Leseurre GL-21 fighters were also evaluated and the latter was chosen because of its lower price. It was found however that the Gourdou-Leseurre had some weak points and 14 Martinsydes were subsequently ordered on 11th February 1927. This batch, numbered MA-24 to MA-37, arrived in Finland over the period March-June 1927 and were joined by the evaluation machine which had been renumbered MA-23. After some modifications, for example deepened seats to accommodate parachutes, the planes served with the fighter unit of the Maalentoeskaaderi at Utti. They were much liked and gave valuable service.

In 1929 the Air Force began to receive Gloster Gamecocks as front-line fighters and the Buzzards were transferred in 1929-1930 to the Aviation School, Kauhava, to be used as trainers. In 1934, nine planes were withdrawn from use, but the others were still flying in 1938, the last being removed from the inventory as late as 28th February 1939.

There were three fatal accidents during the service career of the Buzzard in Finland. The first occurred on 25th February 1930 when MA-32 collided with an Aero A.32 over Utti and the pilot, Lt Lauri Lemminki, was killed. MA-25 spun in at Kauhava on 29th August 1930, killing Flt Cadet Valio Luoma and Sgt Heikki Marklund was also killed at Kauhava during ground attack training when his MA-34 stalled and crashed on 7th September 1934.

The Finnish Air Force Museum has no records of service by Buzzards against the Russian forces. However it is known that R W Kenworthy, long associated with Martinsyde aircraft and particularly the Semiquaver as described earlier, joined the Finnish Air Force as a pilot after being rejected by the RAF at the beginning of the Second World War and rose to the rank of Major. He has stated that he flew a Buzzard sometime during 1940-1 on active service and a photograph exists of him seated in a Buzzard with Finnish markings during this period. His Finnish uniform is now in store at the RAF Museum in Hendon.

The only remaining Buzzard anywhere is exhibited at the Finnish Air Force Museum at Tikkakoski. This is MA-24, which was formerly D4326 of the RAF. It arrived in Finland on 26th March 1927, following test flights made at Croydon by H H Perry on 2/3rd March. It was initially used by the Maalentoeskaaderi at Utti. It was transferred to the Kauhava Aviation School on 12th October 1928. It was damaged on landing on 24th February 1930 and the landing gear was damaged on 8th October 1931. On both occasions, the aircraft was repaired by the State Aircraft Factory. On the second occasion, the aircraft was returned to Utti. On 31st May 1934 it was dismantled and sent by rail to Kauhava. The last flight occurred during the summer of 1934 from

Finnish Martinsyde F.4 MA-29 at Kauhava in the winter of 1929. (Eino Ritaranta)

Laajalahti to Kauhava and the plane was withdrawn from use on 7th July, being dismantled and sent to the Air Force Depot. On 14th November 1934, it was given to the Mechanic School and was preserved for the museum. It was restored over the period 1970-1972 at Luonetjdrvi by Hämeen Lennosto and since 1979 has been on display in the museum. The plane flew a total of 492 hours 10 minutes in 1,320 flights.

Ireland

In June 1921, following a truce in the Anglo-Irish conflict, the British Government agreed to commence peace negotiations with an Irish delegation in London. The Irish delegation was led by Michael Collins, a General of the Irish Republican Army who had previously had a price of £10,000 placed on his head by the British Government. Eventually, after months of negotiations, the Anglo-Irish Treaty was signed. This led to twenty-six of the thirty-two counties forming the Irish Free State, with a constitution allowing total control of its own affairs at home and abroad but subject to membership of the British Commonwealth and allegiance to the King. While this satisfied a majority of the people of Ireland, it did not satisfy a significant proportion of IRA members who had fought for an Irish Republic totally independent of Britain. Serious rioting took place early in 1922 and by the middle of the year a full scale civil war had broken out between Nationalist Government forces which supported the Treaty and the Republicans who did not.

Early in 1922, the Irish Army Air Service was established, commanded by T W McSweeney, who was appointed Major General and Director of Military Aviation. His second-in-command was C F Russell, who was also appointed Major General and Director of Civil Aviation. Both these men had previously been RAF pilots and members of the Irish Republican Army. No.1 Squadron was formed with training aircraft allocated to A Flight and combat aircraft to B Flight. In 1924, following a reorganisation of the Irish Army, the Air Service became the Irish Army Air Corps.

When General Collins went to London to negotiate the treaty in 1921, there was a possibility that he would be detained by the British Government should the negotiations have failed. McSweeney and Russell were instructed to obtain an aircraft, which was to be kept in readiness near London, if it became necessary for Collins to attempt an escape. The Treasurer of the Irish Self-Determination League was persuaded to part with a cheque for £2,600. Russell, who had previously worked on the Canadian rail network, introduced himself to the Aircraft Disposal Company at Croydon as the representative of the Canadian Forestry Commission and negotiated the purchase of a Martinsyde Type A Mark II. The particular aircraft (c/n 217) had been built in 1920 and had been fitted with an engine but had not yet been flown. It was withdrawn from storage and make its first flight, of about 30 minutes, in the hands of Capt Clarke and Mr E C Green, at Brooklands on 24th November 1921.

The escape plan involved Collins and three of his aides making a rendezvous with the aircraft at a place near London. The aircraft would take them south-west of Bristol, skirting the Welsh coast and across the sea to Rosslare. From there Russell would fly them northwards, following the railway to Dublin, where the Leopardstown racecourse on the outskirts had been selected as a landing ground. It was planned that this spot would be held by a heavily-armed force of volunteers under the control of McSweeney.

Russell gave instructions to his superiors in Dublin on

Martinsyde Type A Mark II, 'The Big Fella', at Baldonnel. (Donal McCarron)

how the receiving party should prepare for his arrival:

McSweeney will be able to give all instructions for the landing, but it must be clearly understood that the two men who are to catch the wings and rear struts make sure not to catch the edges of the wings. If this so happens that they misjudge the distance it must be impressed upon them to fall flat on the ground and let the aeroplane pass over.

In the event of our having to cross at night, it would be necessary for your people to mark out an L-shaped figure upon the landing ground, this should be done by means of four petrol tin fires or flares at intervals of 60 yards. The fourth flare would be placed in order to indicate the direction of the wind with the remaining three placed accordingly. The cloth signal to be used by daylight is also a wind signal, the triangular piece should be placed indicating the direction in which the wind is blowing. I will be able to notify you fully of the time at which departure will take place, and the journey is calculated to take between three and four hours.

Although the Aircraft Disposal Company was selling large numbers of many types of aircraft to anyone that may have been interested, Russell was keen not to arouse its suspicions over the true purpose of the venture. As the peace talks dragged on, Russell embarked on a lengthy series of test flights and on each occasion found some minor fault with the aircraft, such as incorrect rigging, suspected tail flutter or a faulty oil gauge, but nothing which would prevent the aircraft from being ready if required.

In the event the aircraft was not needed and after the Anglo-Irish Treaty was signed Russell revealed his true identity to ADC. The aircraft was delivered to Croydon aerodrome three days later on 9th December 1921, where it was first placed in storage and later dismantled and delivered in crates on 16th June 1922 to Baldonnel aerodrome. The aircraft was reassembled at Baldonnel by Army Air Service personnel and made airworthy, as reported by F/Lt Wigglesworth on 21st July:

The five-seater Martinsyde is being erected and has the engine installed, undercarriage fitted but no planes. This machine they are going to use for carrying about Higher

Army Command when necessary. The machine has seating for 4 passengers and is apparently convertible into a seaplane, floats having been supplied.

It was finished silver with the Irish colours on the rudder and on the fuselage sides beneath the cockpit. It was not allocated an Army Air Service serial number but had the inscription *City of Dublin* on the port side of the engine and *Cathair Atha Cliath* on the starboard side. The aircraft was nicknamed "The Big Fella" in memory of Collins.

Combat aircraft were urgently required to provide air support for the Irish National Army against the Republican forces and deliveries of aircraft to the Irish Army Air Service, from the RAF and ADC, commenced in July 1922. Four Martinsyde F.4 Buzzards were purchased from ADC and the first Buzzard (ex D4285), piloted by Major General McSweeney, was delivered to Baldonnel aerodrome on 15th August 1922 and entered service with B Flight, No.1 Squadron, as M1. F/Lt Wigglesworth reported to HQ No.12 Wing on 21st August:

A Martinsyde F.4 and a S.E.5a were delivered last week. McSweeney flew the Martinsyde up to Shotwick and had two forced landings en route through the water connection falling off and then an oil connection doing likewise. In addition the propellers of both machines stripped to the prop boss. Only the Martinsyde has been flown at Baldonnel and this machine is liked very much. The engine in the Martinsyde five-seater has been installed in the old Bristol.

From October onwards, the National Army was engaged on offensive combat operations in the south and west of Ireland, where the majority of the Republican forces were concentrated. A detachment from the Army Air Service was sent south to re-open the former RAF airfield at Fermoy, Co. Cork, from which aircraft could provide air support for the units of the National Army engaged on combat operations in Co. Cork and Co. Kerry. On 1st October 1922, the Buzzard (M1) arrived at the airfield, piloted by a Lt James Fitzmaurice. Incidentally, Lt Fitzmaurice had previously been in command of the Junkers W.33 *Bremen*, the first aircraft to have successfully completed a west-to-east flight over the

Irish Martinsyde F.4 at Fermoy with two D.H.9s and a Bristol Fighter in the background. (Donal McCarron)

Atlantic Ocean.

Operating from the airfield at Fermoy, the Buzzard and other aircraft flew reconnaissance patrols, escorted trains, dropped leaflets and other missions in support of the National Army. On one such mission, when piloted by Lt Fitzmaurice, the engine of the Buzzard failed. In the pilot's own words:

The Government had declared a general amnesty to the Irregular Forces offering a free pardon to those that surrendered their arms by a certain date. My unit was called upon to deliver these amnesty proclamation circulars over the mountains of West Cork and Kerry in order to bring the notice to the attention of those who might fail to see it in the newspapers.

On Saturday morning, 14th October 1922, I set out from my aerodrome at Fermoy in Martinsyde F.4 No.1 carrying a large load of these leaflets, made up of bundles of fifty to be distributed over the Kerry mountains. Upon arrival over the mountainous district outside Ireland's most famous beauty spot, Killarney, my engine failed and I was forced to make a landing. I landed in a field outside Killarney Mental Hospital. I worked on my engine all Saturday and had everything ready to take off on Sunday evening.

Killarney was at this time completely isolated as the telephone wires connecting it with the outside world had all been destroyed and wireless had not at that time been installed in the town. In addition the town was completely surrounded by strong Irregular forces. It was therefore impossible to send any message to my aerodrome regarding my forced landing. They were very anxious regarding my safety and had search parties from every garrison town searching the hills for me.

On Sunday evening at about 1700 hours, with the aid of some local troops, I started my engine and being given a flying start managed to get over some large pine trees at the end of the field. I was beginning to consider myself exceptionally lucky at being safely in the air when I was greeted with some strong bursts of machine gun fire from members of the Irregulars who had been waiting for me to hop off. The wings and fuselage of my machine were riddled with bullets, but fortunately neither myself nor any vital part of the engine or airframe was hit.

By nightfall I had succeeded in reaching the town of Mallow, about 18 miles from my aerodrome but here again, *owing to engine trouble, I was compelled to effect a forced landing about two miles outside the town. On examination the following day, it was discovered that the machine could not be flown out of the field without installing a new engine but as the roads were absolutely impassable at the time owing to trees having been felled in many places and all the bridges were destroyed it was decided to dismantle the aeroplane and store it in the military barracks for the time being. The Martinsyde remained in a shed from 16th October until it was towed to Fermoy by road on 19th November 1922. It was rebuilt at Fermoy and flew again on 8th December 1922.*

The remaining three Buzzards (ex-D4281, D4298 and D4274) were delivered to Baldonnel aerodrome on 14th October 1922. These aircraft (M2, M3 and M4) joined M1 in B Flt, No.1 Squadron. All the Buzzards were finished in standard khaki-green and clear dope finish with struts left in natural wood. The national tricolour was displayed on the rudder and above and below the wings. The serial numbers were painted in white on the fuselage sides just below and in front of the tailplane.

On 4th December, as reported by the *Irish Times* the following day, a scout type aircraft of the Irish Army Air Service became the first to fire its guns in anger during the conflict. This was almost certainly a Martinsyde as the only other scout type aircraft operated by the Service, an S.E.5a, had been destroyed in a crash the day before. To quote the *Irish Times:*

For the first time, an aeroplane has been brought into action against people attacking National soldiers. A party of National troops was travelling between Drimoleague and Dunmanway, Co. Cork yesterday conducting operations in this wide area. About 60 fully armed men sighted the military in two lorries and prepared to ambush them. They took up well covered positions behind high fences on the roadside and when the lorries were passing intensive fire was opened on them.

One soldier was killed. The troops replied with fire but realised that they were outnumbered and that their attackers were in excellent defensive positions and sent for reinforcements. An aeroplane also came. It was of the small scouting type. The plane soon came up with the ambush party, locating them near a wood towards Leap. The pilot descended to a few hundred feet and when just over the ambush party nose dived in their direction. Panic at once seized them. The majority of them threw themselves on the ground. Others, in terror, discharged their arms and sought cover. Bombs were dropped from the aeroplane and the ambush party was filed with consternation. It was then observed that they were splitting up and that the men were scampering in ones and twos towards the wood, seeking any shelter it might afford. The plane however circled the wood and raked it with machine gun fire. The ambush party having been completely dealt with, the plane drew away, returning safely to its base. The dramatic employment of air force against attacks on national troops has made a great impression here in Cork, where for the past week or so it has been used in reconnoitring and probably in despatch carrying.

After the Civil War ended in May 1923, the Buzzards, with the other aircraft in service with the Army Air Service, participated in military exercises and other assignments for the National Army. Apparently the Buzzards were considered to be very unreliable aircraft by the Army Air Service (and later the Air Corps) due to frequent engine failures.

One Buzzard (M4) was withdrawn from service in September 1925, followed by a second Buzzard (M2) in April 1929. On 18th September 1928, one of the Buzzards (M3) was written-off in a crash and on 16th May 1929, a second Buzzard (M1) crashed in a field adjacent to Baldonnel aerodrome. The pilot, Lt Arthur Russell, was seriously injured and the aircraft destroyed. For ten years, the four Buzzards were the only fighters to have entered service with the Irish Army Air Corps until four Gloster Gladiator Is were delivered in 1938.

The Martinsyde Type A Mark II remained in service with the Army Air Service and the Air Corps until 1927. It was used as a personal hack first by Major Maloney, the CO of the Air Corps, and then by his successor, Commandant Fitzmaurice. The aircraft was then used as an instructional airframe for a short period before it was placed in storage at Baldonnel aerodrome. It was broken up and scrapped in 1935 after having flown for only about thirty hours.

The only Martinsyde to be delivered to Japan - an F.4 Buzzard.

Japan

In April 1921, a 29-member British aviation mission, led by Capt The Master of Sempill, arrived in Japan at the invitation of the Navy. Centred around the Kasumigauri Naval Air Station, the British instructors trained Japanese naval air servicemen on the advanced techniques in handling both land and seaplanes. British aircraft imported for the training programme included the Avro 504K, a Short floatplane, the Gloster Sparrowhawk, Parnall Panther, Sopwith Cuckoo, Blackburn Swift, Supermarine Channel and F.5. A single Martinsyde F.4, powered by a 300 hp Hispano-Suiza engine, was also imported into Japan. A British Embassy official visiting Kasumigauri early in 1922 reported that he had seen the newly-erected Martinsyde flying.

Sempill considered one of his duties to be the promotion of sales in Japan of British aircraft. In this aim he was unsuccessful. Besides strong competition from the French, the Japanese authorities were keen to set up their own design and manufacturing facilities and had taken on a number of foreign designers and production engineers, including British ones, in order to produce indigenous designs. Flt Lt W E G Brown of the RAF visited a factory in Nagoya in March 1923 and reported that it was producing single-seat and two-seat fighters designed by Mitsubishi, a torpedo-carrying triplane, a Nieuport design powered by an 80 hp Le Rhône and 300 hp Hispano and 450 hp Napier Lion engines. He also reported that he had seen a machine, almost identical to an F.4 but with a modified tail and fitted with three flotation bags, which had been used for deck-landing trials on the *Hosho*. Following the trials, the cowling had been modified to improve the view over the nose. By replacing the radiator with two cylindrical radiators under the engine and moving the carburettors to positions either side of the engine, it had been possible to incorporate a concave upper surface into the cowling.

Japanese representatives, including Capt T Toyoda, the Naval Attache, and Lt Cdr Kato of the Imperial Japanese Navy, were given a demonstration of the Martinsyde A.D.C.1 at the ADC factory at Croydon during December 1924 but no purchase was made.

A single F.4 Buzzard acquired by the Latvian AF in 1923 and used for training purposes.

Latvia

Detailed records of the Kara Aviacijas Pulks (KAP) or Latvian Aviation Regiment between 1922 until 1929 have not been found. However, by 1929 the LAR was organised into the 1st, 2nd and 3rd Army Division's Reconnaissance Squadrons, the 4th Fighter Squadron, the 5th Reserve Squadron, the 6th Long Range Reconnaissance Squadron, equipped with Letov Smolik S16Ls, and the 7th Squadron at the Aviation School.

A single F.4 Buzzard was acquired by the KAP in 1923 and received the serial number 31. It was supplied without

Three Latvian A.D.C.1s in flight. (Philip Jarrett)

armament and was used for training duties, probably with the Aviation School's squadron. In 1926, it paid a visit of friendship to Kaunas, the capital of Lithuania, in the company of two Ansaldo A.1 Balillas. Its Hispano-Suiza 8Fb engine had been replaced with a 425 hp Armstrong-Siddeley Jaguar engine by 17th August 1928 and, after several mishaps, with a Belgian-made 340 hp Serval V (serial number 5662) by 4th January 1937. This latter modification increased its speed to 225 kph despite a weight increase to 1,256 kg. It served with No.2 Squadron in this form until it crashed on 13th May 1937. It crashed again on 20th August 1938 at Spilve but the pilot, Karlis Grube, survived.

Latvia acquired eight ADC-1s from ADC on 11th June 1926, with the first of these being given the registration G-EBMH while it was being tested by ADC. Acceptance tests were carried out in front of inspectors from Latvia. All the tests were completed to their satisfaction except for a requirement to climb to 10,000 ft in 12 minutes which seemed almost impossible to achieve. However, Frank Courtney was invited to try and achieved the desired result without difficulty, the curve on the barograph looking as if it had been drawn with a pair of compasses. The Martinsydes were transported to Latvia in crates along with some D.H.9s and were assembled at the KAP repair workshops during the winter of 1926/7 by a British engineer provided by ADC. These were test flown by a British pilot before being handed over to the KAP. While testing one of these aircraft, the engine stopped and he force-landed the aircraft on the local race course in Riga, stopping in a distance of about 200 metres and damaging the undercarriage in the process. The aircraft was flown out again after the port wheel had been

replaced.

The aircraft were given Latvian serial numbers 11, 14K, 16, 21, 24, 60, 61 and 66, probably in he same order as the manufacturer's construction numbers (K.502 to K.509). How these related to the British serials is not known for certain. However Latvian serials were normally issued in chronological order, those of written-off aircraft being reallocated to new aircraft. A ninth ADC-1 (serial number 62) was either manufactured locally from the parts of crashed aircraft or built under licence.

The aircraft arrived in their normal all-silver finish. Most but not all were camouflaged dark green on their upper surfaces as and when they were returned to the workshops for servicing.

The Martinsydes were first allocated to 1 Army Division Squadron and were used later in their service history by Nos.1, 2 and 3 Fighter Squadrons. The type gave valuable service, although over a span of ten years or more most of the aircraft were written off in accidents as recounted below and the remainder were taken out of service in 1938.

On 18th August 1927, an ADC-1 (s/n 21), piloted by Serzants (Sergeant) Janis Vistucis, spun out of control into the ground amidst pine trees close to Spilve airfield near Riga and burst into flames, killing the pilot. During the summer of 1928, s/n 11, piloted by Janis Abolins, damaged its starboard wing when it hit a tethered horse on landing at a small airstrip near Krustpils whilst preparing for a flying demonstration at an air show. On 19th July 1930, Virsleitnants (1st Lt) Janis Rucelis was flying s/n 60 from Riga to a summer camp at Daugavpils when he decided to indulge in some low flying. He was flying the aircraft close to the surface of the River

Daugava when its undercarriage struck a steel cable stretched across the river at the ferry at Koknese and it somersaulted into the water. The pilot was lucky to be rescued by the captain of the ferry boat suffering only facial injuries. The aircraft was salvaged and repaired. The aircraft was again repaired after crashing on 31st July 1937 and afterwards served with No.2 Fighter Squadron.

On 28th or 29th August 1931, Virsniekvietnieks (WO) Augusts Lapins was engaged in target practice over the sea near Daugavpils in a camouflaged s/n 11 when he hit the towing cable of the target drone and sheared off one wingtip. The pilot made no effort to parachute to safety and spun into the ground near the seashore and was killed. It was rumoured that he had not been well enough for flying as he had been discharged from hospital only a few days previously. On 24th April 1933 in an unknown A.D.C.1, Virsleitnants Davis Timmermanis survived a crash with multiply fractures when he spun in from about 1,000 metres. Virsleitnants Teodors Svanbergs died when he hit a telegraph pole in A.D.C.1 s/n 16 on 20th July 1934. Whilst serving with No.2 Fighter Squadron, s/n 61 crashed on 5th September 1934 but was subsequently repaired and was known to be serving with No.1 Fighter Squadron in May 1937.

ADC-1 s/n 66 was repaired after crashing on 6th August 1934. It was overhauled on 5th July 1935 and again on 1st September 1935. It was broken up in September 1937 whilst serving with No.2 Fighter Squadron.

Serzants Alberts Gudermanis crashed in an A.D.C.1 (serial unknown) near Spilve on 20th July 1938. On completion of a forty-minute advanced flying exercise at an altitude of 3,000 metres, the pilot decided to lose height by carrying out a series of loops with the engine ticking over at minimum revs. When he was over the airfield at an altitude of 700 metres, he felt a tremor on the port side of the aircraft and saw that a strut near the fuselage had broken and the wings were starting to fold upwards. He pointed the aircraft away from the beach area where people were relaxing and left the engine ticking over. He then attempted to execute a half roll in order to fall out but the aileron control wires had jammed, so he pushed himself out with one leg on the seat, dived over the side and pulled the ripcord of his Irvin parachute when clear of the aircraft. The aircraft crashed in a meadow just north of the Lacaru cemetery.

A similar accident occurred a month later on 20th August, when Virsniekvietnieks Karlis Grube in s/n 31 was carrying out an advanced exercise adjacent to the Spilve airfield. After executing a loop at about 1,000 metres, the rear starboard wing strut broke. The pilot attempted to return to base but the broken strut was damaging the lower starboard wing. The pilot therefore switched off the engine and parachuted to safety, the aircraft crashing between Bolderaja and Riga about ½ km from the airfield.

Lithuania

After Lithuania declared its independence on 16th February 1918, this unfortunate country found itself partially occupied firstly by the Bolsheviks until August 1920 and then by Polish forces. Even after the phony war with Poland ended in December 1927, the south-eastern part of the country and the capital Vilnius remained in Polish hands. In these difficult times, the Lithuanian Government tried to maintain an effective army and air force in the parts of the country under

*F.4 Buzzard of the Lithuanian AF at Kauna airport.
(Edmundo Jasiuno)*

its control. An Aviation Unit was formed as part of the Army on 1st January 1919 and gradually equipped itself with a miscellaneous collection of aircraft, mainly from Germany. This was reformed into the 1st Eskadrile of the Karo Aviacija in the summer of 1920 and the 2nd Eskadrile was formed in 1921, using Fokker D.VII aircraft.

Continual efforts were made to expand the air force and on 2nd June 1921, the President of the Republic of Lithuania, A Stulginskis, assigned 500,000 Auksinas (the temporary currency at that time) to the purchase of two fighters from Britain. Following negotiations by J Simkus, the Minister of Defence and General M Katche, Chief of the General Staff, two F.4 Buzzards, c/n numbers D4306 and D4310, were purchased at a cost of £2,100 c.i.f. (590,000 Auksinas), mainly through donations from American Lithuanians who had previously visited Lithuania during that summer and had been impressed by the fledgling national air force. The price also covered spares, including five propellers, four machine guns, a radiator and undercarriage, machine gun and engine parts. The two aircraft carried inscriptions *Amerikietis* and *Amerikiete*, (American Woman and American Man respectively) followed by *Amerikos Lietuvia Auka* (The Donation of American Lithuanians).

After delivery by sea to Liepaja in Latvia and assembly, the aircraft were test flown by Lieut Jurgis Dobkevicius (later to become an aircraft designer) on 21st September (D4310) and 30th September 1921 (D4306) and were accepted into the inventory (order no.241) of the Aviation Park on 27th September. The Martinsydes were used by 1-moji oro eskadrile (1 Fighter Air Squadron) until 1925, when they were replaced by the Letov Sm-20, and then by a training squadron. D4310 was written off in December 1932 and D4306 was taken out of service on 4th December 1936 after a pilot-cadet had struck telephone wires on landing.

Little is known of their service history, although one incident is recorded when one Martinsyde gave an aerobatic display over a visiting British warship in Klaipeda in 1924. During the flight back to base, the engine cowling acted as a airbrake when it swung back on the rear hinge and rested on the upper wing. Modifications to the locks prevented further problems. Pilots found the aircraft to be faster but less manoeuvrable than the Fokker D.VII and that elevator reversal occurred during a dive. The engine tended to stall during a loop and during a sustained dive.

Polish F.4 Buzzard in its red and white striped markings. (J B Cynk)

Poland

Only one Martinsyde was delivered to Poland. It was an F.4, with the civil registration G-EAWE (ex-H7780), supplied following negotiations between the Polish authorities and a representative of ADC acting on behalf of Handley Page. It was delivered by air on 29th January 1921 to the airfield at Mokotowie and test flown in Warsaw during February by a British pilot, Capt Percy, and by 2/Lt Stephan Pawlikowski. Although it was rated highly, no further aircraft of this type were purchased. The aircraft found its way to 1 Air Regiment's Training Squadron, where it was kept as an example of construction methods. It was air-tested on 28th May and on 19th June it was allocated to the Experimental Section of the Military Centre. It was assigned to Capt Jósef Hendrik on 30th June 1923 as No.4 in a round-Poland flight. However, the aircraft was withdrawn on 4th August after suffering a partial engine failure on the first leg. It was overhauled at the Centralne Warsztaty Lotnicze (Central Aeronautical Works) in 1924. By that time, it was fitted with long exhaust pipes, presumably taken from one of Poland's Hispano-powered Bristol Fighters and its Rafwire interplane bracing had been replaced by cables with turnbuckles covered by lightweight fairings. Between 1924 and 1926, it was used as a personal hack by General Wlodzimierz Zagórski to visit the Puloki Lotnicze (Air Regiments) when he was combining the duties of Chief of the Departament Aeronautyki within the Ministerstwo Spraw Wojskowych (Ministry of Military Affairs) and the Commanding Officer of Lotnictwo Wojskowe. At this time the aircraft was painted in red and white stripes without any other markings, and as a result was nicknamed 'the mattress'. The machine was returned to the training squadron after the coup d'état by Jozef Pilsudski in May 1926. The aircraft was written off following an accident on 9th July 1926 at the Warsaw Mokotow airfield when the undercarriage collapsed on landing. The aircraft nosed over and was badly damaged, although the pilot, the squadron's instructor, H Bohdan Butkiewicz, was hardly hurt.

Portugal

In the spring of 1919, the RAF had made arrangements to fly four aircraft, two D.H.4s, a Bristol Fighter and a Handley Page V/1500, to Lisbon on a long distance endurance trial. Because of competition from the French in Spain, it was decided to arrange a demonstration in Madrid on the way to Portugal and to invite other manufacturers to participate. The only condition was that each manufacturer would buy its respective aircraft from the Air Ministry after its arrival in Lisbon. In the event, although Martinsyde agreed to take part, there was insufficient time for the necessary preparations to be made for the provision of spares and other necessaries.

Martinsyde subsequently made its own arrangements and after gaining the necessary flight approvals from Spain on 2nd October, Raynham flew F.4 G-EANM to Spain on 6th October and from Spain to Alverca, some 15 miles inland from Lisbon, on 11th November. He flew the last leg of 360 miles in 3 hours 5 minutes against a strong headwind. There, the aircraft was bought by British residents and presented to the Portuguese Government. It was christened *Vasco da Gama* by Lady Drummond and formally handed over to the Portuguese Minister of War by the British Ambassador, Sir Lancelot Carnegie on behalf of the donors. The aircraft was first allocated to the Grupo de Esquadrilnas de Aviagco

F.4 Buzzard in the markings of the Portuguese Air Force. (K M Molson)

Republica (G.E.A.R.) at Amadora before going to Tancos. The aircraft was painted silver overall with the national insignia on the rudder and a diagonal red stripe outlined in black and a dark yellow greyhound (the insignia of G.E.A.R. and the unit at Tancos respectively) on the fuselage sides.

Subsequently in 1923, Captain Ribeiro da Fonseca bought three more Hispano-powered F.4 Buzzards, with funds allocated to the Esquadrilna de Treinto e Depuslto, later known as the Esquadrilna No.1 de Caça. These joined the first fighter at Tancos. The three new aircraft were adorned with the greyhound insignia but were not allocated names or serial numbers. These fighters remained in service until 1934 when they were replaced by three Hawker Furies (numbered 50, 51 and 52).

An F.4 Buzzard in Russian markings. (G Petrov via Harry Woodman)

Russia

Two months after the Bolshevik coup on 28th January 1918, Lenin decreed the formation of an air arm of the Red Army called the Raboche-Krest'yanskii Krasnyi Voenno-Vozdushnyi Flot (RKKVF) or Worker's and Peasant's Red Military Air Fleet. By October 1920, when foreign intervention and the civil war had effectively come to an end, the RKKVF had collected about a thousand Russian and foreign aircraft of more than eighty types, of which many were obsolescent and few were operational.

By the end of 1921, many of the units had been

Two Portuguese F.4 Buzzards at Tancos with a Bréguet 14 in the background

A Russian F.4 Buzzard comes in contact with the Motherland. (Andrei Alexandrov)

disbanded and the force reorganised. Some foreign types were being built in Russia and attempts were made to purchase new equipment from abroad. A total of about 270 aircraft were ordered from Germany, Holland, Great Britain and Italy for delivery in the summer of 1922 and more were ordered in 1923 and 1924.

Martinsyde F.4s were amongst the aircraft ordered by the RKKVF authorities to re-equip some of its fighter units. Twenty were ordered by the Soviet Government from ex-RAF stocks held by ADC and arrived in Leningrad on board the *Miranda* in May 1922, followed by another twenty-one in the autumn of 1923. Twenty-five were in service by September 1923 and a year later thirty-eight were on charge. As the original Hispano-Suiza engines wore out they were replaced by 290-hp M-6 Soviet-built copies.

The aircraft were allocated to 2 Otdel'naya Istrebit'elnaya Aviaeskadril'ya based at Ukhtomskaya, near Moscow, and served with this unit until withdrawn from operational use when the unit was disbanded in 1926-27. After having been in service for thirty months, thirty-one of the Martinsydes were presented to the VVS at the Central Airport in Moscow on 17th May 1925, where some 35,000 people had been gathered to witness the ceremony. Soviet railway and waterway workers had subscribed 750,000 roubles to an aviation fund to be used to establish a VVS eskadril'ya to be named Dzerzhinsky after F.E. Dzerzhinsky, who left his post as People's Commissar for Communications to become the first chief (Cheka) of the secret political police. The fighters had been given names such as *Proletarskaya oborona* (Proletarian Defence), *Proletarii* (Proletarian), *Krasnyi zheleznodorozhnik* (Red Railway Worker), *Krasnyi gorets* (Red Mountaineer), *Krasnyi severyanin* (Red Northerner), *Krasnovostochnyi* (Red Easterner), *Strazh revolyuttsii* (Revolutionary Guard), *Vsegda gotov* (Always Ready), *Chekist* (Chekist), *Serg Ordzhonikidze*, *Jan Tomp* and *Pavel Vavilov*.

Some Martinsydes also served in the fighter trainer role with the 1st Higher School of Military Pilots in Moscow and the Strel'bom school at Serpukhov, later moved to Orenburg. On 29th June 1928, the NII VVS received serial number 4280 from Zavod 39 in Moscow, where it had been rebuilt after a crash. At the end of that year, about twenty Martinsydes remained, the Akademiya VVF had one, the 1st and 2nd Schools of Military Pilots each had two, while the 3rd School of Military Pilots (previously Military School of Aerial Combat and Strel'bom) had ten. Those with the 3rd School were withdrawn from use in 1930, but the 1st School

persevered with two until July 1931. Eleven were handed over to Osoaviakhim, but were probably used as instructional airframes and were not flown. The service histories of individual aircraft where known are summarised in the listings of production in the Appendix.

Numbers of F.4 Buzzards in Russian Service

1.10.23 - 25	1.10.26 - 32	1.10.29 - 18
1.10.24 - 38	1.10.27 - 30	1.10.30 - 13
1.10.25 - 33	1.10.28 - 22	1.05.31 - 2

Freddie Raynham in front of F.4 Buzzard G-EANM at Cuatro Vientos, Spain. (The E A Harlin Collection)

Spain

The Spanish Servicio de Aviacion Militar was formed in March 1911, with the formation of an Aviation School at the airfield of Cuatro Vientos near Madrid, and the Aeronautica Naval was formed separately by Royal Decree on 13th September 1917. Although Spain was one of the first countries to use aircraft in military operations, its forces found it difficult to update its equipment during the First World War at a time when the combatants were of necessity making significant technical advances. After the war, Spain therefore became a target for salesmen, principally from Britain and France, keen to dispose of surplus equipment.

Raynham flew to Spain on 6th October 1919 in Martinsyde F.4 G-EANM, one of four civil-registered demonstrators, leaving Brooklands and landing at Vittoria in northern Spain after a stop in France. He made several flights around northern Spain before proceeding to Cuatro Vientos. At the time, this was the best airfield in the peninsula, being large and having a good surface of fine sand. He was there for five weeks during which time he demonstrated the aircraft to the Aeronautica Militar, as it had become known. In one impressive demonstration, he reached a height of 2,500 metres in 6 minutes whilst carrying a 300-lb bomb.

On his return to Britain, he reported that the Spanish air force already operated a number of French machines including Bréguet bombers, Farman F.50s and twin-boom Caudrons, with a variety of engines. He also reported that the peninsula was generally unsuited for commercial aviation due to the mountainous terrain and unsuitable landing grounds. He did however think that there was scope for flying boat services between coastal towns.

When the Spanish air forces came to re-equip in 1920, the dilemma was to choose the best types from the vast array

Six Martinsyde F.4As of the Spanish Aeronautica Naval in flight during 1935; MS-6 and MS-7 are two-seaters.

of war-surplus aircraft which were available. Ingeniero Naval Franco was assigned the task of making recommendations for purchases to the Jef de la Aviacion Naval (Chief of Naval Aviation). The first consideration was to choose a primary trainer and the selection fell naturally on the Avro 504K which was in widespread use. A pair of versatile two-seat Martinsyde F.6 aircraft were also chosen as fighter conversion trainers with the supplementary roles of reconnaissance and bombing. These aircraft were fitted with the 270 hp Rolls-Royce Falcon engine and wheeled undercarriages but metal floats were also supplied. However at that time the problems of converting them at the airfield workshops and transferring them to the marine base precluded their use as floatplanes for the time being.

By the end of January 1921, the Aeronautica Naval had the following aircraft available, in addition to dirigibles and free and captive balloons, with the landplanes allocated to La Escuela (Flying School) at the Aerodromo del Prat: 15 Avro 504K (serials NOAB to NOAP), 6 Savoia flying boats (serials NSAB to NSAG), 2 Martinsyde F.6 (serials NYAB and NYAC) and 2 Felixstowe F.3 (serials NRAB and NRAC).

The naval auxiliary *España No.3* arrived at Barcelona on 8th March 1922 with additional aircraft, including several Avro 504Ls, four more Martinsyde F.6s and two Parnall Panthers. All this equipment was taken to the airfield in crates. It was some time before the Martinsydes were reassembled as priority was given to the Parnall Panthers, these being awaited for trials aboard the *Dédalo*, a seaplane tender with a rudimentary flight deck aft of the funnel.

By the middle of 1922, the strength of the Aeronautica Naval had grown to 33 flying boats at the flying boat base, 16 flying boats and one Parnall Panther allocated to the *Dédalo*,

and 17 Avro 504K/L (six of which were in store and two under repair), five Martinsyde F.6s and one Parnall Panther equipping La Escuela at the Aerodromo del Prat. Plans were laid to equip one of the Avros with skis for landing trials on the *Dédalo* and to convert three of the Martinsyde F.6s to floatplanes for conversion training.

During December 1922, some or all of the Martinsydes took part in an official visit to Italy, the party including the *Dédalo*, several flying boats, some Avro 504s and two airships. By 1923, the Martinsydes were proving themselves as conversion trainers, with the first group of pilots having graduated. The strength of La Escuela at the Aerodromo del Prat on 1st January 1924 was 13 Avro 504K/L (9 flying and 4 under repair), two Panthers (one flying and one under repair), two Blackburn Swifts (both flying) and four Martinsydes (two flying and two under repair).

On 18th January 1923, a Martinsyde F.6, bearing the serial number M-NYAD, suffered an engine failure and overturned while making a forced landing at the racecourse. The crew, consisting of Alfirez de navio (2/Lt.) Dur`n and mechanico Jordana, was uninjured. The damaged aircraft was sent to the workshop for repair the following day. Dur`n was subsequently killed in another Martinsyde accident on 19th July 1926.

Towards the end of May 1924, Teniente de navio (Lt) Gomez Ceballos was sent to Britain for a couple of months. Following his visit, five Martinsyde Buzzard F.4a aircraft were supplied to the Aeronautica Naval by the Aircraft Disposal Company. An inventory return for April 1925 showed that 23 aircraft were available at the Aerodromo del Prat, nine of which were Martinsyde F.4A and F.6 aircraft. These aircraft bore the serials, M-NYAA to M-NYAJ (except

Martinsyde F.6 of the Spanish Aeronautica Naval. (J M Bruce/S Leslie Collection)

M-NYAD). This inventory also showed that five Martinsyde F.3s were available, but in fact these were Felixstowe F.3 flying boats, with serials M-YFBA, M-YFBB, M-YFBC, M-YFBE and M-YFBJ.

During 1926, the Government agreed to a plan submitted by the Dirrecion de la Escuela (school director) to use a Martinsyde to carry out a trial aerial photographic survey of the port of Barcelona and the surrounding coastline, to assess the potential benefits of the technique for carrying out hydrographic surveys for the Navy. The survey was carried out by Teniente de navio Dominguez and Piedra as pilots and Teniente de navio Nuñez and La Rocha as observers at an altitude of 1,600 metres. The trial must have been a success, for two years later, Teniente de navio La Rocha, now of the photographic survey department of the Aeronautica Naval, carried out ten flights in a Martinsyde to produce a detailed 1:3600 scale map of the area where the new free port at Barcelona was to be built.

By 1927 the operational strength of the Martinsydes were beginning to show the effects of attrition and continual usage. An inventory for 1st April showed that their number had been reduced to seven, of which six were in flying condition. By July, the number had been temporarily reduced to six and these were under continual repair and maintenance. Another one was lost in a fatal accident on 19th September 1927. During a flight from the Aerodromo del Prat, an F.6 piloted by Contramaestre (Flight Sergeant) Otero flew into an overhead power cable and crashed into the riverbed of the Llobregat very close to its bank. The aircraft was reduced to a mangled heap of wreckage, the pilot was seriously injured and the passenger, Adolfo Contreras, a captain of a corvette, was mortally wounded and died on his way to hospital.

It was beyond the capabilities of the workshops at the

Aerodromo del Prat to economically repair three Martinsydes which had been badly damaged in accidents and the usable parts were transferred to the workshops of the Aeronautica Militar at Cuatro Vientos, which had experience in repair of similar aircraft. Moreover the Aeronautica Militar offered to loan three replacement aircraft to bring the squadron up to strength in the interim. The repairs were eventually completed by January 1928 and Tenientes de navio Galan and Ceano were delegated to fly them back to the Aerodromo del Prat, which they did without incident.

In 1931, the Monarchy gave way to a Republic and a limited modernisation of the air forces was envisaged, including the possibility of building the Hawker Fury under licence. Some obsolete types were withdrawn and the overall strength reduced to 287 aircraft. The base at Prat was gradually run down and by October 1931 the Martinsydes formed a squadron of ten aircraft in two flights based at San Javier. A Ministry order dated 22nd June 1933 required the surviving Martinsydes to be re-registered EA-EAA to EA-EAJ. The order also required the aircraft to be given numbers in the sequence in which they were first taken on strength. The equivalent numbers to the registrations were EAA 1, EAB 2, EAC 3, EAD 4, EAE 5, EAF 6, EAG 7, EAH 9, EAI 10 and EAJ 8. The numbers were to be painted on the rudders of the aircraft in black in the largest size possible.

By June 1933, it was reported that the squadron had a serious problem of serviceability, with seven of the Martinsydes awaiting repair in the workshops in Barcelona and two of the remaining three being used to keep the instructors at the flying school proficient. This unsatisfactory state of affairs continued through 1934, the total hours flown during the year by the two serviceable Martinsydes at San Javier being about 44 hours out of a total of nearly 1,460

Six Martinsyde F.4As of the Spanish Aeronautica Naval at San Javier in 1936.

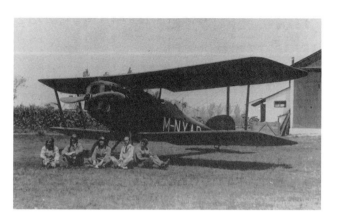

A Martinsyde F.6 of the Spanish Aeronautica Naval with its early serial number and colour scheme.

hours flown by all the aircraft at the base.

The Martinsydes were eventually overhauled at the workshops of the Aeronautica Naval at Casa Antunez, Barcelona. Following their return to service, two of the F.4As were converted from single-seaters to two-seaters with dual control. The improved situation regarding the serviceability of the Martinsydes was reflected in a report of the Central Office of the Aviation Naval in 1935 which gave the number of aircraft at the disposal of the Navy to be about 80 aircraft, of which nine were Martinsydes, seven of which were serviceable and two under repair.

Sometime in July 1935, there were discussions within the Ministerio de Marina concerning the modernisation of the Aeronautica Naval. As part of this scheme, it was proposed to replace the Martinsydes by Hawker Ospreys during 1936 but the Civil War intervened.

Spain had suffered from political instability since the late 1890s and successive Republican governments since 1931 could not stabilise the situation. The inability of the elected government to reconcile the demands of the disaffected Right, the workers and the regional separatists against a background of a depressed economy and growing unrest, led to a coup on 18th July 1936 by a part of the Army which hoped to restore order and unity. This primarily involved the forces in Morocco, commanded by General Franco and supported by rightist politicians and the Catholic church. The title Aeronautica Militar was adopted by the Spanish Nationalist aviation units which merged with the Naval forces which supported the uprising. Loyal government aviation units came under the overall control of the new Fuerzas Aereas de la Republica Espagñola (FARE).

On the outbreak of the war, the remaining Martinsydes formed the Escuadrilla de Acompagañiento y Combate at the naval base at San Javier. Any officers implicated in the uprising were arrested, including the squadron leader, Teniente de navio Manuel de Castro, who was replaced by Alfirez de navio Francisco Piedra Yebenes. The unit consisted of seven Martinsydes in flying condition, two of which were two-seaters, and two under repair. It was found impossible to restore one of these, two-seater MS-1, to flying condition. The remaining aircraft were numbered in the sequence MS-2 to MS-10, MS-6 and MS-7 corresponding to the two F.4As modified to two-seaters.

These aircraft were now painted silver overall, with tricolour cockades above and below the wings, serial numbers

in black on the fuselage sides and the last number of the serial in black on the fin (except for 9 and 10). The rudder had stripes of the national colours of red, yellow and purple. An anchor surmounted by a crown was positioned on the yellow portion of the rudder stripes and a black bee with yellow wings was positioned on the fuselage between the wings (overall yellow for MS-5 and MS-9). At the beginning of the war, the wings and rear fuselage also had red stripes and the serial numbers were superimposed on the red stripes on the fuselage.

On the following day, the aircraft commenced patrols to protect their own airfield and the important naval base of Cartagena nearby. This was accomplished without major incident and the patrols continued into August, by which time the Martinsydes were beginning to show their age. By the end of August, the fighting to the south had intensified and due to a shortage of Nieuport Ni-D 52s at the front, it was decided to reinforce them with two Martinsydes. These were flown under the command of Francisco Piedra from San Javier to their new base at the Aerodromo del Rompedizo near Malaga. A few days later, one of the Martinsydes had engine failure and was grounded. A replacement also had engine failure on its way to Malaga and was forced to land in the countryside near Almeria. It was eventually returned to San Javier where it was incorporated into a new Escuela de Caza (fighter school).

By this time the airframes and engines were clapped out and following a spate of accidents with novice pilots, the Martinsydes were finally withdrawn from service during October and November 1936. They were transferred to the Escuela de Vuelo at El Carmoli and from there they were flown to the Parque de Reserva near San Pedro de Pinatar, where they were stripped of usable engines, propellers, flying instruments and other equipment for use in other aircraft.

There is some controversy as to whether the Aeronautica Militar operated any Martinsydes. Jaime Verlarde Silis in his book *Aviones Espagñols desde 1910* states that the Aeronautica Militar bought about twenty and these formed a squadron at Melilla from May until September 1921 and then operated in the Protectorate under the command of Captain Luis Moreno Abella. He also writes that on 22th June, Tenientes Morenis and Mateo were killed in the first aerial collision over Spain in Martinsydes and that on 11th August Teniente Gomez Spencer reached 7,242 metres over Madrid to take the national altitude record.

Martinsyde Type A Mark II No.10 owned by Pitcairn Aviation

United States

Harold F. Pitcairn is best known for his pioneer work in the development of autogyros. However, in 1924 he also set up Pitcairn Aviation, a commercial aviation business. This was centred on a small aerodrome, called Pitcairn Field, which he developed at Bryn Athyn in Pennsylvania. There he took on Jim Ray to be in charge of field operations and act as chief instructor. Ray set about procuring a suitable fleet of aircraft for carrying flight instruction, sight-seeing, cross-country charters and other contract flying. The fleet when assembled consisted of Pitcairn's personal Farman Sport, four Curtiss Orioles, a Standard Trainer and two Martinsyde Type As (numbered 10 and 11 respectively on the fin). The Martinsydes were said to have been obtained at a knock-down price from a failed sealing operation in Newfoundland. During a ferrying trip, Jim Ray found a sealskin flying helmet under the seat, which he promptly appropriated for his own use in winter.

The Martinsydes are believed to have originated from the Aerial Survey Company Limited. No.10 was certainly similar to a Type A Mark II operated by Sidney Cotton's company in Newfoundland. It had the passenger cabin, unique to the Cotton machine, fitted with both side windows and the special windscreen in the roof of the cabin. The other Martinsyde Type A (No.11), however, was not comparable to any other machine known to have been operated in Newfoundland, fitted as it was with two open cockpits in tandem in front of the pilot's cockpit, each with cut-down sides and dual windscreens for passengers sitting side-by-side.

The fleet was in great demand even before the aerodrome was officially opened in November 1924. However, despite the popularity of the sight-seeing flights, the whole operation showed a loss by the end of 1924 of some $25,000. Much of this loss was accounted for by the start-up costs of the operation. However it was also apparent that although the Orioles and Martinsydes were in great demand at weekends they were under-utilised during the rest of the week. Furthermore the enclosed cabins of the Martinsydes were less popular with the sight-seeing public than the open cockpits of the Orioles. This and the difficulty in obtaining adequate spares to ensure safe operation persuaded Pitcairn to dispose of the Martinsydes after the first season. The eventual fate of these aircraft is unrecorded but it is likely that they were scrapped.

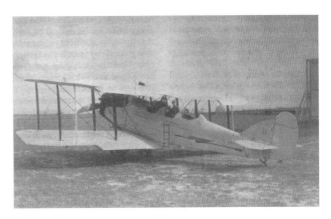

Martinsyde Type A Mark I No.11 used for joyriding by Pitcairn Aviation

The Martinsyde team outside the Woking works after having won the team prize and five gold medals in the 1922 Scottish Six Days Trial. From left to right, J T Bashall, E H Gifford, W H Bashall and A A Symes. (Chris Tait)

CHAPTER 8 - THE MOTORCYCLES

The majority of the Martinsyde motorcycles were fitted with a V twin four-stroke engine, with the cylinders angled at 50 degrees. This engine, as originally conceived by Howard Newman in 1915, was designed in two sizes, 60 mm x 88 mm (498 cc) and 70 mm x 88 mm (678 cc). Either cylinder size fitted the same crankcase and the front and rear cylinders were interchangeable.

The valves were made of stainless steel. The inlet and exhaust valves were mounted vertically in a pocket cast in the side of the each cylinder with their faces opposed. Although the F-head configuration was common to many motorcycle engines such as the Harley Davidson and the Swiss MAG, the Martinsyde was unusual in that the exhaust valve was placed above the inlet valve instead of the other way round. This gave better cooling and avoided cylinder distortion. Thus although the engine was not particularly powerful, it could be run at nearly full throttle for long periods, leading to the reputation that 'you cannot tire the Martinsyde engine'. A casting, containing the exhaust valve guide and a flange to take an elbow connected to the exhaust pipe, had a spigot which fitted inside the exhaust pocket and was bolted down onto a ground face on the cylinder head. The original design had integral supports for the rocker arm spindle but this got far too hot and by 1920 the casting had been replaced by a finned cage with a separate rocker arm support screwed into the head. The inlet valve was placed vertically underneath with the valve seat ground into the

pocket. The inlet port was connected to a Y-shaped induction pipe leading to a carburettor mounted between the cylinders. The valve pockets were streamlined without obstructions to the inlet and exhaust gas flows. The sparking plug for each cylinder was also situated in the pocket.

The exhaust valve was operated by a push rod and overhead rocker arm. The operating mechanism for the valves was kept simple. The timing gear was enclosed in an extension cast on the side of the crankcase. The single cam shaft was machined from the solid, the inlet and exhaust cams being integral. The cam shaft was mounted on ball bearings. The timing wheel incorporated two cams, which lifted in turn all four valves through their respective rockers mounted on independent rocker pins. The standard valve timings according to *Martinsyde Maxims*, (a handbook of useful hints for the use of Martinsyde owners) were inlet 10° BTDC to 50° ATDC and exhaust 55° BTDC to 20° ATDC and magneto setting 35° BTDC (normally set at 40° BTDC). Ball bearings supported the crankshaft and the big end ran on a roller bearing. Later in the life of the engine the exhaust rocker arms above the cylinder were enclosed, improving lubrication and reducing noise.

The pistons were of cast iron with two rings. The gudgeon pins were hardened and ground to fine limits. The crankshaft and flywheel were each manufactured from steel drop forgings. The connecting rods were of H-section. A forked rod carried the roller bearing housing fitted with

The Martinsyde team which won the Team Prize in the 1921 Brooklands 500 Mile Race. No other team completed the course. No.35 is H H Bowen on a 497 cc Martinsyde who finished 11th overall, No.25 is W H Bashall on a 678 cc Martinsyde who finished 13th overall and No.26 is J T Bashall also on a 678 cc Martinsyde who finished 23rd overall. (Chris Tait)

double roller races. The plain rod was bushed with a phosphor bronze bearing, which faced the outside of the hardened and ground housing. The small ends of both rods were bushed with phosphor bronze. The cylinders could be readily removed without taking the engine out of the frame.

The original lubrication system designed by Newman was quite complex and was not adopted by Martinsyde. Instead, all the engine parts, including the big end were splash lubricated. The 1920-21 models were fitted with a Semi-Automatic lubrication system but this was not completely reliable and for later models a Best & Lloyd hand pump with a metering valve and sight glass was used. With this system it was important not to forget to pump every five miles or so.

The induction pipe was manufactured of cast aluminium and attached to the cylinders by a flange fitting and care was taken with the design to ensure good conduction of heat to the carburettor to avoid icing. Various carburettors were used on different models. The early models were fitted with a Special Amac single-lever carburettor. This worked tolerably well and was designed to make driving easier, having just a throttle lever and no air adjustment. This was later replaced by the two-lever carburettor, with both a throttle slide and an air slide. By closing or partly closing the air slide, the mixture could be enriched to assist hill climbing on full throttle. Also the mixture could be enriched for starting by closing the air slide. The float chamber had to be flooded to start the engine with the single-lever carburettor. The standard M.L. high-tension magneto was chain driven and protected by a metal shield, which was kept in position by a light spring, allowing easy access for adjustment.

With the exception of the 1923 Type A 350 cc model, the transmission system consisted of a three-speed A.J.S. style of gearbox, manufactured entirely by Martinsyde, with a chain drive to the rear wheel. The top and bottom gears were engaged by dogs and the middle gear by a sliding pinion. The gear box had a crash second gear. The shafts were mounted on ball bearings. The system was immersed in oil in a casing. The gear change lever was mounted on the right-hand side of the tank. In 1921 Sydney Camm radically redesigned the A.J.S. gearbox, making it neater and more compact. The external kick start quadrant on the near side was replaced by an enclosed kick start housed in an extension of the gearbox cover on the off-side. The clutch, operated by hand from the left-hand side of the handlebars, was of the multiple-plate type, with cork inserts engaging with steel discs. The redesign of the gearbox enabled the rather complicated sheet metal chaincases of the 1920-21 models to be replaced by a neat cast aluminium primary chaincase. A pressed metal shield protected the rear chain.

The early design of frame was intended to give the rider a comfortable seat on a low saddle position. In practice, the frame was not strong enough and had to be redesigned. It was fitted with Brampton Biflex Action forks manufactured under licence. These were heavily raked to absorb bumps in both vertical and horizontal directions but this geometry made it difficult to manoeuvre at low speeds. The oil tank was secured inside the petrol tank, which was itself fastened rigidly to the frame by means of two straps positioned around the tank and engaging clips brazed to the tank. A Brooks saddle and two Brooks long pannier tool bags were fitted as standard.

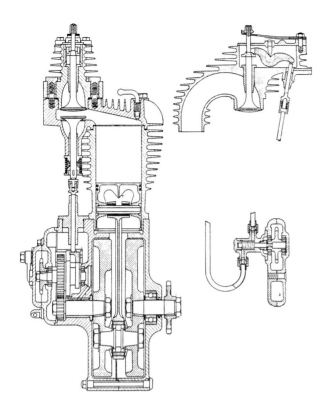

Schematic drawing of the 350 cc Martinsyde engine. This is the only drawing of the Martinsyde engine that has survived but is not wholly representative of the standard engine.
(Chris Tait)

The first model was launched at the 1919 Olympia Show. It was the Martinsyde-Newman 6 hp V-Twin Combination, with a 678 cc capacity engine. It was distinguished from later models by having a square tank with a capacity of two gallons petrol and half-gallon of oil. The brake was a foot-controlled band brake fitted to the rear hub. It had aluminium footboards. The sidecar was mounted on the left side and was sprung by three-leaf Cee springs. The tyres were Dunlop Specials, 650 mm by 65 mm. The motorcycle and the chassis of the sidecar were enamelled black and lined in gold with all bright parts plated. The body of the sidecar was royal blue lined with gold and the upholstery was also royal blue. Every machine came complete with carrier, toolbags, number plates, inflator, oil can and spanners. The price was £170 but the windscreen, hood and storm apron for the sidecar were respectively £4, £5 and 17/6d extra. A Lucas Magdynamo lighting set was an extra at £30.

The prices had been reduced by the 1920 Show, the standard model being offered at £145 for the combination and £125 for the solo machine. In addition, a De Luxe model, with an improved specification and complete with all the above extras plus a spare wheel and leg shields, was available for £215. The M.L. magneto had been replaced with a Lucas L.C.V. Magdyno. A speedometer was offered as an optional extra.

In order to break into the fiercely competitive motorcycle market, the Company decided to enter the competition scene. As well as giving encouragement to amateur riders, both in trials and on the track, Martinsyde formed a works team. The first major success in a sporting event came when the Brooklands Motor Cycle Racing Club organised a 500-mile race for all the major classes of motorcycle on Saturday, 2nd July 1921. It proved to be the first and last of its kind.

Besides cups for the overall winner and two runners-up, there was another cup for the first under-350 cc machine to finish and a team prize for the first trio of riders on machines of the same marque. The race covered 185 laps of the track and in view of its length, started just after dawn at the early hour of 7 am. Altogether there were 64 entrants and, in keeping with the traditions of the course, like jockeys the riders wore coloured jackets, these corresponding to the engine capacity of their mounts; white (250 cc), blue (350 cc), yellow (500 cc), green (750 cc) and red (1000cc).

Martinsyde entered an official team of three riders, Harold Bowen on a 497 cc machine with Harry Bashall and his brother John Bashall on 678 cc Martinsydes. It was claimed by the company that the machines were standard, but it is probable that small modifications were made to lighten the pistons and separate oil tanks were used, a change to be adopted on some later models. Because of the short stub exhausts fitted to their machines, the Martinsyde team wore asbestos gaiters to protect their legs.

Harry Bashall was lying first in the 750 cc Class after 200 miles, at an average speed of 57.29 mph. However, before the halfway stage he received a nasty gash on the leg from a piece of concrete thrown up from the track. In great pain he drew up at the pits for treatment by the track doctor and was advised to retire. However, because he felt that Martinsyde had a great chance of winning the team event, he decided to continue after taking a rest of around thirty minutes. Of course, by then he had lost the lead in his class. However he eventually came second in his class at an average speed of 55.03 mph, a quite remarkable achievement considering his long pit stop due to injury and other stops for fuel and adjustments. None of the Martinsyde entrants came first in their class, J.T. Bashall coming fifth in the 750 cc Class at an average speed of 50.49 mph and H.H. Bowen coming fourth in the 500 cc Class with an average speed of 56.01 mph. As a result Martinsyde carried off the team prize as no other team completed the course. This result substantiated the Company's motto - "The Symbol of Success".

Two sports models introduced the previous August were displayed at the 1921 Show. They sported royal blue panels on the sides of the petrol tank along with an improved logo transfer. The two models had different engine capacities but were otherwise similar. Both were given the two-lever Amac carburettor and were fitted with 650 by 65 mm heavy duty Dunlop tyres. The Type C 3½ hp Solo "Sports" Model was fitted with the 497 cc version of the Newman engine. The M-L HT magneto was retained and the A.J.S type gearbox had a top ratio of 4½ to 1. The square tank was replaced by an oval tank with a capacity of 1½ gallons of petrol and three pints of oil. It was claimed that the machine, which was priced at £120, could easily attain a speed of 60 mph. The Light Delivery Combination had an engine capacity of 678 cc and a top gear ratio of 5½ to 1. It was essentially similar to the 1920 Combination with the sidecar replaced by a special coach-built carrier of 20 cubic feet and 5 to 6 cwt capacity. The carrier was made of an ash frame with plywood covering and had a side door and a rear door, with two drawers inside. The oval tank had a capacity of 2½ gallons of petrol and ½-gallon of oil. The chassis was sprung by flat laminated springs. The finish was similar and the price was £145 with shelves and brass top rails £5 extra.

Martinsyde recorded another success during November 1921 when H H Bowen captured the One Hour Record for 750 cc machines. He only just failed to reach 80 miles in the hour, achieving 77.58 miles on the 24th and 78.13 miles in a

E H Gifford with his Martinsyde Quick Six in 1922 outside the Vickers works at Brooklands. Second from the right is L Pullin of the engine test section and behind him is W H Bashall. (Chris Tait)

second attempt on the 29th. This was a significant improvement in performance compared with the average speeds attained a few months before in the 500 Mile Race and represented an accolade for Bowen and his technical department. It must be borne in mind that the Martinsyde engine, with its tortuous side valve induction tract and primitive valve gear arrangement, was not very suitable for development. For the record attempt, the engine was redesigned in a matter of weeks with a new flywheel, cylinders, cylinder heads, connecting rods and pistons, giving a longer stroke . The Record should however be put in context. At about the same time that Bowen was taking the 750 cc Hour Record, Major F B Halford was taking the 500 cc Hour Record at 76.74 mph. This was achieved with a brand new 4-valve Triumph Ricardo engine. The Ricardo engine was far more capable of development than the Martinsyde engine dating back to 1915. Later, of course, Halford became a noted designer of aero-engines for Napier and de Havilland.

With strong competition from A.J.S and Matchless, it became necessary to rectify a number of deficiencies in the earlier design. Known as the Type B Series 1, the Combination introduced in November 1921 was again powered by the 678 cc version of the engine of a nominal 6

hp and the M.L. HT magneto, Amac carburettor and the modified A.J.S three-speed gearbox were all retained. However, the upper gear ratio was increased to 5.45 to 1. The frame was an entirely new and stronger design, with all the main lugs made from steel drop forgings. A front hand-controlled brake was added. The tyres were now extra heavy 26 x 3 inch. On these Type B models a modification, designed by Sydney Camm, was introduced by which the wheels could be removed easily by unscrewing one nut, removing the spindle and distance piece and pulling the wheel sideways, leaving the chains, sprockets, brakes and mudguards untouched. All the wheels, including the spare, were interchangeable. The chassis of the sidecar was changed to a more luxurious but heavier Millford Modele de Luxe from Coventry with dual tubular side members with a four-point attachment. A sloping door, slightly larger than that on the earlier model, was provided to give ease of access and the rear of the body was designed with a spacious locker capable of taking three cans of petrol. Fitted over the locker door was a stub axle for taking the spare wheel and strong stays were provided which formed a self-contained luggage carrier of sufficient size to take a small suitcase. It retailed at £160 complete.

Martinsyde solo and combination machines were entered

H H Bowen with his 745 cc Martinsyde on the Brooklands track after having broken the 50-Mile and 1-Hour Records in the 750 cc Class at 79.21 mph and 78.13 mph respectively on November 29th 1921. He made two attempts at this record just before the 1921 Motor Cycle Show but just failed to achieve 80 mph. (Chris Tait)

into the Land's End Trial held in April 1922. This was a straightforward run from Slough to Land's End with a speed trial up Porlock Hill and a non-stop section up Lynton Hill. In those days these hills did not possess the metalled surfaces known today but consisted of loose stones and gravel and were therefore not readily negotiated, particularly by the combinations. Of the 122 solo machines and 98 sidecars, only 44 solos and 18 sidecars qualified for gold or silver medals. Amongst these were five of the six Martinsyde entrants, H H Nicholson, E H Gifford and A A F Symes being awarded gold medals on 3½ hp solo models and J T Bashall and G Baxter being awarded silver medals on 6 hp combinations. The remaining combination, ridden by W H Bashall, was the only other Martinsyde to finish the course but did not receive an award.

Martinsyde followed the earlier successes with another in the Scottish Six Days Reliability Trials held between July 11th and 16th, 1922. The Company entered a team of W H Bashall, J T Bashall, E H Gifford and A A F Symes. The Bashall brothers were accompanied by their wives as sidecar passengers. The Martinsydes were in competition with rivals with much larger engine sizes. A.J.S. entered a team with machines of 799 cc capacity and the Matchless machines were fitted with the much more powerful MAG engines of 982 cc capacity. To achieve Gold Medals, the Martinsydes would have had to climb all the observed hills without outside assistance and to have been within the time limits at all the various time checks. Despite their less powerful engines, the Martinsyde team proved the reliability of their machines and shared the sidecar team Gold Medal with Matchless, the A.J.S. team having been eliminated from the Team Prize when one of their number failed to complete the course.

For the 1922 Show, the Touring Combination, known as the Type B1 Series 2, again showed detailed improvements. Because of the considerable weight of this model, particularly when carrying luggage, it was found that the engine could scarcely pull the load up even moderate gradients. It was therefore found necessary to lower the top gear ratio to 5.79

to 1, making the other ratios 10.4 to 1 and 18.75 to 1. A two-lever Amac carburettor, similar to that fitted to the solo models, could be supplied to order. The wheel base was 5 feet 1 inch, width 4 feet 11 inches and the combined weight 495 lbs. The tyres were 26 by 3 inch. The price had by now been reduced to £130, with a comparable solo machine on offer at £107. The Sports Combination or Type B2 Series 2 was similar to the Type B1 except that it had a streamlined sidecar body, footrests instead of footboards and TT pattern handlebars. The sidecar upholstery remained royal blue but the sidecar body was available in blue, yellow or red with a tank panel in a matching colour. The price was the same as the Type B1. Also available with a similar specification to the sidecar models was a Light Delivery Combination retailing at £135. It was claimed that this machine had a petrol consumption of 60-70 miles/gallon and that one gallon of lubricant would last for 800 to 1,000 miles. Unfortunately the change in gear ratios reduced the top gear performance to around 45 mph compared with the lighter and more highly geared 1921 model which could easily exceed 50 mph.

Introduced in May 1922 in an attempt to capitalise on the trials and racing successes and to revive the flagging fortunes of the marque, the Quick Six sports model, or "Quixix" as it was known in some literature, was introduced. It incorporated much of the development work carried out for the Hour Record machine and as a result the design was a significant departure from that of earlier models. The stroke of the V twin engine was increased to 96 mm, giving a cubic capacity of 738 cc. The cylinder heads were improved and made detachable. A new pattern of exhaust valve cage, heavily ribbed with radiating fins, was designed for cooler running and the ports were redesigned to improve breathing. All reciprocating parts had been lightened and Ricardo slipper pistons fitted. The length of the cylinder was designed so that the slipper ring just projected into the head, so preventing a ridge being worn at the top. Connecting rods were made of nickel steel and machined all over. Flywheels were individually balanced for high speeds. The timing gear and camshaft were redesigned to improve efficiency. Special close ratio gearing was chosen, 3.6 to 1 for top, 5.3 to 1 for second and 9.5 to 1 for first. A racing pattern Amac carburettor was fitted. The engine is estimated to have given an output of about 17 bhp compared with about 12 bhp for the standard 678 cc engine. The oil tank was now separate from the petrol tank and was fitted behind the seat support with a foot operated lubricator and a capacity of ½ gallon. The front and rear brakes were on belt rims. The frame was designed for a lower riding position and improved stability. A new pattern of handlebar was fitted which could be adjusted either for road or track work. A lighter pattern of mudguards were fitted without valences and a skeletal pattern of chain guard was fitted to ease removal. As before, the finish was black with a royal blue tank panel. The price was set at £125 with an additional £10 for a Brooklands 80 M.P.H. Certificate.

Also on offer from November 1922, but at the other end of the performance spectrum, was the Type A, with a 2½ hp single cylinder engine of 70 mm bore, 90 mm stroke giving a capacity of 347 cc. It is probable that this engine was heavily influenced by a comparable Beardmore design. It certainly had the same bore and stroke as the 350 cc Beardmore. Designed for cheapness, it differed significantly from earlier Martinsyde designs. The Type A engine had a plain bearing on the timing side whereas the normal engine had a ball bearing on the timing side. Also, whereas with the usual engine the flywheels were integral with the main shaft, with the Type A engine the flywheel was bolted onto the

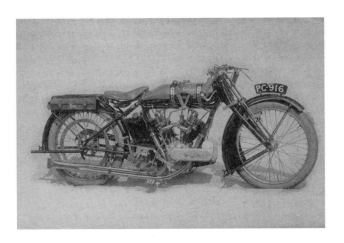

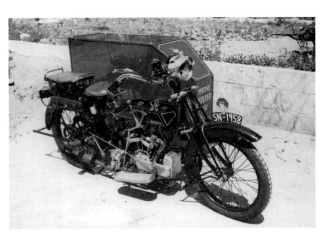

The prototype of the 1922 Quick Six. It was developed from the One-Hour Record machine and was sold with a guarantee of 80 mph. (Chris Tait)

1921 model Tradesman's sidecar belonging to Frank Johnson of Lerwick. (Chris Tait)

crankshaft. Initially the overhead exhaust valve was operated by a new form of rocker assembly which was fitted under a cover plate which could be readily removed to dismount the whole valve gear. The rocker was pivoted on an inverted knife edge and the valve spring was a flat laminated leaf spring. However this system was quickly replaced by a more conventional rocker arm assembly. Mechanical lubrication was employed with a Showell oil pump driven from an idler sprocket on the magneto chain drive forcing oil through a sight glass to the cylinder. A Sturmey-Archer three-speed gearbox was fitted with a kick-starter and controlled by a lever mounted on the seat tube, the ratios being 5.2 to 1.8 to 1 and 1½ to 1. The frame was constructed throughout with straight tubes, butted where necessary, and the forks were of the "Druid" type. The clutch was a multiple plate, composite cork with Ferodo inserts and controlled from the handlebars. The transmission was all-chain, partially enclosed by enamelled sheet metal guards. The oil tank of 3 pints capacity was placed inside a petrol tank holding 1½ gallons. An internal expanding brake was fitted to the front wheel with a dummy belt rim on the rear. The cycle sported the normal Martinsyde finish and retailed at £70 or £72 with Ricardo aluminium pistons and semi-TT bars and footrests.

In 1924, shortly after taking over the Martinsyde motorcycle business, BAT brought out a sidecar combination which incorporated parts from both marques. It would appear that this company had bought about 100 Quick Six engines cheaply from the receiver and decided to use this engine instead of the more expensive J.A.P. engine with which they had long been associated. Although BAT claimed a significant number of improvements to this engine, it was in fact incorporated unchanged. The BAT spring frame was utilised and the footboards and saddle were sprung together, reducing road shocks for the rider. BAT 28-inch wheels were fitted into 1920 Martinsyde forks which had originally intended for 26-inch wheels. It had a 1920's design of stirrup front brake which was quite inadequate and out of date by the time the machine reached the market. Not surprisingly, the machine did not sell and nothing further was heard of it.

BAT was no more successful with the complete Martinsyde machines which they inherited. The Type C Solo model was offered at £60 and the Type B Combination at

£95. Nothing was done to update the models and despite the severe price cutting, few if any machines were sold. In July 1924, BAT published a comprehensive list of Martinsyde spares. In it they offered to convert 3½ hp Type C engines to 6 hp Type D engines for £7-10-0. The sale of these spares could not have brought in much business as other companies were also selling Martinsyde spares. The BAT company finally ceased trading in 1926.

Although the Martinsyde Company had finally gone out of existence in 1923, the motorcycles continue to give service to enthusiasts. In 1969, three of these enthusiasts, Alex Brett, Peter Adorian and Chris Tait, decided to form the Martinsyde Register and in so doing have continued to keep a record of those machines which still survive and arrange events to keep alive the memory of the company. One such event, starting on 2nd July 1972, 51 years to the day after the 500-Mile victory, two Martinsyde motorcycles, accompanied by a back-up team, were ridden to Finland and back to visit the one remaining Martinsyde aircraft, an F.4 Buzzard in a museum in Finland. These machines were basically 1922 6 hp models, incorporating aluminium pistons with a slightly increased compression ratio and some improvements to the brakes. Altogether, the two machines each travelled about 2,050 miles on the road in 7½ days, averaging around 50 mph on the better stretches of road.

It is not possible to detail all exploits and the prizes won in this book. Well over a hundred awards have been won by Martinsyde owners from 1920 to the present time. However, perhaps one should not end this account without putting on record one feat which speaks highly of the mechanical durability of the Martinsyde marque. 1984 marked the 60th anniversary of the first circumnavigation of Australia by any kind of vehicle and this event was commemorated by a similar journey by Australian Neil Bromilow. This was accomplished on a refurbished 1922 678 cc Martinsyde, fitted with a mechanical oil pump and oil tank taken off a 1923 Quick Six. The only other deviation from the original specification was the substitution of a pair of 19 inch BSA C10 wheels, which eliminated the problems with the V-block brakes and obtaining spare tyres. The 9,933-mile trip, which included a 800-mile detour to Alice Springs, was accomplished in an elapsed time of 33 days.

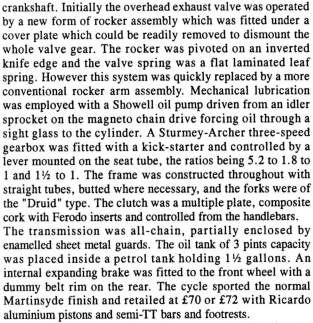

*Single cylinder 350 cc 1923 model
with the Sturmey Archer gearbox, now
owned by Henry Hauptmann in the USA.
(Chris Tait)*

*A battered photograph showing part of a consignment of sixty Martinsyde motorcycles for agents Holmes and Younie Ltd of
Sheffield. The machines include the Two-and-three-quarter-hp and Quick Six models. (Chris Tait)*

Estimate of Martinsyde Motorcycle Production

Year	Model	Approx Prodn
1920-21	Combination Model, including Martinsyde-Newman (square tank)	950
1921	Solo 3½ hp (500 cc), (square (wedge) tank)	< 20
1922-23	Type B Combination Model (large round tank with straps)	550
1922-23	Types C & D Solo Models (small round tank with straps)	350
1922	350 cc Twin Model (tank probably the same as Types C & D)	6
1922-23	Quick Six Model (738 cc) (round tank with straps, separate oil tank)	100
1923	Type A Single Cylinder (350 cc) (round tank, no straps)	10

Note: It is known that about 2000 motorcycles were produced and that about 100 of these were the
Quick Six Model. The rest of the figures are carefully considered estimates.

The Handasyde glider flying over the crest at Firle Beacon. (A J Jackson Collection)

CHAPTER 9 - HANDASYDE AIRCRAFT

Handasyde's designs for his own company are described in some detail below. The products of the other companies for which he worked are also covered but in less detail as the extent of his involvement in the design work is less clear. For more details of the service history of these aircraft, the reader can do no better than refer to the excellent *British Civil Aircraft* in three volumes by A J Jackson in the Putnam series.

The Handasyde Glider

The first aircraft which Handasyde designed after leaving the Martinsyde Company and setting up the Handasyde Aircraft Company was a glider. This was built for Fred Raynham to participate in the *Daily Mail* competition for gliders held at Itford Hill, near Newhaven in Sussex, during the week 16-21st October 1922.

The *Daily Mail* had been encouraging aviation ever since its proprietor, Lord Northcliffe, had met the Wright Brothers before the First World War. Its glider competition for a prize of £1,000 was announced on 23rd August 1922. The event was organised by the Gliding Committee of the Royal Aero Club headed up by its Secretary, Commander Harold Perrin. The competition was open to the world for the longest glide exceeding 30 minutes duration, to be terminated by a landing within 800 yards of the point of departure. The flight had to begin between sunrise and sunset on one of the days within

the stipulated period, although there was no limitation on when the flight should end. Any device using gas lighter than air was excluded, but motive power derived from the activities of the occupants of the glider was allowed.

Although only six weeks elapsed between the announcement and the actual competition, a total of 35 entries were recorded. In the event only 13 flew with any degree of success and many of the entries never arrived at Itford. The serious contenders included two identical gliders designed by de Havilland, two biplane gliders from Antony Fokker, a single-seater and a two-seater, a glider entered by J Jeyes which had been designed by Theodore von Kaman and E C Gordon England in his own machine. Other machines of note were a Dewoitine entered by G Barbot, a monoplane glider built by the Aircraft Disposal Company, the Peyret tandem-winged machine and two further British entries

The Handasyde glider was a clean-looking if somewhat angular monoplane. The wing was a thick cantilever structure with a rectangular centre section and a taper in chord and thickness on the outer panels. The wing was of Göttingen 441 section from the root to four feet from the centre line. The wing was built up on two spars, formed by top and bottom flanges of spruce, with three-ply webs on one side only. Thin three-ply was bent around the leading edge of the inner portion of the wing and extended back as far as the rear spar on both upper and lower surfaces. The rear spar was placed well forward to give a flexible trailing edge, which was made

210

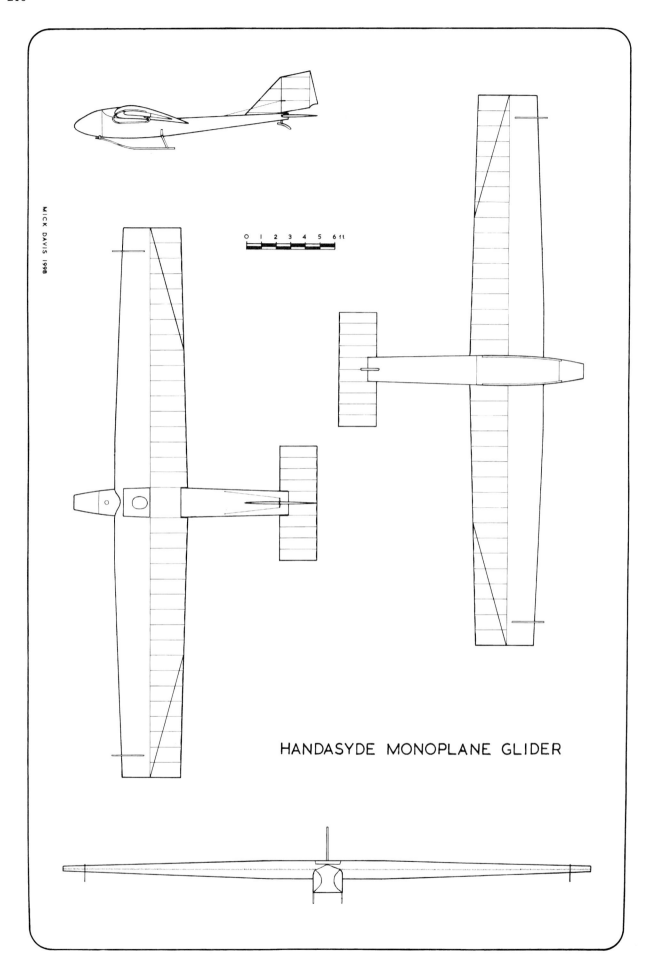

MICK DAVIS 1998

0 1 2 3 4 5 6 ft

HANDASYDE MONOPLANE GLIDER

Raynham in the Raynham-Handasyde monoplane. (A J Jackson Collection)

of wire. The wings were fitted with triangular shape ailerons, with the maximum chord at the tips. These were operated by push rods with the ends of the operating wires fitted to a T-shaped connection. The wings were attached to the fuselage by means of duralumin stirrups. The fuselage had a rectangular cross-section, slightly rounded at the nose from the side view. It was covered with plywood with circular cut-outs in each bay, covered with fabric. This method of lightening the structure attracted some criticism but the fuselage seemed strong enough for its purpose. The front longerons sloped slightly upwards towards the nose and the fuselage tapered horizontally to about two inches at the rear to which was attached a balanced elevator. The thin fin and the rudder were respectively triangular and rhomboid in shape.

The undercarriage consisted of two ash skids, anchored at their front ends to the lower fuselage longerons and supported at the rear by short struts which could pivot backwards when under load. Outrigger skids were fitted near the wing tips and a tail skid. The cockpit was rather small and it is likely that Raynham was actually measured for it as he seemed to fit with little room to spare. The cockpit was placed between the main spars and is covered in three-ply, with a hole cut in it for the pilot's head. It was noteworthy for its unusual control system. There was a conventional rudder bar and the elevator was controlled by means of a short lever operated by the right hand. However because there had not been sufficient time to complete the craft before the meeting, the control wires for the ailerons were not connected to the control column. Instead the cable passed across in front of the pilot and he effected control by pulling directly on an ordinary turnbuckle with his left hand.

The arrivals on the first Saturday and Sunday of the

competition spent their time adjusting their machines and doing short test flights. The competitors had been allocated tent hangars to protect their machines erected near the top of Itford Hill. Raynham's glider shared the upper one with Gordon England's and Jeyes Aachen's machines. According to a contemporary account, Raynham, Camm and half-a-dozen willing helpers carried the Handasyde machine to the top of the hill, whereupon Raynham tried three starts, not attempting to go too far. His machine left the ground at no more than 10 mph and floated along a few feet above the ground, while he tested the controls, and came down gently, stopping within a couple of yards. Lateral control seemed to be rather ineffective and Raynham decided to fit a slightly larger rudder, although in retrospect the small fin area was probably the cause of the problem.

On the Monday, the venue had to be moved to the neighbouring Firle Beacon because of unfavourable winds. The Handasyde glider soon made its mark with a flight of 11 minutes 23 seconds. Raynham was learning the intricacies of gliding as he went along. He nearly stalled as he was catapulted into the air but put his nose down and just cleared the ridge. He gained height for a while but then got into the downwash to the lee of the ridge and had to land downwind. Before the end of the day his time had been bettered by Fokker in his two-seater with a time of 37 minutes 6 seconds.

On the following day, Raynham in the Handasyde stayed aloft for 1 hour 53 minutes to establish a British endurance record. Raynham had left his machine overnight in the lee of a wood just below the top of Firle Beacon. About eight in the morning, he began to drag the machine up the hill and reached the top at about ten o'clock. Before eleven o'clock, he had been launched using rubber bungee cords from the

Raynham and Camm lifting the Handasyde glider to the top of the hill at Itford, with the aid of willing helpers.
(Harald Penrose)

crest of the hill in winds gusting between 15 and 30 knots. After a few minutes, he made a mistake and touched down but he soon got into the air again. This time, instead of gliding into the depression between the ridges as he had done on his flight the previous day, he stayed in an upcurrent along the ridge, keeping between 30 and 70 feet above it. He worked one upcurrent for about 40 minutes before conditions got very bumpy and he then worked up and down the ridge twenty or so times. On this day he was more intent on gaining experience rather than achieving a record. Therefore when Merriam was seen to be making preparations to take off, Raynham sportingly moved out of his way and in so doing lost the lift from the standing wave on the ridge. He nearly lost control and had to land quickly to stay within 800 yards of his starting point as required by the regulations of the contest.

Raynham had found the glider tiring to fly. The controls were sluggish, particularly laterally. Furthermore, he had found the machine to be somewhat nose heavy and had to exert a constant backward force on the stick. After the flight, he worked hard to correct these deficiencies; amongst other things, he increased the movement of the ailerons and fitted a padded loop of wire to the unique aileron control cable to reduce the wear and tear on his left hand. He also fitted a new Smiths airspeed indicator. However all this effort was to no avail as the weather remained unsuitable for gliding over the next three days. To fill in the time, Raynham and a few

others converted a six-wheel trolley into a "sailplane", fitted with a mast, bowsprit and sundry other items, including a broken wing from one of the gliders. A successful trip was accomplished down the hill without injury, braking being aided by a barbed-wire fence.

On the last day of the competition, the weather improved somewhat and Raynham made a short flight. He got his machine back to the top of the hill and decided that as no other competitor looked like improving his record, he would wait until the wind dropped a little. Unfortunately for him, later in the afternoon, a Frenchman, Maneyrol, in the unfancied Peyret tandem-winged glider chanced his arm. It was evident after a short while that he was doing well and eventually landed after achieving a flight of 3 hours 21 minutes 7 seconds to snatch the prize. Despite the unfavourable conditions and approaching darkness, Raynham made one last effort to better the time but failed. In all, Raynham made six flights of 1 minute 38 seconds, 11 minutes 23 seconds, 3 minutes 15 seconds, 1 hour 53 minutes 2 seconds, 8 minutes 30 seconds and 11 minutes 54 seconds for a total of 2 hours 33 minutes 2 seconds.

The last that was heard of the Handasyde glider was when Raynham doubled for the hero in a film called *The Hawk*, and was shot over a cliff at Torquay in the suitably waterproofed glider to rescue the heroine, who was in the act of being carried away by the villain in his private submarine.

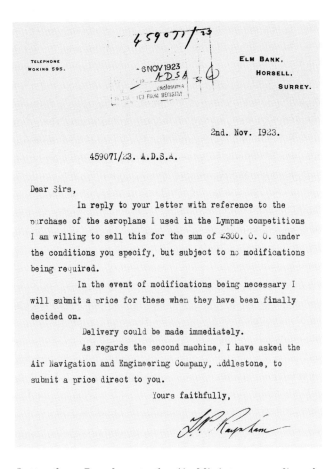

TELEPHONE
WOKING 595.

ELM BANK,

HORSELL,

SURREY.

2nd. Nov. 1923.

459071/23. A.D.S.A.

Dear Sirs,

In reply to your letter with reference to the purchase of the aeroplane I used in the Lympne competitions I am willing to sell this for the sum of £300. 0. 0. under the conditions you specify, but subject to no modifications being required.

In the event of modifications being necessary I will submit a price for these when they have been finally decided on.

Delivery could be made immediately.

As regards the second machine, I have asked the Air Navigation and Engineering Company, Addlestone, to submit a price direct to you.

Yours faithfully,

Letter from Raynham to the Air Ministry regarding the purchase of the monoplane

The Handasyde H.2

Late in 1921, Handasyde began to design a commercial aircraft capable of carrying ten passengers and intended for mail services in Australia. The engine proposed for this aircraft was the 450 hp Napier Lion. It was designed to have a span of 57 feet, a length of 39 feet 6 inches and a height of 10 feet 2 inches. The weight fully loaded would have been 7,000 lb, giving a useful load of 2,000 lb. The projected cruising speed was 100 mph with a maximum speed of 125 mph and a climb to 3,000 ft in 5 minutes.

At the same time, a smaller six-passenger machine, with a useful load of some 1,200-1,500 lb and an all-up weight of 5,000 lb was designed. The power plant was intended to be a Rolls-Royce Eagle IX, which was expected to give the machine a top speed in excess of 115 mph. In the event, the company were unable to afford to fit this engine and the less powerful 350 hp Eagle VII was fitted for trial purposes. It was reported in July 1922 that four of these machines were being built at the Blériot works at Addlestone for the Larkin Company in Australia for service on the Brisbane-Sydney-Adelaide route and that the first was nearing completion.

The prototype of the smaller machine appeared late in 1922. It was a high-wing cantilever monoplane made almost entirely of wood. The fuselage consisted of three box structures of straight taper. Each box structure was made up of four main longerons and a number of stringers supported by shaped formers to give a slightly rounded rectangular section. The forward part, which was made of spruce, encompassed the cockpit. Then followed a straight section also made of spruce which formed the passenger cabin. From

the rear of the cabin, the longerons were made of ash with the lower ones having a pronounced upward taper towards the tail. The sections were butt-jointed, with the joints reinforced with generously sized fishplates. The formers were built up into box sections from ash flanges and plywood walls. It was covered by three-ply, which was fitted to the curvature of the fuselage by cutting V-shapes from the ends of the larger panels and using relatively small panels elsewhere. Joints in the three-py were made by applying a fishplate of three-ply about 4 inches wide to the inside and riveting with hollow rivets of about 3/16-inch diameter pitched about 3 inches apart.

The wings had a bi-convex section at the roots which tapered to a very thin section at the tips with a flat bottom camber. The angle of incidence was constant from root to tip. In plan view, the wing had tapered leading and trailing edges with straight tips tapering slightly outwards to the rear.

It was built up from four main spars - the two forward ones parallel and the two rear ones tapered forwards from root to tip. Each spar was a built-up I-section, the vertical web consisting of two-ply, made from 4-inch strips of spruce set at 45°, crossing at right angles and strengthened with fabric glued to the surfaces. The top and bottom flanges each consisted of two strips screwed and glued either side of the web. There were two stringers top and bottom recessed into the ribs between each spar. The ribs were constructed of three-ply webs, stiffened with vertical and diagonal strips of spruce and pairs of flanges set above and below the stringers. The ribs projected beyond the outer flanges so that they were flush with the wooden wing covering. The wing leading edge was formed with 1/16th-inch three-ply bent to a trough section packed up by strips on the front spar to make it level with the rest of the wing covering. The trailing edge was of solid spruce. The wing covering itself was unusual. It consisted of spruce strips 1/8th-inch thick and 4 inches wide, spindled out internally to form a corrugated section and applied chordwise. Thus although the covering made a contribution to the drag bracing, it did not strengthen the wing span-wise against lift loads and the strips tended to sag somewhat between the ribs where the curvature was greatest.

The pilot was seated immediately behind the engine compartment with his head level and abreast of the wing leading edge. The controls consisted of a standard rudder bar and control column with a hand wheel. The control surfaces were operated by a system of push rods and cranks, coupled in the case of the elevator tube by a chain drive. Behind the pilot was the cabin which could accommodate freight or six passengers. There was a door and three windows on each side. There was an emergency exit through the roof, consisting of a three-ply box projecting through the trailing edge of the wing, fitted with a louvred trap door of aluminium to provide ventilation. A lavatory was fitted aft of the cabin and there was space for luggage under the pilot's seat.

The wings were built in two halves, joined at the centreline by eight bolts placed at the top and bottom of the four main spars. They rested on the top longerons of the cabin. They were accurately located laterally and longitudinally by means of pairs of interconnecting aluminium blocks fitted to each spar and to the upper longerons on each side of the fuselage. Lift loads were transmitted to the main fuselage structure via turnbuckles which connected straps surrounding each spar to corresponding lugs on the main fuselage frames.

The tail assembly was of conventional construction with the tailplane having a spar of straight taper and spindled out

214

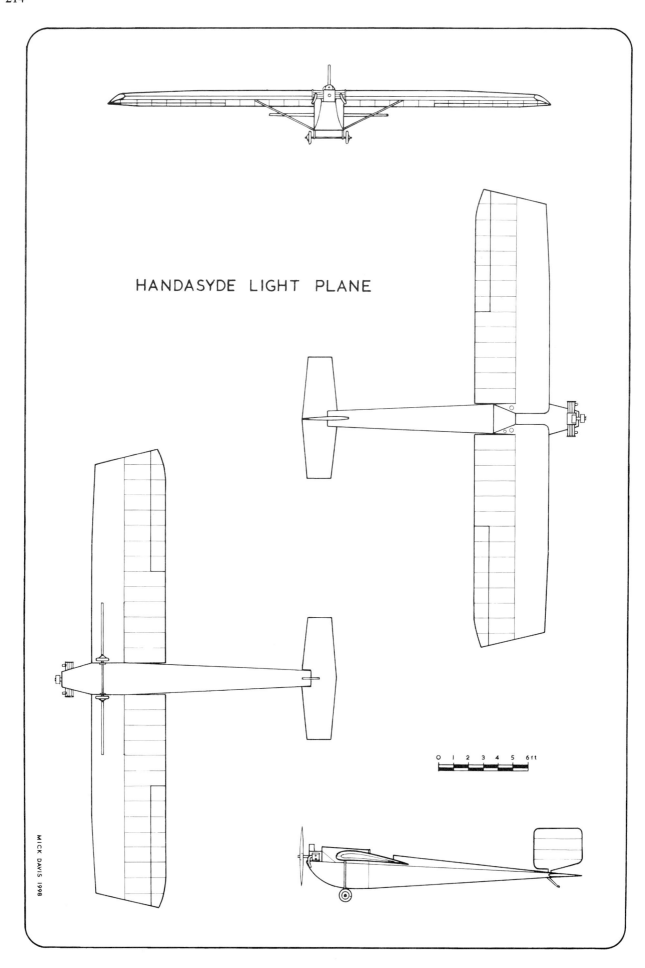

HANDASYDE LIGHT PLANE

0 1 2 3 4 5 6 ft

MICK DAVIS 1998

The Handasyde H.2 at Brooklands. (Brooklands Museum)

to form an I-section. The vertical fin had a stout post fitting into brackets on the back of the stern post and the rudder was fitted to it by eye-bolts. The incidence of the tailplane was adjusted by a worm gear.

The engine mounting consisted of four longerons of ash about 2½ inches square, bolted at the rear to the front of the main longerons and joined at the front with large fishplates at every junction. At the front these longerons were connected by a five-ply former made of spruce. The engine bearers were stout steel tubes resting in sockets in the fireproof bulkhead and the front former and were braced by steel tubes running to the lower longeron joints. Two 50-gallon petrol tanks were fitted in the wing roots which fed, by means of two pumps, a small gravity tank fitted above the engine. In an emergency, the engine could be fed directly by gravity from the main tanks.

The main axles (13-foot track) for the rear pair of wheels of the four-wheeled undercarriage were hinged to the lower fuselage longerons and sprung by means of telescopic struts anchored onto substantial aluminium fittings attached to a wing spar. A bracing cable ran from this fitting to the axle hinge on the lower longeron. The fuselage at this point was reinforced by means of a metal tie rod running under the fuselage to the hinge on the other side. Smaller wheels were fitted on V-struts forward to prevent nosing over and a conventional tail skid was fitted. Brakes were fitted to the main wheels.

Tests on the aircraft began early in December 1922 at Brooklands, with Frank Courtney at the controls. He started by carrying out taxi trials and some preliminary straight hops.

A few days later he carried out more taxi trials but did not venture into the air as there was a strong wing blowing and the engine was not giving full power. One afternoon a few days later, after the engine had been retuned, a few trial hops were carried out but on the third flight after a particularly long landing run one wheel finished up in a foxhole and had to be dug out. Nevertheless, there was sufficient of the day left to make an extended flight. He took off after about a seven-second run and made several circuits at a height of about 500 feet. Afterwards Courtney reported that the aircraft was very light on the controls and expressed general satisfaction with its handling.

It was the intention of the Larkin Company to operate the four Handasyde machines with a Government subsidy of £17,500 on the 760-mile Sydney to Adelaide service and with a subsidy of £11,500 on the 550-mile Sydney-Brisbane-Charleville service. In the event, the aircraft were not delivered before the Handasyde Company went into liquidation. Instead the cabin structure and engine mounts were incorporated by the constructors, A.N.E.C, into a much larger aircraft designed by John Brewster.

The A.N.E.C. III, as it was called, was given a much longer fuselage and high aspect ratio biplane wings, with the top plane having a much wider chord than the lower. Given the long moment arm of the fuselage, the tail unit appeared quite small in comparison. The fuselage was made of wood, the longerons were untapered, the additional strength at the rear that this afforded being compensated by a wider spacing of the formers. Although the spar and rib construction was not too dissimilar from Handasyde's design, the overall wing

The A.N.E.C. III prototype, converted from the Handasyde H.2, outside the T B Andre & Co sheds at Brooklands.
(Brooklands Museum)

construction was much simplified. There were only two I-section spruce spars and the wings were fabric covered. The ailerons were balanced and were fitted to pivots fitted to extensions of the ribs beyond the rear spar. The interplane struts were constructed of streamlined steel tube.

The pilot had an excellent view from the cockpit placed ahead of the wings just behind the engine. The six-seat cabin was retained but the payload was increased to 1,200 lb to allow for the carriage of mails in a compartment under the pilot's seat. A lavatory was fitted behind the cabin and behind that was a luggage compartment with a separate outer door. The Rolls-Royce Eagle IX engine was mounted on steel tube bearers, resting on plywood cradles. The radiator was built into the engine housing below the engine. The petrol tanks were fitted in the roof of the cabin and the fuel was fed to the engine by means of a submerged pump via a small service tank close to the engine. The undercarriage was supported by V-struts and was fitted with rubber cord shock absorbers.

The aircraft was first test flown in March or April 1926. These tests were evidently carried out without much difficulty because the aircraft had been shipped to the Larkin Aircraft Supply Co Ltd in Australia and registered G-AUEZ by 16th August. Two more A.N.E.C. IIIs were registered G-AUFC and G-AUGF on 21st May and 15th August 1927 respectively. On 16th March 1927, G-AUEZ was struck on the ground by Moth VH-UAF and badly damaged. Its C of A was renewed after repairs on 5th October. G-AUFC, named

Satin Bird had only a short life. It crashed on landing at Hay, New South Wales, on 27th December 1927 and never flew again. It was struck off the register on 22nd May 1929. The remaining aircraft were used on scheduled services between Melbourne and Hay and one was used to initiate tourist expeditions into the outback in 1928. The first run was by Capt Frank Neale to Alice Springs, Shell supplying the petrol for the return leg by camel. On the second occasion starting on 4th July, he was accompanied by Capt H J Larkin, the managing director, in a D.H.50. The route went in easy stages to Hermannsburg via Farina Town.

In 1929, two of the A.N.E.C IIIs, G-AUEZ *Diamond Bird* and G-AUGF *Love Bird* were rebuilt as eleven-seaters by Larkin, with their Eagle IX engines replaced by 450 hp Armstrong-Siddeley Jaguars. The whole forward structure was rebuilt using that company's patent steel-tube construction. These aircraft were later re-registered as VH-UEZ and VH-UGF under the new registration scheme. In this form they were transferred to Australian Aerial Services Ltd based in Melbourne, where they carried out passenger and survey work. During 1930, the two aircraft were chartered for carrying out survey work over 40,000 square miles of uncharted territory west of Alice Springs. VH-UGF crashed and was destroyed by fire at Temora, NSW, on 14th July 1931 and VH-UEZ was struck off the register on 9th June 1932.

The Raynham-Handasyde monoplane at Brooklands with the Clubhouse and Test Hill in the background. *(Brooklands Museum)*

The Raynham-Handasyde Monoplane

The last aircraft to be designed by Handasyde was an ultralight aircraft for Raynham to fly in the 1923 Motor Glider Competitions. Small lightweight aircraft with engines of around 10-20 hp were becoming increasingly popular, particularly in France and Germany. British designers were also active and several small single-seaters were under construction early in 1923. The light aircraft movement received a fillip in April 1922 when the Duke of Sutherland, recently given the post of Under-Secretary of State for Air by Bonar Law, offered a prize of £500 for a competition between low-powered aircraft, the details of which were to be decided by the Royal Aero Club. Not to be outdone, two weeks later the *Daily Mail*, which had considered the promotion of aviation to be its own preserve, offered a prize of £1,000 and tried to relegate the Duke's offer to second place. Eventually it was agreed that the two prizes should stand independently without any question of precedence, the only difference being that the *Daily Mail* prize was an open event whereas the Duke's prize was for British competitors and machines only.

The main emphasis was to be on fuel economy. Engines were not to exceed 750 cc capacity, though the pilot could contribute muscle power if able. The winner would be the competitor who covered the greatest distance round a triangular course on an allowance of one gallon of petrol, plus a margin to allow the pilot to regain his starting place. Before the distance flight was attempted, each machine had to pass a transport test to prove that it could be easily removed from a field after a forced landing and could be kept in an ordinary shed or garage. The test consisted of folding or dismantling the wings within a limited time and manhandling the machine over a one-mile course which included a gateway 10 feet wide.

Later, additional prizes were offered by other bodies to make the competition more varied. The Abdullah Company offered a prize of £500 for the highest speed attained over two laps. £150 each was offered by the Society of Motor Manufacturers and Traders and the British Cycle and Motor Cycle Manufactures and Traders Union, for a reliability test consisting of the greatest number of circuits completed, provided that a minimum distance of 400 miles was covered and no alterations were made to the aeroplane or its engine. Later, Sir Charles Wakefield added a prize of £200 for the greatest height attained and the Royal Aero Club gave £100 for a landing competition.

The Raynham-Handasyde entrant was a shoulder-winged monoplane, powered by a 750 cc Douglas motor cycle engine. The aircraft differed in many respects from the Handasyde glider, although they bore a superficial resemblance to one another and the method of construction was similar. The fuselage was of rectangular cross-section and was totally covered in plywood. It tapered to a horizontal knife-edge. The wings and tail were fabric covered. The thick semi-cantilever wing had a Gottingen section and no dihedral and was built in one piece, with the two wing spars boxed with plywood to give it strength and rigidity. The spars were of constant depth over a greater portion of the span, tapering only near the tips. It was attached to the top longerons by simple steel fittings and externally braced to the fuselage by a tube from the front spar and by wire from the rear spar. The aircraft had a partially-balanced all-moving tailplane and an unbalanced rudder without a fin. The undercarriage was very simple, the axle resting in slots in two short wooden supports

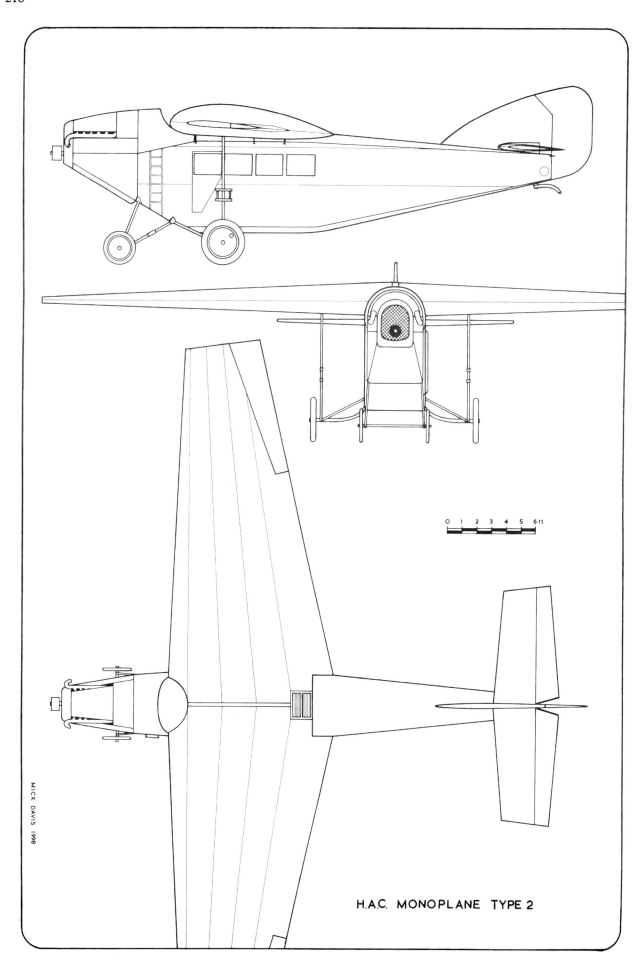

MICK DAVIS 1998

H.A.C. MONOPLANE TYPE 2

0 1 2 3 4 5 6 ft

The F.K.41 after conversion to the Desoutter Mark I. (The A J Jackson Collection)

within a half-tubular transverse member.

The Douglas 750 cc flat-twin air-cooled engine, which developed about 15 hp at 2,500 rpm, was fixed to a simple plate mounted on the front of the top longerons and could easily be removed. There was a direct drive to the propeller which was heavy enough not to require a flywheel. The fuel tank was mounted at about the same height as the engine and was mounted on two transverse beams within a closed fairing about one foot wide which ran from behind the engine to just in front of the cockpit. Petrol was pressure-fed to the engine.

The rather cramped cockpit was positioned between the spars with a cutout in the wing trailing edge to allow access. Although the fuel tank was positioned just in front of the cockpit, it did not obscure the view, which was excellent on landing, although the wing obstructed the downward view during the climb. Some of the instruments were located under the coaming while others were positioned on the top surface of the wing close to the cockpit.

The Raynham-Handasyde was taken to Brooklands for testing and, on 9th September, Raynham made a successful first flight, although difficulties were experienced with engine carburation and the elevator gearing was too high, which made control unduly sensitive. The top speed was found to be around 65 mph and the stalling speed 30 mph. The monoplane was painted in the Raynham racing colours with a dark grey fuselage and yellow flying surfaces. It quickly earned the nickname of 'Goldflake' after the Wills' cigarette packet and several less complimentary names as well. One reporter regretted 'that the terrible mustard and black combination of paint detracted from its pleasant lines' and another commented that 'one wishes that Mr. Raynham would give away that pot of yellow paint'.

The competition for the various prizes took place round a triangular 12½-mile course at Lympne during the week commencing 8th October 1923 in very gusty conditions. The entries closed on 1st October and besides the Raynham-Handasyde there were twenty-three competing machines, including four foreign entries and two other machines manufactured by the A.N.E.C.

The Raynham-Handasyde, which had been given the competition number 13, flew well on the first day of the trials and averaged 65.6 mpg. However the Douglas engine gave continual trouble and only a couple of short flights were made after that. During one of these Raynham managed to reach an altitude of 3,000 feet before the engine malfunctioned. Altogether, the Handasyde flew a total of 162 miles during the competition or thirteen laps of the circuit.

The most common fault with Douglas engines in the competition was breakage of the valve rocker arms, possibly because the valve springs were too stiff. The puzzling thing was that the fault apparently only occurred in the air and not in road applications. Other entrants experienced trouble with flywheels working loose and some with crankshaft failures. Raynham did not experience this fault, probably because the crankshaft extension was properly supported by thrust and journal races positioned well away from the normal front bearing.

The fuel economy prize was shared by a Wren flown by Flt Lt Longton and an A.N.E.C. flown by J H James, with a figure of 87.5 mpg. The altitude prize was won by Piercey in an A.N.E.C with a height of 14,400 feet and the distance prize by Hinkler in the Avro with a total of 575 miles or 46 laps. The landing competition was not held due to the gusty conditions.

The prototype Desoutter Mark II G-AAZI in the colours of Rollason Aviation. (The A J Jackson Collection)

Raynham later flew the aircraft at a light planes meeting at Hendon in October.

The official report on the Raynham-Handasyde was generally critical but did praise its take-off and landing performance. It remarked on the poor climbing performance and the poor visibility during the climb. It also found it unstable fore and aft, with poor aileron control and that the 300 mm wheels were considered too small. Overall, it was felt that the Handasyde was not a practical proposition for everyday use. In common with the other machines constructed by A.N.E.C., the Raynham-Handasyde wing had a three-ply covering over the leading edge which tended to lose shape and it was suggested that additional former ribs were required. It is possible that the poor performance was as a result of concentrating on fuel economy. As *The Aeroplane* commented 'and so not being designed to capture any one prize it did not get any'.

The Raynham-Handasyde had made a favourable impression on senior Ministry observers prior to the results of the competition being known and it was included amongst the five types of machine finally chosen for further evaluation as a basis for a low-cost two-seat trainer. The aircraft was then bought from Raynham for £300 by the Air Ministry under Contract No.487257/24 and given the serial number J7518. The terms of the agreement were that the machine would be overhauled but not otherwise modified, except at an additional cost. The Handasyde went to the A&AEE in August 1924.

Later the machine was seen at the Wembley Exhibition between 19th June and 9th November 1925. The Handasyde was never given a civil registration and its ultimate fate is not known.

Desoutter I and II

Marcel Desoutter employed Handasyde to redesign the Koolhoven FK.41 to conform to British airworthiness requirements. Koolhoven was a Dutchman who first became the designer for the British Deperdussin Company before moving to Armstrong Whitworth, where he designed a series of aircraft, including the FK.3 and FK.8, used by the Royal Flying Corps in the First World War. He then designed for B.A.T. before moving back to the Netherlands. The FK.41 was a high wing monoplane of wooden construction with the fuselage, one-piece semi-cantilever wing and tailplane all covered with plywood. The first prototype made in Holland was fitted with a Siemens engine. The aircraft was intended as a three-seat tourer for the private owner or a commercial plane for light taxi work for a pilot and two passengers.

The second Dutch-built airframe, powered by a 95 hp Cirrus III engine, arrived at Croydon for modification in April 1929. Handasyde made a detailed redesign of the aircraft. He lowered the tailplane from on top of the fin to just above the top of the fuselage and marginally increased the fin area. This brought the tailplane in line with the slipstream of the propeller, which significantly improved its controllability during take-off. Streamlining was improved by sloping the windscreen backwards, the engine cowling was reshaped and a strengthened undercarriage was fitted. The pilot sat in front of the two passengers who were provided with a canvas bench seat. Another airframe arrived from Holland with the modifications incorporated and was promptly shipped to Australia. The first machine was exhibited at Olympia as the Desoutter Dolphin, but this name

The prototype B.A. Swallow fitted with the Salmson A.D.9 radial engine. (The A J Jackson Collection)

was not used again and the design eventually became known simply as the Desoutter I. Following the show, the Desoutter company laid down a large batch, the first of which went to National Flying Services in November 1929. Later the Cirrus Hermes I engine of 105 hp was offered as an option. The sale price was £750 with the Cirrus III and £785 with the Cirrus Hermes. Twenty-nine Desoutter Is were built, twenty-four being first registered in Britain, of which nineteen went to National Flying Services.

In 1930, a much improved version was introduced known as the Desoutter II. The D.H. Gipsy III inverted engine of 120 hp was fitted. This raised the thrust line and allowed the undercarriage to be shortened by some four inches. It also allowed a slimmer front fuselage and a more raked windscreen and deeper side windows which improved the pilot's view without cramping the passengers, who remained seated side-by-side behind the pilot. The depth of the fuselage was reduced by six inches without reducing the headroom. The fuselage structure was strengthened, which allowed the combined window and escape hatch in the roof to be enlarged and two doors to be fitted, each larger than the single door on the Mark I, thus improving access to the cabin. The passengers were provided with two large windows each which could be opened inwards and upwards during flight. The ailerons were redesigned and mass balances were fitted, the tailplane was made adjustable whilst in flight and the fin and rudder were reshaped to a more streamlined appearance. Palmer brakes were fitted. In general the handling was considered satisfactory and the stall was gentle and the low level of noise and vibration was commented upon but the pilot's view came in for some criticism. Thirteen of this new design were built, of which seven were first registered in Britain.

British Klemm and British Aircraft Manufacturing Company Aircraft

In 1933, Handasyde became General Manager of the British Klemm Company, formed to produce an aeroplane suitable for the British market based on the Klemm L.25. The Swallow, as it was known, was a light low-wing cantilever monoplane with two seats in a tandem open cockpit. The wing centre section was built integral with the fuselage, which was a wooden box structure made of spruce and covered with plywood. The wings were ply covered and built on two box-spars with spruce flanges and plywood webs. The ribs were of an open girder construction of spruce. The fabric-covered ailerons were mass-balanced with inset hinges mounted on a false spar. One of the improvements incorporated in the redesign was folding wings. The wings could be folded back by one person, by means of an ingenious arrangement by which the hinge pin and an auxiliary catch could be released by means of a cable operated from the wingtip. The fin was integral with the fuselage and the incidence of the cantilevered tailplane could be adjusted on the ground. The rudder and elevators were fabric covered. Only minor structural modifications were made to British-built versions. The aircraft was very suitable for club use. It was almost spin proof, and had a very low landing speed with little inclination to float. Lateral control was maintained even with the stick pulled right back. The low wing gave good visibility and a degree of protection in the event of a minor crash.

Although fitted with a variety of powerplants, those imported into Britain were generally fitted with the Salmson A.D.9. Only the British-built prototype, G-ACMK, first flown in November 1933, and five others were fitted with the

B.A. Swallow fitted with a Blackburn Cirrus engine. (The A J Jackson Collection)

Salmson engine. The demonstrator, G-ACOW, was fitted with a Pobjoy R and the rest of the production were fitted with the improved Pobjoy Cataract II engine, a 75/85 hp geared 7-cylinder radial.

An improved version, the B.A. Swallow 2, first appeared in May 1935. In order to speed up production, the curvature of the wing tips, rudder and tailplane and the cross section of the fuselage decking were made angular. In addition, the undercarriage was strengthened, as the Swallow tended to sink at speeds just above the stalling speed, resulting at times in heavy landings. While the track and depression under load remained the same, the undercarriage was modified to allow more movement. It was moved forwards, so that the legs were attached to the front wing spar. Modifications to the radius rods allowed the legs to swing forward under load and the damping was improved. The forward section of the fuselage was strengthened by giving it a double skin of plywood, which also had the effect of tidying up the appearance of the cockpit. The seat mountings were strengthened and made detachable. The mounting of the hand-operated brake lever was strengthened so that it did not buckle when forced. A Zwicky hand pump was added to supplement the mechanical fuel pump, which pumped fuel to the gravity tank behind the engine from the wing tanks. The mechanism by which the elevator incidence was altered on the ground was modified so that any adjustment did not affect the tension in the elevator control cables. The wing folding mechanism was left unaltered.

A total of one hundred and five of this version were built, all but seven going to private owners and flying schools in Britain. In 1936, the more powerful Pobjoy Cataract III was fitted and later the 90 hp Cirrus Minor was offered as an alternative and became the standard engine after the seventy-first production machine.

One example of a light cantilever coupé monoplane with two side-by-side seats, called the B.A. Cupid, was built. This was intended for touring and instruction. It was powered by a 130 hp Gipsy Major and dual controls were fitted, consisting of a central control column and duplicated rudder and brake controls. It was given the registration G-ADLR and was flown in the 1935 King's Cup Race before being sold in South Africa in 1936.

In order to meet the burgeoning British market for an advanced touring machine, Handasyde designed a new three-seat cabin monoplane called the Eagle, using the Klemm L.32 as a basis. The passengers were provided with a leather-upholstered bench seat to the rear with the pilot on an adjustable seat situated over the front spar. The wings were of wooden construction with two built-up spars and a plywood skin over ribs and stringers and tapered in chord and thickness. The ailerons were fitted with mass balances below the wing. The wings could be folded at the rear spar, a single lever within the wing and covered by a flap was used to release the upper and lower retaining bolts. The fuselage forward of the rear wing spar, including the engine mountings, was constructed of steel tube and the aft portion was of ply-covered wood. The tail unit was of wooden construction, with the fin braced to the tailplane. The fin and tailplane were plywood covered and all control surfaces were covered in fabric.

Either a fixed or retractable undercarriage could be specified. These were fitted with oleo shock absorbers with steel springs to counter bumps during taxying. On retracting the undercarriage by means of a lever on the pilot's right hand, the wheels folded outwards, the lateral bracing struts being pulled along inclined slides within the wing. The

B.A.IV Double Eagle G-ADVV, one of two on the British register. (The A J Jackson Collection)

wheels were self-locking in the extended position and were held in the retracted position by a catch which could be released by a foot pedal in the cockpit. Differential steering was accomplished by means of Bendix wheel brakes and a parking brake was fitted between the rudder pedals. The first type of engine to be fitted was the 130 hp D.H. Gipsy Major inverted four-cylinder in-line air-cooled engine. Fuel was supplied from tanks in the centre section on each side of the fuselage, by two fuel pumps which could be used separately or in combination.

The prototype, G-ACRG, made its maiden flight in April 1934 from Hanworth. Its top speed proved to be only 25 mph lower than that of the Bulldog, the current biplane fighter in the service of the R.A.F. at the time. The second machine, G-ACPU, was fitted with a 200 hp Gipsy Six. This aircraft was entered into the King's Cup Race of that year and although it was eliminated in its heat, it averaged a respectable 153 mph. The Eagle 2 version appeared shortly after the company was restructured. The fuselage had been deepened and the shape of the tail unit modified to a squatter shape with less area. A total of forty-two Eagles were built. Twenty-three of these were manufactured as Mark 2s and some of the earlier models were reworked to this standard.

Another type of machine appeared in 1936 - the Double Eagle. This was a twin-engined six-seat cabin monoplane, intended for the small airline or charter company. The pilot's compartment was separated from the five-seat cabin by a bulkhead. The cabin was entered by a door on the port side to the rear and was fitted with a lavatory. The fuselage was oval in cross section and was built up of spruce longerons and hoops covered in plywood stiffened with spruce longitudinal stringers. Two aluminium alloy hoops supported the wings through attachment points for the wing spars and bracing struts. The wings were set three-quarters of the way up the fuselage and possessed anhedral as far as the engine mounts,

where the wings picked up parallel bracing struts from the bottom of the fuselage. The wing structure consisted of two laminated box-spars with stressed plywood skinning, strengthened by span-wise spruce stringers. The wing was fitted with split flaps operated by a hydraulic jack, the pressure being supplied by a hand pump. The fin, built integral with the fuselage, and the fixed cantilever six-spar tailplane were both plywood covered. All plywood surfaces were covered with a proprietary treated fabric. The elevator was fitted with a trim tab and the elevators with trim tabs and a servo flap.

The undercarriage was supported by twin oleos and retracted backwards into fairings behind the engine nacelles, the retraction mechanism consisting of a hand-primed hydraulic jack acting on a hinge point on the rear support struts. The engines were two underslung six-cylinder in-line inverted air-cooled Gipsy Majors fed from two 24-gallon tanks located in the wing roots. The oil tanks were in the engine bays.

Only two, G-ADVV and G-AEIN, were registered in Britain, which took part in air races, including the 1936 Johannesburg Race, but were not consigned to customers. One aircraft, ZS-AIY, was bought by the Aircraft Operating Company operating in Africa for aerial survey work and was flown out beginning in early July 1937 by Brian Russell, the chief pilot of that company. This was fitted with special equipment, including a Smith's three-axes automatic pilot, a vertically mounted camera fitted by the side of the operator's seat behind the pilot and the windscreen was modified to give a better downward view. The latest Series II Gipsy Sixes were fitted with D.H. variable-pitch propellers and a small auxiliary fuel tank in the fuselage was provided which could be fed from either wing tank to ensure a steady supply of fuel in the event of one engine failing.

The second prototype B.A. Eagle G-ACPU fitted with a 200-hp Gipsy Six. (The A J Jackson Collection)

The only B.A.3 Cupid built, as flown in the 1935 King's Cup Race by J. Armour. (The A J Jackson Collection)

The second machine at Brooklands fitted with the eight-cylinder JAP side-valve engine and Curva propeller.
(J M Bruce/S Leslie Collection)

APPENDIX A - TABLE OF MARTIN-HANDASYDE AIRCRAFT

1908 Martin-Handasyde Monoplane
12-14-hp Beeston - Humber

Damaged on ground, rebuilt, wrecked on ground at Halifax

1910 Martin-Handasyde Monoplane
Beeston-Humber 40-hp JAP

Re-engined; probably did not fly; flying by 15.6.10; crashed 30.7.10; flying again by 10.10.10; rebuilt as "No.3 Martin-Handasyde"

No.3 Martin-Handasyde
40-hp JAP

Crashed 8.11.10; repaired and flying by 12.11.10; re-engined 35-hp ohv JAP; flying by 11.12.10; re-engined 35-hp Green; re-engined 35-hp sv JAP; flying by 4.6.11; damaged in hangar, Brooklands, 5.6.11; not repaired

Martin-Handasyde Type 4B "Dragon Fly"
50-hp Gnôme

At Olympia 3.11, flew; re-engined 65-hp Antoinette; flown; wings rebuilt by 7.11; crashed 23.8.11

1911 Martin-Handasyde Monoplane
65-hp Antoinette

First flew by 13.11.11; fitted with new wings 2.12; crashed, killing G. Gilmour, 17.2.12

First Monoplane for the R.F.C.
75-hp Antoinette

First flight 27.6.12; to RFC; struck off charge 29.8.13

Military Trials Monoplane (IV.C)
75-hp Chenu

Flew at Military Trials; re-engined 65-hp Antoinette; crashed 24.10.12

Second Monoplane for the R.F.C.
65-hp Antoinette

Damaged 9.11.12; to Farnborough 19.11.12; still at Farnborough 5.12.12

1912 Martin-Handasyde Monoplane
65-hp Antoinette

Flying at Brooklands by 15.12.12; crashed, 24.12.12, killing Edward Petre?

Three or more 1913 Martin-Handasyde Monoplanes
80-hp Laviator

Built and at Olympia 2.13; re-engined 4.13 120-hp Austro-Daimler; first flight 8.5.13; 2nd Whitsun Aeroplane handicap 12.5.13; to Eastchurch 2.6.13; crashed at Brooklands, 13.6.13, killing Lt. J. Kennedy RN

G.102 (A6299) fitted with the Eeman triple gun installation

120-hp Austro-Daimler

Reported under construction 9.13; completed with wheeled under-carriage;, crashed 6.9.13; flying again 11.9.13; (may be two machines); may have been cannibalised for 1914 monoplane

120-hp Austro-Daimler

2nd Aerial Derby 20.9.13; flying at Brooklands 11.13-12.13; fate unknown

1914 Martinsyde Monoplane
120-hp Austro-Daimler

Flown by 9.2.14; Farnborough 4.14, 5.14; Shoreham 2.8.14; bought by government 8.14; cannibalised?

Martinsyde Pusher Biplane
65-hp Antoinette

Entered for 1914 Aerial Derby; not completed

Martinsyde Transatlantic Monoplane
225-hp Sunbeam

Under construction 4.14; not completed on outbreak of war

Martinsyde "Large Monoplane"

Reported under construction 8.14; not completed

One Martin-Handasyde two-seat Tractor Monoplane
(65-hp Antoinette), WO serial number 278

278   RAF Farnborough by 4.13 (not allotted)

Nine Martinsyde S.1 Tractor Biplanes (80-hp Gnôme)
No known Contract numbers. Given WO serial numbers 599, 696, 702, 710, 717, 724, 741, 743, 1601

599   Possibly delivered after 696
696   Impressed at Brooklands; tested Farnborough 25.9.14; Netheravon FS to CFS 23.1.15; Admin Wing to 1 RAS Farnborough 8.6.15; 3 RS Shoreham by 3.16; Northolt, on turn dived in from 3,000ft 20.6.16 (2/Lt G V Aimer killed)
702   1 Sqn to CFS 23.1.15; AP Farnborough to France 24.2.15; 60 Sqn Gosport 6.5.16; 12 Sqn to 3 RAS 4.7.15 - last ref 8.15
710   (non-standard undercarriage); Farnborough by 10.14; movements during squadron mobilisation - 1 Sqn to 12 Sqn 23.1.15; 12 Sqn to Hounslow 7.5.15; 4 Wing to Admin Wing (AID) 28.5.15; 14 Sqn 2.6.15; 17 Sqn to 14 Sqn 9.8.15; 24 Sqn to 27 Sqn 7.11.15; finally to Orfordness for target practice.
717   AID Farnborough 5.11.14, 1 Sqn to 12 Sqn 23.1.15; 12 Sqn to 3 RAS 7.5.15; Admin Wing to 3 RAS 4.6.15; 2 RAS to 3 RAS 13.6.15 - last ref 8.15; to 19 Sqn Castle Bromwich 25.9.15 - last ref 10.15
724   Farnborough for acceptance tests 2.1.15
741   Acceptance test Farnborough 12.12.14; Farnborough by 1.15

The F.1 at Rochford showing the supports for two upward-firing Lewis guns firing through the centre section.
(J M Bruce/S Leslie Collection)

743   1st flight 14.12.14; AID Farnborough 15.12.14 approved 30.12.14; to St Omer 9.1.15, received 16.1.15; 6 Sqn 9.2.15; B Flt 16 Sqn 12.2.15, in action 21/23.1.15 (Capt Holt), to C Flt 16 Sqn attached 4 Sqn 3.3.15, to 1 AP St. Omer 5.3.15 until 8.15; Exp Force to Admin Wing 3.9.15; Northolt 4.9.15, SOC at 1 AP 5.9.15

1601   to Farnborough 21.12.14; Acceptance test 22.12.14; AP Farnborough to AP St Omer 5.1.15; 5 Sqn 9.1.15; damaged on landing (Capt Carmichael) 11.1.15; repaired 11.2.15; to 6 Sqn 29.3.15, to 1 AP 23.7.15, to 6 Sqn 29.6.15, 1 AP St. Omer 21.7.15; 6 Sqn 11.8.15; in combat with Aviatik, Hooge-Polygon Wood, 27.8.15 (2/Lt M K Cooper-King); to 1 AP, 28.8.15; 6 Sqn, in combat with ea at 7,500-8,000ft Ypres 10.9.15 (Capt T W Mulcahy-Morgan); SOC 25.7.17

Two Martinsyde S.1 Tractor Biplanes (80-hp Gnôme)
WO Contract No. A.2810, serial numbers 748 and 749

748   AP Farnborough to France 2.1.15; 6 Sqn by 10.1.15, to AP 16.1.15, to 16 Sqn 9.2.15, to AP 5.3.15, AP St Omer to 1 Sqn 15.3.15; Armed with only 2 revolvers attacked 2 LVG and another EA at 5,500ft near Handzaeme 28.4.15 and damaged in combat near Zandvoorde, 7.5.15 (both 2/Lt MMcB Bell-Irving); to 1 AD 27.7.15; retd Farnborough 28.7.15; 11 RAS; written-off 19.1.16 SOC

749   AP Farnborough to France 4.1.15; tested Farnborough 26.1.15; to 5 Sqn 7.1.15, crashed, Bailleul, 1.5.15 and written off after 30 hrs

Eight Martinsyde S.1 Tractor Biplanes (80-hp Gnôme)
WO Contract No. A.2969, serial numbers 2448 to 2455.

2448   Acceptance test Farnborough 17.12.15; E Flt CFS by 9.15; D Flt CFS 3.4.16

2449   to AP Farnborough 14.1.15; accepted 20.1.15; 1 AP 29.1.15; 4 Sqn 9.2.15, to 1 AP St. Omer 6.4.15; 6 Sqn 15.4.15; Crashed and badly damaged, 26.4.15; combat with Albatros, Ypres-Houthulst at 6,000 ft (Capt L A Strange); in combat with Otto at 8,000 ft over Polygon Wood, 10.5.15 (Capt L A Strange); 1 AP St. Omer 27.6.15, reconstructed 6.15-7.15; reserve aircraft 1 AP 31.7.15; to Farnborough 1.8..15; 9 RAS Norwich 4.15; D Flt 1 RAS 13.8.15; wrecked on landing (Major L Hewitt) 19.8.15; AP 16.10.15; 6 RS to 53 Sqn 17.7.16

2450   Farnborough by 28.1.15

2451   Farnborough by 15.2.15, to 4 RS 7.2.16 - last ref 4.16; 2 RAS 1915

2452   Farnborough by 26.2.15, 2 RAS Brooklands to India 4.7.15

2453   Farnborough by 1.3.15

2454   Farnborough by 1.3.15; 2 RAS Brooklands to 17 Sqn 14.10.15; 24 Sqn 27.10.15; SOC 28.10.15

2455   Acceptance test Farnborough 1.3.15; 2 RAS Brooklands 1915

12 Martinsyde S.1 Tractor Biplanes (80-hp Gnôme)
WO Contract No. A.3121, serial numbers 2820 to 2831

2820   (fitted V-undercarriage) Acceptance test Farnborough 12.3.15; 5 Sqn by 6.15; 3 RAS (later 3 RS) Shoreham by 8.15; last ref 12.16

The F.3 prototype at Martlesham Heath. (J M Bruce/S Leslie Collection)

2821 Farnborough by 12.3.15; Admin Wing to 9 Sqn Dover 5.5.15; 5 Sqn Abeele; 9 Sqn Dover by 6.15

2822 Farnborough by 16.3.15; AP Farnborough to AP St. Omer 18.3.15 (arr 21.3.15); 6 Sqn 24.3.15; combat with ea at 6,000 ft over Poperinghe, 16.4.15 (Capt L A Strange); crashed at AP St.Omer, 23.4.15, written-off after 13.5 hrs, SOC 25.4.15

2823 to AP Farnborough 20.3.15; to 1 AP St Omer 26/27.3.15; 5 Sqn 28.3.15; C Flt 14 Sqn 22.6.15; 1 AP St. Omer 2.7.15; 12 Sqn 14.9.15; HQ FS 20.8.15; 1 AP RS 2.12.15

2824 AP Farnborough to France 25.3.15; 4 RAS Northolt 21.4.15; 11 RAS Northolt by 12.15 - last ref 3.16; 46 Sqn by 8.16

2826 Farnborough by 12.4.15; 15 Sqn to 14 Sqn 11.5.15; 23 Sqn 25.10.15; 40 Sqn 9.3.16

2827 Farnborough by 12.4.15; Northolt 16.4.15; Farnborough 21.4.15; Northolt 5.15, last reference 10.15; 18 Sqn to 26 Sqn 17.11.15; 32 Sqn 8.1.16; to 4 RAS Northolt

2828 Farnborough by 17.4.15 (*Aeroplane* 6.10.15, p.408)

2829 Farnborough by 17.4.15, 9 Sqn Dover from 28.4.15 - last ref 6.15

2830 Farnborough by 5.5.15; 15 Sqn to Admin Wing 15.5.15; 14 Sqn 19.5.15; 23 Sqn 25.10.15; 29 Sqn 17.11.15; 40 Sqn 28.3.16; 2 RS 11.4.16 (temporarily)

2831 Acceptance test Farnborough 5.5.15; Admin Wing to Dover 6.5.15; 9 Sqn to 1 RAS (later 1 RS) Farnborough 14.5.15, last ref 3.16

24 Martinsyde S.1 Tractor Biplanes (80-hp Gnôme)
WO Contract No. 94/A/132, serial numbers 4229 to 4252

4229 Acceptance test Farnborough 20.5.15; 24 Sqn from 27.10.15; 27 Sqn 17.11.15; 12 Sqn by 2.16

4230 Farnborough by 27.5.15; 24 Sqn from 27.10.15; 27 Sqn 17.11.15

4231 Farnborough by 20.5.15; Admin Wing to 15 Sqn 10.6.15; 46 Sqn by 8.16

4232 Farnborough to 4 RS Northolt 7.2.16 - last ref 3.16

4233 Farnborough to 29 Sqn 10.2.16 (allotted 11.15); 40 Sqn 28.3.16; RS 11.4.16

4234 Farnborough by 11.6.15; Admin Wing Farnborough to 2 RAS Brooklands 11.6.15; Admin Wing 17.6.15; 15 Sqn 20.6.15; 46 Sqn by 7.16

4235 Farnborough by 16.6.15; Admin Wing Farnborough to 4 RAS Northolt 26.6.15 (Maj G I Carmichael); last reference 7.15; 18 Sqn to 20 Sqn 17.11.15; 33 Sqn 8.11.16

4236 1 AD to France 16.10.15; 16 Sqn; retd 1 AD to UK 22.11.15

4237 18 RAS Montrose 1.16; 46 Sqn by 7.16; lost speed on turn, dived into ground, 2.8.16 (2/Lt G L Backhouse killed)

4239 46 Sqn by 7.16 - last ref 8.16

4240 Farnborough by 23.6.15; CFS by 9.15

4241 Farnborough by 25.6.15; Admin Wing to 9 Sqn 3.7.15 until 4.10.15; 8 RS

4242 Farnborough by 30.6.15; Admin Wing to 2 RAS Brooklands 6.7.15 last ref 3.16

4243 30 Sqn (MH8), arrived Basrah 26.8.15; destroyed at Ali Gharbi, 7.11.15

4244 30 Sqn (MH6) arrived Basrah 26.8.15; shot down by ground fire near Ctesiphon, 21.11.15 (Major H L Reilly pow)

4246 Farnborough by 22.7.15, Admin Wing to 4 RAS Northolt 6.10.15; 11 RAS Northolt to 8 Wing 3.12.15; 6 RS Montrose to 53 Sqn 17.7.16

4247 Farnborough by 27.7.15; Admin Wing to 6 RAS

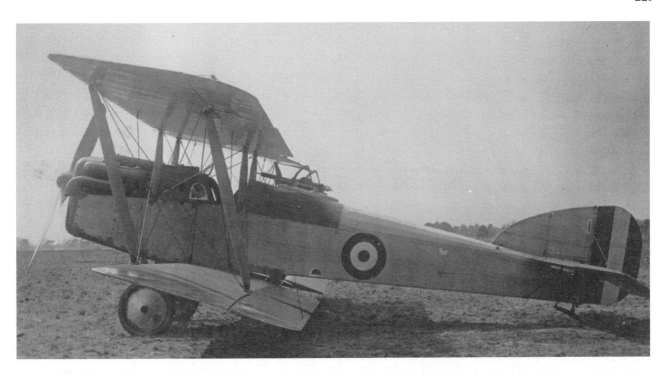

The Martinsyde F.2 at Martlesham Heath. (J M Bruce/S Leslie Collection)

	Montrose 4.8.15; 18 RS Montrose, written-off 30.8.16
4248	Farnborough by 30.7.15; Admin Wing to 6 RAS Montrose 4.8.15
4249	Farnborough by 30.7.15; Admin Wing to 9 RAS Norwich 5.8.15; 4 RAS Northolt by 9.15.
4250	Alexandria 8.15; 30 Sqn, arrived Basrah 26.8.15; lost 22.11.15 (Lt E J Fulton PoW); but also reported 58 TS Suez as crashed in spinning nose dive, 24.6.17 (2/Lt R V Franklin killed)
4251	Farnborough by 9.8.15; AID to 14 Sqn 3.9.15; 27 Sqn 25.10.15; 40 Sqn 9.3.16; 1 RS Gosport 11.4.16 (temporary)
4252	Farnborough by 9.8.15; 19 Sqn by 9.15; 34 Sqn 8.1.16; allotted to 5 RAS Castle Bromwich 12.8.15

One Martinsyde G.100 Elephant Fighter Reconnaissance Tractor Biplane Prototype (120-hp Beardmore)
WO Contract No. 94/A/298, serial no. 4735

4735	AID Farnborough by 25.9.15; CFS Upavon trials by 9.15; 20 Sqn Netheravon 10.15; To 1 AD 29.10.15; 6 Sqn 5.11.15; combat with Fokker at 12,000ft over Gheluvelt, 17.1.16 (2/Lt N A Bolton); to 20 Sqn 1.2.16, in combat 5.2.16 over Forêt de Clairmarais at 9,500 ft (Capt J R Howett); 1 AD 16.3.16; crashed (Lt G E Edwards) after 43.5 flying hrs

12 Martinsyde S.1 Tractor Biplanes (80-hp Gnôme)
WO Contract No. 94/A/295, serial numbers 5442 to 5453

5442	Acceptance test Farnborough 28.8.15; AID to 14 Sqn 30.8.15; Farnborough to 22 Sqn 8.10.15; 45 Sqn 28.3.16; written-off 14.4.16; SOC 18.4.16
5443	Admin Wing to 1 RAS Farnborough 23.9.15
5444	Admin Wing to 6 RAS Montrose 14.9.15
5445	9 Sqn from 21.9.15
5446	Admin Wing to 4 RAS Northolt 29.9.15; 11 RAS Northolt to 6 Wing 20.12.15; 53 Sqn from 13.7.16
5447	19 Sqn Castle Bromwich by 9.15; 34 Sqn 8.1.16

5448	19 Sqn Castle Bromwich by 12.15; 14 RS Catterick, SOC 5.7.16
5449	20 Sqn by 9.15; 7 RAS Netheravon 8.1.16; 4 Wing, written-off 4.7.16 and SOC
5450	20 Sqn; 14 RS Catterick, SOC 5.7.16 but reported by 18 Sqn as crashed, 30.12.16
5451	Admin Wing to 1 RAS Farnborough 6.10.15
5452	CFS Upavon to 60 Sqn Gosport 3-4.5.16
5453	Acceptance test Farnborough 21.10.15

50 Martinsyde G.100 Elephant Bomber Reconnaissance Tractor Biplanes (120-hp Beardmore) ordered 22.11.15 under WO Contract No. 87/A/192 (and also Contract No. 94/A/298?)
serial numbers 7258 to 7307

7258	Del'd CFS Exptl Flight 28.12.15; 27 Sqn to France 1.3.16
7259	49 Sqn; starboard wings came adrift while pulling up sharply out of a dive from 2,000 ft, 8.10.16 (2/Lt H C Baker killed)
7260	1 AD to 20 Sqn 16.3.16; crashed and SOC 12.5.16 (Capt Graves)
7261	2 AD to 27 Sqn 24.7.16; damaged in combat and crashed on landing, 29.7.16 (2/Lt H J W Collins wounded); 2 AD for repair 29.7.16
7262	RFC HQ to 27 Sqn 9.2.16; crashed on arrival (Capt C D Fuller), SOC 9.3.16
7263	23 Sqn; 21 Sqn to 27 Sqn by 8.7.16; damaged during bombing attack, Havrincourt Wood, 22.9.16 (Sgt H Bellerby); to 2 AD 22.9.16, retd UK 13.10.16
7264	Farnborough to EF 27.6.16; 27 Sqn by 8.16
7265	2 AD 11.3.16, 27 Sqn 20.3.16; shot down by Ltn von Bartrab, Jasta 30 6.4.16 (2/Lt J R S Proud)
7266	27 Sqn by 2.3.16; to UK 14.6.16, fitted with Periscope Mk II bombsight ; 49 Sqdn Dover by 10.16
7267	27 Sqn by 2.3.16, broke up in air 8.4.16 (2/Lt W N Thomas killed)
7268	27 Sqn by 2.3.16; shot up NE of Péronne, 6.8.16 (Lt H Spanner); to 2 AD 10.8.16, to 1 AD 9.16; to UK 9.16

The unsuccessful Martinsyde F.1. (E A Harlin Collection)

7269   27 Sqn from RAF HQ 2.3.16, 2 AD 16.7.16, to 27 Sqn 20.10.16

7270   Delivered to 27 Sqn at Dover (via Eastchurch) 8.2.16, France by 2.3.16; Crashed, Fienvillers 27.5.16 (Lt G Joy), 2 AD 22.7.16

7271   Delivered to 27 at Dover (via Grain) 10.2.16; France by 2.3.16, combat damage 6.7.16 (Capt S Smith), repaired (first aircraft to be fitted with rear-firing Lewis gun, 13.3.16)

7273   RFC HQ to 27 Sqdn 2.3.16; damaged in forced landing 27.3.16; 2 AD 2.7.16

7274   Tested Farnborough 20.4.16; 1 AD to 27 Sqn 16.3.16; to UK 11.4.16; 27 Sqn to 2 AD 8.7.16

7275   CFS Upavon by 5.16; to 27 Sqn, crashed 10.5.16 (2/Lt J D Windsor)

7276   1 AD to 27 Sqn (coded "6") 16.8.16; forced down 14.7.17; shot down near Bouilly by Off Stvr M|ller, Jasta 28 21.8.17 (2/Lt S Thompson pow)

7277   1 AD to 27 Sqn 23.3.16, Crashed on landing 8.4.16 (Lt C A Brooks)

7278   1 AD to 27 Sqn by 16.3.16, in combat with Roland and forced down 20.5.16 (Lt M D Basden killed, possibly when wreckage shelled)

7279   18 Sqn by 4.16; badly damaged on landing, 4.5.16; crashed at St. André-aux-Bois, 3.6.16 (Maj G I Carmichael); 27 Sqn; shot down 31.8.16 (2/Lt A J O'Byrne pow, but escaped)

7280   23 Sqn; in combat with 3 Fokkers (AM D A R Chapman) 31.5.16; 2 AD to 27 Sqn 25.7.16; to 2 AD 23.8.16; 27 Sqn by 14.9.16; 49 Sqn 9.15 to 10.16

7281   Farnborough by 14.3.16; 1 AD to 23 Sqn 25.3.16; crashed 27.3.16 (Capt Adams), 2 AD for repair 29.5.16

7282   Tested Farnborough 17.3.16; 39 Sqn from 14.4.16; to France 19.5.16; 2 AD to 27 Sqn 11.6.16; damaged in combat 31.7.16 (Lt R H C Usher wounded); to 2 AD 2.8.16; 27 Sqn; shot down in flames, 31.8.16 (Capt A Skinner killed)

7283   Tested Farnborough 23.3.16; CFS Upavon by 24.4.16; - last ref 5.16

7284   22 Sqdn; Albatros C.I shot down near Pozières 20.5.16 (Capt W A Summers); 27 Sqn 19.7.16; forced to land in combat, 14.9.16 (Lt W H S Chance); to 2 AD 27.10.16; Sheffield to Cramlington via Redcar 19/20.6.17

7285   CFS Upavon by 24.4.16 - last ref 5.16; 27 Sqn 31.8.16

7286   2 AD to 27 Sqn 23.4.16 and 9.7.16, forcelanded behind enemy lines and burned, 17.9.16 (Lt W H S Chance pow)

7287   23 Sqn; in combat with 3 Fokkers (2/Lt J C Griffiths) 29.5.16; 2 AD to 27 Sqn 19.7.16; failed to return 31.8.16 (2/Lt M H Strange pow)

7288   27 Sqn; failed to return 19.7.16 (2/Lt A H W Tollemache killed)

7289   21 Sqn by 4.5.16; to 27 Sqn 8.6.16; damaged in combat 27.9.16 (2/Lt B V S Smith); for repair 29.9.16 but reduced to spares 10.16

7290   1 AD to 27 Sqn 26.4.16; wrecked and to 2 AD 3.9.16; 1 AD 24.1.17

7291   Tested to destruction 18.5.16

7292   49 Sqn Dover by 8.16 - last ref 10.16

7294   49 Sqn by 8.16; 52 Sqn; 51 RS/51 TS Waddington by 3.17 to 8.18

7295   49 Sqn by 8.16

7296   2 AD to 27 Sqn 3.7.16, wrecked 23.7.16 (2/Lt F G Hogarth wounded), to 2 AD 24.7.16

7297   27 Sqn 22.9.16

G.100 7282 from the first batch of G.100s, seen here at No.1 AD St Omer on 27 May 1916 (Peter F G Wright)

7298	1 AD to 27 Sqn 14.6.16; to 2 AD 17.7.16, 27 Sqn; failed to return 24.9.16 (2/Lt E H Wingfield pow)
7299	1 AD to 27 Sqn 1.6.16; shot down in combat by Jasta 1 31.8.16 (Capt O L Whittle pow)
7300	Farnborough to 1 AD 25.5.16; to 27 Sqn 26.5.16; wrecked 4.8.16
7301	RAE Farnborough 27.5.16; 2 AD to 27 Sqn 15.6.16, forced down 9.7.16 (2/Lt Nicholl pow)
7302	Farnborough to Exp Force 20.5.16
7303	23 Sqn, crashed 2.6.16 (Lt S W Price); 27 Sqn; damaged by AA 27.6.16 (Sgt D A R Chapman)
7304	27 Sqn by 8.7.16; shot down 30.7.16 (Lt E R Farmer pow)
7305	39 Sqn by 2.6.16; 46 RS Wyton
7306	RAE Farnborough 1916; 2 AD to 27 Sqn 1.7.16; force-landed 14.9.16 (Capt O T Boyd); wrecked 23.1.17; SOC 24.1.17
7307	2 AD to 27 Sqn 8.7.16; damaged by gunfire, Roisel, 29.7.16 (Lt J C Turner); shot down in bombing attack on Cognelée airship sheds, 3.8.16 (Lt J C Turner pow, later died of wounds)

50 Martinsyde G.100 Elephant Bomber Reconnaissance Tractor Biplanes (120-hp Beardmore) ordered 22.11.15 WO Contract No. 87/A/192, serial numbers 7459 to 7508

7459	30 Sqn by 16.1.17; combat 24.1.17, last ref 2.17; 72 Sqn, crashed and written-off 15.9.18
7460	30 Sqn by 5.1.17; SOC 11.3.17
7461	30 Sqn by 5.17 - last ref 6.17; C Flt Persia by 1.19; written-off 6.3.19
7462	Acceptance test Farnborough 7.6.16; Brooklands by 5.6.16; 1 AD to 27 Sqn 23.6.16; damaged and forced to land 2.7.16 (Capt O T Boyd); 2 AD 5.7.16
7463	RAE by 6.16; tested RAF Periscope Mk II bomb sight 14.7.16; AES Orfordness 18.7.16; 49 Sqn Dover by 8.16 to 9.16; 19 TS Hounslow; caught fire in air on bombing test and crashed, Hanworth; written-off 31.8.17 (Lt A D Roberts killed)
7464	27 Sqn; wrecked 16.5.16, repaired 2 AD by 7.7.16, damaged in combat, Roisel, 29.7.16 (Capt O T Boyd); damaged in combat and forced to land, 19.8.16 (Lt O C Sherren)
7465	2 AD to 27 Sqn 21.7.16; damaged in combat 29.7.16; damaged by Ltn Jv Bertrab, Jasta 30, and forcelanded behind enemy lines, 6.4.17 (2/Lt J P S Proud pow, later died of wounds); flown by Germans
7466	Arrived from UK at Force D for 30 Sqn 11.7.16; combat 7.12.16; SOC 10.5.17
7467	30 Sqn by 11.16; combat 5.12.16; forced down Turkish Fokker monoplane, 27.11.16 (Capt Herring); last ref 1.17; 72 Sqdn; written-off 6.10.18
7468	30 Sqn by 1.17; combat 25.1.17; last ref 5.17; 72 Sqn by 9.18; crashed 4.9.18 (Lt W M Pennington); forcelanded 6.10.18 (Lt Williams); 63 Sqn; written-off 18.7.19
7469	Farnborough by 13.7.16; field trial RAF Mk II Periscope bomb sight 9.16; 1 AD 12.10.16; 2 AD 15.10.16, (fitted with 160-hp Beardmore); to 27 Sqn 20.10.16; to 2 AD 10.5.17
7470	27 Sqn; 49 Sqn 9.16 - 10.16
7471	1 AD to 27 Sqn 22.7.16; shot down near Epigny by Ltn K Wintgens, 29.7.16 (Lt Graham pow wounded)
7472	Recd X AD ex UK 1.9.16; to 14 Sqn; to C Flt 67 Sqn 16.10.16; to X AP 27.10.16; 67 Sqn 26.2.17; shot down by AA fire, 20.4.17 (Lt N Steele); SOC 25.4.17
7473	Recd X AD ex UK 1.9.16; 14 Sqn to X AP 2.1.17; 14 Sqn 16.3.17; X AP 1.7.17; 67 Sqn; crashed and written-

Line up of five F.4s of the Maalentoeskaaderi at Utti in the late Twenties. (Eino Ritaranta)

off, Kantara, 11.17 (Capt O Watt); SOC X AD 25.11.17

7474   Recd X AD ex UK 1.9.16; 14 Sqn 1916; SOC 5.12.16

7475   27 Sqn 12.8.16; shot down near Bus by Ltn Bohme, Jasta 2, 23.9.16 (2/Lt E J Roberts killed)

7476   Recd X AD ex UK 5.9.16; 5 Wing 10.9.16; 14 Sqn to X AP 29.1.17; B Flt 67 Sqn 19.4.17; X AP 20.5.17; 14 Sqdn to X AD 29.8.17

7477   Recd X AD ex UK 5.9.16; 5 Wing 10.9.16; X AP to B Flt 67 Sqn 17.10.16; X AP 6.1.17; 67 Sqn 18.2.17; wings collapsed, 8.7.17 (Capt Brooks killed); SOC 17.7.17

7478   2 AD to 27 Sqn 7.8.16, damaged in combat 26.9.16 (Lt J M McAlery); shot down near Ath, 6.4.17 by Lt Jv Bertrab (Lt J H B Wedderspoon killed)

7479   27 Sqn 13.8.16; shot down in combat with Oblt H Bethge, Jasta 1, 31.8.16 (2/Lt A J O'Byrne pow wounded)

7480   2 AD to 27 Sqn 31.8.16; shot down near Le Transloy by H Reimann, Jasta 2 (2/Lt O C Godfrey killed)

7481   2 AD to 27 Sqn 11.8.16; shot down near Beugny by Ritm M von Richthofen, Jasta 11, 23.9.16 (Sgt H Bellerby killed)

7482   2 AD to 27 Sqn 22.8.16; shot down in combat with Ltn W Fahlbusch, Jasta 1, 31.8.16 (Capt A Skinner killed)

7483   2 AD to 27 Sqn 23.8.16; written-off after fire, 7.9.16

7484   2 AD to 27 Sqn 31.8.16; shot down, Bourlon Wood, 15.9.16 (2/Lt C J Kennedy pow)

7485   2 AD to 27 Sqn 31.8.16; forcelanded and burnt near Oligny, 5.4.17 (2/Lt W T B Tasker pow)

7486   Recd X AD ex UK 25.9.16; 5 Wing 18.10.16; 67 Sqn 3.11.16; crashed, Wadi Hesse, 21.3.17 (Lt F K McNamara awarded VC); SOC 23.3.17

7487   Recd X AD ex UK 20.11.16; 5 Wing 1.12.16; 67 Sqn 18.12.16; crashed, 26.6.17 (Lt Cole); SOC 5.7.17

7488   Recd X AD ex UK 11.16; 5 Wing 1.12.16; 14 Sqn; crashed, 24.2.17 (Lt Tunbridge); to X AD 16.11.17; SOC 25.11.17

7489   Recd X AD ex UK 2.12.16; X AP to 14 Sqn 6.1.17; X AP 15.1.17; SOC 18.1.17; 2 AD to 27 Sqn 22.3.17

7490   Recd X AD ex UK 20.11.16; 5 Wing 1.12.16: X AP to 14 Sqn 18.1.17; X AP 15.5.17; 14 Sqn to X AD 29.8.17

7491   27 Sqn 17.9.17; damaged in combat 27.9.16 (2/Lt R W Chappell); returned crated to UK 28.9.16

7492   2 AD to 27 Sqn 3.9.16; broke up in air, 16.9.16 (2/Lt F D Jackson killed); rebuilt?; 27 Sqn 8.4.17; to 57 Sqn 29.5.17; Scout School 2 AD by 1.8.17. Not listed from 8.8.17

7493   30 Sqn by 3.17; in action (Lt Nuttall) 16.10.17; 17 Sqn; written-off 15.9.18

7494   30 Sqn by 2.17, last ref 6.17; 72 Sqn; destroyed at Eaku 15.9.17 (Lt MacKay); but reported by 63 Sqn as in action 16.10.17 (Lt A E L Skinner); SOC 23.10.17

7495   2 AD to 27 Sqn 15.9.16, shot down by Vzfw L Reimann &/or Hpt O Boelcke, 27.9.16 (2/Lt B S Dendrino pow died of wounds 30.11.16)

7496   2 AD to 27 Sqn 24.9.16; to 57 Sqn 23.5.17, converted to G.102 standard

7497   2 AD to 27 Sqn 22.9.16; wings collapsed in dive near Gorenflos, 6.1.17

7498   2 AD to 27 Sqn 23.9.16; shot down 24.9.16 (2/Lt E H Wingfield); displayed at Delka as war trophy

7499   2 AD to 27 Sqn 25.9.16; damaged in combat 19.3.17 (Lt W S Caster); crashed 16.7.17 (Capt M Johnstone killed)

7500   2 AD to 27 Sqn 26.9.16; shot down by Ltn J Schmidt, Jasta 3, 14.7.17 (2/Lt T E Smith killed)

7501   delivered 23.9.16; 1 AD to 27 Sqn 1.10.16, converted to G.102 5.4.17; in combat 23.4.17 (Lt M H Coote wounded); crashed in fog, 22.11.17, 1 AD 24.11.17

The Martinsyde A.D.C.1 powered by a Armstrong-Siddeley Jaguar engine. (Philip Jarrett)

7502	2 AD to 27 Sqn 28.1.17; wrecked 29.1.17; to 2 AD
7503	1 AD to 27 Sqn 6.10.16; damaged in combat, 6.3.17 (Lt J Gilmour); shot down near Aulnoye by Ltn A Mohr, Jasta 3, 20.3.17 (2/Lt J G Fair killed)
7504	1 AD to 27 Sqn 6.10.16; to 2 AD 31.3.17
7505	Farnborough by 14.10.16; 2 AD to 27 Sqn 27.10.16 - 4.17; 57 Sqn 8.5.17; crashed, 21.5.17 (Maj L A Pattinson), 27 Sqn to Rep Pk 1 ASD 10.12.17
7506	2 AD to 27 Sqn 28.10.16; forcelanded Béthune and crashed at Belle Vue, 20.5.17; to 2 AD
7507	Farnborough by 14.10.16, 1 AD to 27 Sqn (code A2) 6.6.17; to 1 AD 10.12.17; to UK 12.12.17
7508	Farnborough by 14.10.16; 1 AD to 2 AD 1.11.16; to 27 Sqn 3.2.17; shot down near Roisel by Ltn Schlenker, Jasta 3, 19.3.17 (2/Lt T W Jay wounded and pow)

Six Martinsyde "RG" Two-Seat Tractor Biplane Trainers ordered 14.4.16 under WO Contract No. 87/A/395, serial numbers A318 to A323. A320 to A323 not completed.

A318	prototype with 190-hp Rolls-Royce
A319	prototype with 275-hp Rolls-Royce

50 Martinsyde G.102 Elephant Bomber Reconnaissance Tractor Biplanes (160-hp Beardmore, 120-hp Beardmore from A1570?) ordered 21.6.16 under Contract No. 87/A/487, serial numbers A1561 to A1610

A1561	2 AD to 27 Sqn 30.7.16; in action 8.8.16 (Capt R H J Lee wounded); in collision with B.E.12 and wrecked, 21.10.16 (Capt T O D Filley injured)
A1562	2 AD to 27 Sqn 4.8.16; damaged in combat 27.9.16 (2/Lt B V S Smith wounded); wrecked 28.9.16 (Capt O T Boyd); to 2 AD

A1563	2 AD to 27 Sqn 30.7.16; crashlanded after test, 31.7.16?; wrecked after AA damage 3.9.16 (2/Lt F A Wright); 2 AD 4.9.16 then to UK
A1564	2 AD to 27 Sqn 31.7.16; to 2 AD 5.9.16; 27 Sqn; shot down near Rouvroy by Ltn Wolff, Jasta 11, 13.4.17 (2/Lt M Topham killed)
A1565	27 Sqn 8.16; rammed Albatros 23.9.16 (Hans Reimann killed, 2/Lt L F Forbes wounded); 2 AD 24.9.16; SOC 26.9.16
A1566	336 lb bomb trials, Orfordness, 8.16; 2 AD to 27 Sqn 29.10.16; in combat with 9 Albatroses and forcelanded with engine failure; claimed by Ltn Kruger, MFJasta 1, 4.6.17 (2/Lt D T Steeves pow)
A1567	to 2 AD 8.16; to 27 Sqn 5.9.16; damaged by m/gun fire, 8.9.16 (Lt E D Hicks wounded); crashed 1.2.17 (2/Lt R Chappell killed); SOC at 2 AD 22.2.17
A1568	1 AD to 27 Sqn 8.9.16; shot down by Hpt O Boelcke, Jasta 2, 27.9.16 (2/Lt H A Taylor killed)
A1569	2 AD to 27 Sqn 23.9.16; in combat 27.9.16 (Capt H Spanner); shot down in combat, 28.12.16 (Capt H Spanner killed)
A1570	Farnborough by 17.10.16; 2 AD 3.11.16; 2 AD to UK crated 4.1.17
A1571	2 AD to 27 Sqn 14.4.17; force landed and to 2 AD for repair 24.4.17
A1572	1 AD by 1.17; 2 AD to 27 Sqn 10.5.17; shot down near Quivery? by Oblt Bethge, Jasta 30, 14.7.17 (2/Lt G H Palmer pow)
A1573	2 AD to 27 Sqn 24.1.17; shot down in flames by Hpt O Hartmann, Jasta 28, 12.8.17 (2/Lt S C Sillem killed)
A1575	1 AD by 1.17; 2 AD to 27 Sqn 6.4.17; shot down, Villiers, near Cambrai, 2.7.17 (Capt F Wyatt killed)
A1576	Recd X AD ex UK 3.1.17; X AP 12.1.17; 14 Sqn 1.2.17; X AP 26.2.17; SOC 11.3.17

The Nimbus Martinsyde powered by an ADC Nimbus engine developed from the Siddeley Puma. (J M Bruce/S Leslie)

A1577 Recd X AD ex UK 3.1.17; X AP 12.1.17; 14 Sqn 25.1.17; SOC 26.3.17

A1578 1 AD by 1.17; to 27 Sqn 30.1.17; damaged 9.3.17; crashed and burnt, Chateau d'Ossemont, 12 km E of Compiègne, 5.4.17 (2/Lt M Johnstone killed)

A1579 2 AD to 27 Sqn 30.1.17; shot down by AA near Noeux-les-Mines, 13.7.17 (Capt H O Wilkins)

A1580 At Farnborough 8.11.16

A1581 Farnborough by 1.11.16; C Sqn CFS by 4.17; coded ('11') at one time

A1582 Farnborough by 22.11.16; recd X AD ex UK 3.1.17; X AP 26.2.17; 14 Sqn 9.3.17; SOC 25.4.17

A1583 Recd X AD ex UK 3.1.17; X AP to 67 Sqn 26.2.17; hit by AA fire and burnt, 21.4.17 (Lt Cole); SOC 25.4.16

A1584 63 Sqdn; still in service 11.8.19

A1585 Farnborough by 6.11.16

A1587 built as G.102 but restored to G.100; to Middle East Brigade, Egypt, 8.11.16

A1588 Farnborough by 15.11.16; C Flt CFS Upavon by 4.17; 58 Sqn by 10.8.17

A1589 X AD to X AP 21.2.17; 14 Sqn 12.3.17; SOC 9.4.17

A1590 X AD to X AP 21.2.17; 14 Sqn 17.3.17; SOC 3.4.17

A1591 X AD to X AP 21.2.17; 14 Sqn 25.3.17; X AP 19.6.17; X AD;, SOC 25.11.17

A1592 Farnborough by 22.11.16; C Flt CFS Upavon by 5.17; 19 TS Hounslow 9.17; flew into trees, 1.10.17 (Lt B F G Cunliffe injured)

A1593 Presentation acft *Mount Lofty, S. Australia*; recd X AD ex UK 14.4.17; X AP 16.4.17; 14 Sqn 23.4.17; A Flt 67 Sqn 24.5.17; X AP 12.8.17; X AD 17.8.17; 5 FS Heliopolis from 22.9.18; written-off 21.3.19

A1594 Recd Baghdad ex UK 23.5.17; 63 Sqn detd flight Kazvin from 16.12.17; 63 Sqn from 3.1.18; C Flt 72 Sqn from 9.5.18; extant 8.19

A1595 Presentation acft *The White Edenglassie*; Recd X AD ex UK 14.4.17; X AP 16.4.17; A Flt 67 Sqn 8.5.17; X AP 24.10.17; X AD 16.11.17; SOC 25.11.17 but 30 Sqn by 3.18

A1596 Recd Baghdad ex UK 23.5.17; 30 Sqn by 3.18; 72 Sqn; SOC 5.7.18

A1598 Farnborough by 1.12.16; Norwich to Hendon 5.1.17 (Major P E L Gethin); CFS Upavon 7.1.17

A1599 Tested CFS Upavon 1.17; 2 AD to 27 Sqn 30.1.17, to 21 Sqn 17.3.17, 2 AD to 27 Sqn 21.3.17, damaged on landing 9.5.17; 2 AD 11.5.17; retd 27 Sqn by 7.17

A1600 Recd X AD ex UK 6.5.17; 20 RW by 16.7.17; X AP to A Flt 67 Sqn 8.8.17; X AP 24.10.17; 1 Sqn AFC 17.1.18; X AP to 142 Sqn 21.3.18; X AP 3.4.18; 144 Sqn; SOC 14.7.18

A1601 51 Sqn ('4'); SOC 6 AAP Renfrew 12.18

A1602 44 TS Harlaxton by 8.17

A1603 C Flt CFS Upavon 5.17 - 6.17; 30 Wing ARS Turnhouse to 52 TS Montrose 8.11.17

A1604 C Flt CFS Upavon 1917

A1605 Recd X AD ex UK 6.5.17; X AP by 16.7.17; to A Flt 67 Sqn 15.8.17; X Flt 14 Sqn 9.17; X AP 17.11.17; Trg Gp 1.12.17; X Flt Aqaba 4.1.18; 23 TS Aboukir by 3.18; spun into sea from 500 ft, 18.6.18 (2/Lt W Molineaux injured; SOC 20.6.18

A1606 Recd X AD ex UK 6.5.17; X AP 6.5.17; 30 Wing 31.8.17; 22 TS Aboukir to X AD 13.9.17; SOC 25.11.17

A1607 Recd X AD ex UK 6.5.17; 40 Wing 17.10.17; SOC 11.11.17

A1608 C Flt CFS Upavon by 5.17 - 6.17; 52 TS Catterick by 2.18

A1610 C Flt CFS Upavon by 4.17

Two Martinsyde F.1 Tractor Biplane Fighter Prototypes (250-hp Rolls-Royce Mk.III) ordered 16.9.16 under WO Contract No. 87/A/435, serial numbers A3933 & A3934

A3933 Tested at CFS Upavon 11.6.17-22.7.17; Exp Stn Orfordness, HD patrol 22.8.17; HD patrol from Rochford 29.9.17; AP Hendon by 4.18; Hendon 9.4.18; Orfordness 12.4.18; Hendon 1918; RAE Farnborough 21.6.18 last mention 18.3.19 (petrol system tests)

A3934 Not completed

Freddie Raynham's F.6 G-EBDK, which passed through several owners before being dismantled at Brooklands in April 1930. (Philip Jarrett)

70 Martinsyde G.102 Elephant Bomber Reconnaissance Tractor Biplanes (160-hp Beardmore) ordered 11.9.16 under running Contract No. 87/A/487, serial numbers A3935 to A4004

A3935   At Farnborough by 1.1.17; CFS Upavon by 5.17; 44 TS Harlaxton by 8.17; 1 Sqn AFC; accident 13.2.18 (2/Lt H S R Maughan injured)

A3936   C Flt CFS Upavon by 4.17 - last ref 5.17

A3937   C Flt CFS Upavon by 4.17; 19 RS Hounslow by 9.17

A3938   C Flt CFS Upavon by 5.17; 52 TS Catterick by 2.18

A3939   At Farnborough by 3.1.17; CFS; mid-air collision with B.E.2c 7246; both crashed, Wilton, 12.2.17 (2/Lt G T Brown killed)

A3940   Recd X AD ex UK 4.5.17; 30 Sqdn 1.7.17 - last ref 9.17; SOC 8.11.17

A3941   Recd X AD ex UK 4.5.17; 22 TS Aboukir 8.9.17; 23 TS Aboukir by 3.18 - last ref 6.18; 194 TS Amirya, SOC 7.7.18

A3942   22 TS Aboukir 10.17, 23 TS 5.18

A3943   Recd X AD ex UK 4.5.17; 30 Sqn 9.5.17 - last ref 10.17

A3944   Recd X AD ex UK 16.5.17; X AP to 67 Sqn 30.10.17; X AP 17.11.17; 1 Sqn AFC 17.1.18; caught fire on landing at Mejdel, 16.2.18; SOC 20.2.18

A3945   Recd X AD ex UK 16.5.17; 67 Sqn (1 Sqn AFC) 27.8.17; 142 Sqn 13.4.18

A3946   Recd X AD ex UK 16.5.17; 67 Sqn (1 Sqn AFC) 17.10.17; to X AP 3.18; 5 FS Heliopolis; written-off 23.2.19

A3947   51 TS Wye by 5.17; 67 Sqn by 10.17

A3948   AES Orfordness (test mod exhaust, gunsight etc); collected from near Ingatestone by RNAS Chingford 2.3.18 for deletion (presumed crashed)

A3949   10 RS Joyce Green by 4.17; 49 Sqn by 7.17; last reference 8.17

A3950   23 Sqdn by 3.18 - last ref 6.18

A3953   Recd X AD ex UK 3.6.17; 22 TS Aboukir 17.10.17; X AP to 67 Sqn 4.11.17; X AP 9.1.18; 5 FS Heliopolis;

A3954   Recd X AD ex UK 3.6.17; 22 TS Aboukir 17.10.17; X AP to 67 Sqn 1.11.17; X AP 9.1.18; SOC 24.8.18

A3955   Recd X AD ex UK 4.6.17; 67 Sqn (1 Sqn AFC) 17.10.17; 142 Sqn 21.3.18; 17 TDS Abu Suier; written-off 20.9.18

A3956   Recd X AD ex UK 24.6.17; X Flt Aqaba by 25.2.18; written-off 16.9.18

A3957   Recd X AD ex UK 24.6.17; X Flt Aqaba 25.12.17, 23 TS Aboukir 12.6.18; SOC 194 TS Amiria 13.7.18

A3958   Recd X AD ex UK 24.6.17; X Flt Aqaba by 15.1.18; X Flt Aqaba; 23 TS Aboukir 12.6.18; written-off 5 FS Heliopolis 23.2.19

A3959   Recd X AD ex UK 24.6.17; written-off X AD 18.10.18

A3960   X AP by 3.18; 142 Sqn; forcelanded near Kerak and burnt 19.3.18 (Capt A J Evans pow)

A3961   51 TS Waddington by 8.18; crashed and wrecked near Alford, 1918

A3962   crashed

A3963   51 TS Wye by 4.17; 49 Sqn by 6.17, last ref 8.17

A3964   11 TS Scampton by 11.17; SOC 6 AAP Renfrew 12.18

A3965   11 TS Scampton

A3966   11 TS Scampton by 11.17

A3967   Waddington by 12.17

A3968   11 TS Scampton by 11.17; SOC 6 AAP Renfrew 12.18

A3969   75 TS Cramlington; engine failed; hit house, crashed and caught fire, 3.3.18 (2/Lt R W Stobbart died of injuries)

A3970   CFS Upavon by 5.17; forcelanded, 11.5.17 (2/Lt C H Drew)

A3971   19 RS Hounslow by 9.17

A3972   Presentation acft *Gwalior No.2*; at CAD 24.4.17; recd ex UK 18.8.17; 57 RS Abu Suier by 11.17; 30 Sqdn Mesopotamia; SOC 72 Sqn 31.8.18

A3973   Recd Baghdad ex UK 18.8.17; 30 Sqn by 1.18; 72 Sqn; written-off 11.10.18

A3974   Recd Baghdad ex UK 30.7.17; 30 Sqn by 11.17; AP Basrah 2.10.18

A3975   Recd Baghdad ex UK 30.7.17; 30 Sqn by 3.18

F.4 Buzzard of the Lithuanian AF at Kauna airport. (Edmundo Jasiuno)

A3976   1 AD to 27 Sqn 2.7.17, damaged 10.9.17; shot down near Sauchy Lestrie by Obltn H Waldhausen, 24.9.17 (2/Lt W English pow wounded)

A3977   2 AD to 27 Sqn 9.5.17; crashed (2/Lt A E Palfreyman) to 1 AD for repair 4.9.17

A3978   1 AD to 27 Sqn (coded 'B4') 7.8.17; shot down near Quesnoy by Ltn E Hess, Jasta 28, 9.8.17 (2/Lt W R K Skinner pow)

A3979   27 Sqn by 1.17; also 30 Sqn?

A3980   C Flt CFS by 4.17, last ref 5.17

A3981   C Flt CFS by 5.17, last ref 6.17; 52 TS Stirling by 6.17; 17 RS Yatesbury; SOC 6 AAP Renfrew 12.18

A3982   C Flt CFS by 4.17

A3983   C Flt CFS by 5.17; 42 RS Hounslow (coded 3) 1917

A3984   58 Sqn Cramlington by 8.17, last ref 11.17

A3985   C Flt CFS Upavon by 4.17; damaged in collision on landing, 8.4.17 (2/Lt C H Drew); 58 Sqn Cramlington by 8.17; SOC 6 AAP Renfrew 12.18

A3986   1 AD to 27 Sqn 13.7.17; shot down 28.7.17 by Offstvtr Sattler & Ltn Horauf (Capt H O D Wilkins pow)

A3987   SOC 6 AAP Renfrew 12.18

A3988   X Flt 14 Sqn, Aqaba by 4.1.18; 47 Sqn; 23 RS Aboukir, SOC 27.6.18

A3989   21 RS Ismailia; written-off 5 FS Heliopolis 23.2.19

A3990   At Farnborough 15.3.17; 1 AD to 27 Sqn 23.3.17.to 1 AD 25.7.17

A3991   27 Sqn (coded 'C1'); 2 AD 30.3.17, 2 AD to 27 Sqn (coded 'C1') 6.4.17; in combat 9.5.17 (Lt J Stubbs wounded); 2 AD 11.5.17

A3992   2 AD to 27 Sqn (coded 'C3') 6.4.17; collided with A6259 in combat then shot down by Oblt H Bethge, 21.8.17 (2/Lt D P Cox killed)

A3993   2 AD by 30.3.17, 1 AD to 27 Sqn 1.4.17; wrecked (2/Lt A B Cort) 7.8.17 and SOC 7.8.17

A3994   1 AD to 27 Sqn 1.4.17, 27 Sqn to 2 AD 8.4.17

A3995   49 Sqn Dover by 6.17, later with 27 Sqn, last ref 8.17

A3996   49 Sqn Dover by 6.17, last ref 8.17; 10 RS Shawbury

A3997   Martlesham by 6.17, (German radiator tests), HD patrol 12.8.17 (2/Lt G E Cushing)

A3998   1 AD to 27 Sqn 30.3.17, X AD by 31.3.18; written-off at 18 TDS Ismailia 23.10.18

A3999   X Flt Aqaba to 23 TS Aboukir 12.6.18; written-off 5 FS Heliopolis 21.3.19

A4000   X AD to 144 Sqn 3.7.18; written-off 18 TDS Ismailia 23.10.18

A4001   (later re-engined with 120-hp Beardmore); at Farnborough 7.4.17; 10 RS Joyce Green by 4.17; 49 Sqn Dover by 7.17 - last ref 8.17

A4002   51 TS Wye by 4.17, 51 TS Waddington (coded 'B') 15.5.17 - 9.17; HD duties at Higham

A4004   27 Sqn by 4.17; 1 AD to 27 Sqn 28.7.17; crashed, 2.8.17; at 1 AD 3.11; lost in mid-air collision with A6277, 20.12.17 (2/Lt N C Phear killed)

One Martinsyde G.102 Elephant Bomber Reconnaissance Tractor Biplane (160-hp Beardmore) built from spares by SAD Farnborough, serial number A5204

A5204   No information

8E1, The first Martinsyde F.4 delivered to Finland at Utti in the mid-1920s. (Eino Ritaranta)

50 Martinsyde G.102 Elephant Bomber Reconnaissance Tractor Biplanes (160-hp Beardmore) ordered 26.10.16 under Contract No. 87/A/487 and numbered A6250 to A6299

A6250   27 Sqn by 7.17; 1 AD to 27 Sqn 28.7.17; crashed 2.9.17, to 1 AD 14.10.17; to UK

A6251   1 AD to 27 Sqn 15.7.17; shot down by Flakzug 51, 16.9.17 (2/Lt A H Skinner pow)

A6252   (120-hp Beardmore) 10 RS Joyce Green by 4.17; 49 Sqn by 6.17, last ref 7.17; 51 Sqn; 62 TS Dover; crashed into tents on landing, 28.7.17 (2/Lt T H Holiday, 2 on ground killed)

A6253   51 TS Waddington by 5.17 - 9.17

A6254   C Flt CFS Upavon by 1.4.17, last ref 5.17

A6255   1 AD by 3.7.17; 27 Sqn (coded '3') 13.7.17-3.11.17; 1 AD to 27 Sqn 23.11.17; 1 AD 1.12.17; 110 Sqn Sedgeford 2.18 to 4.18

A6256   At Farnborough 23.6.17; Wireless School Chattis Hill for instruction purposes by 5.18, last ref 29.11.18

A6257   1 AD to 27 Sqn 21.10.17; to 1 AD 31.10.17; to 27 Sqn 17.11.17; to 1 AD 14.12.17; RFC Hounslow to Hendon 7.4.18, last ref 11.8.18 (station aircraft)

A6258   2 AD to 27 Sqn 11.5.17; crashed, Clairmarais, 2.10.17 (2/Lt B C Sillem); 1 AD 15.10.17; crashed at Calais, 9.11.17; SOC 6 AAP Renfrew 12.18

A6259   1 AD to 27 Sqn 24.4.17; collided with A3992 in combat then shot down Ltn K Bolle, Jasta 28, 21.8.17 (Capt G K Smith killed)

A6260   2 AD to 27 Sqn 22.5.17; in action 13.7.17 (2/Lt B C Jones wounded); 1 AD 13.7.17

A6261   2 AD to 27 Sqn 14.5.17; shot down by Ltn E Mohnicke, Jasta 11, last seen at 5,000 ft Menin-Ypres, 16.8.17 (2/Lt A R Baker killed)

A6262   2 AD to 27 Sqn (coded 'A5') 21.5.17; to 1 AD 11.7.17

A6263   27 Sqn (coded 'A5') 28.5.17; 1 AD to UK 14.10.17

A6264   1 AD by 13.5.17; to 27 Sqn 25.7.17; damaged by AA and forcelanded, 5.8.17 (2/Lt AE McVitie); 1 AD 5.8.17

A6265   W/T School Biggin Hill 20.5.18; 58 TS Suez

A6266   1 AD to 27 Sqn 11.7.17; shot down near Leffinghe, 14.7.17 (Lt C M de Roche killed)

A6267   At Farnborough 30.7.17; 1 AD to 27 Sqn 16.9.17, to 1 AD 3.11.17, to 27 Sqn 17.11.17, to 1 AD 23.11.17

A6268   RAE Farnborough by 23.6.17

A6269   61 TS South Carlton; broke up in air, 28.7.17 (2/Lt D R Munro killed)

A6270   At Farnborough 23.6.17; 61 TS South Carlton by 9.17

A6271   1 AD to 27 Sqn 10.8.17; to 1 AD 16.10.17; 1 AD to Lympne 18.10.17

A6272   1 AD by 11.8.17; to 27 Sqn 25.9.17; to 1 AD 1.11.17; to 27 Sqn 17.11.17; 1 AD 1.12.17;, 110 Sqn Sedgeford 3.18 to 6.18

A6273   1 AD to 27 Sqn 12.8.17; crashed 2.9.17; to 1 AD for repair 4.9.17

A6274   At Farnborough 16.7.17; 27 Sqn by 11.17

A6275   At 1 AD 18.8.17; to 27 Sqn 21.8.17; 1 AD 19.10.17; W/T School Biggin Hill 20.5.18; Wireless School Chattis Hill for ground instructional purposes by 5.18, last ref 29.11.18

A6276   1 AD to 27 Sqn 17.9.17; to 1 AD repair 20.10.17,

A6277   Presentation aircraft *Baroda No.3*; 27 Sqn; wrecked 22.5.17; retd to 27 Sqn 13.7.17; lost in mid-air collision with A4004, 20.12.17 (Lt H E Darrington killed)

A6278   Presentation aircraft *Kaffraria*; 51 TS Waddington by 8.17; SOC 10.18

F.4 Buzzard G-EANM prior to its flight to Portugal via Spain. (The E A Harlin Collection)

A6279   Presentation aircraft *Gatooma*; 51 TS Waddington; SOC 9.17

A6280   Presentation aircraft *Newfoundland - Reid*; 8 AAP Lympne, HD patrol 12.8.17 (Capt C W Carleton); 1 AD 13.8.17, last ref 16.8.17; 110 Sqdn Sedgeford 1.18 to 3.18; SOC 13.7.18

A6281   (120-hp Beardmore) Presentation aircraft *Malaya No.6, The Choon Guan Peng Siang*; at Farnborough 23.7.17; SOC 9.9.17 but 27 Sqn by 12.10.17

A6282   Presentation aircraft *Malaya No.16, The Menang*; 1 AD to 27 Sqn 17.11.17; to 1 AD 10.12.17; SOC 9.3.18

A6283   Presentation aircraft *Johannesburg No.1*; at Farnborough 16.7.17; SOC 26.7.17

A6284   (120-hp Beardmore) Presentation aircraft *Hawkes Bay, New Zealand*; at Farnborough 11.8.17; UK to 1 AD 30.8.17; SOC 18.3.18

A6285   Presentation aircraft *Jeypores-Vizag*; to 27 Sqn 21.8.17; to 1 AD 18.10.17; to UK

A6286   Presentation aircraft *Rhodesia III*; tested Martlesham 7.17 to 12.8.17; Hendon (station aircraft) by 14.3.18; AES Orfordness w/e 11.5.18; RAE Farnborough by 18.4.18 to 23.11.18; Orfordness 7.7.18; to AES Martlesham 16.9.18; RAE Farnborough 15.3.19

A6287   Presentation aircraft *Punjab No.37 Chambra*; 1 AD to 27 Sqn 15.9.17; shot down by Lt Hanko, Jasta 28, 16.9.17 (Lt N W Goodwin killed)

A6288   Presentation aircraft *Shanghai Britons*, named 22.5.17; 1 AD by 13.8.17; to 27 Sqn 21.8.17; 1 AD for repair 28.10.17

A6289   Presentation aircraft *Malaya No.4, The Wi-Cheng Kim* (then *Mount Lofty, South Australia*); 1 AD by 12.8.17; to 27 Sqn 4.9.17; 1 AD 3.11.17; to UK 13.1.18, SOC 25.3.18

A6290   Presentation aircraft *Lady Ho Tung, Hong Kong*; Southern ARD Farnborough to AAP Lympne 20.6.17; 1

AD 23.6.17; to 27 Sqn 17.7.17; to 1 AD 3.11.17; to 27 Sqn 17.11.17; to 1 AD 10.12.17; to UK 12.12.17

A6291   Presentation aircraft *Liverpool No.1* wef 22.5.17; 27 Sqn (coded '1') 13.7.17; 1 AD to UK 14.10.17

A6292   Presentation aircraft *Ramnad*; 1 AD to 27 Sqn 3.9.17, petrol pipe broke in air, 14.9.17 (2/Lt S H Taylor pow)

A6293   Presentation aircraft *Akim Abuakwa*; 27 Sqn by 11.17; 110 Sqn Sedgeford to 19 TS Hounslow 28.12.17

A6294   Presentation aircraft *Punjab No.15*; 1 AD to 27 Sqn 29.10.17; to 1 AD 3.11.17 and 13.12.17; to UK

A6295   Presentation aircraft *Central Argentine Railway*; 27 Sqn; lost in action 21.8.17 (Capt G K Smith killed)

A6296   Presentation aircraft *Baroda No.6*; 110 Sqn Sedgeford to 19 TS Hounslow 28.12.17; SOC 27.3.18

A6297   Presentation aircraft *Punjab XLIII*; 19 RS Hounslow

A6298   Presentation aircraft *Malaya No.7, The Armenia* allocated EF 12.9.17; 110 Sqn Sedgeford to 19 TS Hounslow 28.12.17; SOC 14.8.18

A6299   RAE Farnborough (experimental Eeman gun-firing); attached 39 Sqn for HD duties; crashed, Stow Maries, on patrol, 19.10.17 (Capt L E Eeman)

Eight Martinsyde G.102 Elephant rebuilds by No.1 (Southern) ARD Farnborough, given serial nos B851, B852, B860, B864 to B866, B872 and B873

B851   1 AD to 27 Sqn 6.10.17; to 1 AD 12.12.17

B852   1 AD by 11.10.17; AAP Lympne 22.10.17; SOC 6 AAP Renfrew 12.18

B860   1 Southern ARD to 1 AD 27.10.17

B864   allocated EF 29.9.17, St Omer to Lympne 22.10.17; AES Orfordness 1.18; 110 Sqn Sedgeford 4.18 to 6.18

B865   110 Sqn Sedgeford; crashed, Sedgeford 9.12.17; Reading by 20.5.18

B866   allocated Exp Force 24.9.17

F.4 Buzzard G-EAWE, formerly H7780, at Johannistal en route for Warsaw. (J M Bruce/S Leslie Collection)

B872	allocated Exp Force 29.9.17; 110 Sqn Sedgeford 1.18 to 4.18; 187 NTS East Retford
B873	allocated EF 29.9.17; 110 Sqn Sedgeford by 2.18; 7 TS Witney 1918

Two Martinsyde F.3 Fighter Tractor Biplanes Prototype (190-hp Rolls-Royce Falcon) ordered under Contract No. 87A435, 19.6.17. First numbered X2, second cancelled

X2	delivered early 1917; to Martlesham Heath 5.1.18

Six Martinsyde F.3 Fighter Tractor Biplane Prototypes ordered under Contract No. AS.29238, serial numbers B1490 to B1495. Duplicate serials H1234 to H1239 allocated and subsequently cancelled.

B1490	(275-hp Rolls-Royce) Delivered Martlesham 26.4.18; AES Orfordness by 19.6.18, last ref 21.6.18
B1491	(285-hp Rolls-Royce) Delivered 4.16; 39 Sqn North Weald Bassett for Home Defence evaluation 1918
B1492	(285-hp Rolls-Royce) Delivered 5.18; 141 Sqn Biggin Hill 1918
B1493	(285-hp Rolls-Royce) Delivered 5.18; 39 Sqn North Weald Bassett for Home Defence evaluation 1918
B1494	Delivered 5.18, in night-flying markings,
B1495	Delivered 5.18, possibly fitted with Lorraine engine

150 Martinsyde F.4 Buzzard Tractor Biplane Fighters (300-hp Hispano-Suiza) ordered 20.11.17 to BR.637 under Contract No. AS.36686 and numbered D4211 to D4360. Duplicate serial numbers H1084 to H1233 allocated and subsequently cancelled. Built May 1918 to February 1919. Mostly to store.

D4214	Sold to French Government
D4251	14 Sqn
D4256	AES Martlesham Heath by 6.18; to France 17.7.18 to 6.8.18
D4259	At Farnborough 2.4.19
D4260	To AES Martlesham Heath 10.3.19 (radiator tests and performance); crashed 4.6.19
D4263	RAE by 4.1.19, last ref 26.5.19 (climb, engine and endurance tests)
D4264	RAE 17.1.19 (engine, endurance and performance tests); AES Martlesham Heath 26.3.19; to RAE 29.3.19, last ref 14.5.19
D4267	Became G-EATD
D4269	RAE by 1.19
D4271	To Russia ex ADC, 1.VshKVL 1.12.22 and 1.6.23
D4272	To Russia ex ADC, 2.OIAE 1.6.23 and 1.6.24, under repair 1924; repair shop 1.12.27; 3.VshL 1.12.28; 3.VShLiLN 1.9.30
D4273	Delivered RAF 22.2.19; CofA 701 to ADC Croydon 8.10.23; to Russia, Aviarabotnik 1.12.27; 3.VshL 1.12.28; 3.VShLiLN 1.9.30

Martinsyde F.4 of the Irish Air Corps at Baldonnel with three newly acquired D.H.9s in the background. (Donal McCarron)

D4274   With ADC, tested 13.4.22; To Irish Air Corps 14.10.22 as 'M4'; B Flt No.1 Sqn Baldonnel, withdrawn 9.25

D4275   Became G-EAYP

D4276   With ADC, tested 14.3.22; to Russia 2.OIAE 1.6.23; repair shop 1.12.27

D4277   With ADC, tested 14.3.22; to Russia 2.OIAE 1.6.23; repair shop 1.12.27

D4279   Became G-EAXB

D4280   With ADC, tested 14.3.22; CofA 689 to ADC Croydon 25.9.23; to Russia ex ADC, 2.OIAE 1.6.24; repair shop 1.12.27; NII VVS 1.12.28

D4281   With ADC, tested 21.9.22; to Irish Air Corps 14.10.22; B Flt No.1 Sqdn Baldonnel ('M.2'); withdrawn 4.29

D4282   With ADC, tested 11.9.22; CofA 690 to ADC Croydon 25.9.23; to Russia; 2.OIAE 1.6.24, repair shop 1.12.27

D4283   To Russia ex ADC; 2.OIAE 1.6.24; crashed 2.OIAE 19.7.26; repair shop 1.12.27; 3.VShL 1.12.28; 1.VShL 1.9.30

D4285   Ex ADC Croydon via Shotwick to Irish Army Air Corps 14.8.22, arrived Baldonnel 15.8.22; (coded 'M1'); B Flt No.1 Sqn; to Fermoy 1.10.22, crashed and written-off, Baldonnel 16.5.29

D4287   RAE by 10.19 (engine and machine test)

D4288   With ADC, tested 7.9.23; CofA 691 to ADC Croydon 25.9.23; to Russia; under repair until 1924; 2.OIAE 1.6.24

D4289   CofA 692 to ADC Croydon 25.9.23; to Russia; VShVBoia 1.12.27 as "5"

D4290   With ADC, tested 1-3.9.23; CofA 693 to ADC Croydon 25.9.23

D4291   With ADC, tested 8.9.23; CofA 694 to ADC Croydon 25.9.23; to Russia; under repair until 1924; 2.OIAE 1.6.24; repair shop 1.12.27

D4292   CofA 703 to ADC Croydon 8.10.23; to Russia; 2.OIAE 1.6.24; repair shop 1.12.27

D4295   Became G-EBMI

D4298   To Irish Air Corps, B Flt No.1 Sqn (coded 'M3') Baldonnel 14.10.22; crashed and written off, 18.9.28

D4304   To Russia ex ADC; 2.OIAE 1.6.23; under repair 1924; 2.OIAE 1.6.24; repair shop 1.12.27

D4306   To Lithuania ex ADC; flew 30.9.21; written-off 4.12.36

D4310   To Lithuania ex ADC; flew 21.9.21; written-off 12.32

D4313   CofA 1113 to ADC Croydon 13.4.27

D4317   CofA 1135 to ADC Croydon 10.5.27

D4324   Delivered circa 11.11.19

D4326   CofA 1092 to ADC Croydon 4.3.27; to Finnish Air Force as MA-24

D4343   CofA 1116 to ADC Croydon 13.4.27

D4350   CofA 1118 to ADC Croydon 13.4.27

D4351   Air Council Inspection Sqn by 8.19; last ref 9.19 (for Directorate of Research)

D4352   (R-R Falcon III engine); 10 TDS Harling Road; from Hounslow to Kenley 30.4.19; became G-EAUR

D4353   (R-R Falcon III engine)

D4354   (R-R Falcon III engine); RAF Communications Wing by 5.19

D4356   CofA 1117 to ADC Croydon 13.4.27; Finnish AF

D4360   Delivered 22.2.19

150 Martinsyde "Special Two-seater" Tractor Biplanes ordered from Martinsyde Ltd, Brooklands & Woking, numbered D4311 to D4460. Order cancelled and numbers reallocated.

Three Martinsyde F.4A Buzzard Mk.IA Long-Range Tractor Biplane Fighters ordered under Contract No. 35a/2939/C.3348, serial numbers H6540 to H6542

H6540   Grain 1919; tested Lewis gun mounting 14.7.20

H6541   RAE Farnborough by 3.9.19; (engine and general testing); AES Martlesham Heath 6.8.20; retd RAE; Howden 3.9.20; RAE by 21.5.21; CFS to RAE 21.2.22-3.7.23

H6542   Grain, tested Lewis gun mounting 14.7.20; AEE Martlesham Heath by 7.22

300 Martinsyde F.4 Buzzard Tractor Biplanes (300-hp Hispano Suiza H) ordered 22.8.18 to B.R.637 under Contract No. 35a/2939/C.3348 and numbered H7613 to H 7912. H7613 to H7780 completed between 15.2.19 and 9.19, mostly to store, H7863 to H7912 cancelled 12.18, H7781 to H7862 cancelled 2.19 (but see H7781 and H7786 below), work stopped 20.9.19

H7613   Photo in hangar, no engine, wings off, probably 2 FS Marske early 1919

H7615   CofA 1134 to ADC Croydon 10.5.27; Finnish AF

Martinsyde Type A Mark I G-CAAX operated by Price Brothers & Co. (J M Bruce/S Leslie Collection)

H7620	CofA 1137 to ADC Croydon 10.5.27; Finnish AF
H7622	CofA 1124 to ADC Croydon 4.5..27; Finnish AF
H7633	To Russia ex ADC; 2.OIAE 1.6.23
H7636	As H7613
H7637	As H7613
H7639	As H7613
H7647	CofA 1113 to ADC Croydon 13.4.27; Finnish AF
H7649	CofA 1114 to ADC Croydon 13.4.27; Finnish AF
H7668	CofA 1115 to ADC Croydon 13.4.27; Finnish AF
H7673	CofA 1093 to ADC Croydon 4.3.27; Finnish AF
H7680	CofA 1136 to ADC Croydon 10.5.27; Finnish AF
H7685	To Russia ex ADC, 2.OIAE 1.6.23
H7686	CofA 678; to ADC Croydon 25.9.23; to Russia; repair shop 1.12.27; VVA UTE 1.12.28
H7687	CofA 679 to ADC Croydon 25.9.23
H7688	Became G-EBFA
H7689	tested ADC Croydon 8.9.23 (Wg Cdr R Stocken), CofA 680 to ADC Croydon 25.9.23
H7690	To Russia ex ADC; 2.OIAE 1.6.23 and 1.6.24; repair shop 1.12.27; 1.VShL 1.12.28; 1.VShL 1.9.30; cancelled
H7691	ADC Croydon by 1920, tested 1.9.23 (Wg Cdr R Stocken), CofA 681 to ADC Croydon 25.9.23; to Russia; being assembled 1924; 2.OIAE 1.6.24; repair shop 1.12.27
H7692	(R-R Falcon engine) tested ADC Croydon 30.5.22 (Wg Cdr R Stocken); became G-EBDM
H7693	To Russia ex ADC; repair shop 1.12.27; 3.VShL 1.12.28
H7698	To Russia ex ADC; 2.OIAE 1.6.23; being assembled 1924; 2.OIAE 1.6.24; repair shop 1.12.27
H7691	ADC Croydon by 1920

H7699	Tested ADC Croydon 14.3.22 (Wg Cdr R Stocken)
H7703	To Russia ex ADC; 1.VShKVL 1922; being assembled 1.1.23 until 1924; crashed 2.OIAE 7.8.25; repair shop 1.12.27; 3.VSHL 1.12.28; 3.VSHLiLN 1.9.30
H7706	To Russia ex ADC; being assembled until 1.1.23; 2.OIAE 1.6.23; VSHVBoia ('12') 1.12.27
H7707	To Russia ex ADC; 2.OIAE 1.6.23; being assembled 1924; VShVBoia ('3') 1.12.27
H7708	Tested ADC Croydon 15.3.22 and 17.3.23 (Wg Cdr R Stocken); to Russia ex ADC; 2.OIAE 1.6.23
H7709	Tested ADC Croydon 14.3.22 (Wg Cdr R Stocken); to Russia ex ADC; 2.OIAE 1.6.23 and 1.6.24; repair shop 1.12.27; 3.VShL 1.12.28; 1.VShL 1.9.30
H7710	Tested ADC Croydon 20.3.22, 25.3.22 (Wg Cdr R Stocken); to Russia ex ADC; 2.OIAE 1.6.23 and 1.6.24
H7711	ADC Croydon by 1920; tested ADC Croydon 15.9.22 with new prop (Wg Cdr R Stocken), CofA 682 to ADC Croydon 25.9.23; to Russia 2.OIAE 1.6.24; repair shop 1.12.27; 2.VShL ('1') 1.12.28
H7712	ADC Croydon, tested ADC Croydon 31.8.23 (Wg Cdr R Stocken), 31.8.22; CofA 683 to ADC Croydon 25.9.23; to Russia; 2.OIAE 1.6.23; repair shop 1.12.27; 3.VShL 1.12.28; 3.VShLiLN 1.9.30
H7715	ADC Croydon by 1920, tested 25-30.8.22; CofA 684 to ADC Croydon 25.9.23; to Russia, being assembled 1924; 2.OIAE 1.6.24; repair shop 1.12.27
H7720	ADC Croydon, tested ADC Croydon 30.8.22 (Wg Cdr R Stocken; to Russia ex ADC
H7723	ADC Croydon, tested 30.8.22; CofA 685 to ADC Croydon 25.9.23; to Russia ex ADC; VSHVBoia ('10') 1.12.27; 3.VShL 1.12.28

One of the Aerial Survey Company's Martinsyde Type A Mark Is. (National Aviation Museum of Canada)

H7724 ADC Croydon, tested ADC Croydon 30.8.22 (Wg Cdr R Stocken; CofA 686 to ADC Croydon 25.9.23; to Russia ex ADC, being assembled 1924; 2.OIAE 1.6.24

H7728 To Russia ex ADC; 2.OIAE 1.6.23; repair shop 1.12.27; 3.VShL 1.12.28

H7735 To Russia ex ADC; 2.OIAE 1.6.23 and 1.6.24; VShVBoia ('2') 1.12.27; 3.VShL 1.12.28

H7749 CofA 687 to ADC Croydon 25.9.23; to Russia; 2.OIAE 1.6.24; repair shop 1.12.27; cancelled 1.VShL 1.9.30

H7751 CofA 688 to ADC Croydon 25.9.23, to Russia, crashed 2.OIAE 7.1.26; repair shop 1.12.27; 2.VShL ('2') 1.12.28

H7753 CofA 716 to ADC Croydon 6.7.24; possibly to Latvia 16.10.24 (reported as c/n 7753); last known flight 20.8.38

H7757 To Russia ex ADC; 2.OIAE 1.6.24

H7758 ADC Croydon, tested ADC Croydon 17.9.22 (Wg Cdr R Stocken); CofA 700 to ADC Croydon 8.10.23; to Russia; 2.OIAE 1.6.24, repair shop 1.12.27

H7774 To Russia ex ADC; 2.OIAE 1.6.23; VShVBoia ('8') 1.12.27

H7775 To Russia ex ADC; 2.OIAE 1.6.23 and 1.6.24

H7780 Became G-EAWE

H7781 AEE Martlesham by 10.20 until 4.21

H7786 Completed as a two-seater F.4A Buzzard Mk.IA; to Spec RAF Type IA; became G-EAUX

H7793 CofA 837 to ADC Croydon 15.10.24

H7794 CofA 836 to ADC Croydon 15.10.24; to Russia; 1.VShL 1.12.28

H7795 CofA 835 to ADC Croydon 15.10.24

H7798 CofA 834 to ADC Croydon 15.10.24

H7801 CofA 838 to ADC Croydon 15.10.24

100 Martinsyde F.4 Buzzard Tractor Biplanes (300-hp Hispano Suiza H) ordered under Contract No. 35a/2730/C.3057, serial numbers H8413 to H8512. Order cancelled 12.18

350 Martinsyde F.4 Buzzard Tractor Biplane Fighters ordered on Contract No. 35a/3361/C3245 dated 4.9.18 from Boulton & Paul, given serial numbers H8763 to H9112, cancelled 19.12.18

150 Martinsyde F.4 Buzzard Tractor Biplane Fighters ordered on Contract No. 35a/3386/C3979 dated 11.10.18 from Boulton & Paul, given serial numbers J1992 to J2141, cancelled 19.12.18

200 Martinsyde F.4 Buzzard Tractor Biplane Fighters ordered on Contract No. 35a/3443/C4053 dated 1.11.18 from Hooper & Co., given serial numbers J3342 to J3541, cancelled 15.1.19

300 Martinsyde F.4 Buzzard Tractor Biplane Fighters ordered on Contract Nos. 35a/3609/C4213 and AS.36283 dated 29.10.18 from Standard Motor Company Ltd., given serial numbers J5592 to J5891, cancelled 1.19

Martinsyde F.4 G-EBMI. (Philip Jarrett)

BRITISH CIVIL REGISTER

A number of Martinsyde civil registered aircraft were quoted as having construction number E4/500 or similar; the reason for this is not known.

Martinsyde F.4 Buzzard, 300 hp Hispano-Suiza

K-152   (c/n E4/500) regd 13.6.19 to Martinsyde Ltd; reregistered as G-EAES 31.7.19

G-EAES ex K-152, no CofA issued, regn cancelled 8.20; to Canada

G-EANM (c/n E4/500), regd 23.9.19 (CofR 353) to Martinsyde Ltd; CofA 244 issued 7.10.19; to Madrid for demonstration 10.19; to Lisbon 11.11.19; regn cancelled; to Portuguese AF 12.19 as *Vasco da Gama*

G-EATD ex D4267 regd 7.5.20 (CofR 521) to Handley Page Ltd (for ADC); regd 12.5.22 (CofR 851) to ADC Croydon 5.22; flown Aerial Derby 29.7.22; No CofA; regn cancelled 13.11.22

G-EAUR ex D4352 regd 15.7.20 (CofR 567) to Handley Page Ltd (for ADC); no CofA issued; to Canada; regn cancelled at census 10.1.23

G-EAUX ex H7786, first flown after conversion at Brooklands 20.5.20; regd 29.7.20 (CofR 576) to Martinsyde Ltd; CofA 418 issued 6.9.20; overseas demonstrator; CofA lapsed 3.9.21, renewed 27.11.22; possibly sold overseas; CofA lapsed 26.11.23; regn cancelled undated

G-EAWE ex H7780, regd 14.1.21 (CofR 625) to Handley Page (for ADC); no CofA issued; left Croydon for Warsaw 29.1.21; sold to Polish Govt. but also reported badly damaged on landing, Lille-Ronchin 27.4.21 (pilot Maurice Piercey) and remains sold by public auction 2.22; regn cancelled 9.1.22

G-EAXB ex D4279, regd 1.6.21 (CofR 664) to ADC, Croydon; no CofA issued; badly damaged in ground collision with S.E.5a G-EAXU, Croydon, 17.4.22; regn cancelled 5.5.22

G-EAYK ex RAF, regd 7.9.21 (CofR 707) to Martinsyde Ltd; CofA 521 issued 3.10.21; overseas demonstrator; CofA lapsed 26.11.23; regn cancelled undated

G-EAYP ex D4275; regd 4.10.21 (CofR 712); CofA 523 issued 13.10.21; overseas demonstrator; CofA exp 26.11.23; regn cancelled undated

G-EBDM ex H7692; regd 19.6.22 (CofR 865) to ADC, Croydon; no CofA issued; regn cancelled 8.6.23; to Portuguese AF in 1923

G-EBFA ex H7688; regd 9.1.23 (CofR 929) 9.1.23 to ADC, Croydon; CofA 852 issued 16.4.25; CofA lapsed 15.4.26; regn cancelled 5.1.27; to Portuguese AF in 1923

G-EBMI ex D4295; regd 10.25 (CofR 1202) to ADC Croydon; CofA 966 issued 15.4.26; CofA lapsed 6.5.28; regd (CofR 2482) 31.3.30 to Lionel E R Bellairs of Southern Aircraft Ltd, Shoreham; sold 8.30 but not regd to Edwin D A Bigg, Woodley; crashed, Woodley, 24.8.30 (S W Giddy killed); regn cancelled 10.30

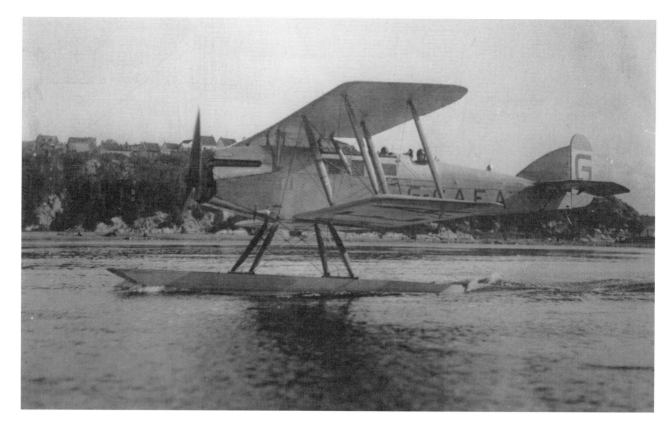

Martinsyde Type A Mark II G-CAEA, operated by Price Brothers & Co. (J M Bruce/S Leslie Collection)

Martinsyde F.4A

G-EAPP   c/n E4-500 regd 21.11.19 (CofR 409) to Martinsyde Ltd; no CofA issued; not flown after Aerial Derby 24.7.20; regn cancelled undated

G-EAQH regd 29.12.19 (CofR 429) to Martinsyde Ltd; CofA 355 issued 1.5.20; crashed 11.20; cancelled 12.20

G-EATX c/n 310; regd 22.6.20 (CofR 546) to Martinsyde Ltd; CofA 433 issued to ADC Aircraft Ltd 4.11.20; reported crashed at Brooklands 12.7.21 (Major S H Long); sold abroad; reg cancelled 4.8.22

G-ABKH modified as "A.V.1" at Croydon; regd 3.31 (CofR 3088) to Charles Amherst Villiers named *Blue Print*; CofA 3081 issued 16.6.31; for sale 7.31; regd 14.10.32 (CofR 3982) to C Brian Field, Kingswood Knoll, Surrey, 10.32; crashed at Bekesbourne, Kent, 5.2.33; regn cancelled 11.35

Martinsyde Semiquaver

G-EAPX c/n S.1; regd 12.19 (CofR 417) to Martinsyde Ltd; no CofA issued; British speed record 21.3.20 at Martlesham (F Raynham); winner Aerial Derby 24.7.20 Hendon and crashed on landing (F Courtney); regd 14.7.21 (CofR 695) to Commercial Aeroplane Wing Syndicate Ltd; unsuccessfully modified with Alula wing; abandoned at Northolt; regn cancelled undated

Martinsyde F.6

G-EAPI c/n E4-500; regd 10.11.19 (CofR 402) to Martinsyde Ltd; CofA 415 issued 24.8.20; regn cancelled 11.20; to Canadian Govt as G-CYEQ; SOC 4.11.25

G-EATQ c/n 61/3; reg 8.6.20 (CofR 538) to Martinsyde Ltd; no CofA issued; sold abroad 1920; reg cancelled at census

10.1.23

G-EBDK first flown Brooklands 29.9.21; reg 16.6.22 (CofR 863) to Martinsyde Ltd; 2nd King's Cup Air Race 9.22 (F Raynham); regd 3.23 (CofR 948) to Frederick P Raynham Croydon 3.23; CofA 655 issued 10.7.23; sold 7.24 and regd 1.25 (CofR 1136) to L C Gerald M Le Champion, Brooklands; regd 11.7.25 (CofR 1188) to Lt Leslie Hamilton, Brooklands; CofA lapsed 1.8.26; renewed 29.10.27; regd 25.11.27 (CofR 1527) to Maj Jack C Savage, Hendon, but possibly based at Brooklands; reported sold to but not regd by Lord Carlow 11.29; regn cancelled with current CofA 4.30 and dismantled at Brooklands

Martinsyde Type A Mark I

G-EAMR c/n E4-500; reg 10.9.19 (CofR 332) to Martinsyde Ltd; no CofA issued; departed Hounslow for Australia 12.12.19; presumed lost at sea off Corfu, 17.12.19 (Capt Cedric Howard & Sgt George Fraser died); regn cancelled 2.20

G-EAPN c/n E4-500; regd 20.11.19 (CofR 407) to Martinsyde Ltd, no CofA issued; regn cancelled in census 10.1.23; almost certainly reworked as Type A Mk.II c/n 217 for Irish Air Corps

The following Martinsyde Type As received Certificates of Airworthiness but were not registered

c/n 15/1 CofA 354 to Martinsyde Ltd 30.4.20; to Canada
c/n 15/2 CofA 370 to Martinsyde Ltd 12.6.20; to Canada
c/n 215   CofA 525 to Martinsyde Ltd 25.10.20
c/n 217   CofA 436 to Martinsyde Ltd 14.11.20, CofA 532 to Martinsyde Ltd 13.12.21; to Irish Air Corps

The A.N.E.C. III in service in Australia on the Melbourne to Hay service in the 1920s. (McGrath Collection)

Martinsyde Type A Mark II

G-EATY c/n 218 regd 22.6.20 (CofR 547) to Martinsyde Ltd;
CofA 474 issued 6.10.20; to F Sidney Cotton and
shipped to the Aerial Survey Co, Newfoundland 10.21;
CofA lapsed 24.10.22; regn cancelled on census 10.1.23

Not reg c/n 216; CofA 483 to R H Nisbet 21.5.21; to Canada

Martinsyde A.D.C.1

G-EBKL c/n K-501; first flown at Croydon 11.10.24; regd
28.11.24 (CofR 1127) to ADC Croydon; CofA 844
issued 1.1.25; CofA lapsed 21.4.27; regn cancelled
1.30; scrapped and burned Croydon 1930
G-EBMH c/n K-502; regd 22.10.25; CofR 1201 to ADC,
Croydon; CofA 990 issued 11.6.26; regn cancelled
7.26; sold to Latvian AF

The following A.D.C.1s received Certificates of Airworthiness but
were not registered;

c/n K.503, CofA 984 issued 9.6.26 to Latvian AF
c/n K.504, CofA 985 issued 9.6.26 to Latvian AF
c/n K.505, CofA 986 issued 9.6.26 to Latvian AF
c/n K.507, CofA 987 issued 9.6.26 to Latvian AF
c/n K.508, CofA 988 issued 9.6.26 to Latvian AF
c/n K.509, CofA 989 issued 9.6.26 to Latvian AF

Martinsyde Nimbus

G-EBOJ c/n K.1001; regd 9.6.26 (CofR 1273) to ADC, Croydon;
CofA 998 issued 2.7.26; CofA lapsed 18.7.29; scrapped
and burnt at Croydon 1930; regn cancelled 12.31
G-EBOL c/n K.1002; regd as Martinsyde F.4A 9.6.26 (CofR
1275) to ADC, Croydon; CofA 999 issued 2.7.26; CofA
renewed 3.3.27; regd 10.3.27 (CofR 1350) to Air Taxis
Ltd, Stag Lane named *Gugnunc*; badly damaged in
forced landing in fog on Epsom Downs inbound from
France, 7.10.27; regn cancelled 18.10.27; remains
stored at Croydon until burned in 1930.

CANADA & NEWFOUNDLAND

"Two Martinsyde Type A Mk.I (Rolls-Royce Falcon III engine)

G-CAAX (C/n 15/1); CofA 354 30.4.20; 21.7.20 Price Bros & Co
Ltd, Chicoutimi, West Quebec; crashed at Lac
Onatchiway, 18.8.20; pilot and passenger injured, one
passenger killed.
G-CADG (C/m 15/2); CofA 370 12.6.20; 21.7.20 Price Bros &
Co Ltd, Chicoutimi, West Quebec; crashed on take-off at
Chicoutimi, 30.5.21.

**Three Martinsyde Type A Mk.II (Rolls-Royce Falcon III
engine)**

G-CAEA (C/n 216-1); CofA 483 21.5.21; 12.6.21 Price Bros &
Co Ltd, Chicoutimi, West Quebec; 7.5.22 to Dominion
Aerial Exploration Co, Toronto; crashed near
Chicoutimi, 11.7.23; unlicensed pilot J Oldham and
passenger L Evans killed.

Two operated by the Aerial Survey Company (Newfoundland)
Limited 1921-23; no registrations; believed sold on to
Pitcairn Aviation, Pennsylvania

Two Martinsyde F.6

G-CYEQ (E4500, previous identity G-EAPI); struck off strength
4.11.25

G-CYER not allocated; may have been intended for G-EATQ;
crashed 25.10.20 before allocated registration.

FINLAND

Martinsyde F.4 Buzzard (300-hp Hispano Suiza)
15 ordered (8E1 in 1923 and MA-24 to MA-37 in 1927)

8E1   ex-ADC, arrived 4.23
MA-23   ex 8E1
MA-24   formerly D4326; CofA 1092 4.3.27; to Utti 3.27; to
Kauhava 12.10.28; damaged 24.2.30 and 8.10.31;
withdrawn 7.7.34; currently in museum

246

Finnish Martinsyde F.4 MA-33 at Utti in the winter of 1928/29. (J M Bruce/S Leslie Collection)

MA-25   spun in 29.8.30 (Flt Cdt V Luoma killed)
MA-32   mid-air collision 25.2.30 (Lt L Lemminki killed)
MA-34   crashed (Sgt H Marklund killed)

IRISH AIR CORPS

One Martinsyde Type A Mk II

c/n 217   first flight Brooklands 24.11.21; to Croydon 9.12.21; CofA 532 13.12.21; to Irish Air Corps at Baldonnel by road/sea 16.6.22; in storage, Baldonnel, 1927; broken up 1935

Four Martinsyde F.4 Buzzards (300-hp Hispano Suiza)
Ordered from the Aircraft Disposal Company 1922

M1   ex-D4285; delivered 15.8.22;B Flt No.1 Sqn, Baldonnel; to Fermoy 1.10.22; crashed and written off, Baldonnel, 16.5.29
M2   ex-D4281; delivered 14.10.22; B Flt No.1 Sqn, Baldonnel; withdrawn 4.29
M3   ex-D4298; delivered 14.10.22; B Flt No.1 Sqn, Baldonnel; crashed and written off 18.9.28
M4   ex-D4274, delivered 14.10.22; B Flt No.1 Sqn, Baldonnel; withdrawn 9.25

JAPAN

One Martinsyde F.4 Buzzard (300-hp Hispano-Suiza)
One ordered from ADC circa 1921

LATVIA

One Martinsyde F.4 Buzzard (300-hp Hispano Suiza)
One purchased from the Aircraft Disposal Company in 1923.

31   Possibly ex-H7753, issued CofA on 6.2.24; fitted with AS Jaguar 17.8.28; tested 17.2.30; crashed 28.2.31; retested 8.9.31; crashed 29.4.32 at Bolderaja (pilot Freimanis); retested 4.6.33; crashed 15.10.35 (pilot Janis Karklins); repaired with 340-hp Serval V; tested and to No.2 Sqdn 4.1.37; crashed 13.5.37 (pilot Karlis Grube)

10 Martinsyde A.D.C.1 (425-hp Armstrong Siddeley Jaguar)
Nine purchased from the Aircraft Disposal Company and one manufactured from spares.

11   Crashed summer 1928 at Krustpils (pilot Janis Abolins); tested 10.9.30; borke up in midair, 29.8.31 (Augusts Lapins killed)
14K   Nosed over 21.8.28 (Alfons Linins); written-off
16   Tested after rebuild 13.5.29; crashed on take-off, 7.12.31 (Krastins); crashed at Salaspils, 9.11.33 (Kltn Dimze); crashed, Krustpils (vltn Teodors Svanbergs); written off
21   Fatal crash 18.8.28 at Spilve (Janis Vistucis); written-off
24   No information
60   Tested 17.11.30; heavily damaged 19.7.30 (Janis Rucelis); tested 19.5.33 and 31.7.36; repaired 31.7.37; No.2 Sqdn
61   Tested 24.1.30; force-landed in ditch, 11.11.30 (Nikolajs Bulmanis; nosed over 1.7.31 (Lodzins); crashed on landing, 17.6.32 at Daugavpils (Kleinbergs); tested 19.5.33; somersaulted on landing, 7.9.34 (Imants Sleiters); crashed 26.9.34; with No.1 Sqdn; 5.37 No.2 Sqdn 6.37
62   Tested 13.11.30; nosed over 3.7.30 (Lodzins); crashed 15.9.30 (Nikolajs Balodis); ripped off undercarriage on landing, 20.10.32 at Jurmala (Kleinbergs); somersaulted, 10.6.32 (Alfreds Ozolins); written-off 24.4.33 Riga (vltn Davis Timmermanis)
66   Tested 1.10.29; crashed 16.11.33 (Janis Udentins); taxying accident 6.8.34 (Karlis Skribo); test after overhaul 1.9.35; overhauled 5.7.37; crashed 22.9.37 at Carnikava (Emils Briedis); 1.38 No.2 Sqdn; 10.38 No.3 Sqdn.

A Jaguar-powered A.D.C.1 in Latvian markings. Eight were acquired from ADC. (Philip Jarrett)

LITHUANIA

Two Martinsyde F.4 Buzzard (300-hp Hispano Suiza)

ex-D4306 ex-ADC ordered 2.6.21; reassembled and flown
  30.9.21; 1 FAS till 1925; training sqn until written off
  4.12.36
ex-D4310 ex-ADC ordered 2.6.21; reassembled and flown
  21.9.21; 1 FAS till 1925; training sqn until written off
  12.32

POLAND

One Martinsyde F.4 Buzzard (300-hp Hispano Suiza)

ex-H7780 ex-G-EAWE; delivered ex-ADC 29.1.21; 1 ARTS until
  1924; hack of Gen Zagorski till 5.26; to 1 ARTS until
  written off, 9.7.26

PORTUGAL

Four Martinsyde F.4 Buzzard (300-hp Hispano Suiza)
One delivered in 1919 and three in 1923 (not numbered)

  ex-G-EANM; ex-Martinsyde; to Spain 6.10.19; to
  Portugal 11.11.19 (Tancos)
  ex-H7692/G-EBDM; ex-H7688/G-EBFA) and one other

RUSSIA

**41 Martinsyde F.4 Buzzard (300-hp Hispano Suiza or 290-hp
M-6)**
  Ordered from ADC in two batches of 20 and 21
4271   1.VshKVL 1.12.22 and 1.6.23
4272   2.OIAE 1.6.23 and 1.6.24; under repair 1924;

Aviarabotnik 1.12.27; 3.VshL 1.12.28; 3.VShLiLN
1.9.30
4273   Aviarabotnik 1.12.27; 3.VshL 1.12.28; 3.VShLiLN
1.9.30
4276   2.OIAE 1.6.23; Aviarabotnik 1.12.27
4277   2.OIAE 1.6.23
4280   2.OIAE 1.6.24; Aviarabotnik 1.12.27; NII VVS 1.12.28
4282   2.OIAE 1.6.24; Aviarabotnik repair shop 1.12.27
4283   2.OIAE 1.6.24; crashed; 2.OIAE 19.7.26; Aviarabotnik
repair shop 1.12.27; 3.VShL 1.12.28; 1.VShL 1.9.30
4288   Under repair until 1924; 2.OIAE 1.6.24
4289   VShVBoia 1.12.27 as "5"
4291   Under repair until 1924; 2.OIAE 1.6.24; Aviarabotnik
1.12.27
4292   2.OIAE 1.6.24; Aviarabotnik 1.12.27
4304   2.OIAE 1.6.23; under repair 1924; 2.OIAE 1.6.24;
Aviarabotnik 1.12.27
4473   2.OIAE 1.6.24
4475   2.OIAE 1.6.23
7685   2.OIAE 1.6.23
7686   Aviarabotnik 1.12.27; VVA UTE 1.12.28
7690   2.OIAE 1.6.23 and 1.6.24; Aviarabotnik 1.12.27;
1.VShL 1.12.28;, 1.VShL 1.9.30; cancelled
7691   Under repair until 1924; 2.OIAE 1.6.24; Aviarabotnik
1.12.27
7693   Aviarabotnik 1.12.27; 3.VShL 1.12.28
7698   2.OIAE 1.6.23; under repair 1924; 2.OIAE 1.6.24;
Aviarabotnik 1.12.27
7703   1.VShKVL 1922; under repair 1.1.23 until 1924;
crashed; 2.OIAE 7.8.25; Aviarabotnik 1.12.27; 3.VSHL
1.12.28; 3.VSHLiLN 1.9.30
7706   Under repair until 1.1.23; 2.OIAE 1.6.23; VSHVBoia as
"12" 1.12.27
7707   2.OIAE 1.6.23; under repair 1924; VShVBoia 1.12.27
as "3"

Martinsyde Type A Mark II operated by Sidney Cotton's Aerial Survey Company. (J M Bruce/S Leslie Collection)

7708	2.OIAE 1.6.23
7709	2.OIAE 1.6.23 and 1.6.24; under repair 1924; Aviarabotnik 1.12.27; 3.VShL 1.12.28; 1.VShL 1.9.30
7710	2.OIAE 1.6.23 and 1.6.24
7711	2.OIAE 1.6.24; Aviarabotnik 1.12.27; 2.VShL 1.12.28 as "1"
7712	Under repair until 1924; 2.OIAE 1.6.23; Aviarabotnik 1.12.27; 3.VShL 1.12.28; 3.VShLiLN 1.9.30
7715	Repair until 1924; 2.OIAE 1.6.24; Aviarabotnik 1.12.27
7720	No details
7723	VSHVBoia as "10" 1.12.27; 3.VShL 1.12.28
7724	Under repair until 1924; 2.OIAE 1.6.24
7728	2.OIAE 1.6.23; Aviarabotnik 1.12.27; 3.VShL 1.12.28
7735	2.OIAE 1.6.23 and 1.6.24; VShVBoia 1.12.27 as "2"; 3.VShL 1.12.28
7749	2.OIAE 1.6.24; Aviarabotnik 1.12.27; cancelled, 1.VShL 1.9.30
7751	Crashed 2.OIAE 7.1.26; Aviarabotnik 1.12.27; 2.VShL 1.12.28 as "2"
7757	2.OIAE 1.6.24
7758	2.OIAE 1.6.24; Aviarabotnik 1.12.27
7774	2.OIAE 1.6.23; VShVBoia 1.12.27 as "8"
7775	2.OIAE 1.6.23 and 1.6.24
VShKVL	Vysshaya shkola krasnykh voennykh letchikov
VShL	Voennaya shkola letchikov
VShLiLN	Voennava shkola letchikov i letchikov-nablyudatelel
VVAUTE	Voenno-vozdushnaya akademiya Uchebno-trenirovochnaya eskdril'ya
VShVBoia	Voennaya shola vozdushnogo bola Aviarabotnik repair shop

SPAIN

Six Martinsyde F.6 (270-hp Rolls-Royce Falcon)
Five Martinsyde F.4A (300-hp Hispano Suiza)
Two F.6 supplied 1920 (M-NYAB and M-NYAC), four more F.6 supplied 3.22. Five remained by mid-1922. Five F.4A supplied ex-ADC 5.24. The ten numbered M-NYAA to M-NYAJ, renumbered EA-EAA to EA-EAJ 22.6.33, renumbered MS-1 to MS-10 14.7.36

UNITED STATES

Type A Mark I (Rolls-Royce Falcon III)

Two bought from Canada in 1924 numbered 10 and 11; fate unknown

Note: Five Martinsydes were exported, CofAs having been issued on 15.10.24. Consignee not identified.

The non-standard cockpits of the Martinsyde Type A Mark I No.11 with Pitcairn in the rear cockpit.

The B.A. Eagle 2 prototype G-ACZT with a deepened fuselage and modified tail. (The A J Jackson Collection)

HANDASYDE AIRCRAFT

One Handasyde Glider (Built by Air Navigation & Engineering Company)

No registration. Entrant for the *Daily Mail* Glider Competition, Itford, 16-21.10.22

One Handasyde H.2 (Built by Air Navigation & Engineering Company, 350-hp Rolls-Royce Eagle VII)

No registration. Tested Brooklands 12.22. Converted to prototype ANEC III.

Three ANEC III (Built by Air Navigation & Engineering Company, one from components of the Handasyde H.2, 375-hp Rolls-Royce Eagle VIII)

G-AUEZ CofR No 141 16.8.26 to Larkin Aircraft Supply Co Ltd, Melbourne as *Diamond Bird*; CofA No 110 20.9.26; damaged on ground, 16.3.27; CofA renewed 5.10.27; 460 hp AS Jaguar installed; CofA exp 11.8.30; rereg VH-UEZ by 31.8.30

VH-UEZ ex-G-AUEZ; to Australian Aerial Services, Melbourne, 21.5.31; CofR exp 9.6.32; struck off register

G-AUFC CofR No 164 21.5.27 to Larkin Aircraft Supply Co Ltd, Melbourne as *Satin Bird*; CofA No 142 5.10.27; crashed on landing at Hay, NSW, 27.12.27; CofA suspended 9.1.28; struck off register 22.5.29

G-AUGF CofR No 175 15.8.27 to Larkin Aircraft Supply Co Ltd, Melbourne as *Lovebird*; CofA issued; rereg VH-UGF by 31.8.30

VH-UGF ex-G-AUGF; to Australian Aerial Services, Melbourne 16.6.31; crashed and destroyed by fire, Temora, NSW, 14.7.31 struck off register 31.8.31

One Raynham-Handasyde Light Aeroplane (Built by Air Navigation & Engineering Company, purchased on Contract No. 487257/24, 750 cc Douglas)

J7518 No civil regn; first flight 9.9.23; Lympne competition (No.13) 8-13.10.23; A&AEE 8.24; to Northolt 18.6.25; Empire Exhibition, Wembley, 19.6.25-9.11.25; by road to Martlesham 10.11.25

250

Buzzard B1492 with No.141 Squadron at Biggin Hill for experimental night fighting trials. (A Thomas Collection)

REFERENCES

General

Bruce J M, *JRAeS*, Vol 72, No. 693, Sept 1968, pp.755-770
Flight 17.6.20 pp.637-41
PRO AIR1/700/27/3/532

Company

Trier & Martin Company records (PRO BT31-17788/89152)
Martin & Handasyde Company records (PRO BT31-22763/139752)
The Aero 24.5.1910 p.407; 25.4.1911 p.257;
Flight 25.4.1914 p.431; 9.4.1915, p.254; 28.8.1919, p.1141
The Aeroplane 28.3.1917, pp.789-92; 24.3.1920, p.642;
    2.6.1920; 22.9.1920, p.567
Aeronautics, August 1914; 13.5.1920, p.375; 24.3.1921,
    p.213; 30.5.1921, p.484
Woking News and Mail, 1.10.1920
Woking News and Mail, 5.11.1920
Woking News and Mail, 12.11.1920
Aeroplane Monthly, 25, 2, Feb 1997 p.24
The Car Illustrated, 4 August 1909, p.508
Martinsyde Motor Cycle Catalogue 1920, p.8-11
Aspley T J, *Cross & Cockade Journal* 20, 2, 1989 p.68
Crosby A, *A History of Woking*, Phillimore 1982 pp.112-5,
    180
Fozard Dr.J W, *Sydney Camm and the Hurricane*, Airlife
    1991, pp. 14, 15, 30, 36, 44
Aeroplane Monthly January 1992
Camm S, *JRAeS*, Jan 1989
Taylor J, *Cross & Cockade Journal* 23, 4, 1992, p.195

Martin-Handasyde Monoplane (No.1)

Lewis P, *British Aircraft 1809-1914*, Putnam 1962, p.352
Barber, *The Aeroplane Speaks*
The Aeroplane 28.3.1917 p.789

Aeronautics 13.5.1920, p.375; 24.3.1921, p.213; 30.5.1921,
    p.484

Martin-Handasyde Monoplane (No.2)

Lewis P, *British Aircraft 1809-1914*, Putnam 1962, p.392
Martin-Handasyde Catalogue (RAeS Ref 3a.132)
The Aero 24.5.1910, p.407; 21.6.1910, p.492; 28.6.1910
    p.514; 5.7.1910, p.17; 27.7.1910, p.72; 3.8.1910, p.94;
    10.8.1910, p.116; 19.10.1910, p.308-9; 9.11.1910,
    p.368; 23.11.1910, p.410; 30.11.1910, p.424,428-9
The Aeroplane 28.3.1917, p.790
Flight 5.11.1910, p.907; 12.11.1910, p.930-1

Martin-Handasyde Monoplane No.3

Lewis P, *British Aircraft 1809-1914*, Putnam
    1962, p.353
Martin-Handasyde Catalogue (RAeS Ref 3a.132)
The Aero 16.11.1910, p.390; 23.11.1910, p.410;
    30.11.1910, p.424-9; 18.1.1911, p.52-3; 22.2.1911,
    p.152; 1.3.1911, p.174; July 1911, p.117
Flight, 12.11.1910, p.931; 26.11.1910, p.969; 17.12.1910,
    p.1038; 24.12.1910, p.1056; 25.2.1911, p.165;
    4.3.1911, p.182; 25.3.1911, p.244-7; 10.6.1911, p.506-
    8

Martin-Handasyde Monoplane No.4B

Lewis P, *British Aircraft 1809-1914*, Putnam 1962, p.355
The Aero, 8.3.1911, p.193; 22.3.1911, p.233; April 1911,
    p.14-15;
Flight 4.2.1911, p.90; 25.3.1911, p.257; 1.4.1911, p.281;
    8.4.1911 pp.307-8; 22.41911, p.352; 24.6.1911,
    p.549; 29.7.1911, pp.662-3; 2.9.1911, p.760;
The Aeroplane 8.6.1911 p.17

Martin-Handasyde Monoplane (No.5)

Thames Valley Times, 21.2.1912
The Aeroplane, 30.11.1911, p.613; 7.12.1911, pp.636-8;
14.12.1911, p.663; 21.12.1911, pp.687-8, 693;
4.1.1912, pp.4,6,16-17; 11.1.1912, pp.35-6; 18.1.1912,
pp.59-61; 15.1.1912, pp.88-9; 1.2.1912, p.111;
8.2.1912, p.124, 132; 15.2.1912, p.157; 22.2.1912,
p.182-3, 185
Flight, 18.11.1911, p.1002; 25.11.1911, p.1021; 2.12.1911,
p.1041; 9.12.1911, p.1060; 16.12.1911, p.1089;
6.1.1912, p.10; 13.1.1912, pp.36-7; 20.1.1912, p.59;
3.2.1912, p.107; 10.2.1912, p.126; 24.2.1912,
pp.172, 174
The Motor, 19.12.11, pp.915-7

Military Monoplane and variants, 1912-14

Lewis P, *British Aircraft 1809-1914*, Putnam 1962, pp.356-7
Lewis P., *British Racing and Record-Breaking Aircraft*,
Putnam 1970, p.60
Bruce J M, *The Aeroplanes of the R.F.C. (Military Wing)*,
Putnam 1982, pp.271-2
Dallas Brett R, *History of British Aviation, 1908-1914*, 1933,
vol 1 pp.167-88
The Aero, June 1912, p.163-5; August 1912, p.233, 239;
Feb. 1913, p.62; March 1913, pp.77-8, 87-8
The Aeroplane, 25.4.1912, p.414; 13.7.1912, p.21;
18.7.1912, p.68; 25.7.1912, p.90; 1.8.1912, pp.116-8;
15.8.1912, p.173; 22.8.1912, p.198; 10.10.1912, p.378;
17.10.1912, p.400-2; 24.10.1912, p.424-6; 31.10.1912,
p.449; 14.11.1912, p.501; 21.11.1912, p.526;
5.12.1912, p.573; 19.12.1912, p.622; 2.1.1913, p.15-
16; 9.1.1913, p.38; 30.1.1913, pp.112-3; 22.5.1913,
p.601; 29.5.1913, p.620, 629; 5.6.1913, p.658;
12.6.1913, p.689; 19.6.1913, p.121,123; 2.2.1914,
p.189; 1.6. 1914, pp.648-9; 18.6.1914, p.700;
25.6.1914, pp.728-9; 29.7.1914, p.120
Flight, 6.7.1912, p.613; 13.7.1912, p.635; 20.7.1912,
pp.654-5; 27.7.1912, pp.681-2; 3.8.1912, p.704, 6;
10.8.1912, p.730; 5.10.1912, p.895; 12.10,1912, p.917;
19.10.1912, pp.932-3; 7.12.1912, p.1138; 14.12.1912,
p.1179; 21.12.1912, p.1200; 4.1.1913, pp.6-9;
15.2.1913, pp.176-7; 22.2.1913, p.222; 31.5.1913,
p.594; 20.9.1913, pp.1031,5,7,1043; 27.9.1913,
p.1060; 9.5.1914, p.494; 22.5.1914, p.545; 5.6.1914,
p.598.
Aeronautics, November 1912, pp.55, 355-7; Feb 1913, p.45;
Mar 1913, pp.97-8, 126-7; May 1913, p.187; Jun 1913,
pp.211-2, 218; Aug 1913, p.311; Oct 1913, pp.378-83;
Dec 1913, pp.455-8

Martin-Handasyde Military Trials Monoplane

Lewis P, *British Aircraft 1809-1914*, Putnam 1962, p.358
Bruce J M, *The Aeroplanes of the R.F.C. (Military Wing)*,
Putnam 1982, pp.271-2
The Aero, Aug 1912, pp.233,4 &7; Sep 1912, p.260; Jan
1913, p.28
The Aeroplane, 25.7.1912, p.91; 1.8. 1912, pp.116,118;
15.8.1912, p.172; 29.8.1912, p.224
Flight, 27.7.1912, pp.681-2; 3.8.1912, pp.704,6-7;
10.8.1912, pp.728-9; 17.8.1912, p.749; 4.8.1912,
p.766; 31.8.1912, pp.793-4; 14.9.1912, p.835;
19.10.1912, p.933; 26.10.1912, p.970; 2.11.1912,
p.1005; 7.12.1912, p.1138; 28.12.1912, p.1213
Aeronautics, Sep 1912, pp.282-8; Mar 1913, p.98; Apr 1913,
p.142; May 1913, p.187; Jun 1913, p.211; Jul 1913,
p.254; Sep 1913, p.340; Oct 1913, pp.378-80; Nov
1913, pp.418-9; Dec 1913, p.455, 458, 469

Martin-Handasyde Waterbus Monoplane

Flight, 23.8.1913, p.941; 20.9.1913, pp.1035-7,1043
Aeronautics, Sep 1913, p.340

Martin-Handasyde Trans-Atlantic Monoplane

Aspley T J, *Cross & Cockade Journal* 20, 2, 1989 p.68
Lewis P, *British Aircraft 1809-1914*, Putnam 1962, p.360
The Sphere, 6.6.1914, p.291
The Aeroplane, 21.5.1914, pp.572-4,6; 18.6.1914, p.698;
1.7.1914, p.20;
Flight, 5.6.1914, pp.595-6
WWI Aero, No.135, pp.47-9

Martin-Handasyde Pusher Biplane

Flight, 9.5.1914, p.494; 20.5.1914, p.539, 543; 5.6.1914,
p.594

Martin-Handasyde 1914 Monoplane

Flight, 7.8.1914, p.842

Martinsyde S.1

Bruce J M, *British Aeroplanes, 1914-18*, Putnam 1957,
p.300-2
Bruce J M, *Air Pictorial*, January 1963, pp.16-9
Bruce J M, *The Aeroplanes of the R.F.C.(Military Wing)*,
Putnam 1982, pp.272-6
Cole, Christopher ed., *RFC Communiques 1915-1916*, No.7
Cole C & Cheeseman E F, *The Air Defence of Britain 1914-
1918*, pp. 35-6
Cutlack F M, *The Australian Flying Corps (The Official
History of Australia in the War of 1914-18), Volume 8*,
pp.1-28
Everidge J ed., *History of No.30 Squadron RAF*
Flight, 6.11.1914, p.1099
Henshaw, Trevor, *The Sky Their Battlefield*, Grub Street
1995
Jones H A, *The War in the Air, Vol 5*, OUP 1925, pp.250-
283
King H F, *Armament of British Aircraft 1909-1939*, Putnam
1971, p.267
Lamberton W M, *Fighter Aircraft of the 1914-18 War*,
Harborough 1960, pp.48-9
Martinsyde Scout Biplane, Report on Test Flight
(PRO AIR/1/765/204/4/236)
Powell Sqn Ldr H S, *Air Home Defence*, Air Publication 956
(PRO AIR/10/973)
Rowell H B R, *Cross & Cockade Journal* 21,3, 1990, p.149
Tennant J E, *In the Clouds Above Baghdad, The Air War in
Mesopotamia*, 1916-1918
Vann R, *Cross & Cockade* 2, 3, 1971, pp.65-79
Warne J, *Cross & Cockade* 12,1, 1981, 30
1 Sqn Daily Routine Orders (PRO AIR1/1336/204/17/68)
1 Sqn War Diary (PRO AIR1/204/17/57a)
Summary of History of 5 Sqn (PRO AIR1/1313/204/13/96)
RFC Organisation in Mesopotamia Nov 16 - Feb 17
(PRO AIR1/506/16/3/38)
Allotment of Aeroplanes to Units in Mesopotamia, Jan-Aug
1916 (PRO AIR1/505/16/3/33)
RFC Mesopotamia Oct 1915 (PRO AIR1/2263/209/61/5)
Establishment of the AP in Mesopotamia
(PRO AIR1/505/16/3/37)
16 Sqn, Daily Routine Orders 12.2.15 to 19.3.15
(PRO AIR1/1344/204/19/25)

Martinsyde Two-seater

Bruce J M, *British Aeroplanes 1914-1918*, Putnam 1957,
p.303
Bruce J M, *J.RAeS*, Vol 72 No 693 Sept 1968, p.763

Martinsyde G.100/G.102 Elephant

Barker R, *The Royal Flying Corps in France, From Bloody
April 1917 to Final Victory*
Bock Dr G, *Cross & Cockade* 11, 2 (1980), pp.78-80, 83
Bowyer C, *The Flying Elephants, The History of No.27
Squadron 1915-1969*, Macdonald 1972, p.30-58

Bowyer C, *Cross & Cockade*, Vol 4 No 4 1973 pp.149-66
Bowyer C ed, *Royal Flying Corps Communiques, 1917-1918*, Grub Street
Bridgeman and Stewart, *The Clouds Remember*, p.74-6
Bruce J M, *British Aircraft 1914-18*, Putnam, 1957, pp.303-8
Bruce J M, *The Martinsyde Elephant*, Profile Publications Number 200, 1967
Bruce J M, *R.Ae.S Journal*, Vol 72, No 693 Sept 1968, pp.763-4
Bruce J M, *The Aeroplanes of the Royal Flying Corps (Military Wing)*, Putnam 1982, pp.276-280
Bruce J M, *Martinsyde G.100 Elephant*, WWI Warplanes Vol One, Albatros, pp.2-10
Bruce J M, *Martinsyde Elephant*, Windsock Datafile 70
Campbell L S, *Cross & Cockade* 14, 3 (1983) pp.126-32
Clarke H S, *Cross & Cockade* 25, 4 (1994) pp.184-94
Clarke R W; *British Aircraft Armament* Vol 2, pp.32-35
Cole, Christopher, *RFC Communiques 1915-1916*, Nos.34, pp.37, 38, 41-49, 53, 55 and 61.
Cole C & Cheeseman E F, *The Air Defence of Britain 1914-1918*, pp. 91, 274, 311-2, 311-2, 344
Cutlack F M, *The Australian Flying Corps (The Official History of Australia in the War of 1914-18*, Volume 8, pp.29-120
Everidge J ed., *History of No.30 Squadron RAF*
Franks N L R et al, *Above the Lines*, Grub Street 1996
Hanmer H I, Lecture on Aircraft in the Palestine Campaign (PRO AIR1/2397/264/1)
Henshaw, Trevor, *The Sky Their Battlefield*. Grub Street 1995
Holder Sqn Ldr F D, *Cross & Cockade* 8,2,(1977) p.60
Jones H A, *The War in the Air*, Vol 5, OUP 1925, pp.160-249, 265-331
Keskinen K, Stenman K & Niska K, *Suomen Ilmavoimen Lentokoneet 1918-38*, pp.74-79
King H F, *Armament of British Aircraft 1909-1939*, Putnam 1971, pp.267-8
Kinsey G; *Orfordness, Secret Site*, p.11
Lamberton W M, *Fighter Aircraft of the 1914-18 War*, Harborough 1960, pp.50-1
Lax M, *One Airman's War*, Aircraft Mechanic Joe Bull's Personal Diaries 1916-1919
Leaman P, *Cross & Cockade* 2, 3 (1971) pp.88-92
Mason T, *Cross & Cockade* 6, 4, 1975, p.171
Orange Dr V, *Winged Promises, A History of No.14 Squadron RAF*, 1915-1945, pp.1-41
Owers C; *'Mimi' and the Elephant*, Aviation News 1990, pp.1052-59
Patent applications 124,777 of 24.3.16, 124,802 of 7.4.16 and 127,033 of 24.3.16
Tennant J E, *In the Clouds Above Baghdad, The Air War in Mesopotamia*, 1916-1918
Thetford & Riding, *Aircraft of the 1914-18 War*, Harborough 1946, pp.24-5
Schaedel C, *Men & Machines of the Australian Flying Corps*, 1914-19
Surrey Adveriser and County Times, 19.2.16
Surrey Herald, 19.2.16
Vann R, *Cross & Cockade* 2, 3, 1971, pp.65-79
Rigging Notes, Martinsyde Scout
Vann R and Waugh C, *Cross & Cockade* 14, 2 (1986), pp.49-105
Vann R and O'Conner M, *Cross & Cockade* 21, 4 (1990) pp.210-15
Warne J, *Cross & Cockade* 11, 1 (1980), p.31
Watson, J C, *History of No.14 Squadron*
Woodman H, *Early Aircraft Armament*, p.193
Wright P, *Cross & Cockade* 15, 1 (1984) pp.33-4
Wright P, *Cross & Cockade* 15, 2 (1984) pp.56-61
The Aeroplane, 8.1.1919, p.44,47
Martlesham Report M.80 (PRO AIR1/1192/204/5/2599)
RFC/RAF (PRO AIR1/689/21/20/14)
Martinsyde periscope sight correspondence (AIR1/756/204/4/91)
Report on the 120 hp Beardmore Martinsyde (PRO AIR2/16MA/Aeroplanes/586)

HQ RFC BEF Correspondence re Martinsyde Scout (PRO AIR1/903/204/5/777 and /778)
1 Sqn AFC (PRO AIR1/2259/209/60/1 to /3)
The formation of service sqns and flts in Egypt and Palestine 1917-18 (PRO AIR1/678/21/13/2090)
Gun for use in aeroplanes to attack German kite balloons, Davis gun (PRO AIR2/17/MA/Misc/949)
Technical Notes, Martinsyde Scout (PRO AIR1/703/27/5/14)
The Air War in Mesopotamia (PRO AIR1/674/21/6/87)
RAE test machines (PRO AVIA1/1 & /2)
CFS Reports 204 & 208 (PRO AIR1/1087/204/5/1740)
Test Reports on various machines 1915/1916 (PRO AIR2/165/MR10723)
1 Sqn AFC War Diary (PRO AIR1/2259/209/60/1)
27 Sqn RFC records (PRO AIR1/1384 to 1388/204/25/1 to /15 & /36, /40, /42)
30 Sqn War Diary (PRO AIR1/2383/226/15/1)
31 Wing & 30 Sqn War Diary June 1916-Oct 1917 (PRO AIR1/2120/207/72/4)
5 Wing War Diary Middle East Feb 1916-Mar 1919 (PRO AIR1/2120/207/72/6a)
72 Sqn History July 1917 to Feb 1919 (PRO AIR1/408/15/237/1)
X Flt (PRO AIR1/2250/209/47/1 to /3)
Notes on the RAF in Egypt and Palestine Nov 1915-Sept 1918 (PRO AIR1/2031/204/326/26/1)
20 Sqn History 1916-18 (PRO AIR1/1358/204/20/3)

Martinsyde RG

Bruce J M, *British Aircraft 1914-18*, Putnam, 1957, pp.308-9
King HF, *Armament of British Aircraft 1909-1939*, Putnam 1971, p.268
Martlesham M.112 (PRO AIR1/1087/204/5/1740)

Martinsyde F.1

Bruce J M, *British Aircraft 1914-18*, Putnam, 1957, pp.310-1
Holder Sqn Ldr F D, *Cross & Cockade* 8,2,(1977) pp.60-1
King H F, *Armament of British Aircraft 1909-1939*, Putnam 1971, p.268

Martinsyde F.2

Bruce J M, *British Aircraft 1914-18*, Putnam, 1957, pp.311-2
King H F, *Armament of British Aircraft 1909-1939*, Putnam 1971, p.268

Martinsyde F.3

Bruce J M, *British Aircraft 1914-18*, Putnam, 1957, pp.312-3
Bruce J M, *The Aeroplanes of the R.F.C.(Military Wing)*, Putnam 1982, pp.280-4
Bruce J M, *Air International*, July 1977, pp.28-32
Cole C & Cheeseman E F, *The Air Defence of Britain 1914-1918*, pp. 291, 312-3, 336-9
King H F, *Armament of British Aircraft 1909-1939*, Putnam 1971, pp.268-9
The Aeroplane, 15.1,1919, p.214
PRO AIR1/204/5/2407
Martlesham M.158 (PRO AIR1/1087/204/5/1740)
Output of Aeroplanes August 1914 to 1919 (unfortunately only from May 1917) (PRO MUN4/6650)

Martinsyde F.4 Buzzard

Bridgeman and Stewart, *The Clouds Remember*, pp.77-8
Bruce J M, *British Aircraft 1914-18*, Putnam, 1957, pp.314-5
Bruce J M, *The Aeroplanes of the R.F.C.(Military Wing)*, Putnam 1982, pp.284-5
Bruce J M, *Air International*, August 1977, pp.82-6
Bruce J M, *Air International*, Sept 1977, pp.131-7
Foxworth T G, *The Speed Seekers*, McDonald & Janes, 1975, pp.79, 315, 431, 434-6, 438-40
King H F, *Armament of British Aircraft 1909-1939*, Putnam 1971, pp.269-70
Kinsey G, *Martlesham Heath*, pp. 136-7

Pilot's Notes Martinsyde F.4
Flight, 26.6.1919, p.845
The Aeroplane, 27.8.1919, pp.812-4, 17.12.1919, pp.1984-6
Jane's All the World's Aircraft 1919-20
Technical Notes Buzzard (AIR1/703/27/5/15)
RAE test machines (PRO AVIA1/1 and /2)
PRO AIR1/454/15/312/29
Martlesham Heath Weekly Reports
   (PRO AIR1/1196/204/5/2600/2)
History of the Martinsyde Buzzard
   (PRO AIR2/56AB.275/8450)
Comparative Charts of New Experimental Aeroplanes
   (PRO AIR1/2089/207/1214)
Output of Aeroplanes August 1914 to 1919
   (PRO MUN4/ 6650)
Surplus Aeroplanes and Engines, 21st May 1919
   (PRO MUN4/6721)

Other Designs Manufactured by Martinsyde

Sturtivant R and Page G, *The S.E.5 File*, Air-Britain 1996

Martinsyde F.4A

Foxworth T G, *The Speed Seekers*, McDonald & Janes,
   1975, p.315
Flight, 23.6.21 p.429, 10.11.21 p.733
Aeronautics, 8.7.1919, p.33
The Aeroplane, 7.7.1920, pp.30-2; 14.7.1920, pp.108-114
Aeronautical Engineering, 14.7.20, p.110

Martinsyde F.6

Foxworth T G, *The Speed Seekers*, McDonald & Janes,
   1975, pp.316, 436, 440-1
Flight, 8.6.22 pp.323-5, 19.7.22 pp.395-8, 10.8.22, pp.447-
   51, 14.9.22 p.531, 30.8.23 p.517, 7.8.24 p.486, 15.6.26
   pp.427-33
The Aeroplane, 17.12.1919, pp.1984-6; 7.7.1920, pp.30-2

Martinsyde A "Raymor" Trans-Atlantic

Foxworth T G, *The Speed Seekers*, McDonald & Janes,
   1975, p.316
Lewis P, *British Racing and Record-Breaking Aircraft*,
   Putnam 1970, p.96
Malott R K, *CAHS Journal*, Spring 1969, pp.22-3
McGrath T M, *CAHS Journal*, Winter 1988, p.124
The Aeroplane, 2.4.1919, p. 1334; 9.4.1919, p.1488;
   14.5.1919, p.1912; 21.5.1919, p.2016; 11.6.1919,
   pp.2310, 2312
Flight, 15.5.1919, pp.635-6, 640.
Jane's All the World's Aircraft 1919
Wallace G, *The Flight of Alcock & Brown*, Putnam 1955

Martinsyde Type AS and A Mk.I/Mk.II

Eustis N, *The Greatest Air Race*, Rigby, pp.65-70
Malott R K, *CAHS Journal*, Fall 1973, pp.76-7
Molson K M, *Pioneering in Canadian Air Transport*, (1974) pp.3-4
The Aeroplane, 5.11.1919, p.590; 10.12.1919, p.1940;
   17.12.1919, p.1972B, 1984-6; 21.1.1920, p.132;
   7.7.1920, pp.30-2; 14.7.1920, pp.108-114
Flight, 6.11.1919, pp.1445-7, 8.7.20 pp.719-21, 15.7.20
   pp.759-61, 17.8.22 pp.463-5
The Aeroplane, 10.12.19 p.1940, 17.12.19 p.1972b
Aeronautics, 8.7. 1919, pp.32-3
Aeronautical Engineering, 27.8.19 p.812, 14.7.20 p.108,
   5.11.19 p.1590, 17.12.19 pp.1984-6, 24.12.19 p.2044-5
Jane's All the World's Aircraft 1920

Martinsyde Semiquaver

Foxworth T G, *The Speed Seekers*, McDonald & Janes,
   1975, pp.316-20
Foxworth T G, *Aeroplane Monthly*, Jan 1976 pp.33-8

Flight, 29.7.20 pp.831-3-9, 5.8.20 pp.862-3, 7.10.20 p.1056,
   21.7.21 p.493, 20.10.21 p.687
Aeronautics, 8.7.1919, p.33, 29.7.1919, p.95
The Aeroplane, 7.7.1920, pp.30-2; 14.7.1920, pp.108-114;
   28.7.1920, pp.240-4, 249, 256

Martinsyde "Alula"

Foxworth T G, *The Speed Seekers*, McDonald & Janes,
   1975, p.439
Lewis P, *British Racing and Record-Breaking Aircraft*,
   Putnam 1970, p.113
Kenworthy R W, *Popular Flying*, October 1937, p.392
The Aeroplane, 21.7.1920, p.182; 4.8.1920, pp.290-1,
   27.2.42 p.251

Martinsyde Aircraft in Overseas Service

Cooke G H, letters to Handley Page F, 27.7.1923 &
   28.7.1923
Keskinen, Stenman & Nisha, *Suomen Ilmavoimen
   Lentokoneet 1918-38*, Tietoteos 1976 p.76-9
Howson G. *Aircraft of the Spanish Civil War 1936-39*,
   Putnam 1990, p.229
Laueau P., *L'Aviation Republicaine Espangnole, 1936-39*,
   Docavia, p.223
Aeronautics, 30.6.1919, p.480
The Aeroplane, 7.1.1920, p.18
Casari R., *WWI Aero* No.146 Nov 1994, pp.3-9
Ritarenta E., letter 1.12.1994
Casari R., letter 2.12.1994
Cummins P J, letter 16.1.95
Cummins P J, letter 7.2.95
Kearns A P, *Scale Aircraft Modelling*, Vol 3 No.10 July 1981
   pp.441-61
MacCarron D, *Wings Over Ireland*, Midland 1996, pp 11-12,
   18-19
Hayes K E, *A History of the Royal Air Force and United
   States Naval Air Service in Ireland 1913-1923*, Irish Air
   Letter, pp.77-80
Barton J, letter 28.7.1994
Judge T R, letter 8.8.1994
Ellis J R, *The Canadian Civil Aircraft Register 1920-1928*,
   Canadian Aviation Historical Society
Griffin J A, *Canadian Military Aircraft, 1920-1968*, Canadian
   War Museum, Pub No.69-2
Register of Canadian Civil Aircraft, National Aviation
   Museum, 1964, pp.11,15
Molson K M, The Martinsydes in Canada and Newfoundland,
   CAHS Journal, Summer 1966, pp.38-41
Molson K M, *Pioneering in Canadian Air Transport*, 1974, pp.3-4
McGrath T M, Early Aviation in Newfoundland, *CAHS
   Journal*, Winter 1988, p.124
Malott Maj R K, First Atlantic Crossing, *CAHS Journal*,
   Spring 1969, pp.22-3
Malott Maj R K, Newfoundland Airmail 1921-23, *CAHS
   Journal*, Fall 1973, pp.76-7
Nowarra H J & Duval G R, *Russian Civil & Military Aircraft
   1884-1969*, pp.59-61
Silis J V, *Aviones Espaqoles desde 1910*, pp.64-5
Smith F K, *Legacy of Wings*, TDA 1981, pp.57-68
Andersson L, *Soviet Aircraft and Aviation 1917-1941*,
   Putnam 1995, pp.175-6
Guardia R, *Cronica D'ella Aeronautica Naval Espanola*, Vols
   I & II (British Library Ref.X.809/27506)
Aeronautics, 30.6.21 p.480
Long Distance Endurance Trials (PRO AVIA2/1701 and PRO
   AVIA2/1789)
Foreign Office Reports; Japan 1921-23 (PRO FO262/1515,
   /1551 and /1577; US 1918-19 (PRO FO/115/2353 and
   /2478)

ADC Martinsyde F.4

Jane's All the World's Aircraft 1924-6
Brown D L, *Miles Aircraft Since 1925*, Putnam, pp.12-14

Martinsyde A.D.C.1

Flight, 27.11.24 pp.742-6, 25.12.24 p.807, 8.7.26 p.416
The Aeroplane, 14.7.26 p.50
Jane's All the World's Aircraft 1925-8

ADC Nimbus Martinsyde

Flight, 3.6.26 pp.316-7, 3.6.26 p.315, 5.7.28 p.536
The Aeroplane, 26.5.26 p.506, 508, 12.7.29 pp.103-4
Jane's All the World's Aircraft 1926-8

Handasyde Glider

Broughton T, *The Story of the British Light Aeroplane*, John
    Murray 1968, pp.22, 28, 30
Penrose H, *Adventure with Fate*, p.19
Fozard Dr. J W, *Sydney Camm and the Hurricane*, pp.36-7
Flight, 20.7.22 pp.412-6, 25.10.22 pp.323, 329, 335,
    19.10.22 pp.608-9, 26.10.22 pp.624-9, 2.11.22 p.640-3,
    14.12.22, 31.1.23 p.87,
The Aeroplane, 31.5.22 pp.387-9, 18.10.22 pp.301-16,
    25.10.22 pp.323-38, 1.11.22 pp.347-54, 31.1.23 p.87
Aeronautical Engineering, 1.11.22 pp.347-50
Jane's All the World's Aircraft 1923, pp.30b-31b

Handasyde H.2 & A.N.E.C III

Cookson B, *The Historic Civil Register of Australia*
    (Pre War), Austairdata
Flight, 20.7.22 pp.412-6, 14.12.22 p.732, 7.3.23 p.180,
    31.5.23 p.290, 11.2.26 pp.78-80, 8.4.26 p.210, 6.5.26
    p.277, 14.10.26, 3.3.27 pp.118-9, 22.11.28 p.999-1000,
    21.11.30 p.1257, 19.12.30 pp.1468-9
The Aeroplane, 13.12.22 p.460
Aeronautical Engineering, 12.10.21 pp.321-2, 31.5.22
    pp.387-9, 7.3.23 p.180
Jane's All the World's Aircraft 1923, pp.30b-31b

Raynham-Handasyde Monoplane

Boughton T, *The Story of the British Light Aeroplane*, John
    Murray 1968, pp.39,40,44-5
Riding R, *Ultralights*, PSL 1987, pp.65-68
Jane's All the World's Aircraft 1924, 41b
Flight, 13.9.23 p.548, 20.9.23 pp.563-6, 18.10.23 p.636
The Aeroplane, 26.9,23 p.324
Aeronautical Engineering, 19.9.23 p.296, 26.9.23 p.324,
    10.10.23 pp.372, 376
Policy Regarding Development of Light Aeroplanes
    (PRO AIR2/243, AVIA2/203 and AVIA2/204)

Desoutter

Jackson A J, *British Civil Aircraft 1919-59 Vol 1*, Putnam
    1959, pp.385-89
Boughton T, *The Story of the British Light Aeroplane*, John
    Murray 1968, p.114
Flight 2.5.29 pp.352-5, 4.7.29 p.548, 11.7.1929 pp.601,
    604-5, 25.7.29 p.751, 29.11.29 p.1259, 20.12.29
    p.1329, 14.2.30 p.219, 28.3.30 p.341, 4.4.30 p.374,
    16.5.30 p.533, 13.6.30 p.633, 11.7.30 p.786, 12.9.30
    pp.1011-4, 1029, 19.9.30 p.1051, 20.2.31 p.155
The Aeroplane, 12.7.29 p.12, 49, 24.7.29 pp.246, 255, 263-
    4, 4.9.29 p.599, 16.10.29 p.930, 20.11.29 p.1203,
    15.1.30 p.95, 12.2.30 p.268, 2.4.30 p.625, 7.5.30
    p.604, 18.6.30 pp.1177-80, 25.6.30 p.1256, 3.9.30
    p.580, 8.10.30 pp.807-30, 21.11.30 p.1286
Aeronautical Engineering, 26.6.29 pp.1070b-d,
Jane's All the World's Aircraft 1929-32

Klemm/BA Swallow

Jackson A J, *British Civil Aircraft 1919-59 Vol 1*, Putnam
    1959, pp.133-6
Flight, 29.1.32 pp.90, 102, 9.11.33 p.1132, 1.3.34 pp.195-7,
    12.7.34 p.705, 19.7.34 p.733,

26.7.34 p.770, 16.8.34
    p.835, 27.9.34 pp.1005-6, 15.11.34 p.1214, 16.5.35
    pp.522-4, 28.5.36 p.574
Jane's All the World's Aircraft 1932-36

Klemm/BA Eagle

Jackson A J, *British Civil Aircraft 1919-59 Vol 1*, Putnam
    1959, pp.137-140
Boughton T, *The Story of the British Light Aeroplane*, John
    Murray 1968, p.159
Riding R, *Aeroplane Monthly*, Nov 1992, pp.42-5
Flight, 5.10.33 p.1006, 19.10.33 p.1059, 9.11.33 p.1132,
    21.6.34 p.614, 12.7.34 p.704, 15.11.34 p.1214
Jane's All the World's Aircraft 1933-36

BA Cupid

Jackson A J, *British Civil Aircraft 1919-59 Vol 1*, Putnam
    1959, p.418

BA Double Eagle

Jackson A J, *British Civil Aircraft 1919-59 Vol 1*, Putnam
    1959, p.418
Jane's All the World's Aircraft 1936

Engines

Beeston Humber engine
Demaus A B & Tarry J C, *The Humber Story, 1868-1932*
The Automotor Journal, Vol 11 1906, pp.343,454-5,484-5;
    Vol 12, 1907, pp.1570-73, 1636-9, 1726-31

J.A.P. 8-cyl engine
The Aero, 19.4.1910, p.317

Austro-Daimler engines
Aeronautics, March 1913, pp.105,109; April 1914, pp.118-9

Laviator
Aeronautics, January 1913, pp.7-8

120-hp Beardmore
Technical Notes (AIR1/703/27/4/2)

Rolls-Royce Falcon
The Aeroplane, 21.7.1920, p.204

Armstrong Siddeley Jaguar
Jane's All the World's Aircraft 1926

ADC Nimbus
The Aeroplane, 17.2.26 pp.174-6
Jane's All the World's Aircraft 1926

Individual Aircraft Histories

Sturtivant R C, letter 7.12.1994
DADAE letter 27.5.1916

Motorcycles

Adorian P, *The Transport Trust News Bulletin*, March 1974
    pp.32-38
The Classic Motor Cycle, Dec 1984 pp.48-51, July 1987
    pp.16-19
Hartley P; *Brooklands Bikes in the Twenties*, pp.36-41
The Brooklands Society Gazette, 3,1, pp.20-25
Martinsyde-Newman Catalogue 1920
Martinsyde Catalogue 1921 Season
Martinsyde Motor Cycles Catalogue 1922
The Martinsyde 1923 Catalogue
The Motor Cycle, 21.12.20 p.702, 8.9.21 p.288, 11.5.22
    p.599, 30.11.22 pp.796,799, 838, 22.5.24 p.735,
Motorcycling, 17.8.15 p.364, 29.11.22 pp.163-4

INDEX

AIR-BRITAIN - THE INTERNATIONAL ASSOCIATION OF AVIATION HISTORIANS - FOUNDED 1948

For fifty years, Air-Britain has recorded aviation events as they have happened, because today's events are tomorrow's history. In addition, considerable research into the past has been undertaken to provide historians with the background to aviation history. Over 16,000 members have contributed to our aims and efforts in that time and many have become accepted authorities in their own fields.

Every month, *AIR-BRITAIN NEWS* covers the current civil and military scene.

Quarterly, each member receives *AIR-BRITAIN DIGEST* which is a fully-illustrated journal containing articles on various subjects.

For those interested in military aviation history, there is the quarterly *AEROMILITARIA* which is designed to delve more deeply into the background of, mainly, British and Commonwealth military aviation than is possible in commercial publications and whose format permits it to be used as components of a filing system which suits the readers' requirements. Also published quarterly is *ARCHIVE*, produced in a similar format to *AEROMILITARIA* but covering civil aviation history in depth on a world-wide basis. Both magazines are well-illustrated by photographs and drawings.

In addition to these regular publications, there are monographs covering type histories, both military and civil, airline fleets, Royal Air Force registers, squadron histories and the civil registers of a large number of countries. Although our publications are available to non-members, prices are considerably lower for members who have priority over non-members when availability is limited. Normally, the accumulated price discounts for which members qualify when buying monographs far exceed the annual subscription rates.

A large team of aviation experts is available to answer members' queries on most aspects of aviation. If you have made a study of any particular subject, you may be able to expand your knowledge by joining those with similar interests. Also available to members are libraries of colour slides and photographs which supply slides and prints at prices considerably lower than those charged by commercial firms.

There are local branches of the Association in Blackpool, Bournemouth, Central Scotland, Exeter, Gwent, Heston, London, Luton, Manchester, Merseyside, North-East England, Rugby, Sheffield, Southampton, South-West Essex, Stansted, W. Cornwall and West Midlands. Overseas in France and the Netherlands.

If you would like to receive samples of Air-Britain magazines, please write to the following address enclosing 50p and stating your particular interests. If you would like only a brochure, please send a stamped self-addressed envelope to the same address (preferably 230 mm by 160 mm or over).

Air-Britain Membership Enquiries (Mil), 1 Rose Cottages, 179 Penn Road, Hazlemere, High Wycombe, Bucks., HP15 7NE

MILITARY AVIATION PUBLICATIONS

Royal Air Force Aircraft series (all prices are for members/non-members and are post-free)

J1-J9999	(£8.00/£12.00)	K1000-K9999	(see The K File below)	L1000-N9999	(£12.00/£18.00)
P1000-R9999	(£11.00/£14.00)	T1000-V9999	(£12.00/£15.00)	W1000-Z9999	(£13.00/£16.50)
AA100-AZ999	(£6.00/£9.00)*	BA100-BZ999	(£6.00/£9.00)	DA100-DZ999	(£5.00/£7.50)
EA100-EZ999	(£5.00/£7.50)	FA100-FZ999	(£5.00/£7.50)	HA100-HZ999	(£6.00/£9.00)
JA100-JZ999	(£6.00/£9.00)	KA100-KZ999	(£6.00/£9.00)	LA100-LZ999	(£7.00/£10.50)
MA199-MZ999	(£8.00/£12.00)	NA100-NZ999	(£8.00/£12.00)	PA100-RZ999	(£10.00/£15.00)
SA100-VZ999	(£6.00/£9.00)	WA100-WZ999	(£5.00/£7.50)*		

Type Histories

The Halifax File	(£6.00/£9.00)*	The Lancaster File	(£8.00/£12.00)*	The Battle File	(£20.00/£25.00)
The Hoverfly File	(£16.00/£19.50)	The Typhoon File	(£4.00/£6.00)*	The Stirling File	(£6.00/£9.00)*
The Anson File	(£15.00/£22.50)	The Harvard File	(£7.00/£10.50)	The Hampden File	(£11.00/£16.50)
The Hornet File	(£9.00/£13.50)	The Beaufort File	(£10.00/£15.00)	The Camel File	(£13.00/£19.00)
The Norman-Thompson File	(£13.50/£17.00)	The Defiant File	(£12.50/£16.00)	The S E 5 File	(£16.00/£20.00)

Hardbacks

The Squadrons of the Royal Air Force and Commonwealth (£15.00/£22.50)*
Royal Air Force Flying Training and Support Units (£20.00/£25.00)
The Squadrons of the Fleet Air Arm (£24.00/£36.00)
Royal Navy Aircraft Serials and Units 1911 - 1919 (£15.00/£22.50)
Fleet Air Arm Aircraft, Units and Ships, 1920 to 1939 (£26.00/£32.50)
Fleet Air Arm Aircraft 1939 - 1945 (£24.00/£36.00)
Royal Navy Shipboard Aircraft Developments 1912 - 1931 (£15.00/£22.50)
Central American and Caribbean Air Forces (£12.50/£18.75)
The British Aircraft Specifications File (£20.00/£30.00)
The K File - The Royal Air Force of the 1930s (£23.00/£30.00)
Aviation in Cornwall (£14.00/£17.50)

Individual Squadron Histories

Strike True - The History of No.80 Squadron, Royal Air Force (£4.00/£6.00)*
With Courage and Faith - The History of No.18 Squadron, Royal Air Force (£5.00/£7.50)*
Scorpions Sting - The History of No.84 Squadron, Royal Air Force (£11.00/£16.50)
Rise from the East - The History of No.247 Squadron, Royal Air Force (£13.00/£16.50)
The Hornet Strikes - The History of No.213 Squadron, Royal Air Force (£20.00/£25.00)
* Currently out of print

The above are available from Air-Britain Sales Department, 5 Bradley Road, Upper Norwood, London SE19 3NT
Access, Visa, Mastercard accepted